Plain English Please

Plain English Please

A RHETORIC

FIFTH EDITION

Elisabeth McPherson

Gregory Cowan

RANDOM HOUSE  NEW YORK

For Leah and Dara

and for Ruth Allen Smith Schane, who started it all

Cover: Arthur Dove. *The Critic.* 1925. Collage. Collection of
Whitney Museum of American Art. Gift of the Historic Art
Associates of the Whitney Museum of American Art, Mr. and Mrs.
Morton L. Janklow, the Howard and Jean Lipman Foundation, Inc.,
and Hannelore Schulhof.

Fifth Edition
987654
Copyright © 1966, 1969, 1976, 1980, 1987 by Random House, Inc.

Library of Congress Cataloging-in-Publication Data

Cowan, Gregory.
    Plain English please.

    Includes index.
        1. English language—Rhetoric.   I. McPherson,
Elisabeth.   II. Title.
PE1408.C66   1987   808'.042   86-15598
ISBN 0-394-36272-1

Manufactured in the United States of America

Preface

Plain English Please has always been a process book. The first edition was based on the belief that all students have things worth saying and that, with guidance and encouragement, they can learn to say those things clearly and effectively in writing. Greg Cowan and I tried to provide that guidance through a structured plan for collecting ideas; for sorting, arranging, and expanding those ideas; and for putting them into final form.

We also believed—and I still do—that inexperienced writers need a taste of success. Failure and frustration have never taught anybody anything much. The step-by-step exercises in earlier editions were not meant to dam or dampen creativity but rather to channel it so that ideas could flow more freely. The idea was—and is—that any student willing to follow the steps carefully could—and can—succeed in producing a satisfactory paper. What inexperienced writers need is a few completed papers of which they can be proud. What they do **not** need is more practice in identifying prepositions, more exercises in distinguishing between *lie* and *lay,* more time spent inserting commas into ready-made sentences.

Recent research in the process of writing has done nothing to change those beliefs. Instead, it has strengthened them. The fifth edition incorporates much of that new knowledge, giving additional emphasis to brainstorming before the actual writing begins and to real revising, with advice from other students, before a paper is considered finished. Check lists for content are given at the end of each chapter, re-emphasizing the need to make a definite point, support that point with convincing details or reasons, and organize the material clearly.

Research reminds us, too, that editing is only the final step, the "good manners" necessary to make life easier for readers. Although what's said is always more important than how it's said, although no amount of careful spelling and meticulous punctuation can redeem a paper that says nothing worth saying, some readers demand edited American English; they reject carelessly edited papers no matter how important the ideas are, no matter how forcefully they're expressed. It's true that when students have finished their last revision, they do need to edit carefully. But students inexperienced in editing aren't helped much by the bare advice, "After you've written something that satisfies you, go back and edit it." This edition, therefore, gives more attention to the process of editing. One problem—how to use apostrophes, for example—is explained at the end of each chapter, and a check list for editing, progressively more inclusive, has been made part of the exercises.

Old friends will find, however, that the philosophy, the style, and the general arrangement of earlier editions remain. Many students still arrive in English class terrified by a belief that college writing demands some mysterious and esoteric quality beyond their experience. They are still paralyzed by the conviction that whatever they write will be "wrong," so they play it safe and fall back on meaningless generalities. The informal, conversational language retained in this edition can help to quiet their fears, and the down-to-earth examples can do more than an excess of unfamiliar terminology to show students what's expected.

The text still begins with giving directions because almost every student can finish that assignment successfully. It goes on to papers of definition, comparison, classification, and analysis, not because life often requires these purposes in pure form but because inexperienced writers need practice in dealing with each purpose separately before they can incorporate those purposes in more sophisticated writing. The difference between objective and subjective language is given special attention in the chapter on reports because students must recognize slant when they use it and when they see it. Personal experience papers are saved until after report writing because by then students can understand that telling what happened to them, and what it meant to them, requires an approach quite different from the other writing they have been doing. Persuasion comes last because good persuasive writing embodies most of the other purposes. The final chapter on fair persuasion reminds students that good writing is always based on clear thinking. The discussion of everyday logic should help them become more critical readers as well as more convincing writers.

Persuasive writing, of course, also includes the ability to summarize. Summarizing, however, has not been given a chapter in this edition, partly because summaries never have a purpose of their own, but mostly because presenting summarizing in an appendix makes it easier for teachers to assign it whenever it seems needed as an aid in either studying or writing.

All the sample papers in this edition are new, and many of them are shown in more than one draft so that students can see the effect of the changes; both first and final drafts contain marginal comments so that students can understand why the changes were made. The sample research paper, which follows the form recommended in the *MLA Handbook for Writers of Research Papers,* Second Edition (1984), is also new, and the appendix on writing research papers has been expanded so that a separate style manual should be unnecessary. Throughout the text outdated examples have been replaced, and key terms and ideas have been printed in boldface type.

These changes, I hope, will make the book easier to use without altering its basic philosophy. Despite the current conservative trend, with its insistence on so-called basics, I still believe that content is more basic than mere correctness. Despite the drift toward elitism in college entrance and placement, I still believe that the first requirement of less well-prepared students is a writing course that will help them become competent writers. This book tries to provide that help.

I am grateful to all the people who have given encouragement and advice on earlier editions: Richard Hawkins, Glenn Leggett, Dean Lewis D. Cannell, Richard Friedrich, Georgia-Mae Gallivan, Barbara Relyea, Deborah Berman, Richard

Larson, David Dushkin, Jim Smith, and Richard Garretson, to name only a few. I am especially grateful to the students and teachers across the country who have used the book and been generous with their comments. For the improvements in this edition, I want especially to thank Thomas H. Barthel, Herkimer County Community College; Edith C. Blankenship, Alexander City State Junior College; Carole L. Edmonds, Kellogg Community College; David Fusani, Erie Community College, North Campus; and Ruby T. Johnson, Wallace State Community College. At Random House, C. Steven Pensinger, English editor, Cynthia Ward, developmental editor, and Jennifer E. Sutherland, project editor, have given me their full support.

Finally, my greatest debt is to Gregory Cowan, my co-author on all the earlier editions. His untimely death in 1979 has left me to write this revision alone, but many of the important concepts are his and much of his wording remains.

ELISABETH MCPHERSON

Contents

Preface   v

A Note to Students   xiii

Chapter 1   Getting Started: Process, Purpose, and Audience   1

Finding a Process	3	Finding Your Audience	14
Finding the Purpose	4	Writing Your Paper	15
Finding a Topic	9	Key Words and Ideas	16
Writing Main Idea Sentences	12	Exercises 1–10	17

Chapter 2   Giving Directions   29

What to Write About	29	A Sample Paper Giving Directions	42
Planning the Paper	30	Key Words and Ideas	46
Main Idea Sentences	32	Exercises 1–10	47
Developing the Plan	33	Exercise 11 with Check List	
Writing the Introduction	34	for Content	63
Writing the Conclusion	35	Exercise 12 with Check List	
Finding a Title	36	for Style	63
Revising Your Paper	37	Exercise 13 with Check List	
Checking for Style	38	for Editing	64
Editing—The Last Step	41	Exercises 14–15	64

Chapter 3   Explaining: Definition   65

How Words Get Meaning	65	Editing	76
Kinds of Definition	66	Sample Paper of Definition	77
General and Specific Words	70	Key Words and Ideas	80
Generalizations and Specific		Exercises 1–13	81
Statements	71	Exercise 14 with Check List	
Supporting Generalizations	71	for Content	99
Planning a Definition Paper	72	Exercise 15 with Check List	
Paragraphing	74	for Editing and Style	99
Developing the Plan	75	Exercises 16 and 17	100

Chapter 4   *Explaining: Comparison*   **101**

What to Compare	102	Key Words and Ideas	116
Collecting Ideas	104	Exercises 1–7	117
Main Idea Sentences	105	Exercise 8 with Check List	
Planning the Order	106	for Content	127
Writing a Comparison Paper	108	Exercises 9–10	129
A Special Comparison—		Exercise 11 with Check List	
Apostrophes	110	for Editing and Style	131
Sample Paper of Comparison	111	Exercise 12	131

Chapter 5   *Explaining: Classification*   **133**

Reasons for Classifying—		Two Sample Classification	
Point of View	134	Papers	143
Classifying and Stereotyping	135	Key Words and Ideas	146
Sorting Up and Sorting Down	136	Exercises 1–12	147
Main Idea Sentences for		Exercise 13 with Check List	
Classification	137	for Content	163
Making a Chart	138	Exercise 14 with Check List	
Developing the Plan	139	for Editing and Style	163
Classification as a Study Aid	140	Exercises 15–16	164
Classifying Commas	141		

Chapter 6   *Explaining: Analysis*   **165**

Operational Analysis	166	Exercises 1–4	177
Main Idea Sentences for		Exercise 5 with Check List for Content	
Operational Analysis	166	in Operational Analysis	181
Developing the Plan	167	Exercise 6 with Check List for Editing	
Causal Analysis	168	in Operational Analysis	181
Cause and Effect	169	Exercises 7–14	183
Main Idea Sentences for		Exercise 15 with Check List for	
Causal Analysis	170	Content in Causal Analysis	195
Developing Your Paper	171	Exercise 16 with Check List for	
Analyzing Homophones	172	Editing in Causal Analysis	195
Two Sample Papers of Analysis	173	Exercise 17	195
Key Words and Ideas	176		

Chapter 7   *Telling What Happened: Objective Reports*   **197**

Reports in Ordinary Life	198	Accuracy	199
Precision	199	Sticking to the Subject	200

Completeness 201
Order 202
Objectivity 203
Fact and Opinion 203
Slanting 205
Main Idea Sentences for
   Objective Reports 206
Writing the Report 208
A Report on Sentence Punctuation 209

Two Sample Reports 211
Key Words and Ideas 214
Exercises 1–12 215
Exercise 13 with Check List
   for Content 235
Exercise 14 with Check List
   for Editing 235
Exercises 15–17 235

Chapter 8   Telling What Happened: Personal Experience   237

Finding Something That Matters 238
Main Idea Sentences for
   Personal Experience 239
Planning the Paper 241
Writing the Paper 242
Sounding Natural 243
Using Quotation Marks 246
Sample Personal Experience Paper 247

Key Words and Ideas 250
Exercises 1–10 251
Exercise 11 with Check List
   for Content 265
Exercise 12 with Check List
   for Editing 265
Exercise 13 266

Chapter 9   Writing to Persuade   267

Discovering a Topic 268
Main Idea Sentences
   for Persuasion 270
Finding Reasons for Your Belief 271
Giving Examples 273
Citing Statistics 275
Using Authorities 276
Predicting Consequences 277
Dealing with the Other Side 277
Planning the Paper 278

Writing the Paper 279
Subjects and Verbs 282
Two Sample Persuasion Papers 283
Key Words and Ideas 287
Exercises 1–14 289
Exercise 15 with Check List
   for Content 313
Exercise 16 with Check List
   for Editing 313
Exercises 17 and 18 314

Chapter 10   Fair Persuasion   315

Slanted Words 316
Glittering Generalities 317
Facts, Inferences, and Judgments 318
Honest Examples 320
Honest Statistics 321
Honest Use of Authorities 323

Honest Predictions 325
Post Hoc Thinking 326
False Analogies 327
Honest Reasoning 328
Inductive Reasoning 329
Deductive Reasoning 330

Guilt by Association   331
Either/Or Thinking and Other
   Bad Logic   332

Suspicion, Stampeding, and Sense   333
Key Words and Ideas   334
Exercises 1–18   335

Appendix 1   Summarizing   363

Summarizing Lecture Notes   363
Summarizing What You Read   364
Putting the Notes into a
   Paragraph   368
Using Your Own Words   368

Using the Help That's Provided   370
Summarizing Graphs   370
Summarizing Fiction   372
Summaries and Reviews   373
Sample Book Review   375

Appendix 2   Writing Longer Papers   379

The Reason for Research Papers   380
Finding Material   381
Taking Notes   382
Planning the Paper   383

A Sentence Outline   385
Giving Credit   386
Using a Style Manual   388
Sample Research Paper   389

Appendix 3   Writing Application Letters   409

Form for Business Letters   409
Application Letters   411
Personal Information Sheets   413

Proofreading   415
Sample Application Letter   416
A Sample Résumé   418

Appendix 4   Editing   421

Spelling   422
Punctuation   430
Paragraphs   442

Capitalization   442
Smoothing Out the Wording 443
Editing In-Class Writing   445

Glossary   447

Index   461

A Note to Students

Don't let anybody tell you you're not "good in English." If you were born in the United States, Canada, or any other English-speaking country, you've been pretty much an expert since you were five or six years old. Before you started school, you had so thoroughly absorbed the shape and pattern of ordinary sentences that you understood nearly everything said to you and could say a good deal for yourself besides. What you had learned, without self-consciousness or drills or any sense of strain, was the English spoken in your neighborhood and your own home. It may have been a little different from the English spoken in other neighborhoods and other homes, but it was the same language. As you grew older and experienced more things, you learned more words and used longer sentences. You discovered that the same thing could be said in more than one way—that your language offered choices. What you could say on the playground, to the applause of your friends, did not always win praise when you tried it at home. You became expert, not just in the structure of your language—how it works—but in appropriateness—when to choose what part of it. What you mastered is a symbolic system so subtle and complex that linguists have not yet been able to describe it completely. But you, like any other normal child, simply absorbed it. Language became as much a part of you as running or breathing, and you used it, most of the time, with as little conscious thought.

In school, however, you had to learn a second system: a method of recording language so people can communicate, or remember, across distance and time. The second system, the writing system, is much less complicated and much easier to describe than the talking system, but most people find it harder to learn. Mastering it becomes a deliberate act. Self-consciously and often with considerable strain, schoolchildren learn to read and write. But they keep right on talking. They ask questions about what they read, complain about their assignments, gossip with their friends, offer and take advice. We all talk, probably, fifty times as much as we read, and a thousand times as much as we write. It's small wonder that most of us feel more comfortable talking, and do it better. We've had more practice.

But even in this electronic age, where television provides much of our news, cassettes can preserve our conversations, and computers can do much of our calculating, talking is not enough. We still live in a literate society, in the sense that we receive most of our general information and do most of our business through print and writing. We're bombarded with printed words: traffic directions and recipes, campaign promises and special sales, textbooks and treatises. Unless you can read with considerable skill, you will have trouble discriminating among this mass of material and pulling from it the information you actually need.

You won't have to write as much or as often as you have to read. But there is no job you can hold, no place you can live, where you won't have to do some writing, unless you opt for a cave in the hills somewhere, and good caves are getting harder to find. When you do write, you will need to write well.

College will give you plenty of practice in the written language, both what other people have written and what you will write yourself. Most of the courses you take will require some reading and some writing. Luckily the two skills are intertwined. When you read an assignment in biology or history, the main value of your reading will be greater understanding of the phenomena of living matter or the clash and strife of political forces. When you pore over the ethical rules of hospital practice, you'll be mostly interested in finding out what the rules are. When you figure out the explanation of a transmission diagram or a wiring chart, your main concern will be learning how the transmission and the electric system work. But you'll get some extra value too. By a kind of transfer process, you will also be learning how to write better. What you read will show you how other writers express themselves and suggest ways of organizing your own ideas and presenting those ideas clearly and forcefully. By the same transfer process, your practice in writing will help you to read with greater understanding and appreciation. You will be better able to follow the plan other writers have used and see why they have found one kind of word choice more appropriate than another.

The material in this book will give you some additional practice in writing, reading, and the clear thinking that must underlie both activities. None of the assignments is intended to stifle your creativity, although some of what you are asked to do may seem rather structured. The exercises you're asked to work through and the process you're asked to follow should lead you to greater freedom in your writing. It will be a more controlled freedom, deliberately directed to the end you want to accomplish. Good writers must always find their own ideas, choose the best words to express those ideas, develop a sensible order, work out their own support and examples, and consider the needs of their readers. Good writing, however, seldom just happens. Good writers have tried first one process and then another and learned to change and revise what they have written.

Good writers have also learned that when they have finally written something that pleases them, they must make it look better by giving some attention to the conventions of the writing system—spelling, punctuation, paragraphing, and so on. Observing the conventions of edited English will make life easier for your readers, and that's always one of a writer's obligations. You will find some advice on editing in this book, but the advice comes after you've written a paper, not before. The thinking and the writing are primary, the editing secondary. No amount of "correctness" can compensate for dullness and disorder. What you say and how clearly you say it are the important parts of good writing.

For years you have been speaking English plainly, probably with some precision, variety, and sophistication. This book offers you practice in writing plainly. It will help you get your ideas on paper with precision, variety, and clarity.

Chapter 1

Getting Started: Process, Purpose, and Audience

Have you ever asked yourself why people write? At first the answer may seem obvious. People write because they have to, or because they'll gain something, or sometimes because they just want to. All these reasons will apply to you, too, for most of your life.

While you are in college you will have to write. You'll have to answer test questions, prepare a paper for your sociology class, complete a report in police science, or keep records in your child care seminar. To hold a job, you will also have to write —a lot or a little, depending on what the job is. Troubleshooters write reports, clerks write collection letters, lawyers write briefs, secretaries write minutes, engineers write specifications, department heads write proposals, politicians write speeches. All this writing has to be done. Getting through college or paying the rent depends on it, and you have a good deal to gain by doing it well.

The writing you do because you want to is a little different. It may include diaries, journals, jottings, love letters, perhaps poetry or stories. We can call this kind **private writing**, even though you may let other people read it or, if you like it well enough, try to get it published. Private writing can be valuable. It helps us understand ourselves and our experiences. It lets us capture a moment we want to remember. It satisfies a deep human need and makes us more aware of our humanity. But it differs from **public writing**—something intended for others to read—in several ways. When we write for ourselves, we can make our own rules, play around with the meaning of words, dart off on tangents, skip or repeat, just as we please. Usually we don't expect other people to criticize or correct what we've written, and we don't much care whether or not they approve of it.

Even though private writing is important, we are not concerned with it in this book. Here we are dealing with public writing, the kind you will need in college and on the job. Somebody else, one person or a hundred, will read what you have written and do something or think something as a result of what they read.

So a second and more difficult question comes up: How do people write? The physical act—picking up a pen or pencil and moving it across a sheet of paper, or punching the keys on a typewriter, or feeding information into a word processor—can be easily observed and explained. What is much harder to explain, and impossible to observe, is how people decide what words to put on the paper, how to arrange them, and when to start and quit. But before you can influence other people by what you write, you must learn to make these decisions. Some of them will be affected by why you are writing (the purpose), and some of them by who your readers will be (the audience).

It will be easier to understand how such choices are made if we look at some of the decisions you are already in the habit of making. Even at home you do some public writing: a list of directions for the baby-sitter, a note to Uncle Ephraim, a letter to the telephone company. In all these situations, of course, you know exactly why you are writing. Unless you remind the baby-sitter to give Angela her medicine at seven o'clock, her cough may get worse. Unless you thank Uncle Ephraim for the fifty-dollar check, he'll be less obliging the next time you need a loan in a hurry. And unless you can convince the telephone company that that forty-minute call to San Francisco was not made from your phone, they'll soon be telling your friends that your line has been temporarily disconnected.

You probably don't worry much about what to include or what words to use. The why controls the how. Because you're worried about Angie, you make the directions you leave for the baby-sitter simple and direct: "One teaspoonful of cough medicine (on the kitchen counter) at seven o'clock." The letter to Uncle Ephraim is a bit more complicated but not much. Your reason for writing is that both good manners and self-interest require it. Your audience—Uncle Ephraim—is well known to you, so you tell him how much you appreciate the money, ask about his arthritis, and mention that your mother has a new job. Your only decision about words and arrangement is to make sure you begin with the thank you and then include enough family details to make the note sound friendly. In writing to the telephone company, you want to avoid paying money you don't owe. You're not sure who will read your letter—the audience is unknown—so in choosing your words you keep to the facts, without adding anything extra. You explain that you were out of town on the day the call was made, you never heard of that number in San Francisco, and you hope they will cancel the charge. This kind of writing is not much different from talking. You write down more or less what you would say if you were face to face with the reader.

But you know that the writing required in college is expected to be more than just talk written down, and the problem of how to do it can sometimes seem overwhelming. When you were writing those directions, that thank-you letter, and even that complaint, you knew nobody would criticize or correct what you wrote—or if somebody did, you wouldn't know about it.

Furthermore, it may seem that the writing you are asked to do in college isn't "real." You don't expect to have any audience except the teacher, and you don't much believe that your teacher will do anything different or think anything different because of what you've written. If you think that, you're partly right. The writing you will do for this class is not real in the same sense as the letter to the phone company, and the record you keep for that child care seminar is not real in the same sense as the report that will be needed when you actually get a job. But unless you think of the writing you do here as real in another sense, as practice for the later writing you'll have to do, you will be wasting your time. Shooting at a basket over and over by yourself is not a real game, but unless you do some of it, you're not likely to score when the actual game takes place. Practicing scales is not a concert, but without that practice, the performance will sound pretty amateurish.

And practice without careful attention is not enough. The successful basketball player has not just tossed the ball without thinking about it; she has concentrated on how she holds her body and when she lets go of the ball. The successful musician has not just let his fingers run up and down, thinking about something else; instead, he has concentrated on the timing and the tone. That concentration is what ties the practice to the real game and the real sonata.

The writing you do in this class, or anywhere else for that matter, will be more effective if you concentrate on three questions: What **writing process** will help me to complete this paper? That is, how can I collect my ideas, how can I arrange and rearrange them, how can I find the right words to say what I mean? What is my **purpose** in writing this paper? That is, what do I hope to do, report something or convince somebody or both? And who is the **audience** for my paper? That is, what do my readers already know and what do they need to be told?

> *Private writing is what you do for yourself—love letters, diaries, poetry, and so on.*
> *Public writing is meant to be read by other people; it's the kind you will be doing in this class.*

Finding a Process

The first of those three questions—what writing process should you use—may be the hardest and, for beginning writers, the most important. Not all successful writers follow the same steps when they sit down to write. Some of them make lots of notes, in their journals or in special folders, on the typewriter or on the backs of old envelopes, but some of them seem to keep their notes entirely in their heads. Some writers make detailed outlines, using Roman numerals and capital letters and complete sentences, but some depend only on a word or two to remind them of the order they want to follow. Some writers get a new inspiration in the middle of a sentence and start over, but some dash off a complete piece of writing and then go back to change it, cutting out some parts and adding others. No single process works for everybody, but whatever the process is, it can usually be boiled down to *think and plan, think and write, think and discuss, think and write again.*

It may occur to you that there's more thinking than actual writing in that process. You're right. Good writing always results from a lot of thinking. Then the question becomes, "How can I direct my thinking so that it turns into writing?" Here are some procedures that have worked for many writers. Whatever your purpose is and whoever your readers will be, following these steps can help you move from a lot of vague thoughts to a finished paper.

1. Collect as many ideas as you can and write them down.
2. Sort your ideas, see how they relate to each other, and get rid of those that seem unrelated.
3. Arrange the remaining ideas in some kind of order and put that order down on paper.
4. Write your ideas out in sentences and paragraphs (a first **draft**).
5. Go over your draft to decide what needs to be added, what needs to be left out (sometimes with advice from other people).
6. Write it again, making the changes you've decided on. (Sometimes it's better to start over.)
7. Polish what you've written to make sure the words are exact and the sentences sound smooth.
8. Edit this last draft for spelling, punctuation, and usage.

Going through all eight of those steps may sound like a lot of time and work for just one short piece of writing. You may be tempted to jump straight to the fourth step, with a little last-minute attention to step 8. Occasionally that may get you by, especially if you have unconsciously worked out some of the other steps in your head, thinking about them while you took a shower or waited at a stop light on the way to school.

More likely, however, you're tempted to skip some of the steps because you have not had enough practice with a system that gets the best results. Directions for a baby-sitter, thank you notes to a relative, and even a quick letter of complaint don't require much in the way of planning, revising, and editing. The exercises in this book are designed to give you the practice you need.

You may find, as you get more practice in writing, that parts of the process suggested here are not the most efficient system for you. Different writers work in different ways. As you become more confident, there's certainly nothing wrong with changing the order of the steps or combining some of them. Almost all successful writers agree, however, that the last two steps should come at the very end. If you get bogged down in polishing and editing each sentence as you produce it, you will not only slow yourself down, you will stand a good chance of forgetting where you intended to go. To use a worn-out comparison, you won't see the forest because you'll be concentrating too soon on the trees.

Different writers use different writing processes, but every process involves a lot of thinking and planning. Whatever the process is, polishing and editing are always the last two steps.

Finding the Purpose

Probably even before you start collecting ideas for a paper, you know what your general purpose will be. Just as you knew at home what you wanted to do before you picked up a pencil—tell the baby-sitter what to do about Angela, tell the phone company why you hadn't paid the bill—knowing what you want to accomplish in your paper will serve as a guide to everything else you do.

Although we can name **writing purposes** in many different ways, such as thanking, advising, protesting, notifying, or reassuring, most of them can be grouped under four general purposes:

> giving directions
> explaining
> telling what happened
> persuading

It's true that these four writing purposes seldom appear in their pure form. Much of what you read seems to have a mixture of many purposes: a bit of explaining, a bit of persuading, a bit of telling what happened. But even though the purposes are mixed, when you read carefully you can usually find what the *main purpose* was and see how the other purposes were used to support it. In *persuading* parents that IQ tests may be unfair to their children, a writer may *tell what happened* when city children were given questions about cows and *explain* how IQ tests are constructed. The persuasion (the main purpose) will succeed, however, only if the telling what happened and the explaining are skillfully done—if the writer has had some practice in using these purposes separately.

Writers who can blend purposes effectively have probably already become pretty good at using each purpose by itself. A good blend is not a hodgepodge but a carefully prepared mixture. Landscape architects can't plan an attractive garden until they have learned whether rhododendrons grow higher than azaleas, whether petunias clash with pinks, and whether wallflowers bloom in the spring or the fall. Gardeners who throw seeds at random are likely to reap chaos. In much the same way, you can keep what you write from sounding chaotic by working on each purpose separately. Then when you need to blend purposes, you'll have a better chance of keeping the emphasis where you want it.

> *The four main writing purposes are giving directions, explaining, telling what happened, and persuading.*

Giving Directions

One common writing purpose is telling other people how to do something—**giving directions**. All of us give directions, and all of us follow them, every day. We follow recipes when we attempt to make chicken cacciatore or even drawn butter. We follow the steps on assembling a TV stand; we read the labels on paint cans, the tissue sheets in dress patterns, and the owner's manual for our microwave ovens. We say eagerly to our friends, "I'll show you!" but if the friends are far away or the project is complicated, we write the directions down. We not only leave notes for the baby-sitter, we post signs on how to operate the word processor. Whenever we offer step-by-step advice on completing any kind of project, we're giving directions.

Writing that gives directions tells readers how to do something.

Explaining

Another common general purpose is **explaining**. In one sense, of course, the experienced cook and the people who built the TV stand are *explaining* to their readers what steps to follow in cutting up the chicken or putting the stand together. Their purpose, however, is to speak directly to readers who will actually do the job, rather than to readers who are mainly interested in the theory behind it. Although giving directions is often very reasonably considered a kind of explaining, directions have some important differences from other explanations. The writer giving directions is saying, "Do this, then do that." In other kinds of explanations, writers never talk to their readers as though the writers were giving commands. These examples show the difference:

> Don't drink alcohol when you're taking antibiotics. [*directions*]

> The combination of antibiotics and alcohol can cause dangerous reactions. [*explanation*]

> Don't run film backward through a projector with the sound on. [*directions*]

> The sound track on a film passes an exciter light, which converts the track to the sound you hear. If the film is run backward while the sound is on, the exciter light becomes overloaded and blows out. [*explanation*]

To avoid confusion, in this book we'll save the term *explanation* for the kind of writing that deals with meaning or relationships—writing that defines or compares or classifies or analyzes.

For instance, if you wrote a paper on IQ tests, you would be explaining when you gave a careful definition of what "standard deviation" means. You would also be explaining when you compared IQ tests and achievement tests, or when you classified the kind of tests given to children in your neighborhood school, or when you analyzed the effects the misuse of tests can have on schoolchildren who are labeled by them. Here are some other examples of explanation:

> A standard deduction is the dollar amount taxpayers are allowed to subtract from their income if they don't want to itemize what they have paid in medical bills, taxes, interest, and so on. [*definition*]

> Although severe indigestion and heart attacks can cause similar symptoms, the first-aid treatment for the two conditions is very different. [*comparison*]

> Lizards, Gila monsters, and dinosaurs all belong to the reptile family. [*classification*]

> In order to understand the working of a welding torch we must consider each of its separate parts. [*analysis*]

Many textbooks—in science or in English, for instance—are made up of explanation. Part of what we are doing here is explaining the difference between one writing purpose and another.

> *Writing that explains tells what something is, what it means, or how it works. Explanation defines, compares, classifies, or analyzes.*

Telling What Happened

Some occasions call for reports instead of explanations. **Reports** are clear and complete accounts of what happened, not attempts to explain why the events occurred or arguments saying they shouldn't have occurred at all. The minutes that secretaries write are one example of a report; the minutes tell what happened in the meeting. Newspaper articles are another example. A front-page news story says, "Thirteen people were killed in weekend highway accidents," or "A severe earthquake left thousands homeless," or "The city council passed a zoning ordinance last night." But news writers do not, in their front-page accounts, warn you to drive carefully or urge you to send sandwiches and blankets to the homeless or tell you the council members are a pack of reactionary idiots. You may find these lectures and appeals and opinions on the editorial page or in syndicated columns, but the news story itself, if it is carefully written, will tell only what happened.

Reports are an objective record of events, with the writer's opinions carefully kept out. Sometimes, however, you will want to write about special events in your own life and make your readers understand why those events were important. You will still be telling what happened, but instead of just producing a record you will be dealing with a **personal experience**—trying to let your readers share the feeling and the mood of your experience. Here is the difference:

> On January 16, 1977, John and Mary Davis were granted a divorce. John Davis was given custody of the two children. [*report*]

> When my parents were divorced and I went to live with my father, I discovered that mothers do more than sew and scold. [*personal experience*]

Telling what happened, either as a report or as a personal experience, is often a useful part of other kinds of writing, and whatever your general purpose is, you will frequently find yourself using it. Reports, however, are so important in much college work and in many jobs that you must be able to recognize them and know what their requirements are.

> *Reports are an objective account of what happened, without giving an opinion about it.*

> *Personal experience papers try to help readers understand why what happened to the writer is important.*

Persuading

Probably the most common writing purpose is **persuasion**—trying to get others to agree with you or do what you want them to do. Perhaps you wrote a letter to the newspaper, urging people to boycott a grocery store that was selling nonunion lettuce. Perhaps you wrote to an airline company, hoping to persuade them to pay for your lost suitcase, or hired a lawyer to persuade a judge that the company should be forced to pay. Perhaps your little sister, or your own child, wrote home from summer camp, pleading for a bit more spending money.

We not only do a lot of persuading ourselves, we read and hear a lot from other people. Half the letters we get in the mail try to persuade us to subscribe to a magazine, vote for a candidate, take out an insurance policy, buy some product we never thought of needing, or send money to somebody's good cause.

In fact, we are overwhelmed by persuasion, some of it masquerading as something else. Senator Goodsell tries to convince the folks back home that voting for him means better schools and lower taxes. Ad writers try to convince us that Twinkle toothpaste will make our teeth a whiter white, that Manheim cigarettes will make us look like cowboys, that because Talaco Oil Company believes in the American way of life, whatever that is, we should buy their gasoline. If you go to church on Sunday, the sermon is designed to persuade you to mend your wicked ways or, if your ways are not wicked, to put some money in the plate. When you were little, your parents tried to convince you that good children pick up their toys, and perhaps you are trying to convince your own children that hitting each other is not acceptable behavior. Editorial writers persuade us that legalized gambling is (or isn't) good for the community, that building a new jail will (or won't) prevent crime, that Senator Goodsell should (or shouldn't) be elected to another term. *Persuading* is the main purpose of any writing that tries to get readers to change their behavior or their beliefs.

In its most straightforward form, persuasion uses such words as *should* or *ought to,* or tells us that we *must* do something or other to make ourselves (or the world) better and safer. Persuasive writing also uses words that praise—*good, safe, beautiful, economical, patriotic*—and words that blame—*bad, dangerous, ugly, expensive, treasonable.* Such words sometimes appear in other kinds of writing, of course, but whenever the main purpose of the writing seems to be getting us to agree that something is good or bad, we can be sure that somebody is trying to persuade us.

Writing that persuades tries to get readers to change their behavior or their beliefs.

Summarizing—A Different Kind of Purpose

While you are in college you will frequently need to use what may seem like a fifth writing purpose—a **summary**. To summarize means to shorten and put in your own words what someone else has written. But what the other person has written always has a purpose of its own. When you summarize, you are doing two things at once—putting what the first writer said into your own words, and following the original writer's purpose.

Perhaps you are answering an essay question in a literature class. The question is, "What happened in the last chapter of *Invisible Man*?" Your answer will be a summary of what Ralph Ellison wrote, but your purpose will be the same as his—to tell what happened. Or a question in a botany test may ask you to identify photosynthesis. Your answer, if it is satisfactory, will be a summary of the explanation in the botany textbook.

In this class, too, summarizing will often be needed. If you are trying to persuade your readers that the city park should be better patrolled at night, you may want to back up what you say by using some ideas from an editorial in the daily paper—summarizing what the editorial said and giving credit to the newspaper for the ideas. In answering those essay questions, of course, you didn't have to give credit. Your literature teacher knew you were shortening what Ellison said, and your botany teacher expected the information to come from the text.

To succeed in college you will need to do a lot of summarizing. You will also need to be able to recognize summaries when you see them. Except in answers to test questions, properly written summaries are not hard to identify because they always mention the source. They begin or end with phrases such as "According to the United States Department of Agriculture . . ." or "As yesterday's paper reported, . . ." If you think you need help in summarizing, you can turn directly to Appendix 1 on page 363.

When you write a summary, you shorten and put into your own words what another writer has said. Summaries always have a purpose of their own.

Finding a Topic

In ordinary life, what you write about is usually chosen for you by the circumstances of your life or the requirements of your job. In college, however, you're sometimes asked to produce a paper with a certain general purpose, and the subject of that paper is left up to you. You must **find a topic**. Knowing that you are going to explain or persuade, naturally, is not enough to start you writing. You have to explain *something*, or convince your readers that they should agree with *something*, and what that something will be can create a problem.

Many beginning writers spend a lot of time worrying about what to write about. They see themselves as ordinary people who have had ordinary experiences and whose information about most things is pretty limited. Caught in the conviction (almost always mistaken) that they aren't experts on anything, they hesitate to expose their ignorance. But we are all ordinary people. It's the way we see our experiences that make them extraordinary, and the way we use those experiences that helps our readers to share them with us. When you write about something you care about, you can make your readers care, too, even if the topic is no more exciting than a ride on a bus or method of cleaning closets.

When you try to decide in this class—or in biology or business or embalming—what the topic of your paper will be, keep two things in mind: First, the topic should be something you know about or are willing to spend some time finding out about. Second, the topic should be something that seems interesting enough or important enough to be worth the time you'll spend on it. If the subject seems dull or trivial to you, it's pretty certain your readers will be bored.

Even though you have chosen a topic you find fascinating, you may think it safer to leave it as wide open as possible. "After all," you say to yourself, "if I write about families, I'll be able to use everything I know—how to get along with in-laws, what happened when my sister got divorced, what's wrong with the laws of adoption, why people say traditional families are disappearing, what a Spartan family was like (from the book we're reading in history), and why I think parents should set a curfew for their kids. My general purpose will be to *explain* about families." If you fall into the trap of a topic that broad, however, you will be saying way too little about way too much. Just as your readers are getting interested in one thing, you'll be off in another direction, and everybody will end up thoroughly frustrated.

Listing that information about families, of course, was a step in the right direction—you were beginning to collect ideas about your chosen topic. Next, you should expand the list:

> getting along with in-laws
> Jake's fight with his father-in-law
> living in cramped quarters
> my sister's divorce
> custody of the children
> joint custody
> children's vacations with their grandmother
> laws of adoption
> one-parent families
> traditional families
> waiting in line for a shower
> aid to families with dependent children
> Medicaid
> Spartan families
> juvenile delinquency
> Bobbie's run-in with the cops
> curfew regulations—set by families or by city?
> people who won't take turns

The list could go on and on. You will be able to think of a lot more, connected with your own family or families you know. This process, known as listing or brainstorming, gives you plenty of ideas from which to choose.

After listing everything you can think of, you are ready for the next step, sorting your ideas to decide which ones are related. Some writers draw circles around the ideas that seem to fit together. Some writers make charts. Some simply choose the idea that seems the most promising and start a new list, keeping anything from the old list that seems useful. If waiting in line for the shower inspires you most—

after all, it took twenty minutes this morning before you could get in the bathroom—you might decide to write about the difficulties of five people sharing a four-room apartment.

Your next list might include:

> living in cramped quarters
> waiting in line for the shower
> people who won't take turns
> finding a place to study
> sharing the cooking and the kitchen cleanup
> arguments over the TV
> closet space
> my sister Hattie is a pig

You have found a general topic—living in cramped quarters—and two problems that are caused by it: lack of space (the closets and the place to study) and the need to take turns (with the shower, the kitchen chores, and the television). The comment about your sister may have to go, unless you can show that she takes more than her share of the closet space or refuses to do her share of the dishes. Whatever you decide about Hattie, you have found a topic, narrowed it to a reasonable size, and made the beginning of a plan.

If you decide you don't like that topic after all, your original list offers plenty of other choices. If you are concerned about the adjustments necessary when a divorce occurs, you may draw circles around a different group of ideas—my sister's divorce, custody of the children, joint custody, one-parent families, aid to families with dependent children, and even vacations with their grandmother. Perhaps your sister is in the middle of an argument about custody, and you don't know much about what the law is in your state. After a trip to the library, you decide to write on joint custody—what it is, who can obtain it, what the results usually are.

It's possible, of course, that a topic has been assigned. "This week's topic is education," the teacher says and disappears down the hall. Now your problem seems especially difficult, since the choice has not been yours and the assigned topic is enormous. Every newspaper you pick up says something about schools; several five-star commissions have announced that American education is failing and tried to explain why; taxpayers have just defeated a school levy; teachers are on strike in four major cities; education in some form has always existed everywhere; and you have been being educated yourself for a sizable number of years.

The only thing to do, of course, is to start brainstorming, but rather than list everything you can think of—that might take you six weeks—try to find one part that interests you or that you know something about. You might limit the topic geographically, to your own city or your own high school. You might limit it in time, to education in ancient Greece or to pioneer days in your area. Think about it for a day or two while you're driving to school, drinking coffee, or trying to go to sleep. And talk about it to anybody who will listen—your roommate, your family, the woman who works next to you. When you've broken the big topic down to a much smaller one, start making your lists and arranging your ideas.

In finding a topic for your paper, choose something you know about or want to find out about, something interesting enough or important enough to be worth your time. Making lists can help both in finding a topic and narrowing it to a suitable size.

Writing Main Idea Sentences

By the time you have collected your ideas, sorted them out, and put them into an order you like, you should have some idea of what your main point will be. Now is the time to work out a **main idea sentence**. A good main idea sentence will make clear what the general purpose of the paper will be—giving directions, explaining, telling what happened, persuading, or summarizing—and it will state the idea or event on which the paper will be based. Here are some samples of main idea sentences on that very broad topic, education:

1. High schools should require three years of math for graduation.
2. Public school teachers should not be allowed to strike.
3. Standardized tests are unfair to many students.
4. British and American colleges operate on different systems.
5. People who oppose school prayer can be divided into three general groups.
6. The school levy failed to pass because retired people were worried about taxes, business leaders were annoyed that some high school graduates can't spell, and editorial writers claimed that teachers have too much free time.
7. Six cases of violence occurred in Woodside High School last year.
8. When I dropped out of school at fifteen, I found that not having a high school diploma does make a difference.
9. To register for adult education classes by mail, you must follow four separate steps.
10. In a recent article in *Library Doings* called "Don't Censor Books," Arden Musgrove points out that students who aren't allowed to read what interests them often don't read at all.

All ten of these sentences have three things in common. First, they all narrow the general topic of education to something much more specific; second, they make clear what the main point of the paper will be; and third, they suggest the general purpose of the paper. The first three main idea sentences will lead to papers of persuasion. They all express the writer's opinion, and the papers will try to get readers to share that opinion. Equally satisfactory main idea sentences could express opposite opinions:

1. For many students three years of math are a waste of time.
2. Public school teachers must be allowed to strike.
3. Standardized tests are the fairest way of measuring how much students have learned.

The next three main idea sentences (4, 5, and 6) will lead to papers of explanation. The paper for sentence 4 will compare British and American colleges, probably without saying which system the writer thinks is better. That for sentence 5 will classify people who are against school prayer and explain the characteristics of each group, again without taking a stand on the issue. From sentence 6 will come an analysis of the reasons for the failure of the school levy.

Sentences 7 and 8 will tell what happened; sentence 7 will produce an objective report, somewhat like a newspaper account, and sentence 8 will introduce details of a personal experience. Sentence 9 will result in a set of directions. Sentence 10, as you can tell by the reference to Arden Musgrove and *Library Doings,* will lead to a summary of what another writer has said.

It shouldn't be hard to write a satisfactory main idea sentence. If you begin with the topic you've decided on and then say something about it, you'll end up with a complete sentence.

> *Topic* — Standardized tests
> *Statement about it* — are unfair to many students.

Not all complete sentences are main idea sentences, however. Certainly the statement, "I am going to write about standardized tests," is, in the grammatical sense, a complete sentence. But the sentence that states your main idea must not contain such obvious evasions as "I am going to write about . . ." or "This paper will be about . . ." To test whether you have stated your idea clearly, strike out all repetitions of the question you began with (What shall I write about?) and examine what remains. After you have crossed out "This paper will be about," do you still have a complete sentence? "Three years of mathematics" is obviously not a complete sentence, but neither is "Requiring three years of mathematics for high school graduation." Such fragments will lead people to ask, "Well, what about it? Are you for it or against it?" "When I dropped out of high school" will force people to ask, "Well, when you dropped out, what happened?" Your main idea sentence must answer such questions before they are asked.

It's a good idea to check your sentence to make sure it's not too narrow. "Sometimes teachers strike" is certainly a complete sentence, and so is "I don't know much about standardized tests," but neither of them will leave you anything to say after you have announced those facts. You have developed a good main idea sentence if the things you could use to support the main idea suggest themselves easily. "Standardized tests are unfair to many students" can be followed by enough examples of unfair questions that readers will understand why you made the statement. "To register for adult education classes by mail, you must follow four separate steps" can lead to what the steps are and the order in which they should be accomplished. If you aren't sure where your main idea sentence will take you, discard it and find another that does provide you with a clear direction.

> *A good main idea sentence makes clear what the purpose is, tells what the topic is, and makes a statement about the topic.*

Finding Your Audience

Knowing who your readers will be—that is, your **audience**—is almost as important as knowing what your general purpose is. In writing that letter to Uncle Ephraim, you considered the state of his health and his interest in your mother's activities. If the letter had been to Aunt Ada, instead, you might have mentioned your mother's new job, but you would probably have asked her how the tomatoes were coming along and skipped the arthritis. Aunt Ada is perfectly healthy, but she does care a lot about her garden.

What's sensible in your personal correspondence is also sensible in your other writing. Knowing who will read your paper should control many of the decisions you make. What do your readers already know and what do they need to be told? If you are writing a report on the treatment of native Americans in the Pacific Northwest, have you assumed that everybody knows who Chief Joseph was? Would it help to give a little background about the Nez Perces before you tell what happened on that tragic thousand-mile flight through Idaho and Montana? If you are writing directions on starting a stamp collection, and you expect your readers to be about twelve years old, is it safe to assume that they'll know what philately is?

Although it's true that most college writing will be read by the teacher who assigned it, don't assume that the papers you write in this class are intended for the teacher alone. The audience for much of your writing should be the other students in the class. You will need to make educated guesses about what their needs are. Not everybody will know the rules of soccer, for instance, or what a byte is, so if you are writing about last week's exciting game, or what to do when a computer disk is full, you'll have to explain some of your terms. On the other hand, if you are writing about the need for better policing on the south parking lot, there's no need to explain what a parking sticker is and how to obtain one, or where the parking lot is located; other people in your class will have that information.

Occasionally, you may be asked to create an imaginary audience for what you write, an audience that is neither your classmates nor your teacher. Perhaps you will be asked to write directions telling twelve-year-olds how to start a stamp collection. In that paper you would want to keep your words fairly short, your ideas fairly simple, and your tone friendly and informal. You would probably use contractions and colloquial expressions. Or perhaps you will be asked to prepare a formal report for the Board of Trustees on the number of foreign students enrolled in technical courses. In that paper you would eliminate contractions—say *will not* rather than *won't* and *cannot* rather than *can't*. You would avoid colloquial expressions—say *appeared indifferent* rather than *didn't give a darn*. You would choose wording that sounds more dignified—say *unable to locate* rather than *couldn't find*.

Who your audience will be controls the words you choose, the tone you adopt, and the amount of background information you give.

Writing Your Paper

Planning your paper and considering the needs of your readers will get you off to a good start, but to write a good paper you will need more than a start. A plan, no matter how complete it is, is not a paper. Now is the time for more brainstorming. Jot down anything you can think of that's connected with what you plan to say—colors, smells, sounds, times, names, memories, contrasts, comparisons. Making such a random list is a kind of exploration, something like a woman who tries on all the clothes in the most expensive departments in the store, even though she ends by buying one ten-dollar blouse because that's all she really needs. Like the woman in the store, you can select what you really need and forget about the rest. But before she bought the blouse, perhaps she consulted a friend. You can do that, too. Ask somebody else to read your first draft and tell you where you need to add something, where you need to leave something out. Or trade drafts with other students in the class. Try to make your next draft answer all the questions that have been raised. Professional writers get this kind of advice all the time. It's only reasonable for you to get it, too, as long as you remember that the final responsibility for what you write is yours, and yours alone.

Different kinds of writing purposes and different kinds of audiences require different kinds of development, but there's no purpose and no topic, intended for any kind of audience, that can't be made interesting by a writer who digs for the right material. There can be a real pleasure in completing a piece of writing that says just what you want it to say. It may be a while before you regard writing as fun, but many people have learned to enjoy the process as well as the product of their writing. They like the intellectual workout of sorting their thoughts, putting mental pictures into words, and finding the best words to help their readers share their pictures and their ideas. Such writers keep the needs of their readers clearly in mind. Their readers won't share the frustration of the poor father who received this letter from summer camp:

Dear Daddy

I'm having a good time.   The nurse thinks it will be OK.   This

letter is about money.

                                     Love,

                                  Timmy

Key Words and Ideas _____

If you know how these key words are used in this chapter, and if you can answer these questions or finish these statements in your own words, you can be fairly certain you have understood the most important ideas in the chapter. If you have trouble with any of them, reread the part of the chapter where the discussion occurs.

1. **Private writing** refers to . . .
2. **Public writing** is . . .
3. What does a good **writing process** involve? Why should **polishing** and **editing** come at the very end in any writing process?
4. What is meant by a **draft**?
5. The four **writing purposes** covered in this book are . . .
6. Writing that **gives directions** tells . . .
7. Writing that **explains** tells . . .
8. A **report** tells . . .
9. **Personal experience** tries to . . .
10. In a paper of **persuasion** you . . .
11. What is a **summary**?
12. In writing, **audience** means . . .
13. What should you consider in **finding a topic**?
14. What does a good **main idea sentence** do?
15. Why should you know who your **audience** will be?

Exercises _____

Exercise 1. Private and Public Writing.   Make two columns and label one column "private" and the other "public." Then list, in the proper column, all the private and public writing you can remember doing in the last two months. Keep these lists in a notebook so you can add to them as the year goes on.

Exercise 2. Brainstorming.   Make another list, this time including all the things you are interested in at the moment and all the things you think you know quite a bit about. Keep this list in your notebook, too. It will help you later.

Exercise 3. More Brainstorming.   For each of these very general topics, list as many ideas as you can think of under each one:

> college
> money
> fun

Then compare your lists with those of other students in your class. Have you all listed the same things? There will probably be some overlapping, but not much; you are all different individuals, with different experiences. Keep these lists, too, in your notebook.

Exercise 4. More Brainstorming.   Working with a group of other students, list all the ideas that occur to any of you on these general topics:

> marriage
> police
> disarmament

Keep these lists in your notebook too. All the ideas belong to all of you.

Name _____

Exercise 5. Identifying Purposes. Which writing purpose does each of these sentences express—giving directions, explaining, telling what happened, persuading? You are not being asked whether these would be good main idea sentences—some of them would not—just what the purpose is.

1. President Kennedy was assassinated in Dallas in 1963.

   _____

2. Be sure to set the brakes before you try to jack up the car.

   _____

3. Success in college depends on four things: reading well, writing well, time to study, and money for tuition.

   _____

4. The college bookstore should sell some mysteries, not just textbooks.

   _____

5. Tornadoes are extremely dangerous.

   _____

6. Last Wednesday a nursing home on Front Avenue caught fire, injuring six elderly residents.

   _____

7. People should protest the government's transporting nuclear waste on public highways.

   _____

8. In spite of Three Mile Island, nuclear power is perfectly safe.

   _____

9. Seven people were arrested yesterday for trying to stop the passage of a White Train.

   _____

10. Washing wool sweaters is easy if you use a mild soap, remember not to wring them, and lay them flat to dry.

    _____

11. Laws against air pollution should be more strictly enforced.

    _____

12. In 1984 a fire in a tire dump in Everett, Washington, burned out of control for more than six months.

    _____

13. The city requires permits for back-
    yard burning.   _____

14. Get a permit from the city fire depart-
    ment before you burn leaves in your
    yard.   _____

15. Several states have passed laws requir-
    ing that small children be in car seats
    in the family car.   _____

16. MADD is an organization of mothers
    who want to stop drunken driving.   _____

17. MADD's proposal differs from pres-
    ent regulations in two ways.   _____

18. The county should set up road blocks
    to search for drunken drivers.   _____

19. Road blocks are bad because they
    assume that drivers are guilty unless
    they are proved innocent.   _____

20. Don't drive if you have had more than
    two beers in the last hour.   _____

Exercise 6. Finding Samples of Writing Purposes.   Look in a newspaper to find paragraphs showing different writing purposes—giving directions, explaining, telling what happened, and persuading. Try to find paragraphs that seem to have only one purpose. Then cut the paragraphs out and paste, staple, or tape them into your note-book, labeling the purpose of each paragraph. Share your paragraphs with other students in the class to see whether they agree as to what the purposes are.

Name _____

Exercise 7. Recognizing Main Idea Sentences.   Which of the following are main idea sentences, written so that you can tell both what the topic is and what the purpose will be? Cross out those that are not main idea sentences. Identify the writing purpose of those that are main idea sentences.

1. The first time I drove a car.   _____

2. This paper will be about learning to drive.   _____

3. Farming in Minnesota is quite different from farming in Georgia.   _____

4. Many small farmers went bankrupt in Minnesota last year.   _____

5. Summers on my grandfather's farm.   _____

6. Explaining how to spray tomatoes.   _____

7. What a difficult time my father had when he tried to get a bank loan.   _____

8. Immigration regulations for Vietnamese orphans should be relaxed.   _____

9. Immigration regulations for Vietnamese orphans should be made more strict.   _____

10. Adopting a baby.   _____

11. My aunt adopted a little Vietnamese girl last year.   _____

12. Advertisements for cigarettes on prime-time television.   _____

13. The Surgeon General's office has adopted new warnings against the dangers of cigarette smoking.   _____

14. The tobacco lobby in the United States Congress.   _____

15. Water skiing requires three kinds of equipment.   _____

16. This paper will explain what water skiing equipment is.

    _____

17. Before you refinish an old chair, make sure you have all the equipment you will need.

    _____

18. I made a terrible mess when I tried to refinish my father's old rocking chair.

    _____

19. Four extracurricular activities for night-school students.

    _____

20. The college should provide more activities for night-school students.

    _____

21. Every high school student should read *The Diary of Anne Frank*.

    _____

22. Some parents have requested that *The Diary of Anne Frank* be removed from the high school library.

    _____

23. The American Civil Liberties Union has filed a suit to stop the censoring of books in the high school library.

    _____

24. Censorship of books should be stopped.

    _____

25. When I went to Chicago.

    _____

26. On my trip to Chicago, I discovered that all big cities are much the same.

    _____

27. The great Chicago fire was started by Mrs. O'Leary's cow.

    _____

28. A dip-stick heater can help to start a car on a cold morning.

    _____

29. Using a dip-stick heater.

    _____

30. Television stations show too many old movies.

    _____

31. Late-night movies can be divided into three major groups.

    _____

Name _____

Exercise 8. Recognizing Satisfactory Main Idea Sentences. Which of these main idea sentences seem suitable for a paper of one or two pages? Mark those you think are suitable with OK and be ready to explain what you think the paper might go on to say. Mark unsuitable ones NO and be ready to explain your reasons. The reasons for your answers are more important than the answers themselves.

1. I ate three helpings of spaghetti yesterday. _____

2. Spaghetti is easy to make if you have the right ingredients. _____

3. Most of my friends like spaghetti. _____

4. The new restaurant on Main Street serves four kinds of spaghetti, all of them equally appetizing. _____

5. Building a garage is not hard if you follow these seventy-five steps. _____

6. Inexperienced carpenters should not try to build a garage. _____

7. When I tried to build a garage, I wasted both my time and my money. _____

8. *The Oxford English Dictionary* is known as the OED. _____

9. Every college student should become familiar with the OED. _____

10. Jogging is a good exercise for three reasons: it's fun, it's cheap, and it's healthy. _____

11. In 1985 a man in a New York subway shot four teen-agers who demanded that he give them five dollars. _____

12. The majority of New York citizens supported the action of a man who shot four teen-agers in a New York subway. _____

13. The sale of handguns should be outlawed.   ———

14. The National Rifle Association opposes any restriction on the sale of guns.   ———

15. In countries where handguns are illegal, the rate of violent crime is much lower than in the United States.   ———

16. The term *vigilante* means a person who punishes a criminal without waiting for the law.   ———

17. Vigilante groups were common in the Old West.   ———

18. Examining the motives of thirty vigilante groups that operated between 1850 and 1900 can provide useful information for today's world.   ———

19. My father knew a man who claimed to have been a cattle rustler in Wyoming fifty years ago.   ———

20. My great grandmother settled on a homestead in Montana in 1908.   ———

Name _____

Exercise 9. Writing Main Idea Sentences.   Go back to the list you made in Exercise 2—things you're interested in. Pick four and write a main idea sentence for each. Then say what the purpose of the paper would be and who would be the readers. Remember that you may have to do some narrowing before you write your main idea sentence. For instance, if you have put "sewing" on your list, you might narrow it to "hemming a dress." Then your main idea sentence might be:

> Two acceptable ways to hem a dress are hand stitching and blind stitching by machine.
> *Purpose:* giving directions
> *Audience:* high school students learning to sew

Or you might narrow the same topic to an account of the first time you made a tailored jacket. Then your main idea sentence might be:

> The first time I tried to make a tailored jacket, it took me three weeks and I thought I would go crazy.
> *Purpose:* telling what happened (personal experience)
> *Audience:* a group of experienced seamstresses

1. *Idea* _____

   Narrowed topic (if needed) _____

   Main idea sentence _____

   _____

   Purpose _____

   Audience _____

2. *Idea* _____

   Narrowed topic (if needed) _____

   Main idea sentence _____

   _____

   Purpose _____

   Audience _____

3. *Idea* _____

   Narrowed topic (if needed) _____

   Main idea sentence _____

   _____

   Purpose _____

   Audience _____

4. *Idea* _____

   Narrowed topic (if needed) _____

   Main idea sentence _____

   _____

   Purpose _____

   Audience _____

Name _____

Exercise 10. Main Idea Sentences for Different Purposes.   Pick another topic from the lists you made in Exercises 2, 3, or 4. This time write four main idea sentences on the same topic, one for giving directions, one for explaining, one for telling what happened, and one for persuading. For instance, if the general topic was "marriage" and one of the items on the list was "teen-age marriages," four satisfactory main idea sentences might be:

Before you decide to marry, consider four things.
Purpose: giving directions
Audience: a group of teen-agers

Many teen-age marriages fail for two reasons.
Purpose: explaining
Audience: your class in social problems

Forty percent of married students dropped out of high school in 1986.
Purpose: telling what happened
Audience: high school students and their parents

Parents should refuse permission for teen-agers to marry.
Purpose: persuading
Audience: members of the high school PTA

Topic _____

Main idea sentence for *giving directions* _____

_____

_____

     Audience _____

Main idea sentence for *explaining* _____

_____

_____

     Audience _____

Main idea sentence for *telling what happened* _____

_____

_____

     Audience _____

Main idea sentence for *persuading* _____

_____

_____

     Audience _____

Chapter 2

Giving Directions

Giving directions sometimes sounds easier than it is. You may understand clearly enough how to do whatever you're writing about—how to bake bread, repair a broken window, or care for an infant with a cold—and it seems simple enough to tell other people to follow your example. If your readers could see you doing it—watch you kneading the dough, removing the broken glass, or hooking up the vaporizer—it might indeed be simple. The difficulty comes in trying to find words for actions that are almost automatic. To write good directions, you must do two things. First, examine your own actions carefully so you won't leave out anything important. Second, find words exact enough so that your readers can see in their minds what you're doing almost as well as if they were watching you.

What to Write About

In many of the directions you write at home or on the job, the topic chooses itself. Angie's baby-sitter needs directions on just what medicine to give and how much. Employees unfamiliar with the office word processor need to be told how to turn it on and what to do next. In writing a paper for English class, the situation is only a little different. You can probably choose **what to write about**, but you are still sharing with your readers something you know how to do.

Your first job is to think of something you can do well, something on which you consider yourself an expert. You may get an inspiration by looking over the lists you made in Chapter 1, or you might do a bit more brainstorming, this time listing everything you can make or do. Don't worry that the topic you select seems "ordinary." If your audience needs the advice, what you say will not seem obvious, and if your readers are trying to do something new, or do something old in a new way, what you write will not bore them.

Choose a topic complicated enough to give you some real practice in direction writing and simple enough that you can do a thorough job. You may be an expert on changing flashlight batteries or putting in new shoelaces, but these processes are too short to give you much practice in writing directions. On the other hand, how to build a garage or program a computer are both much too complicated. If you choose either of these processes, or anything else equally involved, your advice will be so superficial that only people who are already experts will know what you're talking about, and they are indeed likely to find what you say obvious and boring.

Don't choose a topic that requires only three simple steps: "To change a flash-light battery, unscrew the lid, take out the old batteries, and shove the new ones in." And don't choose a topic that requires a long list of equipment and a hundred steps — it might take more than that to explain how to build a garage. Instead, choose something that can be completed in five or ten operations, with not more than five or ten pieces of equipment. How to prepare for a job interview is probably something you could explain thoroughly enough that your readers, by following your advice, might be less awkward and more likely to get the job. How to stop the bleeding until you can get an injured person to a doctor might be advice that could save somebody's life.

As you choose your topic, remember to choose your audience, too. Decide whom you are writing the directions for. People who work in personnel departments are likely to know about preparing for interviews; your directions will be useful to people who have never had a job interview. Nurses know how to deal with bad cuts; your directions will help parents who have never coped with a wound a Band-Aid wouldn't fix.

If you decide to give directions on changing a diaper, you might assume you are writing for a new grandfather who has always foolishly thought that changing babies was woman's work. How to cut a younger brother's hair might be useful advice for teen-agers; how to keep a five-year-old still during a haircut could help young parents. People just learning to sew may not know how to put in a zipper smoothly or how to clean a sewing machine. People who do their own maintenance work may not know how to change the oil in a car. Because you know, you can do a successful job of telling your readers how to do it.

> In finding a topic for a paper of directions, you should consider
>   something you can do well;
>   something you can cover completely in not more than two pages; and
>   who your readers will be.

Planning the Paper

After you have decided on a topic, start **planning the paper** by making two more lists. First, list all the necessary materials and equipment, then list all the steps needed to complete the job. Put down everything you can think of, no matter how trivial it seems. Because the process you are dealing with is very familiar to you, it's easy to leave out something you think is obvious. But your readers are not familiar with that process, and nothing is obvious to them.

When giving directions for baking bread, for instance, make sure you include the flour and specify what kind is needed—enriched white, whole wheat, or self-rising—on your list of supplies and equipment. On your list of steps, don't stop with "dissolve the yeast in warm water." Your readers are not likely to know that if they use too much water, the dough will be sticky, or that if the water is too hot, it will kill the yeast. What seems obvious and maybe even common knowledge to you may be crucial information for your readers. Without that information, they may fail miserably in the whole project.

For the topic, how to paper a bedroom wall, the list of materials might look like this:

> two double rolls of wallpaper
> wallpaper paste
> measuring tape or yardstick
> scissors
> stepladder
> two brushes
> a lot of old newspapers

Is that list complete? It looks all right, but it would be better to be more definite about the kind of brushes, and anybody who has done any papering might suggest a pail to mix the paste in.

For this same topic, papering a wall, the list of necessary steps might be jotted down as they occurred to the writer:

> find stepladder and scissors
> start in corner of wall
> measure first strip
> move furniture and take down pictures
> brush paste on back of paper
> place strip on wall
> smooth with brush
> cut next strip
> follow same steps for each strip
> spread newspaper on long flat surface (floor?)
> match pattern before cutting second strip
> cut off extra paper at top and bottom before next strip
> check to make sure strip is straight
> wipe off extra paste with damp cloth
> clean up mess

The next task is to arrange the steps in the right order. Put in more logical order, these steps would read:

1. move furniture and take down pictures
2. find stepladder and scissors

3. spread newspapers on long flat surface (floor?)
4. start in corner of wall
5. measure strip of wallpaper
6. brush paste on back of paper
7. place strip on wall
8. check to make sure it's straight
9. smooth with brush
10. cut off extra paper at top and bottom
11. wipe off extra paste with damp cloth
12. match pattern before cutting next strip
13. cut strip
14. follow steps 6 through 13 to end of wall
15. clean up mess

Now the writer can see that two of the steps are probably not needed. The step-ladder and scissors are on the list of equipment so readers won't need to be told to find them. And most readers will clean up the mess when they're finished, whether or not they are reminded. It's easier to see, too, that something has been left off the list of equipment—the damp cloth. At least two steps seem to have been omitted in the second list. What about mixing the paste in that pail? Mixing the paste should probably be the second step. Readers need to be told, too, that they should cut the measured strip before they start pasting.

Are the steps in the right order now? Near enough, probably, but we haven't been told what to do with those newspapers spread all over the floor. If they are there to protect the floor from the paste, the writer needs one more step: place the strip of wallpaper face down on the newspapers before spreading the paste.

If, as you plan your own paper, you have listed all the steps you can think of and arranged them in what seems the right order, most of the groundwork will be done. To avoid leaving anything out, however, it's sensible to review the list once more, asking yourself, "Is that everything I do? Is that exactly how I do it?"

As you plan your paper,
   make a list of the material and equipment needed;
   make a list of the steps in the process;
   then put all the steps in the right order.

Main Idea Sentences

Now is the time to work out your main idea sentence. It isn't hard to write **main idea sentences for papers giving directions**. You already know what your purpose is—to give directions—and what your directions will cover—the topic you have selected. Because your lists are completed, you probably have a pretty good idea of what you want to emphasize.

A good main idea sentence for a directions paper will include two things: what the directions will cover and the most important thing readers need to have or do in order to follow the directions. For instance:

> To repair a broken window successfully, the only tools you need are a tape measure, a chisel, and a tack hammer.

Here the job is repairing a broken window. The rest of the sentence lists the three necessary tools and makes the job sound easy by saying "only."

> You can't bake good bread without the proper utensils.

This main idea sentence tells what the job is—baking bread—and what is needed—the proper utensils.

> You can't keep babies from catching colds, but you can keep a baby with a cold more comfortable by following a few simple rules.

This main idea sentence tells what the directions will cover—keeping a baby with a cold comfortable—and gives encouragement by saying that the rules are simple to follow.

A good main idea sentence for how to paper that bedroom wall might be:

> Once you have found some wallpaper you like, it's not hard to cover a single wall if you have a stepladder or a chair, a pair of scissors, a measuring tape, two brushes, and a helper.

> *Main idea sentences for directions papers should include*
> 1. *what the directions will cover;*
> 2. *the most important thing readers need to have or do in order to follow the directions.*

Developing the Plan

Writing your paper involves more than turning the list you've made into sentences, even though you begin with capital letters and end with periods. The student who made the list on page 31 will have to do more than say:

> First move the furniture and take down the pictures. Mix the paste in a pail. Spread some old newspapers on the floor. Start in the corner of the wall and measure a strip of wallpaper. Cut it and lay it face down on the newspapers, brush the paste on the back, and hang it on the wall, checking to make sure it's straight. Then smooth it with the other brush. Cut off the extra paper at top and bottom and wipe off the extra paste with a damp cloth. Before cutting the next strip, match the pattern. Then cut, paste, hang, trim, and wipe again. Do this for each strip till you come to the end of the wall.

Actually, the writer's job is far from finished. All the steps have been included, in the right order, but readers who have never hung any wallpaper won't know how to mix the paste, and they certainly won't know how to trim the paper and match the pattern. The job now is to **develop the plan** into a complete paper.

Instead of merely repeating the list, the writer must get a mental picture of just what happens at each step, and then use that picture to tell in detail what readers must do and how they can do it. Making the directions useful to somebody who has never done the job before will probably mean writing a full paragraph for almost every important step on the list. If you look at the sample paper on pages 42–46, you can see the difference between the writer's first draft, where not enough details were given, and the final paper, where the writer did considerably more than just copy the plan.

Developing your plan means giving complete and definite details about each step on your list.

Writing the Introduction

Like any other paper you write, a paper of directions will sound better if it has an **introduction**. How long should an introduction be? Like a lot of other questions about writing, this one has no absolute answer. The length of the introduction should be in proportion to the length of what you are writing. For very short papers, a short paragraph or sometimes a single sentence is enough, but a ten-page paper may have as much as a page of introduction and a book may have a whole chapter.

The purpose of an introduction is to tell your readers what the writing is going to be about and give them enough other information so that they can decide whether to continue reading. The introduction becomes a contract between writer and readers. You must not go beyond what the introduction agrees to do, nor should you do less than it promises. Perhaps when you wrote your first draft you began with an introductory paragraph, but many writers find it works better for them to write the main part of the paper first and then write an introduction that fits what they have said.

Almost certainly your introduction will include the main idea sentence you have worked out, or some variation of it. If that main idea sentence promises to tell readers how to bake bread, then your paper must be limited to mixing the ingredients, kneading the dough, shaping it, letting it rise, and leaving it in the oven for the right time at the right temperature. You must not get sidetracked into a tirade on whether men belong in the kitchen, unless, perhaps, your audience is men and you want to assure them that they can probably bake better bread than women can. In that case, you may want to include such reassurance in your introductory paragraph.

Although you could let your main idea sentence stand alone as an introduction, you will have a more satisfactory paper if you include more than that. A good introduction may give reasons for doing the job, it may offer encouragement, it may list the necessary equipment, it may justify the need for the first step, or it may simply

arouse interest. The first paragraph should certainly include enough information so that readers can decide whether to undertake the project.

These samples show three ways of introducing a paper giving directions. In each paragraph, the main idea sentence is underlined.

> If you really love the taste, texture, and smell of bread just out of the oven and can't stand that bland, doughy junk the supermarket sells, you may want to try your hand at baking your own. <u>You can't bake good bread without the proper utensils.</u> However, since all you need is a mixing bowl, a spoon, a flat surface (a countertop or cutting board will do), and a baking pan, you probably have everything already on hand.

> <u>You can't keep babies from catching colds, but you can certainly keep a baby with a cold more comfortable by following a few simple rules.</u> New parents, especially, are thrown into a panic when their baby gets sick, but frightened, panicky parents often make babies feel worse instead of better. The thing to do is relax and just follow these rules.

> Everybody who owns a house, or even rents one, is likely to have a broken window occasionally. Some kid will throw a rock, or a ball will go in the wrong direction, or a heavy wind will blow the glass out. You can call the landlord, if you're renting, and wait a month for the repair to get done. If you own your own house, you can pay somebody twenty-five dollars or more to come fix it for you. But it is both quicker and cheaper to fix it yourself. <u>Replacing a broken window is an easy home repair job that requires only a tape measure, a chisel, a tack hammer, and a reasonable amount of care.</u>

Notice that there is no single best place for the main idea sentence. It can come in the middle, at the beginning, or at the end of your introduction. In these samples, the first introduction gives reasons for doing the job and lists the necessary equipment. The second introduction provides encouragement and emphasizes how essential it is for readers to follow the rules that will be given. The third introduction suggests the advantages of replacing your own broken window and mentions the tools that will be required. If you compare the main idea sentence in this introduction with the one given on page 33, you will see that it has been slightly changed. Main idea sentences, like anything else you write, can be revised.

> *A good introduction*
> *serves as a contract, promising readers what the paper will cover;*
> *contains the main idea sentence;*
> *gives enough other information so that readers can decide whether to*
> *follow the directions.*

Writing the Conclusion

Just as a good paper will begin with an introduction, it will end with a **conclusion**. The last paragraph of a paper of directions doesn't need to be very long, but it should give readers the feeling that they have come to the end, not that the writer got tired of writing and just quit. One sentence is usually enough to make a short paper of directions sound complete:

> Now that you know how to bake your own bread, you can have that delicious warm-from-the-oven treat any time you want to—and a wonderful aroma all through the house besides.

> The baby will not only be more comfortable, it will probably get well just as quickly as if you had fretted yourself sick about an ordinary cold.

> When you have washed the finger smudges off the new glass, you can say proudly, "Sure, Mary threw a baseball through the window, but I fixed it without any trouble."

> Now you have a nice cheerful wall instead of an old dirty one.

Single-sentence conclusions such as these are probably all you need for papers of simple directions. But notice that the rather bare conclusion in the last sentence shown above was improved when the writer wrote the final draft. (See page 46.)

Longer, more complicated papers will probably need longer conclusions. But whether the ending of a ten-page paper of explanation uses three paragraphs to summarize the main divisions of the paper, or whether a book defending a point of view includes a whole chapter intended to clinch the argument, all good conclusions have one thing in common: the writer does more than just stop.

A good conclusion makes the paper sound finished.

Finding a Title

There's no right time for deciding what the **title** of your paper will be, but many experienced writers regard it as a final step. Whenever you make the decision, however, remember that simple, direct titles are often the best choice. Especially in a paper giving directions, a phrase that shows clearly what the directions will cover is better than an attempt to be clever. "Baking Your Own Bread" is a more effective title than "To Bake or Not to Bake," or "Rising to the Occasion." The first is a parody of an overworked quotation and the second an obscure pun on the action of yeast. "How to Treat a Baby's Cold" is a better title than "Rockabye Baby," which gives no clue to the real topic of the paper. If you can think of a title that is both clever and clear, fine, but you should worry more about whether the title is direct and appropriate than about whether it is dull.

Although there is no absolute rule about how long a title should be, very short titles may seem to promise too much. "Bread" sounds like an encyclopedia entry rather than a paper on how to make bread, and "Babies" might refer to a report, a personal experience, or even an argument about abortion.

On the other hand, very long titles tell readers more than they need to know at that point. Perhaps the best reason for not making your title too long is to avoid the danger of repeating yourself. If your title is "Almost Anyone Can Read a Subway Map," and the first sentence of the paper is "Almost anyone who learns the basic symbols can read a subway map," readers will find the repetition clumsy and boring. But it would be even worse to make the first sentence "Almost anyone who learns the basic symbols can do it." Although you must give your paper a title, remember that the title is not really a part of the paper.

When you have decided on a title you like, center it at the top of the first page. Capitalize the important words, but don't underline the title or use quotation marks around it. The title for a paper telling readers how to bake bread should look like this:

Baking Your Own Bread

Good titles
  are clear and appropriate;
  are centered at the top of the first page;
  capitalize the first letter of all important words.

Revising Your Paper

Good writers are seldom satisfied with the first draft of a paper; they realize their writing can usually be improved by revising it—adding details, taking out things that don't seem to belong, and sometimes shifting the order around. But they also realize that it's better to wait awhile before trying to rewrite. If you are like most people, whatever you write seems perfectly clear to you while you're writing it. If it didn't seem clear, you wouldn't write it that way. A useful trick is to put the paper away for a day or two and then try to read it as though a stranger had written it. You may find confusions and omissions you didn't know were there.

Even better, let someone else read it. Unless your teacher objects, share your first draft with other students in the class. The questions they ask as they read can guide you in deciding where you need to revise. If somebody asks, "How can you tell it's just a cold and not pneumonia?" you may be reminded to describe what a baby's cold symptoms usually are. If somebody else says, "Everybody knows enough not to take a sick child outside without a warm wrap," you may decide to take that comment out.

Letting your draft cool off before you revise it doesn't mean, of course, that you shouldn't revise as you write. If a good idea for the second paragraph occurs to you in the middle of the fourth paragraph, by all means stop and put it in. Different writers work in different ways. But revising, as the term is used in this book, refers to the content of your paper. It does not mean worrying about spelling and punctuation while you are writing the first draft. That kind of fretting is bound to slow you up and make you lose track of what you are trying to say. Although spelling and punctuation are important, they are matters of editing, and editing is the very last step.

> *Revising your paper means*
>   *adding needed details;*
>   *taking out what doesn't belong;*
>   *making sure the order is right.*

Checking for Style

Style is not some mysterious quality that belongs only to professional writers. *Style* can refer to sounding formal or informal—the difference between saying, "I will be glad to comply with your request," and "Sure, I'll do it." But *style* can also mean whether or not your sentences are clear and easy to read, whether they are long and involved or short and choppy. It can mean whether the words you use are vague or exact. It can mean the difference between sounding apologetic and sounding sure of yourself. It can mean something as simple as using smooth transitions between your ideas or keeping your pronouns straight. All these are matters that beginning writers can control by taking a little care.

Sentence Length

Clarity is important in most writing, but it is essential in giving directions. Just one confused sentence, leaving readers unsure of what you mean, can get them so mixed up that the whole job will be a failure. The following paragraph has a lot of problems. It's unclear for many reasons, but one of them is certainly the length of the sentence:

> Although I'm not an expert on this subject, I think you start with the clay, maybe about five pounds of the right kind—it won't work if you use the wrong kind—and you add the water, less than a cupful, adding it all at once or dribbling it in, it doesn't matter, and work it up, maybe by pounding it or squeezing it, though some people use a kind of shovel and some people tromp it with their feet, and when it's ready you can make a pot and fire it in the kiln, if a person has used the right kind of clay.

Short sentences are more likely to be clear than long, rambling ones. But a string of very short sentences can be equally annoying. This paragraph is no better:

> Although I'm not an expert on this subject, I think you start with the clay. Use about five pounds. It should be the right kind. The wrong kind won't work. Add the water. Use less than a cupful. Add it all at once. Or dribble it in. It doesn't matter which. Work it up. Pound it or squeeze it. Some people use a kind of shovel. Some

people tromp it with their feet. When it's ready you can make a pot. Fire it in the kiln. A person has to use the right kind of clay though.

Try to avoid very long sentences or a string of short, choppy sentences.

Exact Words

Still another problem with those two paragraphs on working with clay is that the wording is very vague. What is the right kind of clay? How much is less than a cupful? What kind of shovel can be used? How can you tell when it's ready? Good directions require exact wording: "five pounds"; "one-fourth of a cup"; "a short-handled garden shovel"; "about the consistency of well-mixed pie dough."

Be sure your words are exact and definite.

Apologies

Another problem with those paragraphs is that the writer's uncertainty shows. Vague wording will make readers wonder whether the writer really knows how to mix clay, but unnecessary **apologies** will make them pretty sure. Whenever you are tempted to say, "Although I'm not an expert on this subject . . ." or "Though I'm not certain, I think . . ." leave it out. If you do know, there's no need for false modesty. If you don't know, find out before you write your paper.

Other phrases that should be cut out as you read over your paper are "in my opinion," "it seems to me," or any of their variations. Your readers can figure out that if it didn't seem that way to you, you wouldn't be saying it. And the phrase "In my opinion" is usually just a way of taking up space, much like the habit some people have of starting every sentence with "you know" when they're talking. Sometimes, though, you may want to make it clear that your opinion differs from that of other people. If that difference is important enough to emphasize, you will do better to come right out and say so: "Many people think . . . , but I think . . ." Naturally you want to be accurate and honest, but the best way to achieve honesty—and accuracy— is to write in a straightforward way, without apologizing. When you're writing directions, you're the expert.

Don't apologize. If you're not sure, find out.

Transitions

Another way to make your writing sound smoother is to take your readers with you as you move from step to step. Words such as *first, next,* and *then* are called **transitions**. If you look again at the two paragraphs on pages 38–39, you'll see that the writer has failed to show the relationship between ideas. The first paragraph uses *and* and *and* and *and* again. The second paragraph doesn't show relationships at all; it reads like a list. Even those choppy sentences would sound better if the writer had added a few words and phrases that suggest order:

> You begin by . . .
> Next . . .
> Then . . .
> After you have . . .
> Before you . . .
> The last step is to . . .
> Finally . . .

Such transitions show how things are related in time, and they help, but overusing any one of them can be tiresome. Try to avoid saying, "*Then* you do this and *then* you do that. *Then* you . . ."

Other transitions show how things are related in space: *in front of, behind, next to, underneath,* and so on. Still others show how things contrast in our minds: *however, nevertheless, but, in spite of, although.* We can call all three of these connectors—those that show time, those that show space, and those that show contrast—**link transitions**. All of them can be useful in writing directions.

Sometimes, however, you will want to show the logical relationship between one group of ideas and the next, and no ready-made transition seems adequate. Then you can pick up a word at the end of one sentence or paragraph and repeat that word, or a slight variation, at the beginning of the next one:

> . . . you will have to *decide* which color to use. Often the *decision* will depend on . . .

We can call this kind of connecting device, which repeats an important word, an **echo transition**. But just as a single link transition can be annoying if it is overused, so echo transitions can annoy your readers if they are used awkwardly. Ending one paragraph with "Now I have explained how to *mix the clay*" and beginning the next with "After you have *mixed the clay* . . ." can sound a bit flatfooted. Besides, your readers may not like to be told that they have been told.

> *Link transitions show relationships of time, space, or contrast.*
> *Echo transitions repeat an important word or phrase.*

Pronouns

Another way to avoid confusion is by keeping the same attitude toward your readers. One way to do this is through your choice of **pronouns**. If you begin by speaking directly to your readers, as though you were face to face, speak to them directly all through the paper. Don't shift from *you* to *a person,* as the writer did in those paragraphs on pages 38–39. Some pronoun changes are so confusing as to be almost scary: "Before *one* can change *their* tire, *you* must stop *our* car." Is "our" car trying to run over "their" tire? Are "you" chasing behind trying to grab the bumper before "one" is smashed to a bloody pulp? Such confusions usually come from writers who have been warned against using *you* and *I* in college papers. No advice could be more mistaken. If you mean "Stop the car before you change the tire," then say so.

Some handbooks still recommend using impersonal expressions such as *people, others, students,* and so on. And it is true that avoiding *I, me,* and *you* will make your writing sound more formal. But struggling for formality often makes for very stilted writing: *one should, one tends,* or even *in the judgment of this writer.* It's better to be too informal than to sound stilted or affected. Such sentences as "One should not stay in the bathtub for more than an hour at a time" will lead some readers to ask "Can two do it?" And such unnatural expressions as *this writer* or *we find* when you mean yourself establish a sense of distance between you and your readers that is surely inappropriate in a paper giving directions.

The best rule is to decide on whatever attitude makes you feel comfortable and then stick with it. If you are comfortable, your readers will probably be comfortable too.

Speak directly to your readers in papers of directions. Don't be afraid to use you *and* I.

Editing—The Last Step

When you're sure your paper says just what you mean, and when you're satisfied with the style, there's still one more step before you are finished. You must **edit** it—that is, you must go over the paper carefully, looking for mistakes in spelling and punctuation. Other departures from the conventions of writing may offend some readers, and you may want to watch out for them too, but misspelled words, misused periods, and missing capital letters are the easiest things for readers to spot. Such matters are certainly not the most important part of writing, but unfortunately if you ignore them, you may be labeled as ignorant. And if your readers see you as ignorant, they may ignore the important things you are trying to tell them.

Look for spelling errors first. Some people believe they can find misspelled words more easily by starting from the end of the paper and going backward. With this system, they can divorce themselves from the meaning of what they have said and look at each word by itself. The system may work for you; it's worth a try. Whatever system you use, if you are not sure how a word should be spelled, use your dictionary. And if you think of yourself as a poor speller, whether or not you are, consult the spelling advice on pages 422–430. Some spelling rules do help, once you learn them and remember to apply them.

Next look carefully at each of your sentences. Make sure that every sentence begins with a capital letter and ends with a period or a question mark, and make sure that every group of words beginning with a capital letter and ending with a period really is a sentence. If you are uncertain, consult the advice on periods on pages 432–433. Commas can be worrisome, too, and you will find some information about using them on pages 434–437. The best general advice on commas, however, is "When in doubt, leave it out." It's better to miss a few than to make your paper look as if there had been a cloudburst of commas in your vicinity.

Spelling and punctuation are not the meat of writing, but they are its good manners. You wouldn't insult your guests by serving their steaks on dirty plates. Don't insult your readers with carelessly edited writing.

Editing means checking for spelling, punctuation, and complete sentences.

A Sample Paper Giving Directions

Here is the first draft of a paper telling how to paper a wall. The comments in the margin include some questions that might have been asked by people who read the first draft.

A Cheerful Bedroom

Title doesn't make clear what the directions cover.

Introduction starts well; it arouses interest. But where is the main idea sentence?

[1] If you wake up some morning feeling depressed because you've been staring at an ugly wall covered with water stains, you don't have to keep feeling bad. A little bit of money and a day or two of your time can change that dirty wall into some nice clean stripes or a cheerful display of flowers.

Do what to one wall? Why not buy single rolls?

Are these comments needed? Why?

What kind of things around the house?

[2] If you are only going to do one wall, you will only need a couple of double rolls of paper, which you can probably get on sale somewhere. Buy some paste at the same time and you're all set. At the wallpaper store they may try to sell you a lot of fancy equipment, like special cutters and plumb lines and things like that, but you really don't need any of that. You can just use things you have around the house anyway.

How do you prepare the wall? What are these newspapers for? How do you mix the paste? What does "big" mean? Will a gallon bottle do? How much is "a little too long"?

[3] Prepare the wall you're going to paper and find a stepladder or a chair to stand on. After the newspapers are spread out on the floor and the paste is mixed in something big, you are ready to start. Measure how long the first piece should be, cut it a little too long, and put the paste on it with a

Are these brushes just "around the house"? If you need a helper, you should say so earlier. Why "up"? Where are you? How do you know where to cut? Writer needs to get clear mental picture of every step in the process.

smaller brush. Then get somebody to hand it up to you and smooth it against the wall with the longer brush. Cut off the extra at the top and bottom and the first piece is up.

How do you fit the paper around the molding? Advice on matching the pattern should come sooner.

[4] After that, just keep on doing the same thing until you get to the end of the wall. If there is a door or a window, it will be a little harder. You will have to cut the paper to fit around the molding. And all the time, of course, you will have to make sure that the pattern matches.

Conclusion is very abrupt.

[5] Hanging wallpaper isn't really hard at all.

Here is the final draft of the same paper. The comments in the margin show how it has been improved.

Title is now clear

How to Paper a Wall

Interesting beginning is kept, but main idea sentence listing equipment and giving encouragement has been added.

[1] If you wake up some morning feeling depressed because you've been staring at an ugly wall streaked with water stains, you don't have to keep feeling bad. A little bit of money and a day or two of your time will let you change that dirty wall into some nice clean stripes or a cheerful display of flowers. Once you have found some wallpaper you like, it's not hard to cover a single wall if you have a stepladder or a chair, a pair of scissors, a measuring tape, two brushes, and an assistant.

Gives reasons for having a helper.

[2] The assistant is important. After some practice you might be able to do the job alone, but if you try it by yourself the first time, you'll probably end up with paste in your hair and more crumpled wallpaper on your clothes than on the wall.

"Double roll" is explained.

[3] If you're going to do just one wall, you will only need a couple of double rolls of paper, and you can usually pick up two rolls of discontinued paper cheap at some sale. The price quoted will be for a single roll, but you can't buy just one roll. Wallpaper always comes in double rolls, so you will have to pay four times the quoted price to get what looks to you like two rolls. Buy some paste at the same time. It's a good idea to get about twice as much paste as the store recommends, because it never goes as far as the box says it will. And

Brushes are described.

unless you can borrow some brushes, better get those too. You will need two—one with long bristles for spreading the paste and one wide, short-bristled brush for smoothing the paper on the wall.

Warning about fancy equipment made briefer.

The store may try to sell you a lot of other fancy things, but don't get taken in. Anything else you need you'll have around the house anyway.

"Big" has been explained— and most houses do have pails or dishpans.

[4]   The first step is to get everything ready. Mix the powdered paste with water according to the directions on the package. A pail or a dishpan or a canning kettle works fine. Then let the paste sit while you're moving the furniture away from the wall,

More definite advice on preparing the wall.

taking down the pictures, pulling out the old nails, and wiping off the cobwebs up by the ceiling. Spread

How to spread newspapers is made clearer.

a lot of old newspapers out on the floor so that they are about a foot wider than the wallpaper and at least a foot longer than the height of the wall. Now you are ready to begin.

[5]   Measure the height of the wall and use the scissors to cut a strip of paper about six inches longer than you will need. Don't worry about cutting it exactly straight because once it is up, you will have to trim it to fit the wall. Then place the strip face down on the newspapers and, using the narrower long-bristled

Directions for measuring, pasting, and cutting are now much more specific.

brush, cover it thoroughly with paste, being especially careful to get plenty of paste on the edges. Get up on the ladder and have your helper hand you the paper, topside up. If you are using stripes, it won't matter, but you don't want flowers to have their stems in the air.

[6]   Starting at the ceiling, put the strip of paper against the wall, leaving it a couple of inches too long at the top. Make sure it hangs straight with the corner

How to hang the first strip is also much more specific.

of the wall of the room. While the paste is still wet —ten or fifteen minutes—you can slide the paper around or even pull it away from the wall until you're satisfied with the way it looks. Use the smoothing brush to make sure the paper is sticking tight, particularly around the edges. Then crease it along the ceiling line with a sharp pencil or your fingernail, get your helper to hand you the scissors, pull the top bit of paper away from the wall, and cut off the extra paper along the crease. Smooth the paper back against the wall with the brush and wipe the smeared paste off the paper and the ceiling with a damp rag. Then get down from the ladder and do the same thing at the bottom.

Advice on matching now given in the right place.

[7] When you cut the second strip, you have to do a little more than measure for length. Hold the paper up against the first strip until the pattern matches before you make your cut. Probably there will be some waste, but it's usually not more than a foot or so. Once this second strip is cut, follow the same procedure, this time making sure that the left edge of this strip fits exactly with the right edge of the strip that's already on the wall and that the pattern matches. Then just keep going until the wall is covered.

Directions for hanging the second strip are more complete.

Directions on how to go around a window or door are better, but readers may still need more help here.

[8] If there is a door or a window in the wall, your job's a little harder. Unless you are very lucky, you'll have to do some vertical cutting. Don't try to measure and cut the paper exactly. Instead, allow the usual couple of inches too much and do your final cutting after the paper is up, just as you did at the ceiling and the floor. If the paper tears a little around the molding, don't worry. The tear won't show after you smooth it down.

Some advice on cleaning up has been added.

[9] When the last strip is up, you and your helper can stand back and admire the job. If you've been careful to put the pasted scraps into a wastepaper basket as you go, instead of letting them paste themselves to the floor, cleaning up won't take very long. Pick up the sticky newspapers, get rid of the extra paste, wash out the brushes, and put the furniture back.

Conclusion refers back to introduction and does a better job of making the paper sound finished.

[10]   When you wake up the next morning, you'll have a clean, attractive wall to cheer you up, and a sense of pride in what you've accomplished.

Key Words and Ideas

Here are some of the important terms and ideas from this chapter. If you have trouble answering any of these questions, reread the part of the chapter where the discussion occurs.

1. When you are assigned a paper of directions, what should you consider in deciding **what to write about**?
2. What are the first three steps in **planning a paper** giving directions?
3. What two things should a **main idea sentence for a paper of directions** include?
4. What is meant by **developing your plan**?
5. Why is an **introduction** called a contract?
6. What does a good **conclusion** do?
7. What makes a good **title**?
8. What does **revising** your paper mean?
9. What is involved in checking for **style**?
10. Why should you avoid **apologies**?
11. What are the two kinds of **transitions**? Explain what each kind is, and give examples if you can.
12. How do **pronouns** show what attitude you are taking toward your readers? What is the best attitude to take in giving directions?
13. What does **editing** mean? Why should editing be the last step?

Exercises _____

Exercise 1. Putting Lists in Order.   In these early plans for papers giving directions, the lists have not yet been put in order. Using your own paper, rearrange the lists in the order that seems most logical. If you are familiar with any of these processes, add whatever steps you think have been left out. Then compare your lists with those of other students in the class.

1. *How to write a paper of directions*
   give it a title
   make a list of the steps
   write a main idea sentence
   cut out all apologies
   check your spelling
   pick something you know how to do
   put steps in logical order
   check sentences for capital letters and periods
   use "you" all the way through
   write introduction

2. *How to roll a sleeping bag*
   begin at foot of bag
   fold straightened bag in half lengthwise
   tie strings with a square knot
   straighten bag out on flat surface
   squeeze roll while rolling it
   brush off leaves, dirt, and sticks as you roll
   wrap weather flap around rolled-up bag

3. *How to make an extension cord*
   buy two plugs, male and female
   remove a half inch of insulation from separated wires at both ends
   separate the two wires for about an inch at both ends
   be sure newly attached plugs are properly insulated
   test finished cord
   measure length of cord you need
   buy electric cord

4. *How to dye shoes*
   use smooth strokes
   pick the color you want
   don't drip dye on clothes
   cover entire surface of shoe
   be sure shoes are clean before dyeing
   dry thoroughly before second coat
   start with a clean applicator
   be sure to purchase shoe dye, not polish
   follow same procedure for second coat

5. *How to paint a room*
   remove rugs and other floor coverings
   take out the furniture
   use overlapping strokes
   cover any furniture too big to move
   mix paint thoroughly
   either a brush or a roller will do
   do woodwork and trim last
   wipe up spilled paint with damp cloth immediately
   remove covers to wall outlets
   wash out the brush or roller
   covering windows with masking tape optional

Name _____

Exercise 2. Main Idea Sentences for Directions Papers.   Mark these main idea sentences *OK* if you think they would be satisfactory for short papers of directions. If you think the topics are unsuitable, mark them *NO.* If the topic seems suitable but the main idea sentence unsatisfactory, rewrite the sentence.

1. I'll tell you how to write a paper of directions.   _____

_____

_____

2. In planning a paper of directions, you should select something you know how to do, make a list of what the steps are, put the list in logical order, and check to see that nothing important has been left out.   _____

_____

_____

3. People who own expensive sleeping bags ought to take care of them.   _____

_____

_____

4. Making an extension cord.   _____

_____

_____

5. Old shoes can be made to look like new by following a few simple steps.   _____

_____

_____

6. There are three ways to get rid of slugs in your garden, but only one way is both successful and ecologically safe.   _____

_____

_____

7. Losing weight is not easy, but it can be done by paying attention to how much you eat, how much you exercise, and how much you want to do it.   _____

_____

_____

8. You can learn to make a quilt if one has a lot of old scraps and a pattern.   _____

_____

_____

9. Only somebody very stupid would not know how to change a tire, but I'll try to tell you anyhow.   _____

_____

_____

10. Startle your guests with magic tricks.   _____

_____

_____

11. To melt ice on your front steps, all you need is a bag of salt.   _____

_____

_____

12. Rebuilding the engine on an old car may take a lot of time, but if you follow these sixty-four steps carefully, you should be able to finish in about two months.   _____

_____

_____

Name _____

Exercise 3. Introductions for Directions Papers. If you think these introductions are satisfactory, underline the main idea sentences. If you think they are unsatisfactory, be ready to say definitely what is wrong with them.

1. This paper is about toys. I don't approve of Cabbage Patch dolls, even though people have been standing in line to try to buy them.

2. The job doesn't take very long, and it's not very hard. It doesn't take much equipment, but you will need to collect everything together before you start. Remember, the most important thing is getting yourself in the right mood.

3. Drugstores sell dozens of different candy bars, but you seldom find packaged fudge that tastes really good. One reason is that fudge is best when it's fresh, and it can get stale within a day or two. Another reason is that fudge is easy to make at home. If you're thinking right now that you'd like something sweet, don't settle for a candy bar. Almost anybody who is careful to measure the ingredients exactly can make rich, creamy fudge in less than half an hour.

4. To change a diaper, you need several things: a clean diaper, a can of baby powder, a wash cloth, and a dirty baby.

5. If you live where the temperature drops down to zero, and if your house is not very well insulated, you can do a few things to keep the water pipes from freezing. Protecting the pipes during cold weather doesn't take any special equipment. But you do have to remember to do it when a cold snap threatens, not after it arrives.

6. Although I've never done it very often, I think I can tell you how to play an old game called "Pit." It's very exciting and noisy. All you really have to do is grab quickly and yell loud. But first you need to be sure that there's nothing breakable on the table.

7. Do you know how to clip a dog? Lots of people don't know and they spend a lot of money in poodle parlors, which scare the dog anyway.

8. You've daydreamed about it hundreds of times. There is a pause during the party when the conversation slacks off and everything is quiet. You step forward, take a deck of cards out of your pocket, and with one deft motion of hand and wrist spread them into a perfect fan. "Take a card, any card," you say. Everyone at the party may think it's magic. But it's not magic. The real secret to doing card tricks successfully is plenty of practice, plenty of patience in trying the basic moves over and over again, and a natural flair for the dramatic.

9. Don't just wish you had a new bookcase. Get some old bricks and build one!

10. Do you have slugs in your garden eating holes in your tender new plants, sometimes destroying them entirely? Most people in this area do. I've heard of three ways to get rid of the pesky things. My grandfather says to put salt on them, and it's true that they shrivel up and die, but that's nasty to look at and takes way too much time if you have as many slugs as I do. The garden store says to buy their slug bait, and that does work, but the package says the bait can be dangerous to pets and kids, and I disapprove of scattering poison around. The best thing is to use some beer.

Name _____

Exercise 4. Conclusions for Directions Papers. If you think these conclusions are satisfactory, mark them *OK*. If you think they are unsatisfactory, be ready to say definitely what's wrong with them.

1. Well, as I already said, it's hard to tell what toys kids will like. _____

2. Now you are finished, and so am I. _____

3. The fudge will be so good everybody in the house will gain two pounds. _____

4. But I guess it might be better to use disposable diapers, even if they do cost more. _____

5. These simple precautions should keep you from having to call a plumber every time the thermometer drops down toward zero. _____

6. The other thing to remember is that every player should be able to reach the center of the table. _____

7. Then sweep up the dog hair that will be all over the floor and stand back to admire your newly groomed dog. _____

8. Practice and patience will pay off, and you can make a sweeping bow to all your envious friends. _____

9. Then put the books in. _____

10. Of course, you could forget about the slugs and just drink the beer. _____

Exercise 5. Titles.   If you think these titles are satisfactory for papers of directions, mark them *OK*. (Pretend that each one is properly centered at the top of the first page.) If you think they are unsatisfactory, be ready to say definitely what's wrong with them.

1. Toys   ———

2. How to Clean a Closet   ———

3. Making Creamy Fudge   ———

4. Changing a Baby's Diaper without Making Either of You Cry   ———

5. Keep That Pipe Warm!   ———

6. "Grabbing Quick and Yelling Loud"   ———

7. Clipping a Dog   ———

8. They Laughed When I Stood up with My Cards   ———

9. Building a Bookcase with Bricks   ———

10. Pesky Garden Pests   ———

Exercise 6. Rewriting Sentences and Using Transitions.   Using your own paper, rewrite these paragraphs of directions so that they are smooth and easy to read. Try for some variety in sentence length, with none of your sentences long enough to be confusing nor so short as to sound choppy. As you rewrite the sentences, use enough transitions so that readers can see the relationships between the ideas. Then compare the paragraphs you have produced with those written by other students. Which paragraphs sound best? Why? Is there a single "right way" to do it? Why or why not?

1. You want to start a campfire. You have no matches. Doing it without matches is easy. You can use a pair of eyeglasses. The glasses work like a magnifying glass. The sun must be out. The sun must shine through the glasses. Collect plenty of paper. The paper must be dry. Collect plenty of twigs and branches. The branches must be small. Leaves can be substituted for the paper. The leaves must be dry. The twigs should be shaved very fine. Hold the glasses so the sun shines on the paper or leaves. This may take a little while. You need to be patient. The paper or leaves will catch fire. Put on the small twigs. They will catch fire. Put on some branches. They will burn. You have the beginning of a campfire. You can add bigger logs.

2. To hem a skirt you need some pins and a needle and thread and a yardstick and you have to decide how high the hem should be and then you turn the bottom edge of the skirt under at the right length and pin the material so it stays up, moving the yardstick five inches along to measure more material, and pin it again, keeping on like this until the skirt is pinned straight all the way around and the same height all the way around. Then you check the hem of the skirt to see if it is pinned okay and thread the needle and lightly stitch around the bottom of the skirt and then remove the pins and press the hem and the skirt should hang straight.

3. Talking to plants makes them healthy. Talking to plants makes them happy. Talking is not enough. Plants can get root-bound. Root-bound plants are unhealthy. The pot is too small. Philodendrons begin to turn yellow. They may need a bigger pot. You can repot your philodendron. It is easy. Get a new pot and some planting soil. The new pot should be the right size. The right size is about an inch bigger around than the old pot. Take the philodendron out of the old pot. Turn it upside down. Tap it on the edge of something. Inside the house a table will do. Outside the edge of a step will do. The philodendron will come out. The soil will come with it. Put a broken piece of pottery in the new pot. Put it over the hole. Put some potting soil in the new pot. Put the philodendron on top of the new soil. Don't bruise the roots. Put more soil around the edges. Put the soil as high on the plant as it was before. Tap the new soil down. Water the plant. It should be healthier and happier. You can talk to it again.

4. If you want to get from the college to the exposition grounds you can drive down Main Street to Rogers Drive, which leads into Exposition Way where the exposition grounds are on the left-hand side. That way you go about three miles to

Rogers Drive and two miles on Exposition Way through the park, which is pretty, but it's easy to get lost there, and it's six miles if you go through the park or you can take the No. 14 bus, which goes straight across the city on Jones Avenue, which is only four miles long, and the bus only costs fifty cents, so maybe it's the best way.

5. Both new and old cars get flat tires. You don't have to despair. You can do it yourself. You have to have a jack and a lug wrench and a spare tire. The spare tire must have air in it. Get the jack. Some jacks fit under bumpers. Some jacks fit in holes in the car body. You push the handle up and down. The jack raises the car. You stop pushing the handle when the wheel is somewhat raised. The tire should still touch the pavement. You must remove the hubcap. You find a screwdriver to go under the edge of the hubcap. You pry hard. The hubcap comes off. The wheel is bolted on. You find a lug wrench. There are four bolts, sometimes more. You loosen the bolts with the lug wrench. You don't take the bolts clear off. This is the first step. Then you jack the car up more. The wheel should be clear off the ground. Take the bolts the rest of the way off. The tire will come off. Put the spare tire on and the bolts back on. Take the car off the jack. Tighten the bolts the rest of the way. Tighten them as hard as you can. Put the flat tire in the trunk. It's all fixed.

Name _____

Exercise 7. Pronouns, Apologies, and Exact Wording. If these sentences seem satisfactory, mark them *OK*. If you think they are unsatisfactory for any reason, rewrite them.

1. In my opinion, buying a preassembled coffee table is a waste of one's money.   _____

    _____

    _____

    _____

2. You begin by removing the old wax and then you scrub the top of the table well and then you rinse it and then one puts on a layer of under-coating and some new wax and then it is polished.   _____

    _____

    _____

    _____

3. The closest videotape store is down past a red light a little way and then you turn right, I think, and go a little farther.   _____

    _____

    _____

    _____

4. If a person has a favorite old chair with an ugly covering, one can make a slipcover for it, at least if you have a sewing machine.   _____

    _____

    _____

    _____

5. You find a lot of people playing poker and they don't know the rules even though you can learn them easily.   _____

_____

_____

_____

6. To improve the taste of your hamburgers, put some seasoning in, just a little, and two or three kinds, and serve them with catsup or mustard or something.   _____

_____

_____

_____

7. This writer had an enjoyable time making cider in an old-fashioned press.   _____

_____

_____

_____

8. It seems to me that you should start with lots of soil and a few pots if you are going to plant three or four or five geraniums.   _____

_____

_____

_____

9. The first thing to do is report the fire because, in my judgment, people should know their emergency number, especially if you live in an old house.   _____

_____

_____

_____

Name _____

10. Be sure the paint is well stirred before you begin.   _____

_____

_____

_____

11. People who forget to stir the paint well will get a streaky job and
     may have to repaint the wall.   _____

_____

_____

_____

12. The writer of this paper once hit her hand with a hammer hard
     enough I had to have four stitches taken in it.   _____

_____

_____

_____

13. Filing your income tax is not too difficult if one follows the direc-
     tions carefully, and I think a person should pay your taxes if you
     don't want trouble with the government.   _____

_____

_____

_____

14. After you have put a little bit of salt into the soup you should, I
     think, taste it, or anyway I would.   _____

_____

_____

_____

15. Put one teaspoon of salt into the soup and then taste it.   _____

_____

_____

_____

Name _____

Exercise 8. Finding a Topic for a Paper Giving Directions.   Make a list of things you know how to make or do. Then circle two that interest you most. Could you explain those processes clearly in papers of about two pages? If not, find two that you think you could explain. Then decide on a suitable audience for each one of them and describe that audience as clearly as you can. Show your completed list to the teacher or to other students in the class. Do they agree that the length would be about right and that the audience would be interested in what you say?

List:

_____

_____

_____

_____

_____

_____

_____

_____

_____

_____

1. *Process* _____

_____

   Audience _____

2. *Process* _____

_____

   Audience _____

Exercise 9. Planning the Paper.   Choose one of the topics from Exercise 8 and list all the steps in the process. If you need to, rearrange the steps in the right order. Then write a main sentence.

How to _____

Audience _____

Steps _____

_____

_____

_____

_____

_____

_____

_____

_____

_____

_____

_____

_____

Main Idea Sentence _____

_____

_____

Exercise 10. Writing the First Draft.   Using the plan you made in Exercise 9, write a first draft of your paper giving directions. Remember to give exact details for each step in the plan. Your paper should do more than just repeat the list. You might try writing the main part of the paper first before you add the introduction, the conclusion, and the title. Then show this first draft to the teacher or other students in the class. Make a note of the questions they ask or the suggestions they make.

Exercise 11. Rewriting Your Paper.   Write another version of the same paper, this time trying to answer all the questions that were asked. Put your paper away for at least a day and reread it to see if you want to make any changes. Then make sure you can answer yes to all the questions on this list.

Check List for Content

1. Have you done everything your introduction promised and no more?   _____

2. Have you told your readers about all the equipment they will need?   _____

3. Have you included all the necessary steps in logical order?   _____

4. Have you given enough details about each step?   _____

5. Does your conclusion make the paper sound finished?   _____

6. Is your title clear and appropriate?   _____

Exercise 12. Checking for Style.   Reread your paper again, looking to see whether you can answer yes to the questions on this check list for style.

Check List for Style

1. Have you rewritten any long involved sentences?   _____

2. Have you combined any short choppy sentences?   _____

3. Have you made sure your words are exact?   _____

4. Have you avoided apologies?   _____

5. Have you used enough transitions to take your readers comfortably from one step to the next?   _____

6. Have you talked to your readers the same way all through the paper? Stayed with *you* if you began with *you*?   _____

Exercise 13. Editing.   The last step is to go over your paper for spelling and punctuation. Make sure you can answer yes to these four questions.

Check List for Editing

1. Have you checked your spelling carefully?   _____

2. Have you used a dictionary when you were not sure?   _____

3. Do all your sentences begin with a capital letter and end with a period or question mark?   _____

4. Is every group of words beginning with a capital letter and ending with a period really a sentence?   _____

Exercise 14. Directions for a Short Journey.   First write your name on a small piece of paper. Then go by yourself and hide the slip of paper somewhere in the building but outside the classroom—anywhere except in the restrooms for men or women. Next write directions exact enough so that another student can find the paper with your name and bring it back. Your directions should start from the door of the classroom. As you write, pretend that there are no written signs in the building—you will have to specify distances, mention left or right, and describe objects that the other student will see. When you have exchanged directions with another student in the class—the teacher may want to supervise these exchanges—try to follow the directions you were given exactly as they were written. If something is missing, don't guess; just stop and return to the room. Your directions have succeeded if the slip of paper with your name on it comes back. If your name doesn't come back, talk about it with the student who tried to follow your directions. Is the problem with the writing or with the reading?

Exercise 15. Directions for a Drawing.   Here's something that's harder than it sounds. Draw four lines at random on a sheet of ruled paper. Then on another sheet of paper write a set of directions exact enough that another student can reproduce what you have drawn without looking at the original. It will help if you refer to the printed horizontal lines as *rules* and the lines you draw as *lines*. Put your drawing away and trade directions with another student in the class. If the other student, by following your directions, can produce a drawing exactly like yours—same size, same proportions, same place on the page—you have both done a good job. If the drawings are not the same, discuss the problem with the other student to see whether the fault is in the writing or the reading. Then try it again.

Chapter 3

Explaining: Definition

When people ask, "What do you mean?" they may be playing for time or showing that they disagree with what has been said. Usually, however, they are asking because they don't understand. Perhaps they want to know what some unfamiliar term means, or perhaps they aren't sure of the precise sense in which you are using a word that can mean several things. Often what they're asking for is a definition.

How Words Get Meaning

Defining words is not as simple as it sounds. We get nowhere with the childish demand, "Just tell me what the **real meaning** of the word is," because words, in themselves, don't *really mean* anything. Words are just symbols, puffs of air that stand for meanings. It's people who put the meaning into those puffs of air. For instance, English-speaking people have agreed that the sound *milk* will represent a nourishing white fluid, but French speakers represent that same fluid by the sound *lait,* Spanish speakers by the sound *leche,* and speakers of Japanese and Swahili by still different sounds. Whatever the sound, the milk stays the same. The meaning exists in the minds of the speakers and listeners. We know, too, that meanings shift and change with time. What do the sounds *a jet* mean to you? Fifty years ago most people would have said, "Something that gushes out with a lot of force, a stream of water from a fire hose, perhaps." Now most of us would think immediately of an airplane.

We learn to give words meaning through our experiences with them, and we all have different experiences. Just as a baby learns what the sound *dog* stands for by hearing it applied to the dogs in the neighborhood, so as we grow older we absorb meanings from the conversations we hear and the books we read. If we all heard exactly the same talk and read exactly the same printed matter, we might all agree on the same meanings. Since we don't, we have to do the best we can.

Remembering that the purpose of language—either spoken or written—is to get meaning out of one mind and into other minds will help. We can never accomplish that aim perfectly, but we can come a good deal closer if we watch out for two things. First, although words don't have any real meaning in themselves, we can't communicate satisfactorily unless the people we're talking to or writing for agree with us as to what the words refer to. Saying *lait* to people who don't understand French won't communicate, and neither will saying *paratoluidine* to people who haven't studied chemistry. Second, we must take the time to explain carefully what we mean by some words whose agreed-on meanings may be fuzzy. Suppose that someone tells you that Regina Angelo, the new mayor, is very patriotic. All of us can agree that *patriotism* means loving your country—any dictionary will say that much. But we still don't understand much about what the mayor believes or how she behaves. Does she open every council meeting with the flag salute and display a large flag in her own front yard? Does she support the Star Wars program because she believes it is necessary for the defense of the country? Or does she show up at nuclear protest marches because she doesn't want the country she loves to be blown off the face of the earth? Until we get a more precise definition of *patriotic,* we can't tell whether or not Regina Angelo fits the meaning we give to patriotism.

Words don't have "real meaning"; people give meaning to words.

Kinds of Definition

Synonyms

The simplest kind of definition is a **synonym definition**—one in which you use another word that means the same, or almost the same, as the word you are defining:

Obese means fat.

Vacuity means emptiness.

A *philatelist* is a stamp collector.

Such definitions are usually satisfactory if they begin with words most people don't know and move to words they do know. They are not much good if they go from one little-known word to another, as this definition does:

To *vacillate* is to oscillate.

You won't get any help unless you already know what *oscillate* means. And this attempt at definition gives even less help:

Vacillation means to vacillate.

The definition goes around in a circle—that is, tries to define a word by a variation of the same word.

Good synonym definitions always move from difficult words to simpler words, and they avoid going in circles.

Class Definitions

Because single words or short phrases often cannot explain some words well enough, a more usual, and usually more satisfactory, kind of definition comes in three parts: (1) the word that's being defined; (2) the big group or class it belongs to; and (3) the way to tell it from other things in the big group. We can call that a **class definition**. Here are some examples:

    1. A *carburetor* (word being defined) is
        2. an apparatus (big group)
           3. for mixing vaporized fuel with air in an internal combustion engine (how a carburetor is different from other kinds of apparatus).

    1. *Vigilantes* (word being defined) are
        2. people (big group)
           3. who take it on themselves to punish criminals without waiting for the law to act (how vigilantes are different from other people).

    1. *Herpes* (word being defined) is
           3. an inflammatory virus (difference)
        2. disease (big group)
           3. that causes watery blisters on the skin (another difference).

    1. *Euphemisms* (word being defined) are
           3. mild or indirect (difference)
        2. expressions (big group)
           3. used in place of harsher, more direct expressions (more differences).

These class definitions are probably satisfactory. If someone tells you that *pass away* is a euphemism for *die* or that *sanitary engineer* is a euphemism for *garbage collector* you can understand what you're being told.

In writing class definitions, it's important to make sure that the third part of the definition, the part that distinguishes the word being defined from other members of the big group, actually does give enough differences. A good definition should fit only the term you are defining and nothing else. Look, for instance, at these unsatisfactory attempts at class definitions:

    1. A *chair* (word being defined) is
        2. a piece of furniture (big group)
           3. for human beings to sit on (difference).

1. *Hydrophobia* (word being defined) is
        3. a virus (difference)
     2. disease (big group).

The problem is not that these two statements are inaccurate—both of them are accurate enough as far as they go. The problem is that they don't go far enough. How is a chair different from a sofa, a bench, or a stool? All of those pieces of furniture are intended for people to sit on, and they often have four legs. The definition of *chair* would be improved if it said:

1. A *chair* is
    2. a piece of furniture
        3. with four legs and a back, intended to seat only one person at a time.

One good way to test the completeness of a class definition is to try turning it around. Does it still make sense?

> All virus diseases are hydrophobia.

Of course it doesn't. Now the definition could apply equally well to herpes, flu, or a number of other human ailments. The job, then, is to add more ways of distinguishing hydrophobia from other virus diseases.

> *Hydrophobia* is a virus disease of the nervous system caused by the bite of a rabid animal.

Now the definition makes sense when it's turned around.

> *Good class definitions put the word being defined into a big group and tell how the word differs from other members of that group. They can be turned around and still make sense.*

Definitions of Abstract Words

In some situations, however, even good class definitions are not enough. What do you mean by *coward,* for instance? A dictionary can offer a three-part definition:

1. A *coward* is
    2. a person that
        3. shows disgraceful fear or timidity.

But when does fear become *disgraceful*? Is fear ever justified by the circumstances?
We run into problems like this whenever we try to explain words that refer to ideas or that describe human behavior or make judgments about the way people behave. And the problems come up not just with unfamiliar words but with ordinary

words that everybody more or less understands: *cowardice, brutality, neglect, racism.* The trouble lies in "more or less understands," and the trouble arises because words like these are **abstractions**. We have *abstracted,* or pulled out, what we think is alike in a lot of different situations and given a name to that likeness.

We see a collie run the other way when a doberman barks at it. We see a prize fighter fall back to the corner of the ring when his opponent aims a blow at his head. We see a soldier run away from the battle rather than toward it. We see a legislator who believes in a sales tax but votes against it because she believes that voting for it might make her lose the next election. We think there is something alike in all this behavior, so we call the likeness *cowardice* and the people who behave like that *cowards.*

There's nothing wrong with using abstractions. It would be hard to get along without them. The trouble comes when we treat them as though they were things rather than just ideas, when we forget that people's experiences have been different and that therefore their definitions may be different too. Some people might say that the collie is not a coward; it's just been trained not to fight. The prize fighter is not a coward either; he's just been made so dizzy by earlier blows that he can't control his actions. The soldier is not a coward; he knows he's out of ammunition. And the state senator, although she favors a sales tax herself, also believes it is her job to represent the wishes of the people who elected her, and the mail has been running five to one against the tax. To define *cowardice* clearly, neither a synonym nor a class definition will be enough.

We can use synonym or class definitions for words that refer to things we can see or hear or touch or count—coffee, computers, sirens, velvet, votes. But to define words like *cowardice* or *disgraceful,* we have to do more than that. We have to show what is happening when we call people's behavior *cowardly* or *brutal* or *neglectful* or *racist.* When we define **abstract words**, we have to limit the kind of behavior that will be included in our definition.

Definitions of abstractions are therefore usually much longer than synonym or class definitions. Showing what happens in one situation will probably not be enough. We'll have to use three or four different situations, and we may have to describe those situations in considerable detail. We may even have to describe situations that our definition does not fit—that's part of how we limit it. But such definitions limit meaning in another way as well. They may limit the meaning to the person who is using it or the occasion on which it is being used. You sometimes hear people say, "For purposes of this discussion, let's agree that freedom means . . ." or "When I say racist, I mean . . ." and then go on from there. These people remember that words cannot be defined absolutely, for all time and all situations, so that everybody always agrees. They remember that words, and especially abstractions, have no "real meaning." Instead, these people try to answer the question, "What do you mean?" by offering definitions that explain what they mean in that discussion or that paper, and they do it in words as specific as possible.

Abstract words refer to things that cannot be seen or heard or touched or counted.

Definitions of abstract words usually require several examples to make the meaning clear.

General and Specific Words

If you aren't used to thinking about words as general or specific, you may need some explanation before you understand the request, "That's too general. Be more specific."

We can explain **general words** by saying that the more things a word refers to, the more general it is. The fewer things a word refers to, the more **specific** the word is. Thus *general* and *specific* are relative terms. *Recliner* is more specific than *chair*. *Chair* is more specific than *furniture*. Looked at from the other direction, *human being* is more general than *politician*. *Politician* is more general than *vice presidential candidate*. And *Geraldine Ferraro* is as specific as you can get, because it refers to one individual. It works like this:

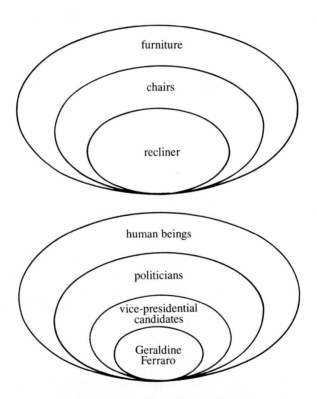

The diagrams should make it easier to see that few words, by themselves, can be considered either general or specific. Whether a word is more or less specific depends on what you are comparing it to.

General and specific words are not bad or good in themselves. Words are bad or good choices depending on whether or not they fit what the writer means to say. A newspaper headline, "TEACHERS GET RAISE," is likely to mislead readers if the cost-of-living increase applied only to Limestone Community College, not to the elementary and high schools in the area. Here, *teachers* is too general a word. On the

other hand, "COACHES GET RAISE" would be too specific if everybody on the staff of the community college got the increase.

Inexperienced writers sometimes deliberately choose rather general words, probably because general words seem safer. If you are not pinned down to anything very definite, there's less chance of being proved wrong. But there's also less chance that what you say will be worth reading. Nobody wants you to be too specific, but you will be fairly safe if you follow this rule:

Always choose the most specific word that will fit what you mean.

Generalizations and Specific Statements

The more general the words you use in making a statement, the more inclusive the statement will be. If the statement refers to a group of people or things, or covers more than one situation, we call it a **generalization**. The statement, "Americans like sports," is a generalization. It includes all the people, young and old, who live on this continent, and it includes all the active recreation you can think of, from watching professional football to water skiing. The statement, "Water skiing is a dangerous sport," is a generalization, too. Although the term *water skiing* is certainly more specific than the general term *sports,* the statement includes all the times that anybody goes water skiing.

Just as there's nothing wrong with general words if they fit the situation and make the meaning clear, so there is nothing wrong with generalizations when they do the same thing. Actually, we would have a hard time getting along without generalizations. If we had to say, "In 1986 there was a hurricane in September," "In 1985 there was a hurricane in September," "In 1984 there was a hurricane in September," and so on, as far back as records have been kept, we'd waste a lot of time and our readers would probably go to sleep. It's much more efficient to say, "September is a bad month for hurricanes."

On the other hand, if we make generalizations too hastily, people are likely to question our statements. If you say, "Teachers at this college grade unfairly," somebody—perhaps a teacher—is likely to ask indignantly, "What do you mean, unfairly? Are you talking about all the teachers at the college?" You are being requested to make a more **specific statement**.

A generalization includes many things or many occasions.

A specific statement is limited to one particular thing that happened at one particular time.

Supporting Generalizations

If a general statement and a specific statement are related, we say that the specific statement is an example of the generalization.

Generalization: The teachers at this college grade unfairly.
Example: Professor Oglethorpe gave me a D on the last botany test, even though I got all the questions right.

Generalization: Amtrak is very unreliable.
Example: The train from Kansas City to Chicago was four hours late last Sunday.

Generalization: Many people believe that water skiing is dangerous.
Example: My Uncle George believes that water skiing is dangerous.

Generalization: First aid, properly given, can save lives.
Example: When my cousin's little boy nearly drowned in Blue Lake last summer, the lifeguard gave him mouth-to-mouth resuscitation until a doctor got there, and the doctor said she saved the child's life.

Notice some things about these pairs of statements. In the first two, the examples relate to the generalizations, but they certainly don't prove them. One D on one test, whether or not it was deserved, does not demonstrate that all teachers grade unfairly or even that Professor Oglethorpe does on other occasions. Neither does one train being four hours late prove that all Amtrak service is unreliable. In the third pair of statements, "Many people" has been made more specific, but the rest of the statement — "dangerous" — is still too general.

Notice, too, that the last generalization says, "First aid, properly given, can save lives"; it doesn't claim that it always does. We are likely to accept this generalization, not just because the example is specific but also because the generalization is more limited. Here the example does support the general statement.

Never make a more general statement than you can justify by enough examples.

Planning a Definition Paper

In life outside the classroom you probably won't have many occasions to write an entire paper that does nothing but make clear what you mean by a word. You will often, however, need to write a paragraph or two of definition as part of papers with other purposes. Practice in writing a short paper entirely devoted to definition will help you when those occasions arise.

Your **plan** for a definition paper should begin with an abstract word for which you think you have a clear, definite meaning. There are a lot to choose from: *success, independence, dishonesty, loyalty, hypocrisy,* and *prejudice* are only a few of the possibilities. Let's suppose that you have decided to define *prejudice*. A synonym definition won't work at all here. If you say "To be prejudiced means to be biased," your readers will know about as much as if you had said nothing at all. So you try again and this time you come up with a generalization: "Prejudice means looking down on Black people because they are different." Notice that your generalization is actually a class definition:

1. *Prejudice* means
   2. looking down on
      3. Black people because they are different.

This definition can serve as a main idea statement, even though it may not be quite what you will actually use. The next step in planning is to make a list of examples that might support your general statement:

> the rocks thrown at Black kids when school integration began
> people making life miserable for Black families who move into all-white suburbs
> apartheid in South Africa
> cross-burning in Black yards
> lynchings by the Ku Klux Klan
> the shooting of four Black teenagers in a New York subway in 1984
> use of derogatory language such as "nigger" or "spade"

But wait a minute. Is prejudice always limited to the way some white people treat Blacks? Doesn't the term "whitey" also show prejudice?

Now you ask yourself more questions. Is prejudice always based on physical differences? Can it be based on sex or life styles? You remember the proportion of women to men in the United States Congress and the Supreme Court. You remember your long-haired friend, a qualified data processor with four years of experience, who habitually dresses in sandals, faded jeans, and a sweat shirt that's none too clean. When he applied for a job at Numbers, Inc., he was told there were no vacancies, but the next day another applicant, with neatly trimmed hair and a business suit, got a job just like the one your friend had applied for. You find it hard to believe that an employee quit within twenty-four hours.

Those ideas lead to another question. Can prejudice be based on religious differences as well as race, sex, and life styles? The questions you've been asking yourself make you realize that you can't cover all kinds of prejudice in a short paper. You decide to limit your definition to religious prejudice and make another list:

> Jews in Nazi Germany
> Jews and Arabs
> Sikhs and Hindus in present-day India
> Catholic father, Mormon son-in-law

Your new generalization reads, "Religious prejudice means looking down on people who have a different faith." That definition will be easier to handle, but it may still be inadequate. The first three examples on your list show more than "looking down." In Nazi Germany, the Middle East, and in India, the prejudice involved the killing of large numbers of people. Maybe the generalization should read, "Religious prejudice means looking down on or slaughtering people because they have a different faith."

To make your meaning even clearer, you may want to include an example of something some people call religious prejudice but which, according to your definition, is not. Maybe you know about a bitter quarrel between two neighbors, one a Buddhist and one an agnostic. The quarrel actually started over the Browns' dog, which bit the Johnsons' little boy, but Mr. Brown goes around the neighborhood saying "Johnson doesn't like me because I'm a Buddhist." You want to point out that not all disagreements between people of different faiths are caused by religious prejudice; sometimes there are other, quite unrelated, reasons.

The next step is to put your list in order. One way to arrange the examples is from the least to the most important. Another way is by time—from the earliest example to the most recent. Using a combination of these methods, your list might look like this:

> Buddhist and agnostic neighbors (not prejudice)
> Catholic father, Mormon son-in-law
> Jews in Nazi Germany
> Sikhs and Hindus in India
> Jews and Arabs in the Middle East

There's no special reason for the order of the last two; violence is still occurring in both places.

Now that you have a satisfactory main idea sentence and a completed plan, you are ready to write the first draft of your paper. Be sure to give plenty of details about each one of your examples. Then write an introduction that includes more than your main idea sentence and a conclusion that restates the same generalization in slightly different words: "Religious prejudice, then, is shown by violent attacks on other people, either by words or weapons, because the others worship in a different way."

Remember, however, that the purpose of your definition is to make clear what you mean by the term, not to argue for your own beliefs. If your definition is part of a longer paper—an attempt to persuade readers to abandon their prejudices—your argument will be more convincing if you have kept your definition impartial. Words such as *ought* or *ought not, good* or *evil,* can be part of a paper intended to persuade, but they do not belong in the definition or the examples that illustrate it. If you have fully described the situations that the examples cover, most readers will realize that religious prejudice can cause great evil; your job is to let them see it, not label it for them. Don't be tempted to write, "Religious prejudice is what's wrong with the world," and think it's part of your definition.

> *A plan for a definition paper*
> 1. *should begin with the main idea statement;*
> 2. *should include enough examples to support the generalization;*
> 3. *may include an example showing what it isn't;*
> 4. *should arrange the examples in order of importance or of time.*

Paragraphing

You know what a **paragraph** looks like. You can recognize it because the first word is indented—set in half an inch or so from the left-hand margin. But you may be a bit uncertain as to when this indenting should be used. That uncertainty is not surprising because there's no very precise definition of what a paragraph is. The best anybody can do is say that a paragraph is a sentence or group of sentences that seem to belong together because they refer to something slightly different from what will be discussed in the next group of sentences.

That's where your plan can help. As you begin to write, try to give each part of the plan a paragraph of its own. You will probably need a paragraph of introduction that will include your generalization and the comments you make about it. You will probably also need a paragraph for each of your examples. Don't worry about making all your paragraphs the same length. Some examples will naturally take less space than others, or perhaps one of them will be so long that it takes more than one paragraph to make your meaning clear.

The best rule is to begin a new paragraph whenever there is a shift in what you're talking about, just as you move from room to room when you shift what you're doing at home. When you finish the example of the Catholic father and move to what happened during the Holocaust in Germany, start a new paragraph, much as you move from kitchen to living room when you shift from cooking dinner to watching TV. If you use several examples in your definition, you may need more paragraphs than your house has rooms, but the idea is the same. The plan you have made has kept your paragraphs in convenient order. Now the transitions discussed in the last chapter can serve as the doors, getting your readers from place to place without stumbling.

Following this rule—giving at least a paragraph to each part of your plan—will keep you from writing a series of tiresome one-sentence paragraphs. By the time you have given enough details to make your examples clear, your paragraphs will have expanded and your readers will have room enough to understand your meaning. A series of one-sentence paragraphs is like an apartment containing nothing but closets: The writer is cramped and the readers are frustrated.

It's true that there is no "right length" for a paragraph, no way of counting words or sentences that will tell you when it's long enough. A glance at any magazine or book will show you paragraphs varying from one to six sentences or longer. But five-sentence paragraphs occur more often than single-sentence paragraphs, which are used only now and then for special emphasis. Most readers are used to how paragraphs look on a page, and if your paragraphs don't look that way, your readers may become uneasy. Appearance—how your paper looks—is one reason for making your paragraphs longer than a single sentence, but successful communication—saying enough so that readers can share your ideas—is a more important reason.

Begin a new paragraph whenever you shift from one part of your plan to the next.

Developing the Plan

One-sentence paragraphs often seem all right to inexperienced writers because they are perfectly certain what those single sentences mean. In their minds, that one sentence expresses all the experience and images and ideas they're thinking about. But for readers who have not shared those experiences, who have not seen those mental pictures, the single general sentence is almost worthless. Not completely worthless, because readers may get a hazy notion of what the writer had in mind and try to supply the rest from their own experiences. But the overlap between the writer's intention and the readers' understanding will be very small.

In that paper defining *prejudice,* for instance, it won't be enough to say, "Catholic parents may try to keep their daughter from marrying a Mormon," and then begin the next paragraph with your next example. All you have done is produce another generalization, only slightly more specific than the one you began with. Adding another sentence that fails to create a picture won't help much either: "That happened last year in a family I know." The picture is probably clear in your own mind. You remember how upset Maggie was when her father wouldn't let Mark in the house, how she cried when her parents didn't come to the wedding, how upset Mark was when he thought the marriage had permanently separated Maggie from her parents. You also know how lonely the parents were. Unless your words create a picture detailed enough so that your readers can see what you see, your example may fall flat.

As you revise your paper, read it carefully to make sure that the picture in your mind will be transferred to the minds of your readers. Add details. Use specific words. Ask a couple of obliging readers to tell you what else they'd like to know and then provide that information. Communication may not be complete, but it will certainly be closer.

Just before you give the finished paper an appropriate title—the term you are defining will probably be enough—read the paper one more time to make sure your readers won't have to ask, "What do you mean?"

Develop each paragraph by using specific words and specific details.

Editing

When you have made your definition as complete as you can, go over it again to make sure that everything you have written makes sense and that none of your sentences will confuse your readers. One thing that might confuse them, or at least slow them down, is not being sure what a **pronoun** stands for. If you have said, "Maggie's father told Mark that he felt sorry for Maggie's mother," your readers won't be able to tell who did the feeling sorry, Mark or Maggie's father. Maybe readers could guess at that one, but some sentences can be even more confusing. "When the newspapers left the presses, the strikers burned them." What was burned, the presses or the newspapers?

Sometimes readers are confused because pronouns don't seem to stand for anything. "Mark had hoped to get a law degree, but the influence of his father-in-law kept him from being one." Who didn't get to be one, Mark or his father-in-law? And what didn't whoever it was get to be? People can't be degrees, but they can be lawyers.

Such sentences are bad, not because they are "wrong," but because they are confusing. Make sure your readers won't be slowed down trying to figure out what your pronouns stand for.

Each pronoun should refer to one definite thing and only to that thing.

A Sample Paper of Definition

Here is the plan for a definition paper:

Definition of *negligence*
Generalization: *Negligence* means not being careful enough in doing the things you are responsible for.
Examples:
    Kids burned to death
    Driver hurts somebody
    Guard at nuclear plant watches ball game
    Explosion at Bhopal
Conclusion: *Negligence* means being careless, but if people are killed, it is criminal negligence.

Here is the first draft of the paper written from this plan:

Negligence

Introduction is adequate but not very interesting.

[1] Negligence is a word you see quite often in the paper these days. Negligence means not being careful enough in doing the things you are responsible for. There are several kinds of negligence, but some of them are more serious than others.

Confusing pronoun: who is burned to death, the children or their parents? If this situation occurs "a lot," the writer should find one definite example and give details. Is it still negligence if the children are not killed?
The second example needs a paragraph of its own; it also needs to be made more specific.

[2] For instance, if children are left by their parents alone in the house at night and the house catches fire and they are burned to death, negligence has occurred. That happens a lot and it's fairly serious. Another instance is if a driver does something careless, like driving with the headlights off at night or running a red light and the people in the other car get hurt, that's negligent driving and it's fairly serious too.

Here the writer may have given all the details that are available, since this is based on a story going around.

[3] There is a story in Oregon about a man who worked at Trojan, a nuclear power plant on the Columbia River. According to the story this man was supposed to be watching the big control panel that showed what was happening in the plant. He was, but he was also watching a championship basketball game on TV. When the red light that meant danger went on, he waited until the game was over before he investigated. Nothing happened, but it could have, and if it did, it would have been serious.

Probably the most important example since it appears last. Much more detail is needed. Details can be found in the library if the writer has forgotten.

[4] Another example of negligence was in Bhopal, India, in December 1984, where a plant owned by Union Carbide let a deadly gas escape and 2,500 people were killed and thousands more injured by negligence that was really serious.

The words "in conclusion" are unnecessary if the writer makes the paper sound finished.
The writer seems to be distinguishing between ordinary negligence and serious negligence. Perhaps criminal negligence is the real topic of the paper.

[5] In conclusion, negligence means being careless, but if people are killed or even could be killed, it is sometimes called criminal negligence.

Here is the final draft of the same paper. The comments in the margin show how it has been improved.

Criminal Negligence

Livelier introduction shows difference between ordinary and criminal negligence and gives an example of negligence that is not criminal.

[1] Everybody is careless now and then about doing what they are responsible for. Students who don't hang up their clothes or do their assignments on time are sometimes accused of being negligent. Probably they are, but their negligence hurts only themselves. It is not criminal. Criminal negligence means people being so careless about their responsibilities that their carelessness could hurt other people.

Example has been made specific.

[2] For instance, Hiram and Hattie Grant couldn't get a sitter one night when they wanted to go to the tavern.

Since their six-year-old son Buddy and his four-year-old sister were asleep, the Grants thought the children would be all right and went anyway. The parents couldn't know the house would catch on fire and the children be killed by the smoke before they could be rescued. The parents felt terrible, but the chance they took just to get a beer or two was criminal negligence.

This example, too, has been made more specific by using an event from the writer's experience. Notice how the use of an echo transition (criminal negligence) between the second and third paragraphs makes for comfortable reading.

[3] Drivers can show criminal negligence, too, if their carelessness causes a serious accident. One day my cousin Jim was very upset about a quarrel he had just had with his wife. He was thinking so hard about the fight that he went right through a red light and hit another car broadside. The woman driving the other car was killed instantly, and both her passengers were critically injured. My cousin was charged with manslaughter. The legal term is different, but the fact is that he was criminally negligent in not watching what he was doing.

Another echo transition. The main part of this paragraph has not been changed much, but the first two sentences and the last two now refer to the "could have been" in the main idea sentence and answer the question of whether there must be a tragedy before the negligence can be considered criminal.

[4] Criminal negligence can occur even though nobody is killed. If it's just good luck that nothing awful happened, the person who was careless should still be held responsible. There is a story in Oregon about a man who worked at Trojan, a nuclear power plant on the Columbia River. According to the story, this man was supposed to be watching the big controls that showed whether everything was safe. He was, but he was also a basketball fan, and he was watching a championship game on television. When the red light went on, the one that showed danger, he decided to wait until the game was over before he investigated. Nothing happened that night, but the ten-minute delay might have meant that radioactive material was scattered all over the Pacific Northwest. Thousands could have been killed and injured.

This paragraph now gives some specific details of what happened in Bhopal and explains why the writer thinks the company's carelessness was more than "irregular."

[5] The outstanding example of criminal negligence occurred in Bhopal, India, in December 1984, when a plant owned by Union Carbide let deadly methyl isocyanide gas leak out. Twenty-five hundred people were killed and thousands more injured. Investigators later found that one of the three safety systems had not been operating for several days and a

refrigeration unit that was supposed to keep the chemical cool had been shut down by the managers several months before. To save money, training of the workers had been cut. And there was no effective system for warning the public. The alarm that did go off sounded the same as the alarm people were used to hearing for practice drills. Newspaper accounts at the time kept talking about "irregularities" and "accident," but the real name for what happened is criminal negligence.

Conclusion restates the main idea in slightly different words and makes the paper sound finished.

[6]   Whatever term the press or the law uses, criminal negligence occurs whenever careless actions or careless failure to act causes, or could cause, death or serious injury to other people.

Key Words and Ideas

Here are some of the key words and ideas used in this chapter. If you have trouble answering any of these questions, reread the part of the chapter where the discussion occurs.

1. Why can't we say what the **real meaning** of a word is?
2. What is a **synonym definition**? What does a good one do?
3. What are the three parts of a **class definition**? How can you recognize a good **class definition**?
4. What is an **abstraction**? How should abstract words be defined?
5. How can you decide whether to use a **general word** or a **specific word** in your own writing? What is meant by the statement, "*General* and *specific* are **relative terms**"?
6. What is a **generalization**?
7. What is a **specific statement**?
8. How can you decide when to make a **general statement**?
9. What should the **plan** for a definition paper include?
10. How can the plan help you in deciding where to **paragraph**?
11. How can you keep your **pronouns** from confusing your readers?

Name _____

Exercises _____

Exercise 1. Synonym Definitions.   Which of these synonym definitions are satisfactory? That is, which ones would help a reader who did not know the meaning of the underlined word? If you think a definition is unsatisfactory, explain what the problem is.

1. <u>Con carne</u> means with meat.

   _____

2. <u>Feasibility</u> means possibility.

   _____

3. <u>Fruitful</u> means fecund.

   _____

4. To <u>delineate</u> is to outline.

   _____

5. A <u>garnish</u> is something that garnishes.

   _____

6. <u>Calumny</u> means slander.

   _____

7. To be <u>disloyal</u> is to be perfidious.

   _____

8. To be <u>specific</u> means to give details.

   _____

Exercise 2. Writing Synonym Definitions. Write synonym definitions for each of these underlined words or phrases. If you can do it from your own knowledge, fine. If not, use a dictionary.

1. A la mode means _____

2. Matrimony means _____

3. To regurgitate is to _____

4. Assignation means _____

5. A yeti is _____

6. A conundrum is _____

7. In street slang, grass means _____

8. A yegg is _____

9. Tempus fugit means _____

10. Yesteryear means _____

Name _____

Exercise 3. Class Definitions. Which of these class definitions are satisfactory? That is, which ones would help a reader who did not know the meaning of the underlined word? If you think a definition is unsatisfactory, explain what the problem is.

1. To <u>fast</u> means to go without eating by your own choice.

   _____

2. A <u>ptarmigan</u> is a bird.

   _____

3. To <u>winnow</u> is the act of winnowing wheat from chaff.

   _____

4. A <u>human being</u> is an upright mammal with the ability to use and understand language.

   _____

5. To <u>bifurcate</u> means to divide into two branches.

   _____

6. To be <u>drip-dry</u> means to be made of a washable fabric that does not need to be ironed.

   _____

7. A <u>patsy</u> is a person who is easily tricked and usually gets blamed for what happens.

   _____

8. A <u>curry</u> is a dish with curry in it.

   _____

9. <u>Canvassing</u> means asking for votes or support from a group of people or from people in a certain area.

   _____

10. A <u>conservationist</u> is a person who wants to conserve things.

_____

11. A <u>conservationist</u> is a person who believes that natural resources should be protected.

_____

12. A <u>dictionary</u> is a book that has lots of words in it.

_____

Name _____

Exercise 4. Writing Class Definitions.   Try to write class definitions for these terms without using a dictionary. Divide your definition into three parts: (1) the term being defined, which is given; (2) the big group it belongs to; and (3) the ways it's different from other things in the big group. Then compare your definitions with those other students have written.

1. A bed is

    Big group _____

    Differences _____

2. To picket means to

    Big group _____

    Differences _____

3. A hotcake is

    Big group _____

    Differences _____

4. Garbage is

    Big group _____

    Differences _____

5. To swim is to

    Big group _____

    Differences _____

Exercise 5. More Class Definitions.   Write class definitions for these terms. If you can do it from your own knowledge, fine. If not, use a dictionary. Again, compare your definitions with those other students have written.

1. A <u>garage sale</u> is

    Big group _____

    Differences _____

2. A <u>dictionary</u> is

    Big group _____

    Differences _____

3. <u>Backlash</u> means

    Big group _____

    Differences _____

4. To <u>repudiate</u> is to

    Big group _____

    Differences _____

5. <u>Unilateral disarmament</u> means

    Big group _____

    Differences _____

Name _____

Exercise 6. General and Specific Words.   Rearrange the words in these groups so that they start with the most general word and end with the most specific. (Not all will need rearranging.)

> *Example:* nasturtium, living thing, flower, plant
>
> living thing, plant, flower, nasturtium

1. animal, human being, native American, Sitting Bull

   _____

2. food, hamburger, meat, beef

   _____

3. transportation, Chevrolet, automobile, four-wheeled vehicle

   _____

4. book, publication, *Huckleberry Finn,* novel

   _____

5. tools, equipment, hammers, claw hammers

   _____

6. printed matter, magazine, weekly magazine, *Newsweek*

   _____

7. bongos, drums, musical instruments, noisemakers

   _____

8. Super Bowl, football, contest, sport

   _____

Exercise 7. General and Specific Words.   For each of these words, find one word or phrase that is more general and one that is more specific. It will be interesting for the whole class to compare answers on this exercise.

	Example: more general		*more specific*
	furniture	chair	rocking chair

1. _____   tree   _____

2. _____   room   _____

3. _____   house   _____

4. _____   adult   _____

5. _____   vegetable   _____

6. _____   college   _____

7. _____   mineral   _____

8. _____   paper   _____

9. _____   dog   _____

10. _____   sport   _____

11. _____   baby   _____

12. _____   human being   _____

13. _____   textbook   _____

14. _____   movie star   _____

15. _____   shoes   _____

Name _____

Exercise 8. Generalizations and Examples. For each of these generalizations, write a specific example that illustrates it. Make sure that your example shows specific people doing specific things in a specific situation, with specific results. If the only example you can think of sounds silly, you may decide that the generalization is unreliable. Here is a sample of what you should do:

> *Generalization:* Eating candy is bad for your teeth.
> *Example:* My sister Ann, who ate a candy bar every day for lunch, had eight cavities by the time she was ten years old.

1. Plants need water.

_____

_____

_____

2. Music cheers people up.

_____

_____

_____

3. Small children should not watch television.

_____

_____

_____

4. Some television programs can help small children learn the alphabet.

_____

_____

_____

5. Regular exercise helps people lose weight.

_____

_____

_____

6. The police are kind and considerate to motorists.

_____

_____

_____

7. The police are rude and inconsiderate to motorists.

_____

_____

_____

8. If you drink, don't drive.

_____

_____

_____

9. People can't be judged by the clothes they wear.

_____

_____

_____

Name _____

Exercise 9. Examples and Generalizations. For each of these specific examples, write a generalization that might be made about it. One example can't prove a general statement, but it can be fun to see what generalizations you come up with if you begin with a specific situation. Compare your generalizations with those other students have written. Do any of the generalizations sound silly? Which generalizations are sound? Here is a sample of what you should do:

> *Example:* A small Boy Scout helped a blind man to cross Grand Avenue last Saturday.
> *Generalization:* Boy Scouts are helpful.

1. My Uncle Bertram lives in a modern house with lots of glass in it. Last Saturday he threw rocks at the kids playing in his front yard, and last night some kids heaved a brick through Uncle Bertram's big front window.

   _____

   _____

2. Algernon Crimple has a lot of conservative relatives; he must be a conservative himself.

   _____

   _____

3. Old Man Tuttle went to bed every night at seven o'clock and got up every morning at six. He died at the age of ninety-nine, when a truck ran over him. When he died, he had a million dollars in the bank.

   _____

   _____

4. This lot is a hundred feet long and fifty feet wide, so it must have an area of five thousand square feet.

   _____

   _____

5. Nellie O'Connell inherited a million dollars, so she must be happy.

_____

_____

6. Socrates was killed for questioning the beliefs held by most of the people of his time.

_____

_____

7. Gwendolyn always uses Cuddle Cologne, so she has lots of dates.

_____

_____

8. At the beach last summer, we put a thermometer in a kettle of hot water and discovered that when the thermometer registered 212 degrees Fahrenheit, the water was boiling.

_____

_____

Name _____

Exercise 10. Paragraphing. Mark where each new paragraph should begin in this short paper of definition. Compare your work with that of other students in the class, and be ready to give reasons for your decisions.

Courage

Courage is a quality that has been valued and praised in every society in every country. Everybody admires people who show courage, but not everybody agrees about what courage is. Actually, there are two kinds of courage, physical courage and moral courage. Physical courage means not being afraid to get hurt. Moral courage is the ability and the desire to hold true to principles and stand up and be counted without thought of personal gain or loss. Physical courage is easier to see than moral courage and is more likely to be praised. Because moral courage is seldom rewarded, and because it is really harder to achieve, the person who has moral courage is showing true courage. For instance, people often consider the war hero brave. They admire a man who plunges through a wall of fire to rescue his smoldering buddy. But even though he risked his life for his good friend, he did not have to use any moral courage. Everybody believes in saving friends. On the other hand, America's classic example of cowardice, Benedict Arnold, may have demonstrated the greatest courage if, when he sold out to the British, he did so because of his personal convictions, because he thought that in changing sides he was actually promoting the best good for the most people. Courage is not always shown in big acts, either. The grimy little boy who can go up to his teacher and stammer, "Mr. Legree, I'm sorry but I cheated on that test," is probably displaying as much courage as the White House aide who says, "Mr. President, I'm sorry, but I lost that file." Although apparently the third grader had a bit of a struggle, both of these people felt strongly enough about honesty to admit their mistakes. Often confessing to somebody else that you have done something wrong requires the highest kind of courage. The word *courage* comes from the Latin word *cor,* which means "heart." Being courageous, then, means that if you believe with your whole heart that something is right, you act according to your belief.

Name _____

Exercise 11. Pronouns.   If any of these sentences is confusing, rewrite it so that each pronoun refers to one definite thing and only to that thing.

1. Jessica Hogg took a course in nurses' training, but she never got to practice it.

_____

_____

2. Maria and Donna discussed the problem and decided that she would clean the kitchen and she would do the cooking.

_____

_____

3. If you want to please both your father and your uncle, find out what he likes.

_____

_____

4. Alonzo does a lot of jogging, which is good for you.

_____

_____

5. That book looks good because it has a cover that shows a chess board, and I think it would be interesting.

_____

_____

6. One should know how to operate a microwave oven even if one doesn't own one.

_____

_____

7. When the police caught up with the gunmen, they shot two of them.

_____

_____

8. Hating something means disliking it so much that you want to destroy it, but according to psychologists, it is a harmful emotion.

_____

_____

9. If you give the floor a good cleaning before you wax it, it will take a good polish.

_____

_____

10. I'm taking dentistry but I'm not sure whether I want to be one.

_____

_____

Name _____

Exercise 12. Planning a Definition Paper. Pick an abstract word that interests you, one you can define without using a dictionary. Write a generalization (probably a class definition) for the word, and find at least three examples—three somewhat different situations—that show the word occurring. After you have found the examples, you may want to rewrite your generalization. Then write a concluding sentence that expresses the same generalization in slightly different words.

Definition of _____

Generalization _____

_____

_____

Examples _____

_____

_____

_____

_____

Example of what it isn't (optional) _____

_____

Conclusion _____

_____

_____

Exercise 13. Writing the First Draft. Using the plan you made in Exercise 12, write a first draft of your definition paper. Make each example you use as specific as you can, telling what definite people did in definite situations. Show your first draft to the teacher, to other students in the class, or to a friend. Make a note of their questions or suggestions.

Exercise 14. Rewriting Your Paper. Write another version of the same paper, this time trying to follow all the suggestions that were made. Put your paper away for at least a day and reread it to see if you want to make any more changes. Then make sure you can answer yes to all the questions on this check list:

Check List for Content

1. Does your introduction contain a generalization in the form of a class definition? _____

2. Have you given at least three different examples? _____

3. Do all your examples fit your definition? _____

4. Is each example detailed and specific? _____

5. Have you stuck to defining and not slipped over into arguing? _____

6. Does your conclusion restate your generalization in slightly different words? _____

7. Have you given it a title? _____

Exercise 15. The Final Step. Now go over your paper one more time, this time reading for spelling, sentences, paragraphs, and pronouns. If you can't answer yes to all of the following questions, make whatever changes are needed.

Check List for Editing and Style

1. Are your sentences a comfortable length? _____

2. Have you used enough transitions to take readers smoothly from one idea to the next? _____

3. Have you made sure none of your pronouns will confuse your readers? _____

4. Have you used a dictionary to check the spelling of any words you were unsure about? _____

5. Do all your sentences begin with capitals and end with periods?   ———

6. Have you given a paragraph to each of your examples?   ———

Exercise 16. Introductions and Conclusions. Pick a different abstract word that you think you can define clearly. This time write only the introductory paragraph and the conclusion. Don't write the middle of the paper, even though you know what would be in it. Trade introductions and conclusions with another student in the class and ask the other student to (1) decide whether what you say in the conclusion fits what you said in the introduction; and (2) write at least one example that seems to fit your definition. Has the other student understood what you mean by the word you are defining?

Exercise 17. Examples.   Pick one of the following abstract terms:

> enthusiasm
> loyalty
> good manners
> child abuse
> persistence

Work out a definition in your notebook. Then on a separate piece of paper write three different examples of the term you are illustrating, without ever using the term itself. Read your examples to other students in the class, or ask the teacher to read them aloud. Have the class decide which of the terms you were defining. If members of the class can't tell which term it was, rewrite your examples.

Chapter 4

Explaining: Comparison

When we explain by looking carefully at one thing and saying what it is, we are defining. When we explain by looking at two things to see how they are alike and how they are different, we are comparing. Comparison is a normal human activity, a way of understanding our world. We make comparisons from the time we are born until we die. A baby compares the sound of voices, then smiles when the voice is familiar and cries when it sounds strange. A two-year-old first sees how cows and horses are alike—both four-legged, both enormous, both scary. Then the child stores away the differences—shape of the heads, mane on the horse and udder on the cow. A girl who has ridden horses all her life sees a zebra for the first time. Will what she knows about horses help her understand the zebra? An eighty-year-old grandfather tries to decide where he should live. Should he keep his city apartment or move into a retirement complex far out in the country? Between infancy and old age we are constantly making comparisons, some of them almost automatic, some of them quite deliberate.

What are some of the **reasons for making comparisons**? One reason is *to get a better understanding of* familiar things. Sometimes we compare two things that seem to be almost alike. That's what the child was doing with the cow and the horse. That's what you are doing when you examine two jackets, for instance, or two part-time jobs. You may have to dig a bit to find the differences. The jackets are both blue, both zippered, both hooded, but when you look carefully, you can see that although one of them has a detachable hood, it has to be dry-cleaned; the other is machine-washable. At first glance the part-time jobs look alike, too. Both are yard work and both pay minimum wage, but in one you will be expected to decide for yourself when the lawn needs mowing and the roses trimmed back; in the other every click of the clippers will be carefully supervised.

Sometimes, on the other hand, a comparison can show that two familiar things which seem quite different actually have much in common. It may never have occurred to you that there are similarities between raising raspberries and raising children, or between painting a picture and preparing a banquet. A detailed examination of these processes, however, can reveal that both the berry bushes and the kids require perseverance, patience, and loving care. Painting a picture and planning a menu both require a sense of color and a sense of proportion. Comparisons can often give you a new insight into familiar things.

A second reason for making comparisons is to gain a better understanding of something that's unknown by comparing it to something familiar. If you have spent summers splashing around at the seashore, a comparison between ocean waves and sound waves will help you see how sound waves operate. If you are a devoted football fan but have never played soccer, a comparison between the two games can help you understand why the soccer players don't use their hands.

In one sense, that's what the elderly man was doing when he thought about leaving the furniture and friends he'd known so long for a different bed and different companions. He was trying to compare something familiar with something unfamiliar, the known with the unknown. One of his aims was a clearer understanding of what moving would involve, but another and probably more important aim was to decide whether or not to make the move. Would it be better to keep his independence and risk lying alone some night with a broken hip? Or would the advantages of skilled help near at hand, meals ready cooked and served at regular hours, outweigh the disadvantage of eating dinner every night with a bunch of old people he might not like?

Choosing between two possible courses of action is the third and very frequent reason for making comparisons. In looking at the two jackets, you were probably deciding which one to buy. In examining the working conditions of the two part-time jobs, you were probably deciding which one to apply for. In the same way, the woman who wants her yard work done will compare the qualifications of the applicants before she decides which one to hire. The family planning a summer vacation will compare the cost and convenience of staying in motels with the adventure and fun of pitching a tent. Before you vote, you may compare the platforms of the two political parties or you may just compare the personalities of the two candidates. After the election, you may compare the behavior of the successful candidate with the promises that were made during the campaign. In either of these situations, you will be using a comparison to evaluate.

> *Comparisons can explain things in three ways:*
> 1. *We can get a better understanding of familiar things by looking at them carefully.*
> 2. *We can learn something new by comparing the known with the unknown.*
> 3. *We can make judgments about objects, actions, or people.*

What to Compare

In ordinary life you seldom have to choose a **topic for comparison**. Both the topic and the audience are determined by the situation. If your car has been totaled by a hit-and-run driver, your comparison will probably be between two secondhand cars, and your audience will be yourself. If you are asked at work to prepare a report comparing the efficiency of two heating units, your audience will be the boss. If a relative from the East wants to know which of two western cities will be the most livable, your audience will be the aunt who asked for the comparison.

Even in college you may be given a ready-made topic. In a class on self-defense, an essay question may say, "Compare and contrast judo and karate." In a literature class a question may read: "Compare and contrast Twain's Huck Finn with Salinger's Holden Caulfield." In such questions, *compare* means show how the two are alike, and *contrast* means show the differences. Your audience will be the teacher of the class, and the reason for the comparison will not be to create new understanding but to demonstrate that you do understand. Nevertheless, the steps you follow in writing your response to these test questions should be the same as those in any other comparison.

In this class you will probably have to choose your own topic, find the reason for your comparison, and decide who your audience will be. The same three reasons for making comparisons in your own life will hold true when you plan a comparison paper, except that now they should be applied to the needs of your readers. Suppose you have decided to compare listening and reading. What can you tell the members of a college orientation seminar to help them see the similarities? They have been reading newspapers and listening to people talk most of their lives. Do your classmates want information on which physical education course to sign up for, whether to pay their tuition by cash or credit card, what fast food restaurant to patronize?

Your audience will be interested in your comparison between listening and reading if you can make them see that both activities take undivided attention, both require connecting what has gone before with what comes after, and both succeed better when the listener or the reader cares about what's being said. Your fellow students can make better informed decisions about which exercise class, which method of payment, or which cheeseburger to select if you give them enough details. Occasionally you may want to end such comparisons with a recommendation, but more often you will just give the facts and let your classmates make up their own minds.

Giving details and examples is as important in comparisons as it is in any other kind of writing. If the topic is too broad, the comparison may be so general that it won't interest anybody much. The writer who says, "I'm going to compare Canada with the United States" has two choices: make a lot of general statements that won't give a clear picture of anything or narrow the topic to something more manageable — economic conditions or political systems, perhaps. It's just as bad to pick a topic that's too narrow. "Carrots and turnips are both root vegetables, but their appearance is quite different" will leave you nothing to say except that one is long and orange, the other round and white.

In deciding on a topic for comparison, you should
  know the reason for the comparison;
  decide who your readers will be;
  pick a topic broad enough so you'll have something to say and narrow
    enough so you can give details and examples.

Collecting Ideas

Perhaps, when you needed some picnic supplies, you wandered into a supermarket on Walnut Terrace, far from your usual shopping area. You saw the big BUYSAFE sign, just like the one on the store near home, but the inside appearance of the strange store astonished you. You decide to compare it with one on Second Street where you regularly shop. You have a topic; now you are ready to **collect your ideas**. How are the two stores alike? How are they different?

The first step is to make two lists, one for each of the stores. **Brainstorming** can help here. *Brainstorming* means putting down everything you can think of, even though some of it seems trivial or silly. Maybe the silliest ones will remind you of something important, and if they don't, they can be discarded later. The lists will be more complete if you work on them for a day or two, adding new things whenever they occur to you. Your final lists might look something like this:

Walnut Terrace	Second Street
lettuce fresh and attractive	lettuce wilted
broccoli 59 cents	broccoli 70 cents
4 kinds of onions, from 39 to 79 cents	2 kinds of onions, all 69 cents
onions clean and graded	onions half rotted
5 checkout lanes	2 checkout lanes, only 1 used
never more than 2 customers waiting	long lines
clean, wide aisles	dirty, crowded aisles
BUYSAFE sign	BUYSAFE sign
Jensen & Trout Co.	Jensen & Trout Co.
redhaired clerk waited on me	
attractive uniforms	soiled aprons
posted hours, 8–11	posted hours, 8–6
4 to 8 brands of cookies, etc.	usually only 1 brand
carry-out service	
specials on coffee, sugar, soft drinks	
	clerks know me
light, warm	dark, overheated
day-old baked goods at reduced prices	

Your lists seem to show that even though the two stores go by the same name, they have some very important differences.

> As you gather your ideas,
>   make your lists as complete as you can;
>   examine them to see whether you want to emphasize similarities or differences.

Main Idea Sentences

Now is the time to write a main idea sentence. You may want to change—or rearrange—it later, but writing it now will help you get started on your first draft. A good **main idea sentence for a paper of comparison** usually has two parts. One part says what things are being compared; the other makes clear whether you are primarily interested in likenesses or in differences. The two parts are usually joined by such **connecting words** or **phrases** as *although, even though, in spite of, except for, notwithstanding,* or *but.* Including such words and phrases can help you avoid useless main idea sentences like "Hamburger Haven and Ben's Beef are both the same and different." A better version would be

> "*In spite of* the differences in their advertising, the food, the prices, and the service at Hamburger Haven and Ben's Beef are very much the same."

Notice that this improved main idea sentence says what is being compared (two fast-food places). It shows that the similarities are more important than the differences ("In spite of the differences . . ."). And it mentions the parts that will be compared (food, prices, and service).

It isn't always necessary to specify the parts of the comparison, but doing so can be a first step in making your plan. If you do mention the parts, you will need to discuss them in the same order as they appear in your main idea sentence. If that order doesn't work out—and it may not—then the main idea sentence needs to be changed to show the changed order. Your main idea sentence as it appears in your introduction is a miniature outline, and your readers will feel cheated if your paper doesn't keep its implied promise.

Here are three more main idea sentences that emphasize likeness:

> *Although* Spokane and Vancouver are different in climate, scenery, and size, both of these Washington cities are good places to live, with only slight differences in schools, recreation, and living costs.

> My two grandmothers were born in different countries and speak different languages, *but* they are much alike in their attitudes toward their grandchildren.

> *Except for* some obvious differences in appearance and cost, Brown's Warmup Model B and McTavish's Heatall No. 764 operate on the same principle, use the same kind of fuel, and provide the same amount of heat.

In the following main idea sentences, the emphasis is reversed, and it is easy to see that the likenesses matter less than the differences:

> *Even though* the Buysafe store on Walnut Terrace and the Buysafe store on Second Street are run by the same company, there are important differences in the choices available, the quality of the food, and the prices that are charged.

Although the voting records of Senator Goodsell and Senator Upright are almost identical, the two senators belong to different political parties, come from different backgrounds, and claim to have different philosophies of government.

Judo and karate may seem alike because they both originated in Japan, *but* as anyone who has seen a karate expert split an oak beam with a bare hand can tell you, the art of karate is quite different from the art of judo.

Good main idea sentences for comparison papers
  always have two parts;
  say what is being compared; and
  show whether similarities or differences are more important.

Planning the Order

There are three main kinds of **order** that can be used in successful comparison papers, but no matter which kind you choose, you will probably want to begin with what is least important and work up to what is most important. That general order will seem natural as you plan what should come first, what next. Your main idea sentence can serve as the beginning of a plan—tell you whether you should start with likenesses or differences—but it won't help much in deciding how to handle the details of your comparison. That decision will depend on what your topic is.

All About One Thing, Then All About the Other

If you were writing a comparison between the two supermarkets, you would probably begin by showing the ways in which the stores are alike—the big BUYSAFE sign in red letters over the door, the same company collecting the profits. Then you might tell everything shoppers see from the time they push through the door on Second Street until they wait in line at the single checkout stand. The last part of your paper would show what can be seen in the wealthier Walnut Terrace store, again from the time the shoppers go through the automatic door until their grocery bags are carried for them to their cars.

In the section on the Walnut Terrace store, the differences can be emphasized by such phrases as "*In contrast with* the scratched wooden door . . . ," "The vegetables, *instead of being* bruised and wilted, . . ." "*Unlike* the dirty floors and broken packages . . ." These phrases are somewhat like echo transitions, but instead of joining two adjacent sentences or paragraphs, these phrases show contrasts and remind readers of what has been said earlier in the paper.

The plan might look like this:

Main idea sentence: Even though the Buysafe store on Walnut Terrace and the Buysafe store on Second Avenue are run by the same company, there are important differences in the choices available, the quality of the food, and the prices that are charged.

Similarities: covered in the introduction

Differences: Second Street store
few choices
stale, wilted vegetables
high prices

Walnut Terrace store
several choices in each section
fresh, appetizing vegetables
lower prices, more specials

This plan would work well for this topic because the shopping trip gives a natural unity to each part, while the contrasting phrases help focus on the differences between the first store and the second, linking the two parts together.

Most Important Part Point by Point

The trouble is that not all topics fit so well into an "all about the first thing, all about the second" arrangement. Unless you are very careful, your comparison may be incomplete, your contrasting phrases may be mechanical and dull, and your paper may wind up sounding like two separate essays. Once the least important part has been covered, it may be better to deal with the more important part point by point, comparing as you go. The writer comparing two heating units might begin with a plan like this:

Main idea sentence: Except for some obvious differences in appearance and cost, Brown's Warmup Model B and McTavish's Heatall No. 764 operate on the same principle, use the same kind of fuel, and provide the same amount of heat.

Differences: Warmup B—green baked enamel; $5,780, installation extra
Heatall 764—unpainted steel; $5,600, installation included

Similarities: both—forced hot air, automatic thermostat
both—natural gas
both—same amount of heat per unit of fuel

This kind of order works best when there are only a few points to cover in the least important part, and you want to emphasize the most important part of the comparison.

Point by Point All Through the Paper

The third kind of order compares both the likenesses and differences point by point. In each part of the comparison, however, the writer usually begins with what seems least important. In the paper on judo and karate, for example, it will be easier to make sure nothing is left out if the writer uses this more sophisticated order. The plan will look like this:

> *Main idea sentence:* Judo and karate may seem alike because they both originated in Japan, but as anyone who has seen a karate expert split an oak beam with a bare hand can tell you, the art of karate is quite different from the art of judo.
>
> I.   Both — Expert must learn and practice certain moves.
>   A. Judo expert learns to throw opponent.
>   B. Karate expert learns to disable opponent.
>
> II. Both — Physical discipline is required.
>   A. Judo expert disciplines all muscles and works for quick reactions.
>   B. Karate expert disciplines certain parts of the body until they are extremely tough.
>
> III. Both — Expert takes advantage of opponent's weight and movements.
>   A. Judo expert takes advantage of balance and gravity.
>   B. Karate expert tries to break arms or legs.
>
> IV. Both — Main use is for defense.
>   A. Victim of judo expert is merely thwarted.
>   B. Victim of karate expert may be dead.

This plan is not as complicated as it looks at first glance. It has been shown as a formal sentence outline, with Roman numerals and capital letters, so you will have a model if you need it. Unless you are specially told to prepare a formal outline, however, you won't have to bother with anything so elaborate. Usually all you want your plan to do is jog your memory as you write, and a few words and phrases will be enough to do that. If you are asked to submit a formal outline, as may sometimes happen, you may either use the outline as a working plan or prepare it after you've finished the paper, as a lot of writers do.

None of these ways of organizing a comparison paper is always better than the others. Choose the one that fits your topic best.

> *The three main kinds of order for comparison papers are*
>   *all about one thing, then all about the other;*
>   *most important part point by point;*
>   *point by point all through the paper.*

Writing a Comparison Paper

When you have worked out a clear plan by whatever method seems best, the preliminary work is done. But as you write your first draft, remember that the plan is only the bare bones. The paper won't be satisfactory if all you do is put that skeleton into paragraphs, adding a few contrasting phrases here and there. Each step in the plan must be carefully **developed**. Go back to those lists you made and begin by looking—actually seeing—the reality of what you are explaining. Let readers see the similarities and differences as clearly as you see them in your mind. Give some examples. Put in some specific details.

The writer of the judo-karate paper could just say that a judo expert works on moves that will land an opponent flat on the ground, whereas a karate expert develops the hands until they become lethal weapons, and then go on to the next point. It will be a better paper, though, if the writer lets readers see how the expertise is developed—the karate expert toughening the side of the hand by hitting a board or table hundreds of times a day, gradually increasing the force of the blows until the hand has developed a horny pad, tougher than the soles of most people's feet, building up hardness and strength until boards, bottles, and bricks can be broken with a single stroke. The first sentence tells, in a general, colorless way, what the karate expert does; the second has been developed with specific details. By the time the writer has explained what the karate expert's hands can do to something as flimsy as the human body, there will be plenty to say, and it will be said interestingly and forcefully.

When you read through your first draft, don't hesitate to change your original plan if you can think of another way that will give a more balanced paper. Maybe your main idea sentence needs to be rewritten to reflect what you have actually said. If it does, change it. Or maybe one part has plenty of details, and other parts have few. Don't take the details out, unless they have nothing to do with the point you're making. Instead, close your eyes, get a clearer picture of the bare parts, and add details.

Then check your first and last paragraphs. How much of an **introduction** is needed will depend on your readers. In answering an essay question or preparing a report at work, the main idea sentence will probably be enough. In an essay intended for general readers, such as the comparison of the two supermarkets, you may want to use the introduction to get their interest and keep them reading.

As you write the **conclusion**, remember that your main purpose is to compare, not to praise or condemn. A single sentence summarizing the main points will do very well: "Shoppers in the poorer neighborhood find the choices more limited, the quality inferior, and everything more expensive." Or the conclusion may simply pick up the most important point and assume that readers will remember the rest: "Judo is for sport; karate is for real."

Even if the point of the paper has been to arrive at a judgment, to decide which of two possibilities would work out better, most of the conclusion should still emphasize what the differences—or the similarities—are. The report comparing heating units will not end by saying "Anybody would be crazy to buy a Warmup Model B." Instead, it will say, "Apparently the Heatall No. 764 will do everything we require and save the company money."

Develop your plan by using specific details.
Don't be afraid to change your plan.
Fit the introduction and the conclusion to the needs of your readers.
In general, just compare—don't praise or condemn.

A Special Comparison—Apostrophes

We can get a better understanding of how part of the spelling system works by comparing some common words that sound alike but are written differently: *its* and *it's, your* and *you're, their* and *they're, whose* and *who's*. The similarity is in the sound. The difference is in the meaning, and the difference is more important than the likeness.

What is the difference between *its* and *it's*, for instance? *It's* means *it is*—we just shove the words together and use an apostrophe to represent the missing *i*. *Its* means that something belongs to something else, as in "The dog knows its master's voice."

To understand the difference, you need to remember two important things. First, we use **apostrophes** in two places in English writing. We use them in contractions to show that letters have been left out, as in "Who's (who is) going to feed that dog?" or "It's (it has) been barking for half an hour." And we use them in possessives to show that one thing belongs to another, as in "The dog knows its master's voice" (voice of the master) or "The dog is Martha's worry" (worry of Martha).

Those two rules seem simple enough. The confusion comes with the second thing you need to remember: seven common possessive pronouns are never written with apostrophes:

> *your/yours   his   hers   its   our/ours   their/theirs   whose*

Four of these pronouns can sound just like contractions:

> *your* (possessive) and *you're* (contraction of *you are*)
>
> *its* (possessive) and *it's* (contraction of *it is* or *it has*)
>
> *their* (possessive) and *they're* (contraction of *they are*)
>
> *theirs* (possessive) and *there's* (contraction of *there is* or *there has*)
>
> *whose* (possessive) and *who's* (contraction of *who is* or *who has*)

In general, it works like this:

> You're (you are) sure to pass your (possessive) next test.
>
> The dog barks so much it's (it is) hard to tell what its (possessive) problem is.
>
> There's (there is) a chance they're (they are) going to get their (possessive) stolen car back today; the one they looked at yesterday was not theirs (possessive).
>
> Who's (who is) going to drive whose (possessive) car?
>
> Martha's (Martha is) the one responsible for Martha's dog (possessive—dog of Martha).

Part of our modern problem was caused by a mistake a grammarian made a couple of hundred years ago. Apostrophes had always been used to show contractions, and this man thought that a word like *John's*, in "John's book," was really a contraction of "John his book." So he made a rule that such words should contain an apostrophe. He was wrong, but we're stuck with the rule—one more thing to watch out for as you edit your papers. Apostrophes are a nuisance, but they're part of the etiquette of writing, and many readers will consider you ill-mannered—they might say illiterate—unless you use apostrophes in the conventional places.

If apostrophes are a problem for you, you can find more information on pages 427–430. Meantime, it may help to read your paper backwards. Look carefully for places where you have shoved two words together. Look carefully for places that show a possessive relationship, where the final *s* could be changed to an *of phrase*. And look carefully to make sure you have *not* used an apostrophe in any of those seven pronouns.

> *Use an apostrophe to show omitted letters.*
> *Use an apostrophe where you could substitute an "of phrase," except in*
>   your/yours, his, hers, its, ours, their/theirs, *and* whose.

A Sample Paper of Comparison

The paper that follows was written in answer to this letter:

Dear Jack:

I've just learned that the company is asking me to move from Michigan to the West Coast, specifically to the state of Washington. Since my new territory will be the whole state, they want me to locate in either Spokane or Vancouver. For some reason, they have eliminated Seattle and the Puget Sound area.

I'm pretty excited by the idea--it will be a considerable promotion--but I've never been west of the Rockies. You've lived out there a long time. Can you send me some information about the differences between the two places? I'm particularly interested in schools, recreation, and costs.

                              In haste,
                              Aunt Louise

Jack made a hasty plan and dashed off a quick letter. When he showed it to his roommate from Spokane, however, the roommate had a lot of questions and comments. The plan looked like this:

Reason: to make a decision

Audience: Aunt Louise

Differences between Spokane and Vancouver:
    climate
    size
    recreation
    cost
    scenery

Here is the first letter:

Dear Aunt Louise:

[1] I think it's wonderful you're going to move out here. I'll get to see you and the kids more than just in the summer.

Where does it rain more? How cold? How hot?

[2] Spokane and Vancouver are both nice places. Spokane is east of the mountains and Vancouver is west, so the climate is quite different. It depends on whether you like rain or snow.

How much bigger? What is there to do? How dead is a doornail? What sports? How far to a ski resort?

[3] Spokane is bigger than Vancouver, so there may be more to do. Sometimes Vancouver is deader than a doornail at night. But I know you like outdoor sports and you would find plenty at both places, only some of them would be different. You aren't too far from skiing at either place.

Can you give some comparative costs? Groceries? Housing? Utilities? Taxes?

[4] Some things are cheaper in Spokane and some are cheaper in Vancouver. It probably evens out. You will need a car either place, but you would have to have one for traveling anyway, wouldn't you?

I don't get "the picture." Where are the fir trees? What about schools? Museums, etc.?

[5] As for scenery, both places are pretty as a picture, but I like fir trees better than pines, maybe because I'm used to them. I won't say where I'd rather live because I'm probably prejudiced. Hope this helps.

Love,
Jack

Jack made a more careful plan and started over. Here is the letter he actually sent:

Dear Aunt Louise:

Main idea sentence emphasizing likenesses.

[1] Although Spokane and Vancouver are quite different in climate, scenery, and size, they are both good places to live, with only minor differences in schools, recreation, and living costs.

Differences are covered first because they are less important.

First difference—climate.

[2] As you probably know, Washington is cut in two parts by the Cascade Mountains. Spokane is east of the mountains, about eighteen miles from the Idaho border. Vancouver is west of the Cascades, seven miles north of Portland, Oregon, and a hundred miles from the Pacific Ocean. Being east of the mountains gives Spokane a much drier climate, and greater extremes of hot and cold.

Specific details about rain and snow.

Specific details about temperature.

[3] According to official figures, Spokane gets seventeen and a half inches of precipitation a year and Vancouver about thirty-eight inches. Much of that precipitation is snow in Spokane, whereas in Vancouver it is mostly rain. Some winters western Washington gets no snow at all, but when it does snow it is usually only two or three inches and melts within a day or two. The same kind of official figures say that the average temperature in Spokane is seventy degrees, in Vancouver, sixty-seven. That doesn't sound much different until you look at some monthly averages: in January, twenty-five degrees in Spokane, thirty-eight in Portland.

Mention of location connects first difference with second difference—scenery.

Specific details about
  trees
  mountains
  lakes and rivers.

[4] The location affects the scenery, too. Forests around Vancouver are mainly Douglas fir, with some cedar and hemlock. Around Spokane the trees are mostly pine. From Vancouver you can see three snow-capped mountains on a clear day—Mt. Hood, which is sixty miles away in Oregon, what's left of Mt. St. Helens forty miles to the north, and Mt. Adams, about eighty miles east. Spokane is surrounded by low mountains, but there are seventy-six lakes within fifty miles of the city, many of them in Idaho. Vancouver has the big Columbia River, but the available lakes are almost all created by the dams on the Lewis River.

Third difference—size.

[5] As for size, Spokane is much larger, with a population of nearly two hundred thousand. Vancouver has only about forty thousand people, but that figure is misleading. The city boundaries have not been changed for years, and unless you see a sign, you can never tell where they are. Counting the unincorporated suburbs, the population is estimated to be over a hundred thousand.

Specific details show the size difference is not very great after all.

[6] Even that doesn't tell the whole story, because Vancouver is so close to Portland that it's really part of that metropolitan area. Portland has nearly four hundred thousand people, not counting its suburbs. Although Spokane is the only large city in what Washingtonians call the Inland Empire and is the business center of an area of about eighty thousand square miles, you might get more feeling of a big city in Vancouver than in Spokane.

Similarities—good schools in both.

Reader's needs recognized; colleges are emphasized.

[7] The kids would find good public schools in both cities. I'd guess you are interested in colleges, though, since Jimmy has only two more years of high school. Both cities have community colleges. Clark College in Vancouver has been in existence since the thirties, and Spokane Community College started in the sixties. Spokane has three private four-year colleges, of which Gonzaga, with about four thousand students, is the best known. Vancouver has only a branch of Evergreen State College, with Washington State University offering a few technical courses. Nearby Portland has the University of Portland, Reed College, Lewis and Clark College, and Portland State University. The first three are private, the last one public. The difference in colleges is not great enough to matter.

Second similarity— outdoor recreation.

Specific details on skiing boating and fishing swimming.

[8] In either place you would be close to good skiing all winter long, an hour and a half drive in Spokane, an hour in Vancouver. Boating and fishing are available in both places, in the lakes around Spokane and in the rivers around Vancouver. In addition, you can fish for salmon on the charter boats that go into the ocean from the mouth of the Columbia, or fish for pogies from the rocks. Swimming, too, is available in both places. The kids can

swim and water ski in the big lakes around Spokane; in Vancouver there's water skiing in the Columbia River, but it's not safe to swim. On the other hand, the Pacific Ocean is only two hours away, where all of you can jump in the waves.

Third similarity— indoor recreation.

Specific details on music museums arboretums zoos.

[9]   Spokane has a symphony orchestra, two museums, an opera house, an arboretum, and a zoo. Vancouver has no orchestra, no zoo, no arboretum, and only two relatively small historical museums, but people in Vancouver can easily take advantage of Portland's symphony orchestra, its opera association, its three museums—art, history, and science and industry— its arboretum, and its zoo. If you want cultural attractions, you can find them in either place.

Fourth similarity—cost.

Specific details on housing food.

[10]   The cost of living is about the same. A three-bedroom house in ordinary condition sells for around seventy thousand dollars in both cities, and three-bedroom apartments rent for around three hundred dollars a month, more if you want a swimming pool. Staples, such as flour, cereals, etc., seem to be a little cheaper in Spokane, but in the summer you can get fresh vegetables and fruit for considerably less in Vancouver if you buy directly from the farmers or, if you want berries, by picking your own.

Specific details on taxes.

[11]   You would not pay a state income tax in either city, since Washington doesn't have one, but you would pay a 7 percent sales tax on everything except food. Many people in Vancouver, however, do a lot of their shopping in Oregon, where there is no sales tax yet. That practice is frowned on, but there is no way of stopping it, except on the purchase of cars. You have to pay sales tax on a car before you can get it licensed in Washington.

Conclusion summarizes the likenesses and refers back to the differences talked about in the first two paragraphs. Conclusion stays neutral— judgment is left up to the reader.

[12]   The two cities are much alike in the things that interest you most—good schools, plenty of recreation, and reasonable costs. People from Spokane swear by their climate, but people in Vancouver think the mountains and the ocean are a great advantage, in spite of the rain—and a lot of us like the rain.

Love,
Jack

Key Words and Ideas _____

Here are some of the important terms and ideas covered in this chapter. See whether you can answer these questions about them.

1. What are three **reasons for making comparisons**?
2. What should you consider in deciding on a **topic for comparison**?
3. How can you **collect your ideas** for a comparison paper? What does **brainstorming** mean?
4. What two things are always included in **main idea sentences for comparison papers**?
5. Why are **connecting words or phrases** important in main idea sentences for comparison papers?
6. What three kinds of **order** can be used in comparison papers? Which kind is best?
7. What is a **formal sentence outline**? When should you use it?
8. What is meant by **developing your plan**?
9. How much **introduction** does a comparison paper need? What should you watch out for in writing the **conclusion**?
10. What are the two places where **apostrophes** should be used? Where should they not be used?

Name _____

Exercises _____

Exercise 1. Finding Topics for Comparison.   Pick out things in your own life—at home, on the job, in college—that you could compare. Then explain the reason for the comparison—to get a better understanding of familiar things, to learn something new, or to make a judgment. For instance, you might compare two ways of keeping up with the news: watching television or reading the daily paper. Why would you make the comparison? Who would your readers be?

> *Example:*
> Comparison of <u>television</u> and <u>newspaper</u>
>
> Reason—<u>better understanding of the news</u>
>
> Readers—<u>other college students</u>

Comparison _____ and _____

Reason _____

Readers _____

Comparison _____ and _____

Reason _____

Readers _____

Comparison _____ and _____

Reason _____

Readers _____

Comparison _____ and _____

Reason _____

Readers _____

Name _____

Exercise 2. Finding Similarities and Differences.   For each of these topics, list some similarities and some differences. Then decide whether the similarities or the differences seem more important.

Two restaurants where you've eaten:

1. _____   2. _____

        Similarities   *Differences*

_____   _____

_____   _____

_____   _____

_____   _____

_____   _____

_____   _____

More important _____

Two teachers you've had:

1. _____   2. _____

        Similarities   *Differences*

_____   _____

_____   _____

_____   _____

_____   _____

_____   _____

More important _____

Two places you've lived:

1. _____   2. _____

| *Similarities* | *Differences* |

_____   _____

_____   _____

_____   _____

_____   _____

_____   _____

_____   _____

More important _____

Two pets you've observed:

1. _____   2. _____

| *Similarities* | *Differences* |

_____   _____

_____   _____

_____   _____

_____   _____

_____   _____

_____   _____

More important _____

Name _____

Exercise 3. Main Idea Sentences.   Here are some possible main idea sentences for comparison papers. If you think a sentence is satisfactory, mark it *OK*. If you think it is unsatisfactory, either say what the problem is or rewrite the sentence so that it is satisfactory.

> *Example:* Divorced men and divorced women both have problems.
>
> *Unsatisfactory* because it doesn't have two parts; it doesn't show which is more important, likeness or difference.
>
> *Rewritten* — Although both divorced men and divorced women have problems, women's problems are usually more difficult than men's.

1. Some people work while they go to college and some people don't, but it makes a difference.   _____

   _____

   _____

   _____

2. Toyotas and Datsuns are both foreign cars.   _____

   _____

   _____

   _____

3. Coffee and tea produce about the same effect on the drinker, despite the difference in taste, aroma, and method of preparation.   _____

   _____

   _____

   _____

4. In this paper I will compare the effects of alcohol with the effects of marijuana.   ———

———————————————————————————

———————————————————————————

———————————————————————————

5. Even though term insurance and conventional life insurance both will protect your family in case of your death, the provisions of the two policies are quite different.   ———

———————————————————————————

———————————————————————————

———————————————————————————

6. The twins, Jonathan and Jacob, seem to look alike, but their hair is a different color.   ———

———————————————————————————

———————————————————————————

———————————————————————————

7. Even though San Francisco and New Orleans may seem very different, the two cities are a lot alike in at least thirty ways.   ———

———————————————————————————

———————————————————————————

———————————————————————————

Name _____

Exercise 4. Writing Main Idea Sentences.   Write a main idea sentence for each of the topics in Exercise 2, basing each sentence on the lists you made earlier.

Two restaurants:

_____

_____

_____

Two teachers:

_____

_____

_____

Two places:

_____

_____

_____

Two pets:

_____

_____

_____

Exercise 5. Collecting Ideas.   Pick one of the topics from Exercise 1, or find an entirely new topic if you prefer. Then make two lists, one for each part of the topic. Put down everything you can think of, no matter how trivial it seems. Use more paper if you need it. After you have finished the lists, decide what the emphasis will be, what the reason for making the comparison is, and who your readers will be. Then write a main idea sentence based on all these decisions.

Comparison of _____ *and* _____

_____ _____

_____ _____

_____ _____

_____ _____

_____ _____

_____ _____

_____ _____

_____ _____

Emphasis _____

Reason _____

Readers _____

Main idea sentence _____

_____

_____

Name _____

Exercise 6. Planning the Paper.   Make a plan for the comparison you were work-ing on in Exercise 5. Use whichever arrangement seems to fit your topic best. (See pages 106–108.)

Main idea sentence _____

_____

_____

Arrangement

_____

_____

_____

_____

_____

_____

_____

_____

_____

_____

_____

_____

Conclusion _____

_____

_____

Exercise 7. Writing a First Draft.   Write the first draft of the paper you planned in Exercise 6. Then exchange drafts with another student in the class. After you have read the other student's paper, make a plan of that paper, showing what you think the arrangement is. Also make a note of any questions you had as you read the paper. When you get your own draft back, compare the plan the other student has made with the one you made in Exercise 6. Do you need to make some changes in the arrangement of your paper? Can you answer the questions the other student asked?

Exercise 8. Rewriting Your Paper.   Write another version of the paper you've been working on. Put this version away for a day or so and then reread it to see if you want to make any other changes. Then make sure you can answer yes to all the questions on this check list.

Check List for Content

1. Does your introduction contain your main idea sentence?   _____

2. Is your main idea sentence in two parts, connected by a word such as *but* or *even though*?   _____

3. Does the main idea sentence make clear whether you're emphasizing similarities or differences?   _____

4. If the main idea sentence indicates the divisions of the comparison, does the main part of your paper follow that same order?   _____

5. Can you justify the order of your plan?   _____

6. Have you given enough specific details so that readers can see the picture you had in your mind?   _____

7. Does your conclusion make the paper sound finished without either praising or condemning?   _____

Name _____

Exercise 9. Apostrophes.   In the following sentences, the apostrophes have been deliberately left out. Circle the words in which the conventions of writing would add apostrophes. Then rewrite those circled words with the apostrophes added.

1. Whos at the door?

2. The doctors not in her office; all the doctors will be out until after lunch.

3. That creams sour.

4. Thats my coat; this must be yours.

5. Its annoying not to know whose parking place this is.

6. Jakes cat hasnt been home for a weeks time, even though its wearing its license tag.

7. Theres little difference between Pats cat and Jakes.

_____   _____   _____   _____

_____   _____   _____   _____

_____   _____   _____   _____

_____   _____   _____   _____

Exercise 10. More Apostrophes. Write some sentences of your own, trying to use each of these words at least once:

whose who's   it's its   your you're

there's theirs   we'll   well   aren't

_____

_____

_____

_____

_____

_____

_____

_____

_____

_____

_____

_____

_____

_____

_____

_____

Exercise 11. The Final Step.   Now go over your paper one more time, this time reading for sentences, paragraphs, pronouns, and spelling, especially the spelling of words with apostrophes. Make sure you can answer yes to all of these questions:

Check List for Editing and Style

1. Are your sentences a comfortable length?   _____

2. Do all your sentences begin with capitals and end with periods?   _____

3. Have you used a dictionary to check the spelling of any words you were unsure about?   _____

4. Have you looked to see that all your contractions contain apostrophes?   _____

5. Have you used apostrophes wherever you could substitute an "of phrase," except for those seven special pronouns?   _____

6. Have you given a separate paragraph to each of the important parts of your comparison?   _____

7. Have you used enough contrasting words and phrases?   _____

Exercise 12. Evaluating Comparisons.   Find a short comparison—it can be just a paragraph or it can be a long article—in some newspaper, magazine, or book. Bring the comparison to class and be ready to explain whether or not you think it is successful, and why.

Chapter 5

Explaining: Classification

When you explain one term, it's *definition*. When you explain the relationship between two things, it's *comparison*. And when you explain the connection between a number of things that are somehow related to each other, it's *classification*. **Classification** is a way of grouping things, of sorting out relationships. You are using a **classification system** whenever you attempt to explain things by sorting them into groups and then sorting each group into smaller groups.

Classifying our experiences is a way of understanding them, of putting order into what has happened to us, what we have learned, or what we have to deal with. Ranchers classify cattle, librarians classify books, doctors classify diseases, automobile dealers classify cars, lawmakers classify crimes. Classification, in fact, is a method commonly used in specialized fields whenever people need to make the work easier and the subject more understandable. But classification is not reserved for specialists. It's a method of explanation anybody can use, and it can be applied to almost anything. In fact, it's impossible to be human and not classify things.

Occasionally you hear a very small child call all little animals "kitties." The child has taken a first step in classifying; it's clear that puppies and kittens and squirrels belong in a different group than trees or people. As the child grows older and sees more animals, however, it becomes apparent that although puppies and kittens and squirrels all belong to a big group of small furry creatures, there are enough differences that people call these animals by different names. That is, people put them into different groups. Indeed, if we didn't learn at an early age to classify, our lives would not have much order.

Language itself is a giant classification system. If you hadn't learned, well before you started to school, which words fit which positions in English sentences, you wouldn't be able to talk or to understand what others said to you. It would never occur to a four-year-old to say: "A bit dog man the," because the child learned very early to classify *dog* and *man* as nouns and *bit* as a verb, without ever hearing those technical terms. The child also knows that either "a dog bit the man" or "a man bit the dog" makes sense—and "makes sense" is a sign that the words fit properly into the system.

Language helps us classify in other ways, too. We see things in the physical world as separate objects because we have words to separate those things. In English, we can say, "That's an orange shirt; those slacks are red," because our language classifies those colors into different groups. In other languages, where colors may be classified differently, people may regard an orange shirt and red slacks as being the same color, only slightly different in shade, just as we see light blue and dark blue as belonging to the general group of "blue."

So we classify to separate bits out of the whirling chaos surrounding us, to label those bits, and to group similar bits together. Classification is a convenient shortcut for helping our experiences "make sense." For instance, we only have to learn once about telling time. Thereafter, we recognize "clocks," whether they are wristwatches, grandfather clocks, cuckoo clocks, giant neon announcements flashing above a shopping center, or tiny digital stick-ons that we can buy for $1.95 plus tax. We can recognize each new, unexperienced timekeeper as a "clock" and fit the new thing into the framework of information we already possess. If we had to figure each separate thing out each time we encountered it, we wouldn't have much time or energy for anything else.

> *Classification is a method of bringing order to our experiences and our knowledge.*

Reasons for Classifying—Point of View

Cars or clothes, jobs or jewelry, furniture, foods, or fads—you can and do classify any of them. All you need is a system for the classification. Almost any subject can be classified in a number of ways, and the system you use depends on your reason for making the classification.

For example, college students can be classified according to income, age, marital status, grade-point average, activities, or even their reasons for coming to college. Students can be classified as contributors or consumers, as audience or activists. The system you choose depends on what you want to know about students and what you want your readers to know. In other words, it depends on your **point of view**. If you are writing for the Board of Trustees, who are considering whether to raise tuition, you can classify students by income; your reason might be to explain how many students won't be able to return next year if costs are too high. If you are writing for a committee trying to decide whether the child care center should be expanded, you can classify students by marital status, in an attempt to discover whether there has been, or will be, an increase in the demand for nursery school services. Knowing why you have chosen the system helps you stay with a single point of view—keeps you from talking about grade-point averages when you start out with income.

Choice of a classification system depends on the reason for classifying. The reason determines the point of view.

Classifying and Stereotyping

Sometimes we classify physical things—recipes, rock music, clocks. Sometimes we classify events—exciting, boring, frightening, and so on. Sometimes we classify people—and it's when we start classifying other human beings that we may run into trouble. We may slide over into stereotyping. **Stereotyping** means putting one label on a person or a group of people and then assuming that everybody with that label is exactly alike; it means forgetting that people are individuals and disregarding all the other ways they could be classified. When somebody says, "Queeny Monroe is a woman's libber; that's all I need to know about her!" or "All South Africans hate Blacks," that person is stereotyping. Stereotyping is a special kind of classifying—a faulty kind—and although it, too, works as a shortcut and a timesaver, it is nearly always used to "prove" something unpleasant. People who stereotype generalize about a whole human being from partial evidence. They start with one part of a person—name, hair style, skin color, age, nationality, occupation, or whatever—and forget about the rest of the person.

Suppose, for instance, somebody says, "Richard Arnold's a cop, isn't he? You know what they're like," and goes on as though there were nothing else worth saying. But Richard Arnold is thirty-five years old, a Black veteran majoring in political science. He lives two and a half miles from the campus with his wife and two small daughters. He voted Democratic in the last election, and he goes bowling whenever he has time. It's true that he works as a police officer from 4:00 to 9:00 P.M., and it's also true that he is a member of the American Civil Liberties Union. This short description shows a dozen different ways of looking at one man, at least a dozen classification systems into which he would fit. Whether you classify Arnold as a police officer or a bowler or a Black depends entirely on whether you are interested in finding out about occupations, hobbies, or affirmative action. If you are classifying college students according to marital status, for instance, neither Arnold's age nor his political beliefs have anything to do with it. Whatever classification system is used, part of the "real Mr. Arnold" is left out. But if you remember that a classification system is set up from a single point of view, for one reason, and probably for only one time, you will realize that the classification cannot put a permanent label on Richard Arnold.

Those who stereotype, on the other hand, get hold of one detail and think they have the whole Mr. Arnold. They assume that because of one part of him, he can be placed permanently in a single group and that he shares all the other characteristics of that group. Students who are only eighteen might stereotype him as "typically middle-aged" and thereby dismiss his character, opinions, accomplishments, and potentials as not worth bothering about. On the other hand, the Chief of Police, who is sixty-five, may think of Arnold as too young to have good judgment and disregard his opinions for that reason. Racial bigots, white or Black, will think they know all they need to know by simply looking at his skin color.

If, when you classify people, you remember that you're doing so from a particular point of view, for a particular reason, and for that reason only, you can avoid stereotyping. You will say, for example, *"For now, because I'm interested in part-time jobs,* I'll group Richard Arnold with other police officers." You will not say, "Don't trust him—he's a cop." Honest classification is a way of thinking clearly; stereotyping is a kind of short circuit that prevents thinking.

Stereotyping means putting a permanent label on people on the basis of one thing about them and ignoring everything else.

Sorting Up and Sorting Down

Honest classification can work in two directions. It could start with Richard Arnold and place him in a group of police officers, then in a somewhat larger group of working students. That group, in turn, could be placed in the even larger group of college students. We can call this kind of classification **sorting up**. Or the system can begin with a big group and divide it into smaller and smaller groups, much like a woman unpacking a suitcase. She starts with a big batch of clothes and sorts them into piles of underwear, skirts, slacks, tops, and shoes. She may then sort the tops into turtlenecks and blouses, and then sort the blouses into those that go with suits and those that go with jeans. We can call this process **sorting down**.

In sorting up, for example, you might begin with cats and explain that they are members of a larger group, felines, which includes jaguars, lions, and tigers; mention what characteristics that group shares; and move up once more to put felines into a larger group, mammals. What you are doing here is much like what you did when you were working with general and specific words. When you sort up, you begin with a specific term and go on to increasingly general terms.

When you sort down, you get more and more specific. You might divide cats into smaller groups—pedigreed and common—and then divide pedigreed cats into smaller groups, according to breed, perhaps—Siamese, Persian, Maltese—or by hair length—short, medium, long—or by disposition, rarity, sex, or anything else that interests you. You would not, however, discover anything useful if you further divided Siamese cats by disposition, Persian cats by hair length, and Maltese cats by sex. Whether you are sorting up or down, you must stick with one system. The woman unpacking that suitcase is not likely to stop in the middle of separating slacks and skirts and decide to sort them according to how much they originally cost. Such a shift in system, in the middle of her unpacking, would destroy the reason for the classification—getting the clothes put away in the closet.

Sorting up starts with one thing and puts it into larger groups.
Sorting down starts with a big group and divides it into smaller groups.

Main Idea Sentences for Classification

All of us classify almost automatically most of the time, but when we undertake a more formal classification, starting with a **main idea sentence** may help. When you write a classification paper in college—or more likely, a classification paragraph, as you may need to do in many of your classes—the main idea sentence will show the direction you plan to take. A good main idea sentence will tell what is being classified (the topic); what method of explanation is being used (classification); and the point of view (what the first division is based on).

Here are some main idea sentences for classification papers:

Prehistoric people had tools made of horn, tooth, and bone, each kind used for a specific purpose.
Topic: prehistoric tools
Point of view: material tools were made from

Depending on the amount of training they have had, nurses fall into three general groups—registered nurses, practical nurses, and aides.
Topic: nurses
Point of view: amount of training

Three kinds of people consult fortunetellers: those who believe, those who are not sure, and those who are just spoofing.
Topic: people who consult fortunetellers
Point of view: degree of belief

Dentists can be divided into two groups, those that talk a lot and those that keep quiet.
Topic: dentists
Point of view: amount of talking

It's just as important in classification as in other writing to remember who your readers will be and what they need to be told. A classification of prehistoric tools will demonstrate, probably to a teacher, that the writer has the information and understands the subject. The classification of nurses might be written for high school students investigating a career in the health sciences. "Three kinds of people consult fortunetellers . . ." might introduce the first paragraph of a more general essay on fortunetelling, intended for readers who are curious about the topic. "Dentists can be divided . . ." might be a humorous account of one person's experiences, intended to amuse fellow students; it certainly doesn't sound as if it were intended for a class in dental hygiene.

Main idea sentences for classification should make clear
  what the topic is;
  what method of explaining is being used;
  what the point of view is.

Making a Chart

Just as a main idea sentence can remind you of the direction you plan to take, a **classification chart** can serve as your writing plan. Often such a chart is quite simple:

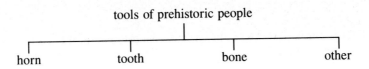

The category "other" has been added, even though it doesn't appear in the main idea sentence, as a kind of insurance against leaving anything out. Although the writer may mean to concentrate on tools made of horn, tooth, and bone, it seems probable that early people did use rocks or stones for some purposes.

A chart placing nurses into groups according to the training they have had will be almost as simple, although the writer may want to add one more step to the chart, breaking down the kind of training that registered nurses may have:

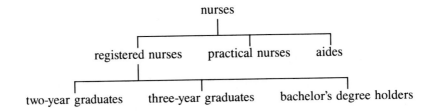

If the writer is quite sure there are no other possibilities, it won't be necessary to add an "other" category at either step.

It is necessary, however, to make sure that the categories are real divisions and that they don't overlap. A chart of people who go to fortunetellers would get both writer and readers seriously muddled if it looked like this:

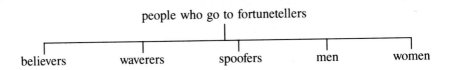

The problem here is that all of the first three categories already include both men and women. If you want to include Mary Jones, who bases all her actions on what is shown in a crystal ball, where do you put her? Under women or under believers? A better chart, one that avoids overlapping, might look like this:

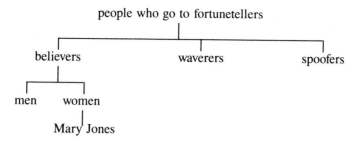

It would be possible, of course, also to divide waverers and spoofers into men and women, but this second chart seems to show that the writer's main interest is in believers.

In these charts, and the main idea sentences that go with them, the writers are quite sure of the point of view they will take. Suppose, however, that the teacher of an early childhood education class has asked for short papers on day-care centers. Several points of view are possible:

> licensed and unlicensed
> size
> with or without structured learning
> government sponsored or private
> religious affiliation or nonaffiliated
> cost
> hours that care is available

The first division establishes the system the rest of the classification will follow. The student who begins with licensed and unlicensed may go on to divide both categories according to cost, and then further subdivide the unlicensed centers according to the hours that care is available. On the other hand, dividing the centers into those with a religious affiliation and those without might lead to a second step showing whether or not the centers provide structured learning. A third step might show the kinds of learning that is provided—Bible verses, group games, craft work, color recognition.

A good classification chart
   includes all possible categories at each step;
   avoids overlapping categories.

Developing the Plan

Like any other plan, a classification chart is just that—a plan. When it is **developed** into a paper, or even a paragraph, it must give examples and details. The test question on prehistoric tools will be better answered if the student gives an example of a drinking vessel made of horn, jewelry shaped from a mastodon tooth, and a bone needle used to sew animal furs. The high school students can better understand the distinction between registered nurses and nurses' aides if examples are given—perhaps of the registered nurse assisting at an operation, the aide bathing a patient and making a bed.

The writer planning the fortunetelling paragraph may already have done some brainstorming. Certainly before she goes much further she will need to do more—get a mental picture of one fortuneteller, with a dark turban around his head and a robe covered with signs of the zodiac; see the half-darkened room at the top of the narrow stairs; picture the crystal ball with its black velvet cover. She will imagine the waverers wondering whether they might really come into some money quite soon, and the scoffers treating it all as a huge joke. She will hear, in her mind, Mary Jones's timid voice asking whether she should change jobs and her sigh of relief when the fortuneteller assures her that if she stays where she is, she will get a surprise. If the writer herself is one of the nonbelievers, she might go on to consider the amount of money Mary Jones spends every week in that dingy room, money that could be spent on a much needed new raincoat.

The writer may begin her paragraph with the main idea sentence that has already been written, or she may decide to change it slightly. Maybe the paragraph will now begin, "Of all the people who consult fortunetellers—those who believe, those who are not sure, and those who go simply for a joke—the ones who really believe are the ones to be pitied." After she has described one fortuneteller and one room, she will probably give a sentence or two to the waverers and the scoffers, just enough that readers can understand their attitudes, and then spend the rest of the paragraph on the true believers, using Mary Jones as an example. The paragraph may end with a sentence about the money that could have gone toward a raincoat, or it may end with a comment that the reassurance Mary Jones gets seems to Mary—but not to the writer—to be worth the cost.

Specific examples are essential in classification papers.

Classification as a Study Aid

If you have followed your chart carefully and written your paper clearly, readers should be able to reproduce the chart from which you were working. Good readers often make such charts as they study, either in their minds or actually on paper. Just as classification charts can help you sort out your own thoughts before you write, so **reconstructed charts** can help you sort out the ideas behind other people's writing. For example, a chart of writing purposes as they have been presented in this book would look like this:

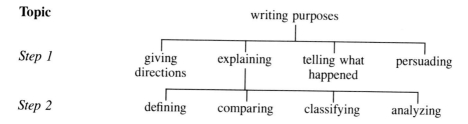

Topic

Step 1

Step 2

Notice that step 1 includes all the writing purposes mentioned in the first chapter. Step 2 includes the four kinds of explanation that the book discusses. It would also be possible to subdivide *giving directions* in step 2; it could be separated into *making things* and *doing things,* in the same way that *telling what happened* will later be separated into *reports* and *personal experience.*

This chart shows the process of stepping down, from the more general *writing purposes* to the more specific *explaining.* The other divisions that could be made in the second step have been omitted because the main point right now is to explain *classification.* Although charts such as these are primarily useful in straightening out what you have learned, they can also serve as writing plans if you are answering a test question.

Making charts of what you read can help you see and remember relationships.

Classifying Commas

Of all the punctuation symbols writers are supposed to use as they edit, **commas** are among the most confusing. Professional writers don't always agree on where commas are needed. Handbooks often give eight or nine different rules, all of them in terminology that's hard to understand. And some readers regard a "comma splice" as very nearly a capital offense. In spite of the problems, however, commas remain part of the editing process, and unless you confine yourself to kindergarten sentences — *"Prehistoric people had tools. Some tools were made of bone. Some were made of horn. Some were made of . . ."* and so on—you will need to use them. In modern practice, the most important uses of commas can be classified like this:

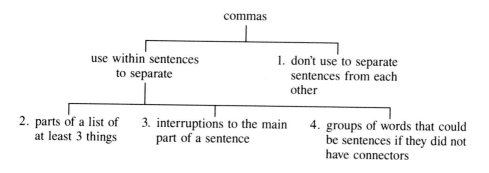

Like other charts, this one is not much help without some examples, so here they are:

1. *Don't use* commas to separate sentences from each other:

    Mary Jones was very hard up, she needed a new raincoat badly.

    Mary Jones, who was very hard up, needed a new raincoat and a lot of other clothes, she kept going to fortunetellers anyway.

    Here the underlined commas are separating two separate sentences and creating what's called a comma splice. These commas should be changed to periods, unless the writer wants to add some connectors.

2. Use commas to separate parts of a list of at least three things:

    bone, horn, tooth, and other material (four things)
    those who believe, those who aren't sure, and those who are merely scoffing (three things)

3. Use to separate interruptions from the main part of a sentence:

    However, some people are comforted by crystal balls.
    Mary Jones, *who is very hard up,* needs a new raincoat badly.
    Uncertain of what choices to make, Mary Jones goes, *at least once a week,* to see her favorite fortuneteller.
    On January 10, *1985,* she even went twice.
    "Please," *she said,* "tell me what I ought to do."
    She spends five dollars a visit, *money she can ill afford.*

    Here the interruptions are shown in italics. As you will notice, interruptions can come at the beginning, in the middle, or at the end of sentences.

4. Use to separate groups of words that could be sentences if they were not joined by connectors:

    Because Mary Jones was very hard up, she needed a new raincoat badly.
    Mary Jones needed a new raincoat and a lot of other clothes, *but* she kept going to fortunetellers anyway.

    Here the connectors are shown in italics.

Looking at a chart such as this, even studying the examples with care, won't make you an expert on the uses of commas. Most writers who can edit skillfully have not learned what they know about commas from either rules or charts. Instead, they have unconsciously absorbed an understanding of where commas fit from all the reading they have done, in much the same way that children absorb an understanding of the structure of their native language. Such writers never have to ask themselves,

"Is this a list of at least three things? Does this phrase interrupt my main thought?" As they give a finished paper a final reading, however, they may sometimes ask, "Will a comma here make my meaning clearer or will it just confuse my readers?" Commas, like all other conventions of writing, are intended to make life easier for readers.

As you edit your own writing, you can ask yourself that same question. And if commas continue to worry you, you can find more information on pages 434–437.

> *In modern English, commas are used to separate*
> *parts of a list of at least three things;*
> *interruptions to the main part of a sentence;*
> *groups of words that could be sentences if they did not have connectors.*

Two Sample Classification Papers

Paper One

This paper was written for an examination question in a class on the nature of language. The question was: "Identify and explain three different meanings of the word *grammar.* The student quickly realized that this question required a paragraph of classification and made a brief chart:

Here is the paragraph that was turned in:

> Nelson Francis said that what people understand by "grammar" can be divided into what he calls grammar 1, grammar 2, and grammar 3. Grammar 1 is the real grammar, grammar 2 is talking about it, and grammar 3 is correcting it.

When the answer received only half credit, the student was indignant and wanted to know why. The teacher—an unusually generous type who believed that the purpose of tests is to teach—gave some advice and allowed the student to rewrite the paragraph. Here is the second, much improved, version:

Satisfactory main idea sentence has been kept.

Nelson Francis said that what people understand by "grammar" can be divided into what he calls grammar 1, grammar 2, and grammar 3. Grammar 1 means the way a language actually operates. That knowledge was built into us when we learned

Grammar 1 is explained by a general statement supported by a specific example.

Grammar 2 has also been made more specific.

Grammar 3 has been given two examples.

Short paragraph doesn't need a formal conclusion.

to talk, and that knowledge lets us understand sentences we've never heard before. It's the thing that tells us the difference in English between "John ate the pig" and "The pig ate John," even though the words in both sentences are the same. Grammar 2 means analyzing how grammar 1 works. It's what we do when we learn about subjects and predicates and verbs. Grammar 3 really refers to conventional usage. That's the kind people mean when they say, "If you're an English teacher, I'll have to watch my grammar." It's also the kind parents mean when they tell their kids that saying "ain't" is "bad grammar."

Paper Two

This is the final draft of a paper written for an English class, with the hope it could be used in the college literary magazine.

The Captive Patient

Why is the main idea sentence saved until the end of the paragraph? What does the first part accomplish?

[1]   Don't let anybody tell you that dentists are all alike. I've been to a good many in my life because my mother is a firm believer in "Brush your teeth twice a day and see your dentist twice a year." We've moved around a lot, so her motto could have been "See two dentists a year." The ones I was forced to visit can be divided into two groups: dentists that don't talk and dentists that do.

What is there in the main idea sentence that tells you nontalkers will be discussed first?

[2]   The nontalkers can't keep totally quiet, of course, but they do the best they can. After the assistant has tucked me into that enormous bib and left me to stare for fifteen minutes at the glittering array of torture tools spread out on the counter, the dentist finally walks in and says "Open." After a long while he says "Close," and then "Open." If he's feeling really chatty, he sometimes says "Wider." When he's through with the thing in the chair—the "thing" is me, since this automatic tooth-fixer has managed to make me feel like an object—he walks out and leaves the assistant to deliver the big speech of the day: "Don't chew on that side for twenty-four hours."

How does the writer let readers know that there's a shift from nontalkers to talkers?	**[3]** When I go to a new dentist I can't tell at first whether he's a talker. He comes in with a pleasant "Good morning" and tends quietly to his business until he gets my mouth propped open as wide as it will go. Then he begins.
Why doesn't the writer quote the actual conversation in this paragraph?	**[4]** One talking dentist I knew was a basketball fan. He used to tell me, play by play, about the big game he'd seen on television the night before. That is, he'd tell me all about it until he got to the really exciting part, when the star of the game was about to throw the basket that might break the tie. That always happened just when the dentist got to the exciting part of the cavity he was filling. Then he'd stop the story and concentrate on the tooth. I never did find out how the game ended.
Actual conversation is not quoted in this paragraph either, until the last sentence. What is the effect of quoting that one sentence?	**[5]** That could be pretty frustrating, but it was better than the line of talk my Uncle Ollie turned out. We once lived for nearly a year in the town where Uncle Ollie was practicing, so of course I had to go to him. He told me a lot of stuff I didn't want to hear—gossip about one of my aunts, tales of the terrible time he was having with my cousins. I thought most of it wasn't true, but I was a captive in the chair and couldn't contradict him. Then he finished it all off by saying at intervals, "If you don't sit still, I'll tell your mother."
Why do you think all the conversation is quoted here?	**[6]** But the worst kind of talker is the one that asks questions. First he stuffs my mouth full of cotton wadding, in case holding it open won't immobilize me enough. Then he asks, "Are you new in town?"
	[7] "Glug," I say.
	[8] "Where does your family come from?"
	[9] "Glug."
	[10] "How do you like it here?"
	[11] "Glug."
	[12] "Where do you go to school?"
	[13] "Glug."
	[14] "Who used to be your dentist?"

Does the paper sound fin-
ished? Why or why not?
Could you make a classification chart of this paper?
How can you tell who the
readers are expected to be?

[15]   It goes on like that for half an hour. By the time he finally says, "You can rinse your mouth out now," I've forgotten what the questions were, and so has he, so I just say "Glug" very politely and go home.

Key Words and Ideas

Here are some of the important terms and ideas covered in this chapter. See whether you can answer these questions about them.

1. Why is **classification** an important human activity?
2. What does the choice of a **classification system** depend on?
3. What is meant by **point of view** in classification?
4. What is **stereotyping**? Why should it be avoided?
5. What is the difference between **sorting up** and **sorting down**?
6. What should the **main idea sentence** for a **classification paper** do?
7. What does a good **classification chart** include? What does it avoid?
8. In **developing a classification chart** into a paragraph or paper, what is it especially important to remember?
9. How can **reconstructed classification charts** help in studying?
10. What are the three main uses of **commas** in modern English writing?

Name _____

Exercises _____

Exercise 1. Classification in Ordinary Life. List eight or ten things that you classify in your own life, more or less automatically. The list can include almost anything, from the mail you receive to the men or women that you know. Then pick two of those things and explain the reason for classifying them.

> *Example:*
> *Thing classified:* contents of closet
> *Reason:* to separate summer clothes from winter clothes

Things you classify:

_____

_____

_____

_____

_____

_____

_____

_____

Thing classified _____

Reason _____

Thing classified _____

Reason _____

Exercise 2. Point of View.   Give three points of view from which each of these topics could be classified. There's no "right answer" to this exercise, but it should be interesting to compare your answers with those of the other students in the class.

> *Example:* Contents of closet
> summer and winter clothes
> indoor and outdoor wear
> worn-out and still good

1. Radio programs _____

   _____

   _____

2. Toys _____

   _____

   _____

3. Doctors _____

   _____

   _____

4. Vacations _____

   _____

   _____

5. Motorcycles _____

   _____

   _____

Name _____

Exercise 3. Recognizing Stereotyping.   Which of these statements indicate stereotyping and which show honest classification? If you think a statement shows stereotyping, explain how you decided. If you think there is an honest attempt at classification, give the probable reason for the classifying. Compare your answers with those of other students in the class.

1. *Voter:* "You can't depend on what Senator Upright says. He's just a politician."

_____

2. *Voter:* "Senator Upright is one of three candidates who promised to vote for lower taxes."

_____

3. *Mother:* "I don't let Bobby play with Carlos because I don't want him getting any of those dirty germs. Carlos's father is a migrant worker."

_____

4. *Mother:* "Bobby's kindergarten teacher says that five of the children in his class speak Spanish and three speak Vietnamese."

_____

5. *Neighbor:* "It must have been teen-agers who stole my garden hose; they're all out of control."

_____

6. *Teen-ager:* "You can't expect old man Hawkins to understand kids; he must be at least seventy."

_____

7. *Father:* "You're going out with Cleveland Archer? Don't you know what they say about preachers' sons?"

_____

8. *Man:* "That must be a good suit; it cost more than anything else in the store."

_____

9. *Man:* "That suit is the most expensive piece of clothing I ever owned."

_____

10. *Personnel Director:* "I never hire women if I can help it—they spend too much time fixing their faces."

_____

11. *Friend:* "I sure pity you. I hear your mother-in-law is coming for a visit."

_____

12. *Woman:* "I'm sure he's charming. He belongs to the same club as my brother."

_____

13. *Woman:* "One of my brother's friends drives a Mercedes, one drives a Porsche, and four drive Lincoln Continentals."

_____

14. *Gardener:* "Can this possibly be a new variety of slug?"

_____

15. *Extension Agent:* "Five varieties of garden slugs are found in this area."

_____

Name _____

Exercise 4. Sorting Up and Sorting Down. All of these situations involve classifying. Decide whether you think the person doing the classifying will be *sorting up* or *sorting down*. Give the probable reason for the classification, and then compare your answers with those of other students in the class.

> *Example:* copy of the phone bill you just paid — sorting up
> *Reason:* to file it with other utility bills for the year

1. A shipment of medical supplies received by a hospital   _____

   Reason _____

2. Sacks of outgoing mail at a post office   _____

   Reason _____

3. Letter addressed to New York City received at a post office   _____

   Reason _____

4. A new angleworm discovered by a zoologist   _____

   Reason _____

5. A shipment of textbooks received by the college bookstore   _____

   Reason _____

6. An unused textbook returned to the bookstore   _____

   Reason _____

7. A miscellaneous collection of nails and screws   _____

   Reason _____

Name _____

Exercise 5. Main Idea Sentences for Classification. Which of these sentences would be good main idea sentences for classification? If you think a sentence is OK, list the topic and the point of view. If you think a sentence is unsuitable, say why.

1. Political candidates can be grouped according to the offices they are running for— local, state, or national.

Topic ___OK___

Point of view ___level of political office___

If unsuitable, why? _____

2. Political candidates can be grouped according to age, sex, and popularity.

Topic ___NO___

Point of view _____

If unsuitable, why? _____

3. People who oppose abortion for women on welfare do so because of religious objections, financial considerations, or class prejudice.

Topic ___YES___

Point of view _____

If unsuitable, why? _____

4. Long-distance telephone rates vary according to the time of day the call is placed —during business hours, in the evening, over the weekend, or late at night.

Topic ___NO___

Point of view _____

If unsuitable, why? ___Over lapping catigories___

5. Long-distance telephone rates are too high, too different, and too hard to understand.

Topic _____ NO _____

Point of view _____

If unsuitable, why? VAGUE _____

6. Airplane tickets vary in cost according to whether you are traveling on supersavers, regular coach, first-class, or at a special rate.

Topic _____ NO _____

Point of view _____

If unsuitable, why? TO LIMITED _____

7. Airplane seats are coach, first-class, or uncomfortable.

Topic _____ NO _____

Point of view _____

If unsuitable, why? TO LIMITED _____

8. Rock music can be classified in several ways.

Topic _____ NO _____

Point of view _____

If unsuitable, why? TO BROAD _____

9. Native Americans can be classified according to the areas in which they lived.

Topic _____ Yes _____

Point of view _____

If unsuitable, why? _____

Name _____

Exercise 6. Writing Main Idea Sentences.   Write a main idea sentence for a classification paper on each of these topics. Be ready to explain who the readers of the
paper might be.

Trees _____

_____

_____

Teachers _____

_____

_____

Popular music _____

_____

_____

Crimes _____

_____

_____

Movies _____

_____

_____

Jogging shoes _____

_____

_____

Name _____

Exercise 7. Classification Charts. Make classification charts for any two of the main idea sentences you wrote in Exercise 6. Be sure you keep the point of view shown in the main idea sentence.

Main idea sentence _____

_____

_____

Chart:

Main idea sentence _____

_____

_____

Chart:

Exercise 8. Order in a Classification Paper. The sentences in this classification paper have been scrambled. On your own paper, rearrange the sentences so that the result is a complete, well-ordered essay, with an introduction, a main part, and a conclusion. If you keep each point in its own paragraph, you should come out with six paragraphs. Then compare your paragraphs with those of other students in the class.

Four Ways to Travel

Traveling by car, however, is tiring, and if you choose to drive straight through—a drive of about eighteen hours—you run the risk of falling asleep at the wheel. People who want to get from Seattle to San Francisco have a choice of four methods: car, bus, plane, or train. A few years ago there was a boat, too, but now the regular passenger boats no longer run and the only water travel is by private yacht or by freighter. The bus is the cheapest way if you are traveling alone, but buses offer little in the way of sightseeing, and the trip can become very boring. Airplanes are by far the fastest method, but they are also the most expensive, even if there is a price war on. Since freighters run for their own convenience rather than for yours, and since very few people have access to yachts, going by sea is not practical enough to be considered. Traveling by Amtrak is more expensive than the bus ride and less expensive than the plane trip. Meals at bus stops are hurried and usually not very good. People who drive their own cars can leave whenever they wish, travel as fast as the law and their own state of exhaustion will allow, and choose whatever route suits their fancy. Each of these methods of travel has its own advantages and its own drawbacks. Travelers who can afford it and are not afraid of air travel will choose the plane. Moreover, travelers whose legs stiffen when they sit in one position for several hours may find the bus ride very uncomfortable. Travelers must decide whether they value speed, economy, sightseeing, or comfort and make their choice accordingly. The train track goes through the high mountains and provides some dazzling scenery. Unfortunately, part of the trip through the mountains takes place at night, but the traveler can still get good views of the countryside during the eighteen hours the trip takes. Then all they have to do is fill the gas tank or buy the tickets, and the slowest of these methods will get them to San Francisco in less than twenty-four hours. Cramped legs can be stretched by a walk down the aisle, and food is available, although not very good, on the train. A more sensible decision, to spend the night in a motel, makes the trip take about twenty hours.

Exercise 9. Another Classification Chart. Make a classification chart showing the divisions and subdivisions of the paper you rearranged in Exercise 8.

Exercise 10. Commas. Write three sentences of your own, illustrating the three uses of commas discussed on pages 141–143. Then rewrite your sentences, leaving out all of the punctuation. Exchange your rewritten sentences with another student in the class. After the other student has put in the punctuation, see whether that student's commas are in the same places that yours originally were. Do both of you agree on the reasons? If there is disagreement, talk to the teacher about it.

Name _____

Exercise 11. Planning a Classification Paper.   Pick a topic, either one you have already worked on or an entirely different one if you prefer. Decide on a point of view. Imagine who your readers would be. Write a main idea sentence. Make a classification chart. Then do some brainstorming; make a list of specific details and examples for each division in your chart.

Topic _____

Point of view _____

Readers _____

Main idea sentence _____

_____

_____

Chart:

Details and examples

_____

_____

_____

_____

_____

_____

_____

_____

_____

_____

_____

_____

_____

_____

_____

_____

_____

_____

_____

_____

_____

Exercise 12. Writing a First Draft.   Write the first draft of the paper you planned in Exercise 11. Exchange drafts with another student in the class, asking the other student to make a classification chart based on your paper. Then compare that student's chart with the one you were working from. Are they exactly the same? Do you need to change your chart? Do you need to rearrange the order of your paper?

Exercise 13. Rewriting Your Paper.   Write another version of the paper you've been working on. Put this version away for a day or so and then reread it to see if you want to make any other changes or additions. Make sure you can answer all the questions on this check list:

Check List for Content

1. Does your main idea sentence show clearly what your point of view is?   _____

2. Is that same point of view maintained all through your paper?   _____

3. Have you included all the possible categories in the first step of your classification?   _____

4. Have you avoided overlapping categories?   _____

5. If your main idea sentence mentions the categories in the first division, are those categories discussed in the same order in the rest of the paper?   _____

6. Have you given specific details and at least one example for each division in your classification?   _____

Exercise 14. The Final Step.   Now go over your paper one more time, this time reading for sentences, paragraphs, pronouns, spelling, apostrophes, and commas. Make sure you can answer yes to the following questions:

Check List for Editing and Style

1. Are your sentences a comfortable length?   _____

2. Do all your sentences begin with capitals and end with periods?   _____

3. Have you used a dictionary to check the spelling of the words you were unsure about?   _____

4. Can you explain all the apostrophes you've used?   _____

5. Have you checked to see whether there's a reason for your commas?   _____

6. Have you given a separate paragraph to each of the important divisions of your classification?   _____

7. Do your transitions and contrasting words help readers to follow the order of your ideas?   _____

Exercise 15. More on Point of View.   Working in groups of four or five students, decide on a system for classifying the students in the class and make a chart using that system. Try to have your chart include at least two steps. Then compare charts. How many points of view have been used? Does the first division of each chart include all the students in the class?

Exercise 16. More on Order.   Working with the same group of students as in Exercise 15, write a paragraph based on the chart you made in that exercise. Then scramble the sentences, as was done in Exercise 8, page 159. Exchange the scrambled paragraph with another group of students. Can they find the order your group originally used? If they can't, is the problem with the writers or the readers?

Chapter 6

Explaining: Analysis

When defining or comparing or classifying is not enough to explain something thoroughly, we can use a fourth method—analyzing. We analyze when we explain something by looking at the parts that make it up.

Cooks are defining when they say that clam chowder is a soup whose main ingredient is clams. When they go on to say that New England clam chowder contains clams, potatoes, onions, and sometimes celery, but that Manhattan clam chowder adds tomatoes, carrots, and other miscellaneous vegetables, they are comparing. When they explain that chowder belongs to the bigger group of soups, and soups, in turn, belong to the even bigger group of nourishing foods, they are classifying. But when you order a bowl of that chowder in a restaurant and try to figure out what's in it—the clams, the potatoes, the onions, the cream, maybe some bits of bacon, certainly some seasoning—you are analyzing. You are also analyzing if you try to figure out the next morning whether it was the chowder or the cheesecake that gave you heartburn.

We use **analysis** whenever we try to discover the parts of something or tell other people what those parts are and how they relate to each other. We are also analyzing when we look at some event—that bad case of heartburn, for instance—and try to decide what caused it.

In ordinary life, we use analysis for two purposes, to explain how and to explain why. Often the two kinds of analysis work together. First you examine a zipper to see how it works—how the teeth mesh and how the tab pulls them together or forces them apart. Then when the zipper in your slacks gets stuck, you try to find out why it won't work—find the thread that's caught around one of the teeth so you can pull it out. Auto mechanics have to know how a brake system operates before they can discover why your car takes thirty feet to come to a full stop. When your optometrist was going to medical school, she examined the parts of the human eye to see how a normal eye works. When she examines your eyes, she's trying to find out why you see two fuzzy letters where there is only one clear letter. We call the first kind—

looking at something to see *how* it works—operational analysis. We call the second kind—looking at some event to see *why* it happened—causal analysis.

Analysis explains the whole by examining the separate parts that make it up.

Operational Analysis

Operational analysis is often used to explain a process that works the same way over and over. We can explain the principle on which carburetors work by looking at the mixing chamber, the air intake, the gas intake, and the jet. We can explain how blood courses through the human body by analyzing the parts of the circulatory system—the heart, the arteries, the veins, and the lungs. We can analyze how the United States is governed by looking at the three branches—executive, judicial, and legislative.

A great deal of what you learn in college is concerned with how things work, and many test questions ask for a paragraph or two explaining what the parts of something are and how those parts relate to each other. In other words, those test questions ask for a short paper of operational analysis.

Operational analysis explains how things work.

Main Idea Sentences for Operational Analysis

Main idea sentences for operational analysis are not hard to put together. They start with the thing being analyzed (*the whole*) and go on to mention the parts. If the thing is fairly simple, the main idea sentence can name the parts, or it can simply say how many there are.

If the question on a physiology test, for instance, asks: "Explain how the circulatory system works," your main idea sentence might be:

> The circulatory system (*the whole*) is composed of the heart, the arteries, the veins, and the lungs (*the parts*).

Notice that it is always a good idea to repeat a part of the question in your main idea sentence. Don't begin with "*It* is composed of . . ." and expect the teacher to remember which question you're answering.

Here are some other main idea sentences for operational analysis:

> A carburetor (*the whole*) cannot operate unless it has a mixing chamber, an air intake, a gas intake, and a jet (*the parts*).

The federal government (*the whole*) has three branches: executive, which enforces laws; legislative, which makes them; and judicial, which interprets them (*the parts*).

All cameras (*the whole*) have four basic parts (*the parts*).

A water faucet (*the whole*) has five parts: a pipe, a handle, a stem, a disk, and a washer (*the parts*).

The first three of these main idea sentences might be useful in responding to test questions in automotive mechanics, political science, or photography. Even the last one might appear on a test if you were taking an extension course in easy home repairs.

Main idea sentences for operational analysis begin with the thing being analyzed and go on to mention the parts.

Developing the Plan

Once you have written your main idea sentence, your plan is more than half made. If you have already named the parts, your paper will follow the same **order** you used in listing them. In a paper on the branches of the federal government, you will begin with the executive branch, go on to the legislative, and end with the judicial. If, as you write, you think of a more logical order—getting laws passed before they are enforced—you can easily rearrange your main idea sentence.

It's true that during a test you won't have much time for rearranging. In that situation, it's important to get your entire main idea sentence just the way you want it before you begin to write. Plan out in your head, or jot down with a pencil, what the parts of your paper will cover. Then begin with a main idea sentence that will serve as an outline for the rest of your answer.

In responding to test questions, you won't have to arouse the interest of your readers. The teacher, who will probably be the only person to read your answer, is interested in finding out whether you know what the parts are and how they work together. You probably won't need many examples, either, unless the question specifically asks for them. And after dealing with each part, you can stop. A test question doesn't usually require a conclusion.

When you are writing for a more general audience, however, you may need more introduction than your main idea sentence can provide. If the explanation of how a camera works is meant for readers who have never done more than click the shutter and let the drugstore develop the film, you may want to begin with something like this:

In spite of the built-in light meters, flash attachments, range finders, and other fancy gadgets that come on a lot of cameras these days, all cameras are built on the same principle. In order to operate, any camera must have four basic parts—a box, which keeps out light until it is wanted; some film, on which light can register; a lens, which will let the light in; and a shutter that opens and closes the lens. These four things are essential. Everything else is extra.

It will probably take at least a paragraph to explain each of the four parts in some detail. Here examples and quick comparisons may help. You may want to explain why the box has to be completely light-proof and why the film must be kept in the dark except for the second or so that the lens is opened. You may want to compare the opening of the lens with the blinking of a human eye or the shutter with a window blind that can be opened and closed.

After you have explained all the parts, you will probably add a sentence or two to make the explanation sound finished:

> A light meter can measure the light, and a flash bulb can brighten it. A range finder can measure the distance accurately, and these gadgets do help. But the basic parts remain the same: a box, a lens, some film, and a shutter.

The main part of the paper should follow the same order as the main idea sentence.

Causal Analysis

Explaining how something works can be fairly straightforward if you understand the process clearly, but analyzing why something happens (or happened) the way it does (or did) is a bit more complicated. In **causal analysis** you still begin with the whole, the event:

> When you click the switch, the light doesn't go on.
>
> Your favorite aunt didn't send you a card last Christmas.
>
> You got an F in biology.
>
> Toxic material has been found in a nearby lake.
>
> The cost of groceries keeps going up.

And then you go on to the parts. But whereas the parts in operational analysis are things that can be seen and counted, or the parts of a process that can be observed, the parts in causal analysis are reasons, or possible reasons, that you are trying to discover.

If the event is fairly simple and concerned with physical things, you can probably list all the possible causes and check them out one by one. Why doesn't the light go on? Maybe the bulb is burned out. If the bulb is all right, maybe a fuse has blown or the circuit breaker has been thrown. If that's all right, maybe the power is off all over the neighborhood. You find the cause by a process of elimination, and you can be fairly sure you have gotten it right. It would be very bad luck if the bulb burned out at the same time the power was cut off.

It may be less simple to discover why your aunt didn't send you a Christmas card. Has she lost your address? Did she break her wrist in December? Did she decide to save the money she usually spends on paper and postage and give it to charity instead? Or does she disapprove of some of your new friends? Has she heard a lot of gossip about the accident you had last spring? Is she offended that you didn't visit her last summer? You can write and ask her, of course, and if the reason was a lost address, a broken wrist, or a charitable impulse, she will probably tell you so. But if the reason was any of the last three possibilities, or some others you haven't thought of, you will probably never be sure. It's much harder to find a single reason for events that involve human behavior and human attitudes.

As for that F in biology, you may think you know why it happened because, after all, you were the person involved. Did you fail the course because the teacher didn't like you? Because you got the flu and missed two weeks of school? Because your car broke down and you were late a lot? Because your roommate made so much noise you couldn't concentrate? Or was it a combination of all those things and a few more? You are human too, and being human, you may find it hard to separate your own feelings from what actually caused the F.

The toxic material that's poisoning the fish in the nearby lake is a physical thing that can be measured and observed. You can find out that a paint company located on a stream a mile away has been dumping waste containing lead into the soil. The soil has been washing into the stream, and the stream empties into the lake. That's certainly the primary cause. But why has the dumping occurred? Were the workers who did it unaware of the possible damage? Did the owners who knew it was happening care more about profits than about pollution? Are the laws so lenient that what the paint company did was perfectly legal? When physical events have human causes, those causes, too, can be difficult to pin down.

And you will have even more difficulty trying to determine why a sack of groceries is more expensive this month than it was four weeks ago. The statistics say that the cost-of-living has gone down, but your supermarket doesn't seem to have noticed. Perhaps milk and cheese cost more because the government has paid dairy farmers to reduce their herds, or oranges cost more because the weather was bad in Florida. But dairy products and citrus fruit are only two items; everything has gone up. Obviously, there are many contributing causes, and the question is too complicated to handle in a short paper—it might take two months and twenty pages. Even then you couldn't be sure you'd found all the causes. Trained economists can't agree on what's causing the increase, and unless you're asked to respond in a test question, you will do well to leave that problem alone. If the question does come up in a course on marketing, the most sensible plan is to summarize the causes that have been discussed in class, with a quiet aside to yourself, "According to some authorities . . ."

Causal analysis tries to explain why something happened.

Cause and Effect

The more complex an event is, the more most of us are tempted to oversimplify it. Has the cost of milk gone up *just because* the government has been paying dairy farmers to raise fewer cows? Has the cost of everything gone up *just because* the middlemen—those mysterious creatures that operate between the grower and the grocer—are becoming millionaires while the poor public barely squeezes by? Did your aunt ignore you last holiday season *just because* there was some gossip about that accident? Are you failing biology *just because* you had the flu?

When we look at **cause and effect**, we may forget that most events involving people have, or can have, several causes and instead settle for simple and incorrect explanations. As we have seen, some events do have only one cause. The light didn't go on because the bulb was burned out. The picture didn't turn out because the film was in the camera backwards. And if you talk to your biology teacher about that F, you may discover that the main reason for your failure is that you have a weak background in science. The teacher may recommend that you take a general science course before you attempt biology again. Before we can say definitely that there is one cause, and only one cause, of any event, we need to be sure there are no other possible causes. Unless you can find those other possibilities and eliminate them, you need to consider them in your analysis.

Another way of going wrong is to suppose that because one thing happened after another, the first thing caused the second. It's true that you did neglect to visit your aunt last vacation, and it's true that she didn't send a Christmas card. Are you justified in thinking that the lack of a visit caused the lack of a card, only because one occurred before the other? Perhaps you decide to take an umbrella on a cloudy morning, and then the sun shines brilliantly all afternoon. Are you justified in saying that carrying an umbrella caused it not to rain?

People who believe that walking under ladders causes accidents forget to ask whether the accident could have been caused by anything else. At ten o'clock Rupert walked under a ladder. Ten minutes later he tripped over a pail of paint and broke his ankle. Did walking under the ladder cause him to fall over the bucket? His friend Reggie walked under the same ladder. Why didn't Reggie break his arm? Tansy caught a bad head cold, sneezed miserably for five days, and on the sixth day tried a new cold pill she'd seen advertised on television. Two days later the cold was gone. Did the pill cure her cold or would she have gotten well anyway? Her colds usually last about a week.

> *Before you decide that one thing caused another, ask two questions:*
> *Could there have been any other possible causes?*
> *When the cause is there, does the effect always follow?*

Main Idea Sentences for Causal Analysis

Good **main idea sentences** for papers of **causal analysis** have two parts: the event (*the whole*) and the cause or causes (*the parts*). Because it's hard to be absolutely sure what the causes are, it's a good idea to include some qualifier: "The *main* cause . . . ," "The *most important* cause . . . ," "*Although possibly* . . . ," and so on.

Sometimes, of course, you can consider and eliminate all other possible causes of some event and be left with only one possible cause. A nail in a tire caused it to go flat, for instance, or falling out of the cherry tree caused Billie to break her arm. When events are that simple, however, there isn't much to say about them. A brief report will do; you don't need a paper of causal analysis.

Here are some main idea sentences that would do for short papers analyzing causes:

> The main cause for the vandalism in the gymnasium (*the event*) seems to have been anger over the cancellation of the championship game (*the cause*).

> Four major factors (*the causes*) contributed to the Wall Street crash of 1929 (*the event*).

> More people are riding the city buses (*the event*), not because the fares are reasonable and the service courteous, but because traffic is congested and the cost of parking a car in the city has skyrocketed (*the causes*).

> Although other things may have helped, Sadie Gallico won the election (*the event*) because she was qualified, because she was honest, and because she worked hard (*the causes*).

> The paint company on Gifford Creek is entirely responsible (*the cause*) for the toxic waste in Clear Lake (*the event*).

If you look carefully at these main idea sentences, you will notice that the first four use words such as *main, seems, major, not because, although,* and *may.* All of them, except the last sentence, avoid sounding absolutely sure. And if there are no other factories located on Gifford Creek, and no other streams that empty into what used to be a clear lake, the writer can probably demonstrate that the paint company did cause the pollution. In general, however, careful readers will consider what you say more seriously if you concede that there might be other contributing causes.

> *Main idea sentences for causal analysis say what the event is and what (probably) caused it.*

Developing the Paper

Just as main idea sentences for operational analysis provide a preliminary plan, so main idea sentences for causal analysis give a rough outline of what the paper will cover. **Developing** a causal analysis paper, however, is not quite as simple. You will need to do some more brainstorming—make the usual list of examples and specific details for each of the causes the paper will cover. Even if you are only answering a test question, as you may be doing in explaining the factors that contributed to the Wall Street crash, you will need to do more than give a single sentence to each one. You must explain in more detail what each factor was and show how it contributed to the crash.

A paper on vandalism in the gymnasium might begin with some specific details about the importance of the championship game, the way the announcement was made, and the extent of the destruction. That could be followed by examples of the angry reactions you observed and how that anger led students to break windows and throw paint on the doors of the building.

In writing about the greater numbers of people riding city buses, you should be specific about what the fares are and how the bus drivers behave before you go on to give examples of the two-hour wait behind an overturned truck, the bumper-to-bumper lineup between seven and nine every weekday morning, the headaches people get from breathing the exhaust fumes of the car ahead of them. You will also need examples of people driving around and around looking for a parking space, the annoyance of paying five dollars a day when they finally do find a vacancy, and the frustration of arriving two hours late for work. Then you can show how the city buses sail by in the "buses only" lane and how relaxed the passengers look as they read their morning papers.

You will need an introduction, too, to get your readers interested enough in the event to care what caused it. You might begin by contrasting the way Clear Lake used to be with the way it is now. You might start by describing the paint-spattered exterior of the gymnasium and the money it will cost to remove that paint. Or you might start with an example of one driver, in one car, on one morning when the traffic was particularly heavy.

After you have analyzed the causes, you will need a conclusion that reinforces your main idea or reminds readers of what you think the main cause was. You might say:

> We need paint for our houses and jobs for our citizens, but we also need to keep our lakes clean and wholesome.

> If the administration had explained the need for canceling the game, the destruction might have been prevented.

> Bus tickets may not be cheaper than gasoline, and drivers may sometimes be cranky, but people are beginning to realize that the disadvantages of riding the bus are far outweighed by the disadvantages of fighting traffic and supporting the parking lots.

Good papers of causal analysis give specific details and examples.

Analyzing Homophones

You already know, of course, that some words that sound alike are spelled differently—*its* and *it's* or *whose* and *who's,* for instance. The word for such pairs is **homophones.** *Homo* means "alike," and *phone* means "sound." You probably also know that some other sets of words without apostrophes present a similar problem—*to, too,* and *two* or *compliment* and *complement,* for instance.

When you stop to think about it, you know that *to* is used in phrases such as "*to* go *to* the store." You also know that *too* is used for *also* ("I went *too*") and for showing extent ("*too* angry"; "*too* little"). But knowing those differences and knowing that *two* means "twice one" doesn't do much good when you're writing hastily. On a first draft it may not matter, but when you are editing a finished paper, it does matter. Your readers are likely to care. As you edit (*the event*), stop to discover why you are using one spelling rather than another (*the cause*). Such careful analysis will pay off in the greater respect your writing will receive.

Deciding when and where one spelling is preferred to another will sometimes be easy. You won't have much difficulty with *to/too/two* or *your/you're* or *here/hear* if you take the time to examine them. But pairs such as *compliment/complement* and *principal/principle* may still leave you guessing. If you aren't sure, use a dictionary.

Word processors sometimes have built-in spelling checks, but word processors do not have your ability to analyze meanings. One college teacher who dictated a report found, when it came back typed up, that the phrase "the *principle* cause" occurred all through the paper. When the teacher complained about the misspelled word, the typist said he'd asked the computer, and the computer had responded with *principle.* You have an advantage over technology, no matter how advanced it is. You can analyze what you mean, consult an authority that explains the difference, and get the spelling right.

When you have a choice of homophones, stop to analyze what you really mean.

Two Sample Papers of Analysis

Here is a paper of operational analysis:

How a Faucet Works

First sentence shows paper is meant for a general audience.

Here *principle* means the rule by which faucets work.

[1] Whether the faucet opens a galvanized pipe outside the house or releases hot water into a shiny porcelain tub, the operating principle is the same. All faucets have five essential parts—a pipe, a handle, a stem, a disk, and a washer.

Pipe comes first in the main idea sentence, so it is explained first.

[2] First, there must be a pipe. The pipe carries water from a central source, either a well in the country or a central main in the city. Outside you can often see the pipe running along the edge of the building. In the house the pipe is concealed within the walls. On the inside of the pipe, at the point where the rest of the faucet is attached, is a small flat surface.

Next comes the handle, with its appearance described.

[3] Except for the opening at the end of the pipe, the handle is the only part of the faucet that is visible. On the outside of the house the handle is often a

small round wheel that can be turned from left to right. Inside it is usually in the shape of a small bar that you pull toward yourself.

Then the stem, with explanation of what it does.

[4]   Attached to the handle but invisible to the user is a stem in the shape of a screw. As the handle is turned or pushed, the stem twists up. As the handle is turned or pushed in the opposite direction, the stem twists down. At the bottom end of the stem is a small flat disk.

"Disk" provides an echo transition between paragraphs.

Comparison to a dime helps readers see the size.

[5]   This disk is built so that it will hold a washer. Faucet washers are small flat circles about the size of a dime. Once they were made of rubber, but now they are usually made of some composition material. These washers are removable so that when they become hard and brittle, they can be replaced.

Explains how the parts work together.
The pattern of outside/inside is followed in the early part of the paper and at the end—first outside the house, then inside.

[6]   Whether you are sprinkling the garden or taking a hot shower, the process of obtaining water is the same. You move the handle to the left and the stem moves up, lifting the disk and washer away from the flat spot in the pipe. Turning the handle a little way moves the disk up slightly, and a small stream of water comes out the opening in the end of the pipe. Turning the handle as far as it will go lifts the disk to the top of the pipe and a lot of water gushes out.

Would it be better to move the comment about the washer to the paragraph where washers are discussed? Does the last sentence make the paper sound finished?

[7]   When you have finished with the sprinkler or the shower, you move the handle to the right. The stem turns the disk and washer until it rests on the flat spot in the pipe and the water stops. If it keeps dribbling out, the washer needs to be replaced.

Here is a paper of causal analysis:

To the editor:

The event—Sadie Gallico won the election.
The causes—what she is and did. But notice "part of the reason" and

[1]   I've read a number of articles lately trying to explain why Otis Goode lost the election. I think it's about time somebody explained why Sadie Gallico won. I'm sure that some of the things Goode did and didn't do were part of the reason for Goode's defeat,

"more important reasons." Introduction ends with main idea sentence.

Transitions at the beginning of each paragraph separate the three causes—"To start with," "Furthermore," and "Finally."

Example—funds for the library.
Comparison—what Goode didn't do.
Why what Gallico did got votes.

Second cause

Examples—stand on abortion and taxes.

Comparison—what Goode did and didn't do.

Why what Gallico said got votes.

Third cause

Examples—ringing doorbells, talking at meetings.
Comparison—Goode bought advertising but Gallico talked to people.

Conclusion considers other less important causes.

but I'm equally sure that what Sadie Gallico is and what she did were more important reasons for her victory.

[2] To start with, Gallico is very well qualified to be mayor. She has a law degree, with honors, from Eastern State's law school, and she has served two terms on the city council. Goode is a lawyer, too, and a former council member, but it was Gallico who got the measure for more library funds on last year's ballot and kept at it until the measure passed. If Goode supported library money, he kept very quiet about it. Lots of people around here think libraries are important, and they tend to like people who can get things done.

[3] Furthermore, Gallico is, and was, honest. She didn't mind admitting, when she was asked, that she is pro-choice, even though she knows that many people in town are right-to-lifers. She told people frankly that taxes would have to be raised if roads were to be repaired, the sewer system modernized, and better fire protection provided. She said she would work for a tax increase. Goode kept quiet again, except for saying once or twice that he didn't see why the potholes couldn't be filled without taxes going up much. People don't like taxes, but they do like streets without holes, a sewage system that doesn't smell, and fire trucks that get there when they're needed. Most voters are smart enough to know that paving streets costs money, no matter what Goode says. People preferred honesty to hypocrisy.

[4] Finally, Gallico worked hard to win. She rang doorbells and talked to people about her convictions. She spoke at at least thirty meetings. She didn't spend as much money as Goode did on advertising, but she talked face-to-face with more people. Without ever running Goode down, she convinced most voters that she would be a better mayor.

[5] So it wasn't just that Goode didn't spend enough money or get enough endorsements. It wasn't even Goode's assumption that no woman could be elected mayor in this town. Maybe his thinking that, and

Last sentence restates the main idea that the rest of the letter has explained.

therefore not campaigning very hard, had something to do with the outcome. But the main reasons for Sadie Gallico's victory and Goode's defeat are that she is well qualified, she is honest, and she worked hard.

Hiram Arthur
Clear Lake

Key Words and Ideas

Here are some of the important terms and ideas covered in this chapter. See whether you can answer these questions about them:

1. How does **analysis** explain things?
2. What does **operational analysis** do?
3. What two things should a **main idea sentence for operational analysis** contain?
4. What **order** should a paper of **operational analysis** follow?
5. What does **causal analysis** do?
6. What two questions should be asked about **cause and effect**?
7. What should a **main idea sentence for causal analysis** contain?
8. How should a paper of **causal analysis** be **developed**?
9. What are **homophones**? How can you choose between them?

Name _____

Exercises _____

Exercise 1. Main Idea Sentences for Analysis.   Which of these statements would be suitable main idea sentences for short papers of analysis? If you think a sentence is suitable, say whether the paper would be operational or causal analysis. If you think a sentence is unsuitable, say why.

1. A guitar has six parts: finger board, strings, tuning pegs, bridge, anchor, and soundbox.

    _____

    _____

2. There are four steps involved in getting an initiative measure on the ballot— drafting the measure, collecting signatures to the petition, having the signatures verified, and filing the finished initiative with the clerk of elections.

    _____

    _____

3. The initiative to consider steelhead a sport fish passed because, among other reasons, people who fish wanted steelhead exempt from the provisions of the Indian treaties.

    _____

    _____

4. To understand how a computer works, you have to examine several hundred parts.

    _____

    _____

5. The office computer broke down because a thunderstorm knocked out a transformer.

    _____

    _____

6. All stringed instruments work on the same principle: a soundbox, a set of strings that can be made to vibrate, and something to make the vibrations take place.

_____

_____

7. The word *homophone,* which comes from Greek, means words that sound alike but mean something different.

_____

_____

8. The reasons for the large attendance at last week's concert were the heavy advertising, the popularity of the soloist, and the free admission.

_____

_____

9. There are three popular styles of piano: spinets, uprights, and grands.

_____

_____

10. Shinyclean toothpaste is composed of baking soda, sodium fluoride, mint flavoring, and some thickening material.

_____

_____

11. War has a large number of causes.

_____

_____

Name _____

Exercise 2. Planning a Paper of Operational Analysis.   Make a list of four or five sample gadgets with which you are familiar—such as a ball point pen, a fishing reel, a retractable measuring tape, a pulley.

Gadgets

_____

_____

_____

_____

_____

Next pick one gadget and list its parts.

Parts of the gadget

_____

_____

_____

_____

_____

Write a main idea sentence for a paper of operational analysis for this topic.

Main idea sentence _____

_____

_____

Now make another list of four or five processes with which you are familiar—such as opening a checking account, registering to vote, planning a party.

Processes

_____

_____

_____

_____

_____

Next pick one process and list the steps in the process.

Steps in the process

_____

_____

_____

_____

_____

Write a main idea sentence for a paper of operational analysis for this topic.

Main idea sentence _____

_____

_____

Exercise 3. Writing a First Draft. Write a first draft of one of the papers you planned in Exercise 2. Find somebody else who is familiar with the gadget or the process you're analyzing and ask that person to read your paper and make suggestions as to how it could be improved.

Exercise 4. Another Draft. Write a draft of the other paper you planned in Exercise 2, this time leaving out the main idea sentence and the name of the gadget or process you're analyzing. Exchange papers with another student to see whether that other student can tell what the gadget or the process is. Don't treat this as a riddle. The more easily the reader can tell what you're analyzing, the better the job you've done.

Exercise 5. Rewriting the Paper. Write a finished version of one of the papers you've been working on in Exercises 2 through 4. Put this version away for a day or two, then reread it to see whether you want to make any other changes. Can you answer yes to all the questions on this check list?

Check List for Content

1. Does your main idea sentence tell what you are analyzing and mention the parts? _____

2. Does the rest of the paper follow the order indicated in your main idea sentence? _____

3. Have you considered who your readers will be? _____

4. Does your paper sound finished? _____

Exercise 6. The Final Step. Now go over your paper one more time, this time tending to the manners of your writing. Can you answer yes to all these questions?

Check List for Editing

1. Have you given a separate paragraph to all the important parts of your analysis? _____

2. Have you made sure all your sentences really are sentences? _____

3. Have you checked your punctuation, with special attention to commas? _____

4. Have you checked your spelling? _____

5. Have you given special attention to homophones? _____

Name _____

Exercise 7. Homophones.   List at least six pairs of homophones, trying not to use any of the examples given in the chapter. Then write a short sentence showing how each member of the pair should be used.

> *Example:* die: Everybody must *die* sometime.
> dye: Why not *dye* that old sweater?

Homophones		*Sentences*
1. _____	a)	_____
_____	b)	_____
2. _____	a)	_____
_____	b)	_____
3. _____	a)	_____
_____	b)	_____
4. _____	a)	_____
_____	b)	_____
5. _____	a)	_____
_____	b)	_____
6. _____	a)	_____
_____	b)	_____

Exercise 8. More Homophones.   Go back to the pairs of homophones you listed in Exercise 7, or think of new ones if you prefer. Then make a quiz for other students in the class. Your quiz should look something like this:

Sue didn't think it was _____ to have to pay for the bus _____ twice just because she lost her ticket.

<u>(fare or fair)</u>

1. _____

_____

_____

2. _____

_____

_____

3. _____

_____

_____

4. _____

_____

_____

5. _____

_____

_____

6. _____

_____

_____

Name _____

Exercise 9. Cause and Effect.   Here are some cause-and-effect statements. What questions should be asked about each one in deciding whether the cause was really responsible for the effect? Be as specific as you can about the questions.

> *Statement:* After a black cat crossed her path, Hattie had her purse stolen.
> *Questions:* Does something bad happen to Hattie every time a black cat runs in front of her?
> Was her purse stolen because she left it in an unlocked car?

1. Drinking two cups of coffee last night kept John awake until three in the morning.

   _____

   _____

2. Tony didn't read all the book, so he failed the test.

   _____

   _____

3. Annie broke a mirror and cut her foot cleaning up the mess.

   _____

   _____

4. The car won't start because the battery is dead.

   _____

   _____

5. There are three main reasons why Jamie can't play basketball—he can't dribble, he works after school, and he's only five feet tall.

   _____

   _____

6. The car won't start because it's below zero outside.

_____

_____

7. School was called off today because everything was covered with an inch of ice.

_____

_____

8. Harold takes carotene every day, so he hasn't had the flu all winter.

_____

_____

9. No wonder I spilled the gravy; we had thirteen people to dinner.

_____

_____

10. When the mayor came to office in 1980 there were thirteen hundred people in town. Now there are five thousand. We'd better reelect him. You can't beat a record like that, can you?

_____

_____

11. Enrollment in the data processing program has increased because Ms. Semple is a popular teacher.

_____

_____

Name _____

Exercise 10. More Cause and Effect. List all the possible causes you can think of for these events. Then put an *X* by those you consider the most likely. Compare the causes you have listed with those listed by other students in the class.

> *Event:* Your glasses are not on the bedside table in the morning.
> *Causes:* You knocked them under the bed in your sleep. *X*
> A burglar stole them.
> You left them on the kitchen table last night. *X*
> The cat dragged them off.
> They're tangled up in the bedclothes. *X*

1. The back door is standing wide open when you get home.

   _____

   _____

   _____

2. The car won't start.

   _____

   _____

   _____

3. A kindergarten child is an hour late getting home from school.

   _____

   _____

   _____

4. When you open the refrigerator door, the light doesn't come on.

   _____

   _____

   _____

5. A woman who was hired a year after you gets the promotion you expected.

_____

_____

_____

6. You catch the flu.

_____

_____

_____

7. The plane due in at 7 P.M. has not arrived by midnight.

_____

_____

_____

8. Your friend doesn't invite you to a party he's giving.

_____

_____

_____

Name _____

Exercise 11. Main Idea Sentences for Causal Analysis.   Which of these statements are suitable as main idea sentences for short papers of causal analysis? If you think a sentence is suitable, say who you think the readers would be. If you think a sentence is unsuitable, say why.

1. The old opera house collapsed because there were termites in the foundation, the city had no funds to repair it, and the capacity audience stamped their feet all the time the rock band was playing.

_____

_____

2. There were four main causes of the American Civil War.

_____

_____

3. The American Civil War was fought between the North and the South.

_____

_____

4. Nobody knows for sure what causes people to catch a cold.

_____

_____

5. There are three main causes of poverty in America.

_____

_____

6. People can't spell correctly because they don't care about spelling.

_____

_____

7. Defense contracts have a lot of cost overruns because the contractors pay several hundred dollars for an ordinary hammer.

_____

_____

8. Although the news release said he wanted to spend more time with his family, there were at least three political reasons for Coach Thompson's resigning.

_____

_____

9. People who picket against apartheid in South Africa do so because they believe the treatment of Blacks in that country is everybody's concern.

_____

_____

10. There are many, many reasons for the fluctuations of world money.

_____

_____

11. There's only one reason for the high divorce rate in this country.

_____

_____

12. People subscribe to the *Morning Bugle* because they like to work the crossword while they drink their first cup of coffee.

_____

_____

Name _____

Exercise 12. More Main Idea Sentences. Write a main idea sentence for a paper of causal analysis on each of these situations.

1. A fast food store (The Old Tar Fish Market) is losing customers.

_____

_____

_____

2. Thirty-five percent of the economics class failed the last test.

_____

_____

_____

3. The women's softball team has lost four games in a row.

_____

_____

_____

4. Only ten people attended the last school dance.

_____

_____

_____

5. Your dog bit the neighbor's little boy.

_____

_____

_____

Name _____

Exercise 13. Planning a Causal Analysis Paper. Pick some important event in your own life and list all the possible causes. It can be something that pleased you or something that troubled you, but either way it should be something that might have been prevented.

Event _____

Causes _____

_____

_____

_____

_____

Decide which of the causes you listed are the most likely or the most important and write a main idea sentence of causal analysis based on the event.

Main idea sentence _____

_____

_____

For each of the important causes, list as many specific details as you can. Use more paper if you need it.

Specific details:

First cause _____

_____

_____

Second cause _____

_____

_____

Exercise 14. Writing a First Draft.   Write the first draft of the paper you planned in Exercise 13. Then read it to a group of other students, asking whether they think your reasons are convincing and whether you need to add more details.

Exercise 15. Rewriting Your Paper.   Write another version of the paper you've been working on. Put it away for a day or so and read it again to see whether you want to make more changes. Then make sure you can answer yes to all these questions:

Check List for Content

1. Will your introduction catch the interest of most readers?   _____

2. Does your main idea sentence include both the event and some mention of the causes?   _____

3. Have you allowed for other possible causes?   _____

4. Have you given plenty of specific details about each cause?   _____

5. Does your conclusion make the paper sound finished?   _____

Exercise 16. The Final Step.   Now go over your paper one more time, this time tending to the manners of your writing. Can you answer yes to all these questions?

Check List for Editing

1. Have you given a separate paragraph to all the important parts of your analysis?   _____

2. Have you made sure all your sentences really are sentences?   _____

3. Have you checked your punctuation, with special attention to commas?   _____

4. Have you checked your spelling?   _____

5. Have you given special attention to homophones?   _____

Exercise 17. More Causal Analysis.   Working with a group of three or four other students, decide on some controversial event in your college or your community. Write a letter to the editor of the college paper analyzing the causes of either the event or the controversy surrounding it. Read the draft of the letter to the rest of the class and ask for their suggestions. Revise and edit the letter carefully. Then mail it to the college paper, signing the names of everybody in the group.

Chapter 7

Telling What Happened: Objective Reports

A **report** is an account of something that has happened, written in such a way that somebody who wasn't there can understand clearly just what did occur. Reports don't usually tell people how to do something or coax them to do it. Reports seldom bother with why an event occurred, and they don't praise or condemn. They simply say that it happened. When you fill out your income tax report, for instance, you don't explain to the government why you made that much money—or that little. You don't—in the report, at least—plead with the government to let you pay at a different rate. Instead, you tell the Internal Revenue Service how much money you earned, how much interest you paid on your house and your charge accounts, how many children you supported last year. Sometimes people who think the tax is unfair take the issue to the courts or don't make the report at all, but if they do file, they stick to the financial facts.

Sometimes, however, the term *report* is used more loosely than it is being used here. High school teachers ask their students for "book reports" when what the teachers really expect is for students to give their opinion of the books they have read. When stockbrokers print "reports" recommending which oil stock to buy, they are actually trying to predict the future—guessing how much crude oil the new wells will produce or what OPEC will do next year. Looked at in one way, these things do contain reports. In his book report Edgar Lawson is telling about one thing that happened (Edgar did read *I Know Why the Caged Bird Sings*) before he goes on to say why he liked Angelou's book. The investment company is telling what happened, too—the oil company did drill two new wells and a firm of engineers did analyze the rock formations beneath the ground—before going on to predict what next year's dividends will be. In this book, however, the term *report* will not include comments or analyses or predictions.

A report tells only what happened.

Reports in Ordinary Life

Everybody's life is full of reports. Your bank statement is a report of how many checks you wrote last month and how much money you deposited. Your telephone bill tells you what the basic rate is and how many long distance calls you made. When the college gives you a copy of your transcript, you can read a report on what classes you have taken and what credit you received. When you glance at the front page of the *Evening Bugle,* you are reading reports of what happened in the city, in the nation, and in the world. All these things are **objective reports**; they give just facts, without including any comment or opinion.

Whatever your job is, you will probably be writing reports as well as reading them. Some of the reports will be on ready-made forms that guide you in deciding what to say. An income tax form is one example of such a ready-made guide. An accident report form is another. If your old Volkswagen slides into the back of the garbage truck, you'll have to fill out blanks on a printed form. The form will remind you to tell where the collision occurred and when, how fast you were going, whether the streets were wet or dry. The clerk at the admissions desk in a hospital will probably use a form to report how many patients were admitted on a given night, who their doctors were, what insurance they carry, and what rooms they were assigned to. A teacher's aide will probably have a form for reporting which children were absent, which ones came in late, which ones lost their lunch money. A TV repairman may have to fill out a form reporting what houses he called at, how many tubes he installed, how much time he spent doing it. All these forms help by reminding the writers what must be included in the report.

But other occasions require reports, too, and frequently there are no forms to act as guides. The secretary of the Firwood Neighborhood Association writes the minutes of the October meeting—a report. A biochemist runs a series of tests on cancer in mice treated with nicotine and writes up the results of the experiment—a report. A journalist spends a day with the city council and records what new regulations were discussed, what the mayor said, and how the council members voted—a report. A health officer investigates ten children who got lead poisoning from flaking paint and turns the findings over to the housing bureau—a report. The housing bureau sends an inspector to examine the apartment building where the children live —another report. If these reports are satisfactory, they will have several things in common even though they deal with different kinds of events.

Good objective reports are
  precise—don't leave readers guessing;
  accurate—don't get the facts wrong;
  to the point—don't get off the subject;
  complete—don't leave out any of the facts;
  orderly—don't tell what happened next before what happened first;
  objective—don't give the writer's opinions.

Precision

Reports, especially, need to be precise. Being precise means being exact. In writing, **precision** means finding exactly the right word to tell what happened instead of settling for some other word fairly close to it.

The teacher's aide who writes "A few boys were absent" will not have a satisfactory report; the form must say "seven boys" and probably give their names. The TV repair report cannot say, "An old television set"; instead it must say "a twenty-one-inch Trutone Model X-489, with the picture tube gone." The biochemist must say "two milligrams" rather than "a little bit," and the housing inspector must write "lien against the property" rather than "owner owes some money." The nurse will probably write "dysphasia" rather than "can't talk very well." In making all these choices, the writers use exact wording—they want to be precise.

Nevertheless, before you choose an uncommon word, ask yourself, "Does this work better than a familiar, ordinary word? Is it really more precise?" The answer will depend somewhat on the kind of report you are writing, but more on who your readers are. If the nurse is reporting to the child's parents, rather than to a specialist in speech therapy, she may say "can't pronounce consonants clearly." If you are writing a chemistry report instead of a recipe, you will need to say "sodium chloride," not "salt." In chemistry there are many kinds of salts, and a good report will make clear which kind you mean. If, on the other hand, you are reporting on conditions in the college cafeteria, it would be silly to say that some tables are supplied with pepper but not sodium chloride.

In reports, as in other kinds of writing, if there is a common, easily understood word for what you want to say, that word is usually the best choice. The word most people know is the word everybody is likely to understand. A teacher's aide who writes, "The elementary educator operating in the learning situation to which I was assigned provided the students with assistance in philately," is merely showing off. "The sixth grade teacher I worked under helped the children with their stamp collections" is a much better choice. "Sixth grade teacher" is not only easier to understand, it's more precise than "elementary educator." The journalist will say, "The council members from Wards 26 and 21" instead of "a couple of guys," which is vague, or "a duo of duly elected representatives of the people's will," which is pretentious.

Use ordinary words when their meaning is precise enough for the situation, but you don't have to stay with a "See-Spot-run" vocabulary. When you come across new words in your reading, don't ignore them just because they sound strange or new, but don't use them in your writing just for their fine sound, either. Examine them to see whether they are more precise than the common words they're replacing, and decide whether the audience you're writing for is likely to understand them.

Use ordinary words whenever they are exact enough for the situation.

Accuracy

Good reports are always precise, but they must be **accurate**, too. A biochemist who says "a little bit" and a journalist who says "a while back" are not being precise.

When they change their reports to say "two milligrams" and "in 1980," however, it's important that the amount actually was two milligrams, not three, and that the prisoner actually was put on probation in September 1980, not January 1979. September 1980 and January 1979 are both *precise* but only one of them is *accurate.*

Customers at the Best Brands Market will be justifiably angry if the halibut advertised for sale at $.79 a pound actually costs $2.79, and they won't be much soothed when the manager says, "Sorry, that was a mistake. It's lard that's $.79. The price got in the wrong column." If a newspaper reports, "Cyrus P. Witherspoon, of 4612 East Main Street, was arrested Saturday night for growing marijuana in his garage," when actually it was Cyril B. Witherspoon, who lives at 462 West Main, that newspaper could find itself on the unpleasant end of a lawsuit.

Whenever a report includes names and dates and numbers—and most reports will, for reports deal in exactness—the names and dates and numbers must be right. Guessing isn't good enough. The writer has to know. And what the writer knows is what must actually be in the report. The TV repairman, who worked from 1 to 5:30 P.M., obviously can't say "Installing the picture tube took a long time." But if his report says "Time: 2 hrs., 30 min.," Mr. Smith may sign, but the company will lose money. To be accurate, the report should read "Time: 4 hrs., 30 min."

Most of us trust the reports we read, just as we trust the makers of yardsticks to make all their inches the same length, and the bus company to hire only drivers who have passed the driving test. Because most readers do trust reports, you have a special obligation to make sure the facts you give are not just exact but also accurate.

Accuracy means getting the facts right.

Sticking to the Subject

Good reports **stick to the subject**. Whenever a writer gets sidetracked and gives readers a chance to say, "What does *that* have to do with it?" the report is off the subject. The journalist will not comment on the odd way the mayor's husband was dressed, even though she could barely keep her eyes off his bright red bandanna and his purple and orange plaid pants. The housing inspector will not comment on how dead the philodendrons look, or the number of comic books on the living room floor; he will confine his report to the flaking paint.

And the minutes of the Firwood Neighborhood Association will not be very satisfactory if they read like this:

> Fifteen members and two guests attended the meeting at Ernest Jack's house on October 13, 1986. Jack's house is very well furnished, but it isn't really satisfactory for a meeting—too many kids running around. The secretary read the minutes of the September meeting and they were unanimously approved. I don't know why nobody complained. They didn't seem very good. Barbara Yates moved that we go immediately to the question of better police protection. That must be because her son-in-law was mugged last year. . . .

It's obvious that only three sentences belong in this report—the first, the third, and the fifth. The rest of the information—actually, the opinions—are suitable only for a bit of gossip over a cup of coffee.

A good report sticks to the topic of the report.

Completeness

Although it's easy enough to see that the secretary included too much in his report, it's not as easy to see what he may have left out. Perhaps Barbara Yates went on to propose that the neighbors patrol the playground in four-hour shifts every weekend, and the motion was discussed and tabled until the next meeting. Even though the secretary disagrees vigorously with that proposal and hopes that by November everybody will forget it, he must not leave that discussion out of his report. If another member corrects the minutes in November, the secretary can say it was merely an oversight, and probably get away with it. But if the investment company pushing oil stock neglects to say, in the report of the engineering study, that two trial wells were completely dry, the stock buyers may accuse them of fraud.

If a report is to be honest, it must be **complete**. But sometimes writers who are not deliberately dishonest produce incomplete reports, and an incomplete report is not much use. If readers recognize that the report is incomplete, they will be annoyed. If they have no way of knowing that it's not complete, they will go away with a wrong impression of what actually happened. Members of the Firwood Neighborhood Association who missed the October meeting will never realize that the secretary left an important discussion out of the minutes.

People who read this account of the biochemist's experiment, however, will know that something important has been left out, and they will find the omission frustrating:

> Last week I inoculated some mice with a nicotine solution in sugar water. Now about half of the ones in the cage are looking all right. Of that half, three are very frisky. Next week I plan to . . .

Such a report is incomplete in two ways: it is inexact, and it doesn't go far enough. For exactness, we need to know when she began the experiment, how many mice were inoculated, how much nicotine and how much sugar the solution contained, and what "about half" and "looking all right" mean. We also need to know what happened to the half that did not look all right. Are they dead? Did they sneak out through a hole in the cage and run under the refrigerator?

The amateur biologist will help both her readers and her own records if her report reads more like this:

> On September 16 I inoculated ten white mice with a solution containing 2 milligrams of nicotine in a 2 percent sugar solution. On September 17 two of the mice refused to eat.

On September 18 five refused food and four would not move, although they were still breathing. On September 19 five mice were dead but three appeared to be eating and moving normally.

This report could be made even more complete. We still don't know whether the mice that died on the nineteenth were the same ones that refused food the day before, or what condition the two that are not eating normally are in.

On the other hand, we probably don't need to be told how big the cage was or what kind of food the mice were given, assuming that it was suitable for a mouse diet. That the mice did not eat must be included in the report because loss of appetite is one of the symptoms of nicotine poisoning. But so is lack of movement, and the biochemist will be overemphasizing the appetite loss if she gives lots of detail about the food and almost no information about the tails that didn't twitch or the mice that just lay there when she poked them with a stick.

Although the accident form you fill out asks for "complete description of the car," the insurance company doesn't care that it's pale blue, the back upholstery has two tears, and the horn won't work. They do care about the make, the model, and the year, and if you forget to give some of that information, you may have trouble collecting for the repairs.

> *In deciding what details to include in a report, ask yourself these questions:*
> *Do the details have something to do with how the event turned out?*
> *Am I giving too much information in one part of the report and too little in another?*
> *Can readers understand just what happened without the details?*

Order

A satisfactory report sticks to the subject without leaving out any important facts, but it also keeps those facts in the right **order**. A report that jumps around, putting in the details of what happened just as the writer chances to remember them rather than as they occurred, will also confuse its readers. The biochemist's report should not read like this:

> On September 16 I inoculated ten white mice with a solution containing 2 milligrams of nicotine in a 2 percent sugar solution. On September 19 five mice were dead but three appeared to be eating and moving normally. Two days earlier two of the mice refused to eat. Two of the mice that died would not move on September 18.

Readers should not be forced to read a paragraph twice, sorting out for themselves what happened first, what happened next.

The secretary of the Firwood Neighborhood Association will have equally unsatisfactory minutes if he writes them like this:

Fifteen members and two guests attended the meeting at Ernest Jack's house on October 13, 1986. Two motions were made but only one carried. Barbara Yates moved that we go immediately to the question of better police protection. Before that the chair had called the meeting to order. That one carried unanimously. She also moved that neighbors patrol the playground in four-hour shifts every weekend. I forgot to say that the minutes were read and approved. Barbara's second motion was tabled.

Such an arrangement may be excusable in a first draft, but before the minutes are mailed out to the members, the secretary must rearrange them in chronological order.

The best order for a report is what happened first, what happened next, and what happened after that.

Objectivity

Objectivity is probably the most important characteristic of reports. When you write **objectively** you keep yourself out of what you say; when you write **subjectively** you put yourself in. People who write subjectively see an event in relation to themselves and their own reactions. Of course, we all see things from our own point of view simply because it is impossible for us to *be* anybody else. It is possible, however, to remember this tendency and make a great effort to stay neutral, to keep our own opinions out of the reports we write.

But keeping opinions out involves more than remembering not to say "I like it" or "I didn't like it." Some kinds of opinions are obvious. Most of us realize that the TV repairman's report should not say that the Smiths' TV set was disgustingly dirty, and that the newspaper report, when the Cyrus/Cyril apology is printed, should not say "Cyrus Witherspoon is an upright citizen, who could never be suspected of breaking the law, whereas Cyril is a pretty shady type." Other kinds of opinions, however, are harder to recognize. In order to identify them, we have to know the difference between statements of fact and statements of opinion.

Being objective means keeping your opinions out of your writing.

Fact and Opinion

A **factual statement** can always be checked. If your son tells you that it's raining outside, he has made a factual statement. What he says may not be accurate; maybe the rain stopped an hour ago. *But statements do not have to be accurate to be factual.* The only requirement is that they be verifiable. Unless you are sick in bed, you can go outside and see whether it's raining.

An **opinion statement**, on the other hand, lets the speaker's judgment creep in, even though the statement may seem factual. If your son tells you the weather is lousy, he has given you his opinion, and you cannot possibly check his statement for accuracy. Both of you mean the same thing by *rain,* but your son wants to play baseball and you want the garden watered. In the winter, when your son wants to go sledding, he may think 45 degrees and bright sunshine are "lousy weather." You have made a factual statement if you tell your son that the temperature is 45 degrees. He can check the thermometer if he doesn't believe you. You have made an opinion statement if you tell him, "What a beautiful winter day!"

Perhaps you have read a brochure on Granite City, in which the writer refers to it as a large and prosperous town. Is that a factual statement or just the writer's opinion? Though *large* and *prosperous* may seem like facts, they are really opinions, because *large* and *prosperous* both depend on what the writer's experience has been. People who grew up on a farm, where the nearest shopping center was a village with a population of five hundred, may think Granite City, with its five thousand inhabitants, is a big place. But to people who grew up in Chicago or Los Angeles, Granite City may seem very tiny. *Prosperous,* too, has different meanings to different people. To some readers, *prosperous* means that most of the houses are painted, smoke is still coming out of the factory chimney, and only a handful of people are sleeping in the streets and under the bridge. To others, *prosperous* means that everybody in town can afford a new car, three pairs of shoes, and steak for dinner every night. Politicians argue endlessly over whether an 8 percent unemployment rate is normal and unavoidable, or whether it shows a recession.

All such words as *large, small, lousy, beautiful, ugly, prosperous,* and *depressed,* are subjective. Such words depend on the writer's point of view, and we all have our own ideas of what they mean. No statements that contain such words can be checked. If you are thinking about moving to Granite City, a statement that tells you it's large and prosperous won't help much. You need a report that says Granite City has a population of five thousand, that it has two grade schools and a consolidated high school, that the furniture factory employs ninety workers, that the business section contains a hardware store, three grocery stores, a bank, and a tavern, all of which have been painted within the last two years. Then, if you doubt the report, you can go to Granite City, count the schools and businesses, visit the factory, and look at the paint. While you are there, you will form your own opinion of Granite City's relative size and prosperity. But if you write a report for your employers, who are thinking of opening a branch there, you must include just the factual information and let your employers, in turn, form their own opinions.

It's not possible, of course, to check all factual statements in person. You can't go from house to house in Granite City, counting the residents, but you can check its population in an atlas that gives the most recent census figures. In the same way, you can check events that occurred long before you were born by looking in encyclopedias, histories, and other reference books. We assume that such records are accurate and complete. But what historians tell us should be given the same test as the language in any other report. That Abraham Lincoln was shot in Ford's Theater in April 1865 is a factual statement. That he was the greatest president that ever lived is opinion, no matter which history text says it. A factual statement, then, is anything that could have been checked if you had been there or if you had done the counting.

Most of the knock-down, drag-out arguments people get into could be avoided if we all remembered that some terms always rest on opinion. Was Lincoln a *greater* president than Franklin Roosevelt? Are the Green Sox a *better* baseball team than the Blue Sox? Is baseball a *better* game than softball? Are the teen-agers of this generation *worse* than their parents were at that age? Is the small child next door *naughty*? Or is the child *neglected*? None of these arguments can be settled until the people arguing agree on what they mean by *greater, better, worse, naughty,* and *neglected.* They must define their terms. If they can agree that *better* in baseball means home runs hit, bases stolen, or games won, they have something that can be checked. The sports section of the newspaper can probably provide these statistics.

And before we decide whether today's teen-agers are *better* or *worse,* we have to decide what kind of behavior we want to consider. Are we talking about grades in school? Willingness to mow the lawn when requested? Number of accidents and arrests? Do we mean everybody between twelve and twenty? All the students in Overland High? All the young people on our block? Or just the sixteen-year-old twins across the street? Until we make the discussion precise, and until we produce the facts on which our opinions rest, the opinions aren't worth much.

The purpose of reports is to tell what happened, not to interpret the events. The teacher's aide who tells the school nurse, "Tommy's face is flushed and he has four red spots on his forehead. He has sneezed four times in the last four minutes and his nose is running," is reporting. The aide who says, "Tommy doesn't feel very well," is interpreting. The first report includes only events that can be checked. The second tells what the teacher's aide thinks they mean.

Opinion statements reflect the speaker's point of view. Factual statements can be, or could have been, checked.

Slanting

Even when we try to report just the facts, our own attitude toward what happened tends to influence our choice of words. When we talk about people of other races, the words we choose often reveal more about us and our attitudes than about the people we are discussing. Whether white tenants call their Black landlord *a darky, a colored man, a nigger, a negro, a spook, a Black,* or just *a man,* has very little to do with the landlord; it has a lot to do with the tenants—how old they are, what magazines they read, what their prejudices are. In the same way, the Black tenants who call their white landlord *Mr. Charley, whitey, the man, honky,* or *sir* are not really revealing anything about the man who collects the rent; they're revealing themselves.

Unfortunately, not all **slanting** is that easy to recognize. If the local newspaper calls David Meddlar *a local businessman,* we'll get quite a different impression than if he is called *an entrepreneur* or *a bookie.* Whether Sadie Gallico is referred to as a lawyer, a housewife, or a women's libber will affect our vision of her and may make the difference between whether she wins the election or loses it. The *referent* of the words (the actual thing or person the words refer to) has not changed at all. Sadie Gallico *does* practice law, she *does* mop the kitchen and get dinner, she *does* belong to NOW (the National Organization for Women) and lecture in favor of comparable worth. All the terms that can be used to describe her are accurate enough in one sense, but using any one of them alone slants because, like stereotyping, it selects just one part of Sadie Gallico's life and ignores the rest of her.

Suppose a headline in the *Evening Bugle* says "Overton Demolishes Granite City in Season Opener." As you read the article, you find out that the final score was 28–14—a fairly large point spread but not exactly "demolishing." You keep reading and discover that Granite City led Overton at the end of the third quarter. In the first play of the fourth quarter, Granite City's defensive tackle was injured. Then Overton completed several crucial passes and won the game. A turn of events seems to have helped Overton win. The only thing that was "demolished" about Granite City was the injured tackle, and he was just hurt, not demolished. That headline, which might seem objective at a glance, is actually slanted against Granite City.

It's also possible to slant toward, rather than against. The headline in the Granite City paper may say "Injury Lets Overton Slip by Local Team." The story goes on to say that "weak defense" by Overton kept Granite City in the lead for the first three quarters, and that only "bad luck" kept them from winning. An unslanted headline would read "Overton 28–Granite City 14."

Good reports avoid slanting, either for or against. They neither purr nor snarl. *Purr words,* according to S. I. Hayakawa, who invented the term many years ago, are words that express our approval and not much else; *snarl words* express disapproval. In writing reports, talk about a seventy-year-old woman instead of "an old hag" or "a sweet old lady." Say "The car was traveling at forty miles an hour" instead of "tore recklessly through the intersection" or "crawled along like a snail." Say "came without noise" instead of "sneaked"; say "said" rather than "boasted" or "admitted"; say "walked unevenly" rather than "staggered." If the facts are presented in neutral terms, readers can make their own interpretations.

Slanting means using words that color readers' understanding of what happened.

Main Idea Sentences for Objective Reports

For some of the reports you make, you don't have to develop a main idea sentence. The form itself will provide it, and all you have to do is furnish the details. The main idea sentence for an income tax report, for instance, is "We, _____ and _____, who live on _____ Street in _____ city, are reporting to the government how much money we made and some of what we spent last year." The main idea of an insurance report is that you, the insured, are reporting a loss and asking the company to reimburse you for it. There are many kinds of report forms. Some of them are complicated, like an IRS 1040 form. Some are simple, like a gas bill. In filling out these report forms, writers need to be precise and accurate, complete and objective, but the forms do the rest of the work for them. Forms provide the main idea and a ready-made plan, and, through the kind of information they ask for, nudge the writers into sticking to the subject.

Other kinds of reports, however, leave us on our own. We must provide our own main idea sentences and our own plans. Writing a good main idea sentence will not ensure that your report is complete and orderly, but, as usual, it can help. If your main idea sentence is accurate and objective, it will be easier to keep the rest of the report accurate and objective too.

The **main idea sentence of a report** should make clear *what* event is being reported, *when* the event took place, *who* took part in it, and, unless it would be obvious to readers, *where* it happened. Here are some main idea sentences for several different kinds of reports:

> The regular meeting of the Firwood Neighborhood Association took place at Ernest Jack's house on October 13, 1986.

> On September 16, I inoculated ten white mice with a solution containing 2 milligrams of nicotine in a 2 percent sugar solution.

> During January 1986 three children under the age of five, all living in the Grand Ronde Hotel, were diagnosed as suffering from lead poisoning.

> On March 1, I inspected all eight apartments in the multifamily dwelling at 798 Chevy Chase Avenue, known as the Grand Ronde Hotel, checking for the type of paint used in the living quarters.

> Cyril B. Witherspoon, 462 West Main Street, was arrested Saturday night on suspicion of growing marijuana.

> Margaret Wastradowski, who has been called the most outspoken of the protesters against the nuclear armaments being transported through the city, lectured at the library yesterday evening.

All these main idea sentences give exact details. They include names, addresses, dates, numbers, and events. With one exception, they avoid using opinion words, and even that one—the sentence about Margaret Wastradowski—tries to stay factual by claiming that somebody else said it. If the sentence had said, "The mayor called her the most outspoken of the protesters," it would be clearly factual. We could check to see whether the mayor had expressed that opinion.

In the third sentence, *suffering* is probably not an opinion word. As medical people use the term—"suffering from a cold," for instance—*suffering* means "has a cold." In more ordinary usage, *suffering* does express opinion: "Take that ribbon off that cat! Can't you see the poor thing is suffering?"

Main idea sentences for reports tell who, what, when, and where.

Writing the Report

Most of these examples of main idea sentences could serve as the first sentence of the report itself. Reports need much less introduction than other kinds of writing because many of them are written for a special audience. Probably nobody except the members of the Firwood Neighborhood Association will read the secretary's minutes. Only the biochemist's teacher, or perhaps other students, will read the report of her experiment. The health officer's report is read by the housing bureau, and the building inspector's report is read by that same bureau. A great many more people will read the reports on Witherspoon's arrest and Wastradowski's speech, but there too the main idea sentence will probably begin the article. Journalists are trained to begin their reports with who, what, when, and where.

The main idea sentence, in fact, usually serves as the introduction. The purpose of a report is to give information, and people who do not want to be informed will not read past the first sentence anyway. If you stick to the facts, the interest will take care of itself.

Planning the report is usually less trouble, too. You know that the order should be chronological; you know what the principal facts are. If you don't, you shouldn't be writing the report. The main things to decide are what details are important enough to be included, what details are needed to make the report complete. As you write, be careful to make sure that the words you use are precise and accurate, and be sure to keep your opinions out, neither stating them openly nor letting them creep in through the words you use.

If you are reporting events in which you were involved, keeping your own attitude out will be particularly difficult. Suppose you are writing a report of what happened to you when your parents were divorced, and you begin like this:

> When my parents were divorced in 1977, in the same month that I became eleven years old, I had to live with my mother, but my brother, who was fourteen, got to live with my father, where things were much more exciting.

Even without the open statement of opinion ("much more exciting"), this report is slanted by the use of "had to" and "got to." One way to get around this almost inevitable slant is to write the report as though you were somebody else telling what happened to you. Instead of "I," use your name.

> When Luther and Estelle Bennett were divorced in 1977, the same month that Stella became eleven years old, she was placed in the custody of her mother, and her father was given custody of her brother Luke. Mrs. Bennett remained in the same suburban house where the family had previously lived, and Stella continued to attend the same school. Mr. Bennett moved to an apartment in the city. . . .

If you are writing a report on something in which you are not emotionally involved — a performance you attended, perhaps, or an accident you witnessed — take notes as the event occurs, if you can. If that is impossible, write a set of notes as soon afterward as possible, before you forget any significant details. As you write, the notes will refresh your memory and help to keep the report accurate.

If your report concerns something controversial – the picketing of an abortion clinic, perhaps – find somebody whose position on abortion is different from yours and ask that person to read a draft of your report. If that person decides what you have said is fair, you have probably avoided slanting the account of what happened.

Just as reports don't need much in the way of introduction, so they need little in the way of conclusion. When you come to the end of the event, you have come to the end of the report:

The meeting adjourned at 9:30 P.M.

By September 22 all ten mice were dead.

Lead-based paint was found in all but one of the apartments, where the tenant herself had scraped and repainted.

Witherspoon was released on a recognizance bond.

Stella Bennett continued to live with her mother until high school graduation.

Even though you have been carefully neutral through most of the report, it's always a temptation to use the conclusion to interpret the events, especially if you feel strongly about the subject. But the secretary should not end his minutes by adding, "That was the dullest meeting I ever attended," and the building inspector must not say, "That landlord ought to be jailed."

Reports can be used to support arguments, of course, and very often are. In fact, the best and most successful attempts to persuade are always supported by facts. The local newspaper may run an editorial about the disgraceful conditions at the Grand Ronde Hotel and use the cases of lead poisoning and the building inspector's report as facts to support the argument that city ordinances must be more strictly enforced. But the argument will be stronger if the reports on which it is based are completely objective.

Reports should be precise, accurate, complete, orderly, and free of opinion and slant.

A Report on Sentence Punctuation

In modern English, seven punctuation marks are commonly used to show the structure of sentences. Of these seven **sentence punctuation marks**, three are the most important.

Periods (.) separate one sentence from another. Other uses of periods, in abbreviations, for instance, have nothing to do with sentence structure.

The clock struck one. Then everybody left.

Question marks (?) substitute for periods when the sentence is a question instead of a statement.

Did everybody leave when the clock struck?

Commas (,) separate

1. parts of a list of at least three things:

   Coffee, tea, and cake were served at midnight.

2. interruptions to the main part of a sentence:

   The coffee, a blend of Jamaica and French roast, was very strong. Trying to be polite, most people drank it anyway.

   In the corner stood the clock, a family heirloom.

3. groups of words that could be sentences if they didn't contain connectors:

   When the clock struck one, everybody left. It was early, but everybody left anyway.

The following four punctuation marks are less important.

Parentheses ( ) sometimes separate more serious interruptions or explanations, but usually commas could be used instead of the parentheses. When parentheses are used, they always come in pairs.

The guest of honor (Mrs. Black from New York) was the last to leave.

Dashes (—) separate interruptions that are even more abrupt. If the interruption comes in the middle of a sentence, the dashes come in pairs. If the interruption occurs at the beginning or end of the sentence, one dash is enough. Usually a comma could be used instead of the dashes.

Mrs. Black—though I don't understand why so much fuss was made about her—was the speaker.

Semicolons (;) sometimes separate two sentences that seem closely related. Periods, however, could be used instead.

The clock struck one; everybody left.

Semicolons also sometimes separate parts of a list when the parts are long and complicated, but here commas could be used.

Colons (:) can separate a formal list from the sentence that introduces the list, but that colon could usually be replaced by a comma. The other use of a colon, after the salutation in a letter, has nothing to do with sentence structure.

In modern English the following seven punctuation marks are commonly used to show the structure of sentences: periods, question marks, commas, parentheses, dashes, semicolons, and colons.

You should understand the purpose of these last four, but acceptable papers can be written without using any structural symbols except periods, commas, and occasional question marks. *These three punctuation marks are essential.* All the other structure symbols are more sophisticated refinements. Unless you are sure that these more sophisticated symbols will help your readers, don't use them. If you think these symbols will help your readers, be sure that you use them in the conventional places in the conventional ways.

Periods, commas, and question marks are the three symbols that must be used when they are needed.

Two Sample Reports

Here is a report of an assigned class visit.

Visitation,
May 3, 1985

"Visit" would be better than the jargon word "visitation."

Main idea sentence tells who, what, when, and where.
More on "what" — the purpose of the session.

[1] On May 3, four members of our physical therapy class visited an exercise session at the swimming pool in the Moreland Civic Center. The exercises are supposed to help people who have arthritis and can't do regular exercises without water to make it easier.

"Old" is an opinion word — is there a better way to indicate the age of the bathers?
How many men? Women? Is "wife" an opinion here?

[2] I counted sixteen people, all of them old. They were a mixture of men and women, and some of them came in wheelchairs or on crutches. One old man had to have somebody help him into the pool, and at the end his wife, I think, and another man helped him out.

Could information about the number and type of exercises be more precise?

Entire last sentence of this paragraph should be omitted, with its "I think" and "looked very funny."

[3] The session started at two o'clock and lasted forty minutes. The session included ten different exercises, half of them without any equipment and half of them with empty plastic bottles of the type that bleach or milk comes in. I think the purpose of the bottles was to hold up the people who could not swim, but it looked very funny to see all those white bottles bobbing around.

"Young and friendly" is another opinion.
What the instructor wore is off the subject, and does talking have anything to do with the main point?

[4]   The instructor was young and friendly. She stood on the edge of the pool, dressed in an attractive exercise suit and a sweatshirt and talked to a lot of the people who were in the water.

Information in this paragraph should come earlier in report. Name should be given when instructor is first mentioned.

"Probably" indicates a guess rather than a fact.

[5]   Before the class started, a few of the people in the pool were swimming laps and some of them were playing with the bottles. Aside from the instructor, whose name was Madeline Glen, there are three special things for these exercise classes: a lifeguard, who is there to watch out for heart attacks, probably; a ramp that helps the crippled people get into the pool; and water that is fairly warm, about 85 degrees.

"Got bored" is opinion.

[6]   I noticed that all the people did the first half of the exercises, but one of the men got bored and started swimming laps again. All of the women did everything.

This paragraph makes the report sound finished.

[7]   After the class we talked to three of the women. One said the exercises made her arthritis better and another one said her doctor thought they might help. Another woman said she wanted to lose weight.

Julie Smith
Physical Therapy 110

Here is another report on the same visit. Compare the information in this report with that in the earlier one. Which is more complete?

An Arthritis Exercise Session

Main idea sentence tells who, what, when, and where.

Rest of the paragraph gives specific details of what—the exercise session. Readers must take accuracy of the details on trust.

[1]   Four members of Physical Therapy 110 visited an exercise session at the swimming pool at Moreland Civic Center on May 3, 1985. These sessions, which are given every Monday, Wednesday, and Friday at two o'clock, are intended for people who have arthritis. The instructor is Madeline Glen, who has a degree in physical therapy from Eastern State University. There is no registration fee for these sessions, but each person is required to pay the regular

Age of bathers shown by fact — entrance fee paid.

pool admission fee each day — one dollar for adults and seventy-five cents for senior citizens. We did not see anyone pay more than seventy-five cents.

Specific details about the bathers.

[2]   On the day we observed the session there were sixteen people in the pool, nine women and seven men. Two of the men and one of the women came in wheelchairs. One of the men, who appeared to be severely crippled, had to be helped out of the chair and into the water. Three other women were using canes or walkers, but they went down the ramp without assistance. For these sessions, the pool is equipped with a special ramp that slopes from the side of the pool to its bottom, with hand rails the entire length of both sides.

Is "severely crippled" an opinion here? Does "appeared to be" and the fact of the help support it as fact?

[3]   As they entered the pool area, each bather took two plastic gallon bottles from a bin and arranged them at the side of the pool. The bottles were empty, but the lids were screwed on.

[4]   At five minutes after two, the instructor came in and told the bathers to jog across the pool for four minutes. When the four minutes were up, she had them slide back and forth across the pool, spreading their legs as far apart as possible. Then she asked them to place their backs against the side of the pool, hold on with their arms, and kick. After that they faced the sides, still holding on, and with their legs spread apart, walked their feet up the sides and back down.

Details about the exercises, given in chronological order.
Are the details specific enough that readers can visualize what happened?

New paragraph here because of change in type of exercise.

[5]   Next the instructor said, "Get your bottles and bicycle." The bathers put the bottles under their arms and crossed the pool by moving their legs in the motions used by bicycle riders. Three other exercises involved using the bottles. In one, the bathers held the bottles at arms' length and swung their legs from in front of themselves to behind themselves. In another, they rotated their bodies in a complete circle, using the bottles as balance. In still another, they swung their arms, touching the bottles together in front of themselves and then together behind themselves. The session ended with another four minutes of jogging.

[6]   When it was over, the man who had been helped

No judgment is made about the relationship of the man and the woman.

Does "apparently" justify this guess?

into the pool was pushed up the ramp by two other people and lifted into the wheelchair. A woman who was with him waited until the women's dressing room was empty and wheeled him in there, apparently so that she could help him dress.

Gives more specific details of what the women said. Does the first report contain facts that should be included in this report? The lifeguard? The water temperature?

[7]   In the women's dressing room after the session we interviewed three of the women. One of them, who was using a cane, said she had been coming three times a week since January. At the beginning, she was unable to get into bed alone, but now she can do it without assistance. The second woman said her arthritis was not really crippling, but her doctor thought the exercise might keep it from getting worse. The third woman said she came because she enjoyed it, the water was pleasant, and she wanted to lose some weight.

Sharon Brown
May 8, 1985

Key Words and Ideas _____

Here are some of the important terms and ideas in this chapter. See whether you can answer these questions about them.

1. What does a **report** do?
2. What are the characteristics of a good **objective report**?
3. What does **precision** mean? How can you decide whether to use ordinary instead of unusual words?
4. What does **accuracy** mean? How does accuracy differ from precision?
5. How can you tell when you are not **sticking to the subject**?
6. What questions can you ask in deciding whether a report is **complete** enough?
7. What should the **order** of a report be?
8. What does being **objective** mean? What does being **subjective** mean?
9. Distinguish between **factual statements** and **opinion statements**. Do factual statements need to be accurate to be factual? Why not?
10. What does **slanting** mean?
11. What should the **main idea sentence of a report** contain?
12. What three **sentence punctuation marks** does every writer have to use?

Name _____

Exercises _____

Exercise 1. Precision.   Which of these pairs of sentences would be the better choice for a report? Pay special attention to the italicized words and phrases. Then explain your decision in terms of what the purpose of the report is and who the readers will be.

Choice

1. a. The experiment began with two *hypotheses.*
   b. I started out with two *guesses.*   _____

Purpose _____

Readers _____

2. a. The shipping department has made *a bunch of mistakes lately.*
   b. The shipping department made *fourteen errors in zip codes in the last two weeks.*   _____

Purpose _____

Readers _____

3. a. Joe Schane was treated for *chest trouble.*
   b. Joe Schane was treated for *emphysema.*   _____

Purpose _____

Readers _____

4. a. I *apprehended the subject not far from his home.*
   b. I *arrested the driver at the corner of Waterford and Bly.*   _____

Purpose _____

Readers _____

Choice

5. a. Fashion Footwear is underselling us *quite a lot* on *some men's shoes.*
   b. Fashion Footwear is underselling us *by two dollars* on *Brazilian-made Devonshire boots.*   _____

Purpose _____

Readers _____

6. a. The boycott had no *observable efficacy vis-à-vis* beef prices.
   b. The boycott had no *obvious effect on* beef prices.   _____

Purpose _____

Readers _____

7. a. *Some snake plants* were *received in damaged condition.*
   b. *Two dozen sansevieria* were *dead when they arrived.*   _____

Purpose _____

Readers _____

8. a. *Owing to the obligatory nature of his pecuniary involvements,* Mr. Clark was refused credit.
   b. Mr. Clark was refused credit *because he owes a thousand dollars.*   _____

Purpose _____

Readers _____

9. a. *To decide definitely now* would *seem silly.*
   b. *To reach an unalterable decision at this point in time* would *indicate a certain lack of judgment.*   _____

Purpose _____

Readers _____

10. a. The *kid* swallowed *some kind of poison.*
    b. The *infant* swallowed *a teaspoonful of sodium hydroxide.*   _____

Purpose _____

Readers _____

11. a. The *cost of the plan* must be *explained in detail.*
    b. The *monetary objectives* must be *supplemented by a careful analysis of budgetary obligations.*   _____

Purpose _____

Readers _____

12. a. *Notwithstanding its apparent validity,* the referee's decision was made *pursuant to established and codified procedures.*
    b. *In spite of the way it looked,* the referee's decision was made *according to the rules.*   _____

Purpose _____

Readers _____

13. a. There was *an insufficiency of sodium bicarbonate* to make the biscuits.
    b. There wasn't *enough baking soda* to make the biscuits.   _____

Purpose _____

Readers _____

14. a. *Sodium bicarbonate* was used in the experiment.
    b. *Baking soda* was used in the experiment.   _____

Purpose _____

Readers _____

Name _____

Exercise 2. Accuracy.   Some of these statements are accurate, some inaccurate. Mark the accurate statements *OK,* and rewrite the inaccurate ones. (Many of these facts you will already know; the rest can be checked in a college dictionary or an up-to-date almanac.)

1. There are 24 hours in a day and 276 hours in a week.   _____

_____

_____

2. The English names of all the winter months contain the letter *r.*   _____

_____

_____

3. None of the English names for the summer months contain the letter *r.*   _____

_____

_____

4. Thanksgiving is always on the second Thursday in November.   _____

_____

_____

5. A kilometer is the same length as a mile.   _____

_____

_____

6. Alaska is the largest state in the union.   _____

_____

_____

7. More boy babies than girl babies are born each year.   _____

_____

_____

8. Ronald Reagan is the oldest man ever to be president of the United
   States.   _____

_____

_____

9. Sodium bicarbonate is another name for table salt.   _____

_____

_____

10. The first Super Bowl game was played in 1967.   _____

_____

_____

11. An Emmy is a statuette awarded annually for notable achievements in
    radio broadcasting.   _____

_____

_____

12. Cape Horn is located at the southern tip of Africa.   _____

_____

_____

13. John F. Kennedy was assassinated in Galveston, Texas, in 1963.   _____

_____

_____

Name _____

Exercise 3. Sticking to the Subject.   In each set of details listed, cross out the ones that are off the subject. Be ready to give reasons for your decisions.

1. *A report to the police about a car accident*
    Two cars were involved.
    Woman in rear car cried a lot.
    Driver of first car refused to take a blood test.
    It was raining.
    First car skidded twenty feet.
    Second car was hit broadside.
    First car needed painting.
    Driver of first car had no driver's license.
    Driver of first car had no coat on.

2. *A report to a newspaper about a basketball game*
    Auburn defeated Tech 78–63.
    Two thousand people attended the game.
    Cheerleaders for Auburn wore their new sweaters for the first time this season.
    Tech's stage band performed at half time.
    Game was fifth win in a row for Auburn.
    Tech is 0–2 for the season.
    Stevens was high-point man, with 22 points.

3. *A report to the class on a botany field trip*
    We went to Oldfield State Park.
    Trilliums were blooming along the nature walk.
    Skunk cabbage was in bloom in the swamp.
    Dogwood was in bud but not yet in blossom.
    Dogwood is the prettiest of the flowering trees.
    We gathered no specimens because it is illegal to pick the flora in a state park.
    It was so chilly I had to wear gloves.
    Nobody could identify one tall blue flower.

4. *A report on a committee meeting*
    Meeting was called for 5:30 P.M.
    Only four committee members came.
    Two of those were late.
    It takes nine for a quorum.
    It's disgraceful that people accept appointments and don't come.

Exercise 4. Completeness.   Use your imagination to supply three more details that should (or could) have been included in each report planned in Exercise 3. Remember that reports should include who, what, where, and when.

1. The accident

_____

_____

_____

2. The basketball game

_____

_____

_____

3. The botany field trip

_____

_____

_____

4. The committee meeting

_____

_____

_____

Exercise 5. Order.   Use your own paper to arrange the following details in the order a good report would follow, and be ready to give reasons for the order you use. Change the wording slightly if you need to, but don't change the facts.

1. *A report of the final exam committee*
   A survey conducted in May 1982 indicated that 18 percent of the instructors did not give final exams.
   The university currently has no set policy on final exams.
   Three days are set aside at the end of the term for finals.
   Eighty percent of the students surveyed in the fall of 1982 stated that final exams should be optional.
   The College of Arts and Sciences faculty handbook says that finals are required in every course.
   A committee was formed in June 1982 to establish a final exam policy for the entire university.
   In May 1982 five out of six colleges within the university said that they wanted to set their own policies.
   The May 1982 survey was conducted by the college paper.

2. *A newspaper report of a marathon run*
   Plans for next year's race are already under way.
   "I never thought I'd make it," said Rosa Alba, car salesperson and mother of four.
   Thousands of spectators lined the route.
   Carl Walker came in first.
   Rosa Alba came in third among the women over forty.
   Twenty states and five foreign countries were represented.
   Carl Walker is a teacher at Robert E. Lee High School here.
   Nancy Blair is a lawyer from Pocatello, Idaho.
   The course covered a distance of 26 miles and 217 yards.
   There were 943 official entries.
   Blair set a new women's record with a time of 2 hours, 58 minutes, 27 seconds.
   The fourth annual May Day marathon was held in Oak Meadows yesterday.

3. *A substitute teacher's report to the regular teacher*
   Today the class covered problems 1–16 on page 89.
   Six students were absent.
   I won't be able to come tomorrow.
   I assigned problems 17–30 on pages 89–90.

Name _____

Exercise 6. Fact and Opinion.   Some of these statements are factual, some are not. Mark the factual statements *OK,* remembering that statements don't have to be accurate to be factual. Then rewrite the opinion statements as factual statements on which the opinions might be based. Don't turn any of the opinion statements into factual statements just by saying that somebody else said it. That is, don't turn the opinion statement "*Zowie* is a wonderful movie" into a factual statement by making it read "My sister says *Zowie* is a wonderful movie." That your sister said it may be a fact, but for purposes of this exercise, that rearrangement won't do.

> *Example:*   1. Hondas are Japanese cars.   *OK*
> 2. Hondas are wonderful cars.   *(not factual)*
>
> *Rewritten:* My Honda gets forty-two miles to the gallon.

1. Agatha Christie wrote good mystery stories.

  Opinion _____

  _____

2. Agatha Christie's mystery novels are boring.

  Opinion _____

  _____

3. Cuba is not very far from Key West, Florida.

  Where How far is very far? _____

  _____

4. John Zablanski came in first in the Boston marathon.

  OK _____

  _____

5. John loves Mary.

  _____

  _____

6. John and Mary got married last Saturday.

_____

_____

7. My father made an omelet for breakfast on Sunday.

_____

_____

8. My father is a good cook.

_____

_____

9. Baseball is America's favorite sport.

_____

_____

10. *Dracula* is a story about a vampire.

_____

_____

11. Stories about vampires are exciting.

_____

_____

12. The Pizza Palace makes delicious pizzas.

_____

_____

Name _____

Exercise 7. More Fact and Opinion.   Follow the same procedure you used in Exercise 6 — mark factual statements *OK* and rewrite opinion statements.

1. The area of San Francisco is six square miles.

   _____

   _____

2. There is one person every square yard in San Francisco.

   _____

   _____

3. Sunday is the pleasantest day of the week.

   _____

   _____

4. Pencils are made from graphite and cedar.

   _____

   _____

5. There are five *c*'s in the word *people.*

   _____

   _____

6. Gina Smith is a very talented girl.

   _____

   _____

7. Gina Smith won first prize for a quilt at the county fair.

_____

_____

8. A knife is a dangerous instrument.

_____

_____

9. My cousin Roger has bad table manners.

_____

_____

10. Roger ate his peas with his fingers last night.

_____

_____

11. Roger is a spoiled child.

_____

_____

12. Aunt Miriam is too lenient with Roger.

_____

_____

13. Uncle Mark is cranky.

_____

_____

Name _____

Exercise 8. Slanted Words.   For each of these slanted words or phrases, find a more neutral term.

> *Example:* economically underprivileged — poor

boob tube   _____

brat   _____

clunker   _____

gobbled   _____

officer of the law   _____

mumbled   _____

pigheaded   _____

Polack   _____

shiftless   _____

statesman   _____

scrawny   _____

pleasingly plump   _____

agitator   _____

mutt   _____

elderly gentleman   _____

waddled   _____

slum   _____

mouthpiece (in court)   _____

nagged   _____

Exercise 9. Criticizing Reports. Working in groups of four or five students, comment on these reports for precision, accuracy (if you can tell), sticking to the subject, completeness, order, and objectivity. Keep talking until you can all agree on what the problems (if any) are and how the problems could be corrected. Then compare what your group decides with what other groups have decided.

Report 1

The meeting of the Raglan College Service Club was called to order at 3:15 P.M. in Room 304, Hannah Hall, by the president, Cathy Shaw, on March 8, 1985.

Cathy called for new business, and Elsie Dinsmore mentioned that the party scheduled for June 10 would have to be canceled because no transportation is available to the Townsend Hotel. A motion was made and carried by a vote of 8–3 that we charter a bus for the trip. Liz Borden made that motion.

There was no further old business.

Molly Flanders had some new business. She suggested the club sell "No Peddlers Allowed" signs to raise money for the club charity. Mandy Christian was appointed head of a committee to look into this possibility.

Before there was any discussion of business, Nancy Drew, the secretary, read the minutes of the December meeting and they were approved.

The meeting adjourned at 4:05.

Nancy Drew
Secretary

Report 2

On March 23, the day after the vernal equinox, I commenced my custodial duties at 6 A.M. mountain standard time, and had just emerged from the antiquated enclosure where the outworn and discarded garments used for increasing the luster of the furnishings are kept when it dawned on my consciousness that all was not well in the oversized edifice devoted to student assemblages. I slunk on little cat feet to an orifice and peered in. Some unmitigated scoundrel had molested school property. I was shocked to see the shambles that had been made of those beautiful, expensive folding chairs and all those handsome, festooned with roses maroon draperies that our gallant Parent Teachers' Association sold so many stale doughnuts to pay for.

At 6:30 A.M. mountain standard time I bounded to the nearest telephone and communicated with the fearless arm of the law, informing him that I suspected foul play.

Report 3

The two years that I served with the Peace Corps in Arreta, Bodgiklotsque, from 1979 to 1981, saw several changes in the living habits of the village.

When I first arrived with two other Peace Corps volunteers, the 103 village inhabitants lived in eight by ten foot huts made of tree bark. Their chief food was a root that is native to that region, supplemented occasionally by milk and meat from a flock of about twenty-five small sheeplike animals. There were no public buildings, no school, no teachers, and no government.

In the winter of 1979 we instructed the men of the village in the planting of corn and wheat, and the next spring we helped them plant and cultivate these two crops. Late that summer and in the early fall, after the harvest, we worked with the village people to erect a twenty by forty foot building made of mud bricks, thatched with bark, and glazed with glass brought overland more than one hundred miles by donkeys. This building was used both as a school and a public meeting room. We later encouraged several families to make houses of mud brick thatched with bark. Five families had completed such houses, which were about ten by twenty feet, and when we left, in October 1981, four other families had started to build.

When we left after two years, the people of Arreta had two new crops, which they used for both food and trade. They had a building usable for a school and for a public meeting room. They had a teacher and a mayor. They were holding classes in reading and arithmetic for children and in farming methods for adults.

Arreta was not completely changed, but the differences are measurable. Now that I am home, I'm not sure that all those changes were a blessing.

Exercise 10. Sentence Punctuation.   Write seven sentences of your own showing the use of the punctuation marks listed on pages 209–211. Show your sentences to the rest of the class to see whether they agree with the way you have used the seven kinds of punctuation marks.

Name _____

Exercise 11. Main Idea Sentences for Objective Reports.   Write a main idea sentence for an objective report on each of these events, making up whatever details you need. For each main idea sentence you write, say who the readers of the report will be.

1. A fire   *Readers* _____

_____

_____

2. An accident   *Readers* _____

_____

_____

3. Minutes of a meeting   *Readers* _____

_____

_____

4. A safety inspection   *Readers* _____

_____

_____

5. A trip   *Readers* _____

_____

_____

6. An arrest   *Readers* _____

_____

_____

Exercise 12. The First Draft of a Report.   Attend some campus function—a lecture, a concert, a game, or a social event—and take notes on what goes on. Arrange your notes in order. Then write a first draft of an objective report that might be published in the college newspaper. If you can, show your draft to another student who attended the same event. Does the other student agree that you have covered all the important parts of the event? Make whatever changes you need in your draft.

Exercise 13. Writing the Report.   Write a finished version of the report you worked on in Exercise 12. Then go back over it, making sure you can answer yes to all the questions on this check list.

Check List for Content

1. Does your main idea sentence tell who, what, when, and where?   _____

2. Are your facts precise and accurate?   _____

3. Does everything you say stick to the subject?   _____

4. Is your report complete? Does it include all the important facts about the event?   _____

5. Have you avoided opinion words and slant?   _____

Exercise 14. The Final Step.   Now go over your paper one more time, this time tending to the manners of your writing. Can you answer yes to all these questions?

Check List for Editing

1. Have you given a separate paragraph to each important division of your report?   _____

2. Have you made sure all your sentences really are sentences?   _____

3. Have you checked the important symbols of sentence punctuation—periods, commas, question marks?   _____

4. Have you checked your spelling?   _____

5. Have you used a dictionary for any words you aren't sure about?   _____

Exercise 15. Another Report.   Write an objective report of what happened in this class so far today, assuming that your reader will be a student who is absent. When you have finished, exchange papers with the student sitting next to you to see whether you have included the same things.

Exercise 16. Looking for Slant.   Although newspapers claim to report objectively on what happens, sometimes their reports are slanted. Find a report that seems to you slanted, underline the slanted terms, and bring the report to class. Read it aloud to a small group of students to see whether they find the same slant you found.

Exercise 17. Slanting Deliberately.   Write a short report (not more than half a page) of some event, being as neutral as you can. Then rewrite your report, deliberately slanting it so that readers get a favorable or unfavorable impression of the event, but don't change or omit any of the facts. Make sure the slant occurs in the words you use rather than in an openly expressed opinion. When you bring both versions to class, see whether other students can tell which one is neutral, and what your attitude in the slanted version is. (This exercise isn't easy, but it can be fun.)

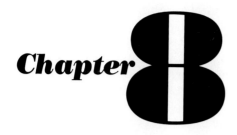

Chapter 8

Telling What Happened: Personal Experience

It's hard to write about an event with which you are personally involved without letting any of that emotion creep in. If you have watched a neighbor's house burn down, for instance, you may have to struggle to keep your report objective. It can, however, be done:

> A house belonging to Edward Brown, 4213 Auburn Road, was damaged Saturday evening by a fire believed to have started from a defective electrical appliance. The blaze was reported at 11:15 P.M. Saturday by a passing motorist who saw smoke coming out a first floor window. Two fire trucks from District 3 responded to the alarm, and by midnight the fire had been extinguished. One fireman, John Perry, was treated at City Hospital for smoke inhalation and released the same night. The Brown family was away from home at the time of the fire, but Mrs. Brown said today that damage was estimated at more than $40,000.

It may seem easy, on the other hand, to produce a **personal experience paper** describing that same event. Now, you think, you can pour out all those emotions you felt as you heard the sirens come closer and closer. Perhaps you produce something like this:

> I saw the Browns' house almost burn down last Saturday. It was awful, but kind of exciting, too. I kept thinking what if it was our house, and then I started worrying that maybe it would be our house if the firemen didn't get the blaze put out in time. A lot of people came out in the street to watch, and I wondered why people like to watch things like that. I was out watching too. It was too bad that the Browns weren't home, but then I thought maybe it would have been worse if they had been. And I kept thinking how I'd never liked Mrs. Brown much, but then I felt sorry. I always thought she was careless, so maybe it was her fault. And then I felt mean. But all the time I was scared to death. I was never more frightened in my whole life.

This account of the same fire is very personal indeed—so personal that there's very little about the fire. But letting yourself go—putting down everything you thought in very general terms, without letting readers *see* what was awful or exciting or frightening about it—won't interest readers as much as the objective report. At least the report contained some details. Watching the fire undoubtedly had a lot of meaning for you, but just saying so over and over won't help readers share your experience.

When you're writing just for yourself, the kind of private writing you do in a diary or journal, naturally you can write anything that pleases you in any way you please. But when you write to share your experiences with your readers, you must have a definite reason for telling those experiences, and you must make that definite reason clear. Unless your writing makes a point, it won't interest anybody else, no matter how exciting the experience seemed to you.

Are you writing about the fire because, in spite of your sympathy for the Browns, you realized that your main concern was for yourself and your own house? Because you realized that deep inside you were really enjoying somebody else's disaster? Because seeing the house in flames made you feel mean about your attitude toward Mrs. Brown? Or simply because you want to express the genuine sense of terror you felt?

Although the paragraph on page 237 hints at all those reasons, although it suggests several meanings the fire might have had for you, it doesn't follow up on any of them. If you can show your readers—not just tell them—why the event mattered to you, it will matter to them too. But showing them involves more than just rambling on—"I thought and then I thought and then I thought . . ."—a lot more.

When you write about your personal experiences, you must let readers see *why the experience was important.*

Finding Something That Matters

Perhaps you think nothing exciting ever happened to you. You've never witnessed a spectacular fire, saved anybody's life, or even been taken to jail on suspicion. Fortunately, events like that are rare in most lives. But you don't have to have watched a house burn down or received a citation for bravery to find something worth writing about. It isn't always the big dramatic experiences that make the best papers.

You probably see yourself as an ordinary person, leading an ordinary life. You say, "But I've never done anything interesting," and sit staring at a blank piece of paper. If you find yourself in that situation, you can try something that almost always works. Make a list of things you remember from more than a year ago. Go back into your childhood and jot down whatever makes a vivid picture in your memory. What have you done that made you proud of yourself? Did you take care of your little brother when he gashed his leg open with a butcher knife? What have you done that made you ashamed? Did you lose your wallet on the way to the store and tell your mother you were ripped off? Were you snowed in for nearly a week? Was your favorite cat hit by a car? Can you remember a family weekend at the beach or in the mountains or at your grandmother's house? All these things are **experiences**, and they are neither ordinary nor trivial if you can still see in your mind a picture of what happened. All these experiences are worth writing about if you can make your readers see them too.

The next step is figuring out why you remember the experience so vividly after all that time. When you tied a scarf around that bleeding leg and rushed your brother to the doctor all by yourself, did you discover that you could indeed cope with an emergency? When you lied to your mother about the wallet that wasn't stolen, did the loving sympathy you received make you feel worse than ever? When you were snowed in for a week, did you become aware of all the conveniences you'd taken for granted? Did burying the mangled cat in the garden slow down the speed of your driving for a long time afterward?

When you've finished the list and examined each event to see why it was significant enough to be remembered so clearly, you'll have plenty of experiences to choose from.

An experience is any event from which you learned something important.

Main Idea Sentences for Personal Experience

Once you've decided on an experience you want to write about, it's time to construct a main idea sentence. You may want to change it later, and you may never use it in the paper at all, but putting it into words can be a help.

It's obvious that the **main idea sentence for a personal experience paper** must be more than a statement of what happened. "Three years ago we were snowbound for a week" won't do. Such a sentence doesn't say why that week was important. "I'll never forget the week we were snowbound" isn't much better. That sentence sounds uncomfortably like "I'm going to write about . . ." Ask yourself why you won't forget it. Is it because of the snow that kept relentlessly piling up all day and all night, blocking the doorway and hiding the road? Trying to walk in the drifts, falling, laughing, and falling again? The trips to the garage to bring in load after load of wood when the power went off? The smell of caps and mittens drying in front of the fire? Getting along without a telephone because the snow and the ice had torn the wires down? Don't lose any of these vivid details. They're all part of what you remember, and you can use them when you write the paper.

What you're looking for now is *why* you remember, what you discovered during that storm. A good main idea sentence for a paper of personal experience usually has a two-part pattern. The first part of the sentence is the event; the second part is the discovery.

Event	*Discovery*

(1) When Freddy gashed his leg open, (2) _____.

(1) Losing my wallet on the way to the store, (2) _____.

(1) During a weekend our family spent at the beach, (2) _____.

(1) The time we were snowed in, (2) _____.

Even though many kinds of discoveries will fit into the second blank, some of them won't be usable. "When Freddy gashed his leg open, I discovered that it is two miles from my house to the hospital" is useless for two reasons. First, it's a "So what?" discovery. Nobody, except your family or a prospective buyer of your house, cares how far it is from your house to the hospital. But even if there were readers who would find this fact interesting, what else can you say about it? Once you have announced the distance, you're through.

"During a weekend our family spent at the beach, I discovered that the tide goes out and comes in every twelve hours" is no good either, even though you found that information fascinating. If you want to write about the trip to the beach, you'll have to find a discovery less universally known. If, on the other hand, you want to write a paper of explanation, telling what tides are and how they behave, "The tide goes out and comes in every twelve hours" might be an acceptable main idea sentence. Notice, however, that your weekend at the beach has faded completely out. The tides come in and go out whether or not you are there. But that doesn't mean you must give up on the beach weekend. Did you get stuck on the fishing rocks and have to wait six hours before you could wade off? Did you learn that it's safer to know what you're up against before you go exploring? Now you have a different kind of discovery, and the basis for a good paper.

The kind of discovery that makes a good paper must grow out of the experience, and it must have a meaning that will carry over into other experiences. Learning that it's foolish to take off without knowing what the risks are is one example of the right kind of discovery. Learning that your grandfather was not the pompous old stuffed shirt you had always thought him is another. Did he refrain from scolding, or even laughing, when you finally got off the rocks? Did he keep your mother from worrying herself sick by saying, "The boy has more sense than you give him credit for"? And when you finally waded off, feeling extremely silly, did he tell you about the foolish things he did when he was your age? This discovery—that people you thought were old and unsympathetic once had feelings much like your own—will carry beyond that particular experience.

Here are some main idea sentences showing significant discoveries:

When Freddy gashed his leg open, *I learned that I could cope with emergencies without losing my head.*

The time we were snowed in, *I discovered that people can get along without all the conveniences we take for granted.*

Losing my wallet on the way to the store *taught me that lying can cause more trouble than it cures.*

These discoveries may not be the kind of earthshaking thing you usually think of as significant, but they all have two things in common: they show clearly why the experience meant something to you; and they can lead to thoughtful and interesting papers.

Main idea sentences for papers of personal experience say what the event was and why it had significance for the writer.

Planning the Paper

The next step is to list the **specific details** that make the experience so vivid in your memory. Put down sounds and smells and sights, taste and touching. Put down what other people said and what they did. Try not to include "I thought" or "I wondered" as you make this list. What you're looking for is not what you thought but the details and events that prompted the thought.

snowed 36 hrs. without stopping
snow piled 2 ft. high
5 ft. in drifts
doorway blocked
road hidden
power off
phone lines down
furnace stopped working
carried wood in 3 times a day
tried to walk outside
fell in drifts
laughed and fell again
clothes soaked
smell of wet wool
sister cried
sister 10 yrs. old—curly hair, brown eyes
mother kept saying "Has to stop soon."
mother not very tall
3rd day snowed again
no way to find out if others snowed in too
stew cooked over fireplace
smell mixed with wet wool and wood fire
stew tasted good even 3rd day
no electricity—no TV
well pump electric—no water
snow melting in pot over fireplace
hands chapped and rough from hauling icy water
gloves fuzzy green
down parka, blue

This list is probably only a beginning. Don't stop until you have put down everything that comes into your memory, no matter how minor it seems. The list will provide the material you need to make your experience come alive for your readers.

As you write the first draft, remember that your aim is to help readers share the experience almost as completely as if they had been part of it. Don't tell them about it. Let them see it. Perhaps your first draft begins like this:

> Two years ago we were snowed in for a week. My mother and my sister and I were at home at the time. My mother is pretty but not very tall. My sister was ten years old. She has curly hair and brown eyes. We went to bed one night and everything was normal. We got up in the morning and it was snowing hard. It snowed all day and all night and all the next day. When it quit, the door was blocked and the road was hidden. I had to carry wood in three times a day. When we went outside, we fell in the drifts, but we laughed and got up and fell again. My sister cried and my mother kept saying, "It has to stop sometime," but it didn't. The next day it snowed again.

Plenty of details, all right, but have you forgotten what your main idea sentence was? ("The time we were snowed in, I discovered that people can get along without all the conveniences we take for granted.") How does your mother being pretty and your sister having curly hair and brown eyes relate to that discovery? Does your mother not being tall have something to do with your bringing in the wood? Couldn't she reach the top of the woodpile or is that just another detail that has nothing much to do with your discovery? And if the door was blocked, how did you get outside? Could you give a more vivid picture of crawling through a window and clearing the snow from the door, shovel by shovelful?

You can begin with a description of the snowstorm—how long it lasted, how deep it was, how it looked—because that will help readers visualize what it was like. But you need to go on very soon to the details that relate directly to your discovery —that you could get along without the furnace, without the electric stove and the electric light, without the telephone, without the television, and even without running water.

Specific details are as important in writing about personal experiences as they are in writing reports, but the kind of details and the way they are used are different. Reports give the facts; personal experience papers create pictures. In reports, your aim is to provide information; in personal experience papers your aim is to share your experience and the meaning it had for you.

Choose specific details that relate to the point of your paper.

Writing the Paper

Personal experience papers need introductions and conclusions, but the **introduction** sets the scene for the experience rather than serving as an unmistakable contract. In giving directions, in explaining, in reporting, your main idea sentence usually appears in the introduction, often as the first sentence in the first paragraph. In papers of personal experience, your main idea sentence may not appear at all. After readers have finished the paper, they should be able to think back to the introduction and understand how it prepared them for what happened, but when they read the first paragraph, they may not be able to guess what the point is going to be.

In writing the paper about the week you were snowbound, you might start with something like this:

> Although we've always lived out in the country, our house had all the conveniences of a city apartment. An electric thermostat controlled the furnace heat, and the open fireplace was only for pleasure. Nothing much needed to be done, and my little sister and I had plenty of time to watch television. Mother got most of our meals ready-made from the deep freeze, and if she needed something extra for dinner, she just phoned my father to bring it out when he came home from town. It's true that our water came from a well, but we weren't really aware of that. When I turned the faucet on, the hot water came gushing out, just as it would in town. Then one week, before my father could get home, it snowed. And snowed. And snowed.

Just as the introduction is less direct than in other kinds of writing, so is the **conclusion**. What you discovered during that snowstorm may not be clearly stated until the end of the paper, and even then, maybe it will be only implied:

> When the storm was over and the electricity repaired, I was glad enough to run a tub of hot water and soak for an hour. It was nice to settle down in front of the TV again, but it was even nicer to know that I could, if I had to, wash in cold water and read a book by candlelight.

If you've done a good job in the main part of your paper, readers will be able to figure out for themselves what your main idea sentence was.

> *Papers of personal experience don't need to contain the main idea sentence, but the introduction should hint at it and the conclusion should emphasize it.*

Sounding Natural

In all the writing you do, the more natural you sound the better, and the more comfortable your readers will be. You already know that if an ordinary word is just as precise as a long, unusual word, the ordinary word is the better choice. That rule is especially important in personal experience writing, where the style should be more informal than in explanations or objective reports. After all, you are writing about your personal life; it makes sense to use a personal style. Riding a patrol car, having a baby, shopping at a co-op—all are more convincing and more interesting if they **sound natural**, if they are written in the language of conversation. Stilted and pedantic language can only bore readers—or possibly amuse them unintentionally:

Shortly after I had, for the first time, assumed the vestments of an on-duty police officer, I encountered an individual who seemed to take exception to my occupational role. He spoke to me in abusive and disrespectful language, even though we had never seen each other before.

Such writing is fine for parody, awful for naturalness. Any reader would be quick to see that *vestments* is a most unusual word for clothing. The "individual who seemed to take exception to my occupational role" could probably be translated into "a man who didn't like the police." That's how most of us would say it. And what did the "individual" really say? We are told that it was "abusive and disrespectful," but repeating the actual words spoken would be more detailed, more lively, and certainly more accurate.

The word order, too, is strained. If the writer is talking about his first day on duty, he should say so, not mess around with "Shortly after I had, for the first time . . ." Written in more natural language, the paragraph might sound like this:

On my very first day in uniform, I ran into a man who just plain didn't like the police. Although I'd never seen the man before, he walked up to me, called me a dirty copper, and asked how many kids I'd shot lately.

When you've finished your first draft, read your paper aloud to yourself. If your voice stumbles in places over what you have written, rewrite that section to make it sound more natural. In informal accounts of your experience, if you would feel silly saying it, don't write it.

Though the language in papers of personal experience should sound natural, it can't be exactly like conversation. For one thing, we have to be clearer in writing, since readers can't interrupt to ask questions or give us a puzzled look. When we talk, we rely on feedback to tell how we're doing. When we write, we have to get along without any help from our readers. A sentence that's quite clear in conversation may be confusing when it's written down. If somebody says, "When the people come for their cars, be sure they're clean," you know it's the cars that must be clean, not the people. In writing, it's hard to tell.

Another difference between talking and writing is the number of fragments or incomplete sentences we use when we talk. A perfectly normal conversation might go something like this:

"Coming?"
"Guess not."
"Damn. Why?"
"Psych test."
"Worried?"
"Ought to be."
"Oh, come on!"
"Can't be done."
"Well, . . . luck, anyway."

To the speakers, this conversation is perfectly satisfactory, but written down it sounds incomplete.

When we talk we not only use fragments, we often repeat ourselves without any awareness of sounding like a stuck phonograph record:

> "My, but this is a good dinner. This is one of the best meals I ever ate. Isn't this chicken good? I was just telling Agnes that I sure like the way Aunt Mary fixes chicken. Henry, don't you think this is good? I think this is the best meal I've had for a month. It's sure good."

If everybody is enjoying the dinner, probably nobody will notice how repetitious these remarks are, and Aunt Mary will be pleased with the whole speech. But written down, the repetition is too much.

You have probably also noticed that in talking, many people string their sentences together, using almost no connectors except *and* and *so*. Even in conversation the effect is a kind of breathlessness, a seeming unwillingness to let anybody else speak:

> I was telling my wife about how hard my job was in the cannery and how long the hours were and how hot and steamy it was and how the floor shook and how the place smelled, and she said to me, "Well, how long ago was that?" and I realized it was nearly fifteen years ago, and she kind of smiled and then laughed and said, "Well, it sounds like you worked a full shift just yesterday," and I smiled back and laughed a little and said, "Yeah, I guess I better get over that," and I realized that fifteen years is long enough to complain about a job.

Are you still there? The content of the paragraph is not bad. It's full of specific details, and there's a discovery at the end, but the general effect is tiresome. The writer can make it much pleasanter to read by using connecting words that show more precise relationships—*nevertheless, in spite of, although, before, while,* and similar words.

> *As* I was telling my wife about how hard my job at the cannery used to be, I really got into it. "*Even though* you'd think the twelve hours a day were the worst part, they weren't. It was a hundred twenty degrees in there, and so much steam you couldn't see across the room. *On top of all that,* the machinery smelled awful and the floor never stopped vibrating."
>
> *When* I stopped for breath, she looked up and smiled. "How long ago was that?" she asked.
>
> *Because* I had been so involved in my story, her question really brought me up short. "Fifteen years ago," I said.
>
> She smiled a little more, *then* laughed. "Well, it sounds like you worked a full shift just yesterday."
>
> *In spite of myself,* I had to laugh, too. "Yeah, I guess I'd better get over that. Fifteen years is long enough to complain about a job."

In this revised version, the writer has made a few details more specific and quoted more of the conversation, but the main improvement is in the more varied connectors. Surprisingly, this version sounds more natural.

Another temptation in trying to make your writing sound just like you'd talk is to use too much slang. A bit of slang may make your paper sound lively, especially if it's quoted, but too much can be as tiresome as too many *and*'s. Besides, many slang words are not lively at all—they're as worn out as old Kleenex and just about as deadening to thought.

As for swearing, there's always been a problem. No words are "bad" in themselves, but because some people think some words are bad, using those words will turn those readers off and destroy the effect of whatever else you're saying. We all know what the words are, and we know where and when and with whom we can safely use them. We should also know when we can't use them safely. Writing intended for general readers is one of those places. Robert Louis Stevenson said the hardest thing about writing *Treasure Island* was to create convincing pirates who didn't swear. But he succeeded so well that we don't miss the profanity; we take "Shiver me timbers" and "Avast thar, matey," as powerful oaths, and no readers are offended.

Profanity and slang, carefully used, may give flavor to your writing in much the same way that pepper flavors soup. Tastes vary as to how much is acceptable. Whatever your own taste is, remember that though a careful sprinkling gives spice, dumping in great quantities to conceal the absence of thought is like using pepper to conceal the fact that the soup is spoiled.

It sounds like a tall order to write personal experience papers that make a point, use significant details and events, and sound natural without being an exact copy of the way you would talk. Such papers do take more thinking out than a series of generalizations or a list of details strung together with a lot of *and*'s and *so*'s. But they are certainly a great deal pleasanter to read, and they do provide you with excellent opportunities for examining the meaning of your own experiences.

> *Personal experience writing should sound natural, but it should avoid*
> *too many fragments;*
> *too much repetition;*
> *too many sentences strung together with "and";*
> *too much slang or profanity.*

Using Quotation Marks

You can help readers share your experience by quoting exactly what people said rather than just telling about it. Quotations can be handled in two ways. You can make very slight changes in what was said and introduce it by using *that:*

He said that I was a dirty copper and asked me how many kids I'd shot lately.

Or you can repeat the speaker's exact words:

"Dirty copper! How many kids have *you* shot lately?"

Quotation marks show that the speaker's exact words are being used. Notice that the first method, called indirect quotation, does not require quotation marks. But the second method, which does require quotation marks, gives readers more feeling of being there, of actually hearing what was said. If you are quoting more than one speaker, you always begin a new paragraph when you change from one speaker to another:

> "The stove won't work," I said.
> "Mama, I'm cold," my sister whined. "I'm hungry and I want to watch TV. I want to play outside but it makes my fingers hurt. When will it stop?"
> "I know," mother answered. "But it has to stop sometime."

Notice, too, that the quotation marks come only around the material that is actually quoted. When the quotation is interrupted by an explanation—*mother answered* or *my sister whined*—there must be two sets of quotation marks.

Don't use quotation marks for indirect quotations.
Do use them when you repeat the exact words of the speaker.

A Sample Personal Experience Paper

Here is the first draft of a personal experience paper:

A Misunderstanding

Introduction does arouse readers' interest, but details could be more specific.

[1] Judy and I had been best friends since the second grade. We did everything together and we talked on the phone a lot. We were together so much that sometimes people mixed us up. We didn't have any secrets from each other and we took turns spending Saturdays at each other's house. I knew her parents and she knew mine.

Could we hear some of this conversation instead of being told about it?

[2] Then one Friday when we were in high school I asked her what she wanted to do on Saturday. It was her turn to come to my house. She said she thought she'd stay home. When I asked why she said she just thought she would. When I kept nagging, she finally said she wasn't coming and why didn't I leave her alone.

Some of these "and/so" connectors need to be replaced.

Again, some direct quotation would help.

[3] My feelings were hurt and I was sure she was going to spend Saturday with somebody else, so I decided I'd show her and I asked Sharon, a girl Judy didn't like very well, to come and go to a movie with me, and I made sure Judy heard it and when my mother

asked me where Judy was, I said she was sick. All next week at school I acted like Judy wasn't there. I didn't call her on the phone, and when my mother asked me how she was, I said she had a bad sore throat and couldn't talk.

It's plain that this experience meant something to the writer, but readers aren't sure what the meaning was.

[4]   Then on Friday afternoon I went into the restroom and Judy was in there crying. I thought it served her right and if she wanted to be friends again, she'd have to be the one to ask. So I pretended I didn't see her and went out and left her crying. When I got home my mother asked me why I hadn't told her that Judy's father had been arrested. Then she asked me if Judy really had been sick, and why I'd said so. I felt awful but I didn't know what to do, and my mother just kept looking at me. Finally she told me I ought to call Judy up, so I did.

Paper sounds unfinished. Readers want to know what was said in the phone call.

Here is another version of the same paper, written after a discussion with other students in the class.

Best Friends

First sentence stays the same but more specific details help.

[1]   Judy and I had been best friends since the second grade. We got roller skates the same Christmas and skinned our knees the same day. When she got a new blue parka, I got one like it. We called each other every night and did our math over the phone. We talked so long that my father had to say, "Ruth, hang up. You don't have a private phone." At school we were together so much that sometimes people called her Ruth and me Judy, even though her hair is brown and mine is reddish. We had secrets from other people, but not from each other. We spent every Saturday together, and I thought I knew her parents as well as she knew mine.

Quoted conversation all through this section also helps.

[2]   Then one Friday I asked her what she wanted to do the next Saturday. It was her turn to spend the day at my house.

[3]   "I think I won't come," she said, not looking at me.

[4]   I was so startled I couldn't say anything for a minute.

"Why, Judy? Why?" I finally said. When she didn't answer, I just kept saying "Why? Why not?"

[5] Then she said, "I'm not coming. Why don't you leave me alone?"

Using better connectors makes this paragraph read more smoothly.

[6] My feelings were hurt. I was sure she was going to spend the day with somebody else, and I thought to myself, "I'll show her!" I asked Sharon, a girl I knew Judy didn't like very much, to go to a movie with me, making sure that Judy heard me ask and Sharon accept.

[7] On Saturday my mother asked, "What happened to Judy?" but I just said, "She's sick."

Better details here, too.

[8] All the next week at school I acted like Judy wasn't there. She asked me on Monday if I liked the movie—it was one we'd been planning to see together—but I walked away, pretending that I hadn't heard her. When she sat down next to me in English class, I got up and moved away. I didn't phone her all week, and when my mother asked if Judy was better, I said, "She's all right, but she's got laryngitis and isn't supposed to talk." That was so my mother wouldn't call up to ask about her and find out she wasn't sick at all.

[9] Then on Friday afternoon I went into the restroom and found Judy crying. "Serves her right!" I thought. "If she wants to be friends again, she'll have to do the asking!" I pretended I didn't see her and backed out as quick as I could.

This paragraph makes what happened much clearer.

[10] The first thing my mother said to me that night was "Why on earth didn't you tell me that Mr. Harrod was arrested for embezzlement last week? It was in last Sunday's paper, but I missed it, and didn't find out until Anita Loftus told me this morning. Is Judy terribly upset? Have you been able to help her at all?"

Now readers can tell that the main idea sentence must have been something like "When Judy's father was arrested, I learned the hard way that friends have to trust each other."

[11] I didn't say anything, but my face must have gotten red, because my mother went on, "Is that why you told me she was sick? I bet she hasn't been sick at all. Didn't you know I'd want to see her? What do you think friends are for, Ruth?"

[12]   I felt awful, but I didn't know what to do and my mother just kept looking at me. I could feel my face getting redder and redder. At last, when I said, "I didn't know, Mom, really I didn't," she asked me, "Are you going to ask Judy over for supper or shall I?"

[13]   When I got Judy on the phone, I was crying harder than she was, and all I could say was, "Oh, Judy. Judy." My mother had to take the phone away from me and do the asking.

Ending is much improved; readers aren't left wondering how it turned out.

[14]   But Judy came. She's a nicer person than I am. She hugged me without saying a word about last week. She didn't even say she thought I didn't want to know her any more, but that must have been what she thought. When I managed to mutter, "I'm sorry," she just hugged me again and we sat down to supper.

Key Words and Ideas

Here are some of the important terms and ideas discussed in this chapter. See whether you can answer these questions about them.

1. What is the difference between telling what happened in objective reports and telling what happened in personal experience papers?
2. How can you find an **experience** worth writing about?
3. What are the two parts of a **main idea sentence for papers of personal experience**?
4. How can you decide what **specific details** to use?
5. What is the difference between the way a **main idea sentence** is used in papers of personal experience and the way it is used in other kinds of writing?
6. What should the **introduction** and **conclusion** of a personal experience paper do?
7. In making your writing **sound natural**, what four things should you avoid? Why?
8. Explain where **quotation marks** are used.

Name _____

Exercises _____

Exercise 1. Main Idea Sentences for Personal Experience Papers.   Complete these sentences so that they could be used as main idea sentences for papers of personal experience. If you haven't had such an experience, use your imagination. Then compare your sentences with those of other students. Are all your discoveries broad enough to apply to other situations?

> *Example:* When I moved away from home, I discovered that <u>families do more than provide food and shelter.</u>

1. When I had a flat tire, I discovered that _____

   _____

   _____

2. Getting fired from a job taught me that _____

   _____

   _____

3. During a tornado, I discovered that _____

   _____

   _____

4. When my parents were divorced, I found out that _____

   _____

   _____

5. After a quarrel with my father, I decided that _____

   _____

   _____

6. When our team lost the game, I discovered that _____

_____

_____

7. A month of baby-sitting showed me that _____

_____

_____

8. When I got lost in New York, I discovered that _____

_____

_____

9. Wearing the wrong clothes to a party made me realize that _____

_____

_____

10. When our apartment was vandalized, I learned that _____

_____

_____

11. After a night in the hospital, I was sure that _____

_____

_____

12. When I took part in a peace rally, I learned that _____

_____

_____

Name _____

Exercise 2. Using Specific Details.   Replace these very general statements with the details on which they could have been based. Don't repeat the general statement; instead, say something specific from which readers could form their own general statement.

> *Example:*
> *General statement:* The clerk was very nasty.
> *Specific statement:* The clerk snatched my money and said, "If you don't like it here, go shop someplace else."

1. The party was disappointing.

   _____

   _____

   _____

2. The weather was terrible.

   _____

   _____

   _____

3. My uncle is stingy.

   _____

   _____

   _____

4. That store is too expensive.

   _____

   _____

   _____

5. The bus driver was very obliging.

_____

_____

_____

6. The new owner is a nice man.

_____

_____

_____

7. The new owner seems cranky.

_____

_____

_____

8. The substitute instructor is unreasonable.

_____

_____

_____

9. The room was a mess.

_____

_____

10. He seemed to be in a hurry.

_____

_____

Name _____

Exercise 3. Sounding Natural.   Rewrite these sentences to avoid unnatural word order and stilted language.

> *Example:* Extinguish the illumination upon departing.
> Turn out the light when you leave.

1. In-class sleeping is not, by most educators, looked upon with favor.

   _____

   _____

2. My wife then encouraged me to attempt once again to release the lock and thus enable the door to open.

   _____

   _____

3. I made each individual present acquainted with the educator responsible for enabling me to master the intricacies of solid geometry.

   _____

   _____

4. Due to the fact that I was insufficiently prepared for the examination, the final result was less than my parents felt desirable.

   _____

   _____

5. Opening the mail, I discovered a chiding letter written by a computer, rebuking me for the failure to remit a monthly installment.

   _____

   _____

6. The person responsible for chairing the meeting requested input on the probable causes of there being an inadequately large attendance.

_____

_____

7. While you are riding a public conveyance, you are politely requested to refrain from extended discussions with the operator of the vehicle.

_____

_____

8. Extinguish all smoking materials until the plane is completely at rest at its final destination.

_____

_____

9. That is an unjustified regulation up with which I will not put.

_____

_____

10. Kindly be advised that you and your dependents are being requested to vacate said premises.

_____

_____

11. At that point in time, an intimate acquaintance implored me to imbibe with him the cup that cheers but not inebriates.

_____

_____

Name _____

Exercise 4. Fragmentary Talk and Repetitions.   Just for fun, see if you can rewrite this conversation so that somebody who wasn't there can tell what was going on. Then exchange what you've done with another student in the class. Whose version is clearer? Does it still sound as though it might be a real conversation?

> "No. Never."
> "Why not?"
> "You know very well."
> "No, I don't."
> "Use your head."
> "I don't understand at all."
> "I'll just say it again. I won't do it!"

_____

_____

_____

_____

_____

_____

Now rewrite this speech to avoid some of the repetition. Can you keep it sounding natural? Again, exchange with another student and talk about what both of you have done.

> "I really like that photograph. It looks just like you. That's why I like it so much, because it's really a good likeness. I don't remember ever seeing a picture that looked more like you. Don't you think it's good? Don't you think it looks like you? I really like it, don't you?"

_____

_____

_____

_____

Exercise 5. Slang.   Make a list of eight or ten slang expressions you and your friends are currently using. Opposite each expression, write what you think it means. Then get together in groups of four or five and compare your lists—both the slang expressions and their meanings. How much agreement is there? Can you agree on which expressions might give flavor to papers of personal experience and which would be inappropriate?

Slang expression   *Meaning*

_____   _____

_____   _____

_____   _____

_____   _____

_____   _____

_____   _____

_____   _____

_____   _____

Ask some older person to explain four or five slang expressions that used to be common but are no longer used. List them, then tell what effect using those slang expressions would have in a paper of personal experience.

_____   _____

_____   _____

_____   _____

_____   _____

Name _____

Exercise 6. Using Better Connectors.   Rewrite these sentences, using more precise connectors in place of some of the *and*'s and *so*'s. You may change the wording
slightly as long as you keep the original meaning. You will probably want to make
some of the longer ones into more than one sentence, but use your own judgment.
Then compare your sentences with those other students have written. What differences are there? Do the differences matter?

1. I was afraid of the water so I couldn't swim, but I wanted to learn so I took some
   lessons and I kept trying and I learned to float and I felt better about myself so
   I kept on trying.

   _____

   _____

   _____

   _____

2. The speed limit was twenty miles an hour and it was a school zone and I was
   driving thirty-five and so I was arrested.

   _____

   _____

   _____

3. We've been practicing for a week and almost all the actors know their lines and
   the costumes are ready and the tickets are mostly sold and I hope it will be a big
   success and I hope it doesn't snow that night.

   _____

   _____

   _____

   _____

4. So I told my husband about the accident so he phoned the insurance company so they said to take it to the nearest garage so they said it couldn't be fixed so we got a new car.

_____

_____

_____

_____

5. The nurse said my brother was very sick and I asked what the problem was and she said it was pneumonia and I asked if he would get well and she said everybody hoped so.

_____

_____

_____

_____

_____

6. I took my girl out to dinner and the bill was higher than I expected and I didn't have enough money and she had to pay for half the meal and she saw it embarrassed me so she asked me if I didn't believe in the equality of the sexes.

_____

_____

_____

_____

_____

Name _____

Exercise 7. Quotations.   Turn each of these indirect quotations into direct quotations. Try to vary the arrangement a little; don't start every sentence with "He said . . ." And don't forget the quotation marks.

1. The math teacher said for us to skip questions 8 and 9 if we had any trouble with them.

   _____

   _____

   _____

2. She complained that she'd be caught dead before she'd be seen riding in that dirty old car.

   _____

   _____

   _____

3. The man cried out that we should watch where we were going because there was a car coming.

   _____

   _____

   _____

4. That he couldn't hear the sopranos at all was what the director actually said.

   _____

   _____

5. Mrs. Eagleton asked us when we planned to bring the car back.

   _____

   _____

Exercise 8. More Quotations.   For each of these general statements, quote what the speaker actually said.

> *Example:* The fat man complained about the food.
> "This spaghetti has a dead fly in it," the fat man complained.

1. She insisted she was innocent.

_____

_____

2. The child begged to go home.

_____

_____

3. She complimented me on my appearance.

_____

_____

4. Dennis was polite about the dinner.

_____

_____

5. He threatened me with bodily damage.

_____

_____

Name _____

Exercise 9. Planning a Personal Experience Paper.   Make a list of events and experiences you remember from more than a year ago. Then ask yourself why you remember them. This list is for your own use; you don't have to show it to anybody else
unless you want to. Then pick one of those experiences and fit it into a main idea
sentence for a paper of personal experience.

Main idea sentence _____

_____

_____

Under your main idea sentence, list all the specific details you can remember. Try
to include sights, sounds, smells, taste, and touch.

_____

_____

_____

_____

_____

_____

_____

_____

_____

_____

_____

_____

Next, try to write down all the conversation that occurred during the event. Use the exact words of the conversation, just as you remember it.

_____

_____

_____

_____

_____

_____

_____

_____

_____

_____

_____

_____

Now look back at the list of specific details and the conversation. Have you left out anything important? If you think of anything else, add it here.

_____

_____

Exercise 10. Writing the First Draft.   Write the first draft of the paper you planned in Exercise 9. You probably won't use all the details you listed, and you may not want all the conversation, but be sure to refer to those lists as you write. Don't include your actual main idea sentence in the paper. When you have finished the draft, read it to one or two other students to see whether they can figure out what your main idea sentence was. If they can, fine. If they can't, rewrite your paper so that the point you're making is clearer.

Exercise 11. Writing the Paper.   Write a finished version of the paper you worked on in Exercises 9 and 10. Then go back over it, making sure you can answer yes to all the questions on this check list:

Check List for Content

1. Does your first paragraph set the scene for your experience?   _____

2. Have you used plenty of specific details—enough that readers can see what happened?   _____

3. Do the details you have used have some connection to the meaning of your experience?   _____

4. Have you quoted enough conversation that readers can hear what happened?   _____

5. Does your conclusion make your paper sound finished without actually including your main idea sentence?   _____

Exercise 12. The Final Step.   Read through your paper one more time, this time tending to the manners of your writing. Can you answer yes to all the questions on this check list?

Check List for Editing

1. Have you made sure all your sentences really are sentences, except when you are deliberately using a few fragments to make your conversation sound natural?   _____

2. Have you checked the important symbols of sentence punctuation—periods, commas, question marks?   _____

3. Have you used quotation marks around all your direct quotations but not around indirect quotations?   _____

4. Have you started a new paragraph each time you quoted from a different person?   _____

5. Have you checked your spelling?   _____

Exercise 13. Reading Personal Experience Papers.   Trade papers with another student in the class—not the one who read your first draft. After you have read the other paper, write down what you think the main idea sentence was. Is your sentence fairly close to the one the writer started with? If there is much difference, talk about it. What else could the writer have included? What might have been left out?

Chapter 9

Writing to Persuade

Persuasion, and attempts at persuasion, go on all around us all the time. Other people try to persuade us, and we try to persuade them. We have been using persuasive techniques since we were born, and we'll keep using them till we die. Babies bawl for the breast or the bottle. Children scream and stomp, smile and coax. Adults argue, plead, and sometimes slaughter each other. All these kinds of behavior—bawling, begging, and battering—have one thing in common: they are attempts to get other people to give us what we want, to do what we want them to do.

Between the methods of the baby and the methods of the businessman or bureaucrat, however, there are some important differences. A new infant's crying is instinctive, a reaction to hunger and discomfort. But soon instinct turns to calculation. Even very small children's attempts at persuasion can become emotional. Anger makes them holler and hit, and if their parents are tired enough, or the other child is small enough, anger can be a successful technique. Observant children, though, learn early that anger doesn't always work, and they develop new ways of persuading. They discover that sometimes a smile and an appealing glance, a muttered, "Momma, I love you," get them further than temper tantrums do. These children are learning to play on other people's emotions, not just to indulge their own. Many of them discover that personal charm can take them a very long way toward getting what they want.

And some adults don't go much beyond these elementary methods of persuading. They rely on anger; they curse and condemn ideas they don't like, often convincing others that an emotional reaction is the only possible alternative to what they see as evil. Or they plead for our pity, flatter our egos, and coax us so enchantingly that only real curmudgeons can avoid saying, "Of course, of course." Such emotional methods do work, sometimes in writing, but especially in face-to-face situations. The wife who can aim a skillet accurately enough usually gets her husband's attention without much delay. The husband who can shout obscenities loud enough can usually cow his wife. Lovers respond to soulful eyes and tear-streaked faces. Employers promote stock clerks who make ordinary supervisors feel like vice-presidents. A candidate who appears on television looking like a benevolent uncle and telling us that all will indeed be well if we just leave it to him usually gets elected.

Beyond instinctive reactions and emotional appeals, however, is another, more adult method of influencing other people, sometimes called **rational persuasion**. Rational arguments rely on reasons, not just emotions, for getting people to do one thing rather than another. The emotional appeals that almost always work when people are face-to-face with one another, or sitting in front of a television set, sometimes fail when people are separated in space or time. When we think seriously about them a bit later, emotional appeals often lose their force. We need to remember that when we write, readers can't see that drooping mouth, that worshipful look, that benevolent beam. All they can see are the words on the paper. Good readers demand reasons, and successful written persuasion should produce those reasons. In writing, as in talking, you succeed if you are a skillful persuader, but you must persuade through sound performance, not just sound.

Rational persuasion deals in reasons, not just emotions.

Discovering a Topic

In an ideal world, all persuasive writing would represent the writer's honest convictions. No writer would try to convince readers about anything the writer didn't really believe in. Unfortunately, in the actual world that isn't always true. Advertising agencies are hired to convince the public that one headache pill is better than another. Editorial writers are told whether to be for the new garbage dump or against it. Public relations departments, and sometimes ordinary employees, are forced to support their employer's point of view. A public relations woman who puts out a release showing that her university is not trying very hard to meet affirmative action goals, or a public relations man who hints that half the dollars collected in the campaign to fight cancer were spent on champagne dinners, will be looking for a new job rather suddenly.

As a writer, you may occasionally find yourself in a situation where you have to argue for or against a belief you don't care much about. Perhaps you will have a job that requires you to take a stand you don't really believe in. Or you may have a teacher in college who assigns a paper contrary to your convictions. When that happens, you will of course put your own beliefs to one side and do the best you can. Most of the time, however, nobody will tell you what to believe in or what side to support. You won't be asked to change your opinions as easily as you change your clothes. Instead, you will be asked to examine your own opinions and your own convictions and choose a **topic** that seems to you really worth writing about.

As you try to decide which of your beliefs you will use for your paper, remember that your aim is to get your readers to do something or believe something. If your paper succeeds, it will result in either changed actions or changed attitudes. Advertising agencies and public relations experts to the contrary, writing that really convinces usually comes from writers who are themselves convinced. Unless you are writing about something you care about, you will find it very hard to make your readers change either their behavior or their beliefs. But unless you are writing about something your readers also care about, you will find it even harder.

Suppose you begin by listing some of your genuine beliefs. You are against nuclear war, and you think murder is wrong. You believe in love and brotherhood. You are strongly convinced that the people next door should keep their poodle out of your petunias, that the college cafeteria ought not to charge a dollar for a cold hot dog, that your history teacher shouldn't force you to take a final exam. All these convictions meet the first test—you believe in them. How many of them meet the second test—will your readers care?

Probably almost all readers do care about nuclear war and murder. Like you, they're against them both. No matter how vigorously you maintain that nuclear war is a great evil and that the government should *do something,* no matter how often you assert that killing other human beings is terrible, you won't change any minds because your readers already agree. Do you know anybody who wants a nuclear war or who argues that murder is right? Readers care about brotherhood, too. They're for it, although they may be against affirmative action or against welfare or against the Russians. The trouble with being against nuclear war and murder or in favor of brotherhood is that these beliefs are much too broad. They're too general and too widely accepted. Arguing for them is a waste of your time.

If, on the other hand, you can bring these beliefs down to size, if you can center in on these topics at a level where there is some disagreement, you may change people's minds. There is disagreement about how to prevent a nuclear war, and if you have a wide knowledge of world affairs and unlimited time, you may be able to present a sound argument showing that a new international policy will increase the chances of a permanent peace. Nobody can do it in a short paper, however, and many readers will already have a strong emotional investment in either disarmament or increased military spending. In the same way, you might be able to trace people's attitudes toward killing through several different cultures, from the beginning of civilization, and come up with a clear distinction between acceptable and unacceptable forms of human slaughter, but that's a semester's project. If you want to deal with either nuclear war or murder, you will need to narrow your topic even more, to find a place where it touches your readers' lives more closely. Should the police arrest peace activists who sit on railroad tracks to prevent nuclear warheads from passing through the city? Should the legislature pass a new capital punishment law or repeal an existing one? Should the police fire at suspects trying to escape? Should private citizens shoot at suspected pickpockets? Almost all readers will care about these more specific questions.

Let's go back to that list. It seems pretty obvious that most readers won't care much about your petunias, your cold hot dog, or your problems in American history. And even if they did care, what is there to say beyond pointing out that the flowers are dead, hot dogs should be hot, and your history final frightens you? But before you discard all these beliefs as too narrow or too personal, ask yourself whether your readers might be troubled by similar problems. You're not the only person with a garden. Should the city council pass a new leash law or enforce the law that already exists? You're not the only student who eats in the cafeteria. Can you start a campaign to get the food service improved and the prices reduced? You're not the only person worried about final exams. Should the college make them optional? Now that the questions have become slightly broader, you'll have plenty to say, and many of your readers will care about the problems.

> *Before you decide on a topic, ask yourself these questions:*
>   *Do you really care about it yourself?*
>   *Is it specific enough that readers will care?*
>   *Is it specific enough that you can cover it in a short paper?*
>   *Is it general enough that readers will care?*
>   *Is it broad enough that you will have something to say?*

Main Idea Sentences for Persuasion

Before you select a topic, make a list of things that you are really concerned about. Decide which ones are suitable for short papers by answering those five questions. Then try to put your belief into definite words by asking yourself questions about each possible topic. Should peace activists be arrested for nonviolent protests? Should private citizens be allowed to carry handguns? Should the leash law be more strictly enforced? Should husbands help with the housework? Is a state lottery a reasonable way to support schools? Remember that a great many people disagree on all these questions. Either yes or no is a possible answer to all of them. The question you ask is not a main idea sentence, but the way you answer it is. Your answer becomes a statement of what you believe and what you are trying to get your readers to believe.

Main idea sentences for papers of persuasion are easy to recognize because they are always *definite statements* and because they always contain *opinion words*. Usually they use words like *should* or *should not, must* or *must not, ought* or *ought not*. Sometimes they use words like *fair* or *unfair, better* or *worse*.

> Garbage rates in Granite City *should* be reduced.
> The garbage rates in Granite City *cannot and should not* be reduced.

> Peace activists *should not* be arrested for nonviolent protests.
> Anyone who breaks the law, including peace activists, *should* be arrested.

> Private citizens *must be allowed* to carry handguns for their own protection.
> Private citizens *must not* be allowed to carry handguns.

> Men *ought* to help with housework and child care.
> Men *ought not* to have to do housework and care for children.

> Food and service in the college are both *terrible*.
> The college cafeteria provides *good* food at *fair* prices.

A state lottery is the *best* way to raise money for education.
A state lottery is a *bad* way to raise money.

In all these main idea sentences, the opinion words—the words that show the writer's belief—are in italics.

Main ideas for persuasion always make a definite statement and they always contain opinion words.

Finding Reasons for Your Belief

The next step is to ask yourself why you believe whatever it is. A strong feeling that something ought or ought not to be so is not enough. Readers, unless they already share your feeling, will demand that you **support your beliefs** with reasons. Insisting that "I just know it, that's all," or "Anybody with any sense knows that!" won't convince anybody, no matter how many exclamation marks you use to emphasize your belief. In the coffee shop you can pound the table. At home you can shout, maybe loud enough to keep your listeners from asking, "Why? What makes you think that?" But when you write, the readers' "Why?" is always in the background. If the reasons aren't there, the readers won't be there long either.

Before you begin your first draft, make another list, this time putting down all the reasons that might support your main idea sentence. Suppose we take as an example the belief that the charge for picking up the garbage in Granite City should be reduced. The main reason for wanting the charges reduced, of course, is that you think they're too high, but that's the belief, not the reason for it. It's merely a repetition of the main idea in slightly different words. After thinking for a while, you might come up with a list like this:

1. Poor people can't afford to have their garbage hauled away.
2. The high rates make the public mad at the company.
3. Some cities provide free garbage collection.
4. Garbage dumped along the roads looks awful.
5. Garbage piled up outside houses is unsanitary.
6. The garbage company is making a huge profit.
7. The garbage dump is polluting the nearby streams.
8. The company has a franchise from the city—no competition.
9. The owner of the company drives around in a Mercedes and goes to Las Vegas twice a year.
10. Calling the garbage company "The Granite City Sanitary Disposal Service" is just showing off.

Now let's look at that list again. Which of these are real reasons and which should be thrown away? The first reason sounds all right. It's true that having refuse from every house collected at least once a week, from the poor as well as anybody else, is important to the community. And if the Granite City Sanitary Disposal Service has the only franchise (see reason 8) then people on low incomes, or no income at all, have no other choice.

What about the second reason? It's probably true that the company would prefer that their customers be satisfied—too many dissatisfied customers might keep them from getting their franchise renewed. But they aren't likely to lower their rates just to keep everybody smiling. That reason had better go.

The third reason, that some cities provide free garbage collection, is probably worth considering, especially if you can show that those towns are about the same size as Granite City and have about the same income. But notice that this reason refers to no rates at all rather than a reduction of the rates that do exist. The main idea sentence would have to be changed to read "Granite City should provide free garbage service to all its citizens."

What about reasons 4 and 5? These reasons are clearly related to each other. Both of them deal with what happens to garbage when people can't afford to have it picked up. And both of them relate to the first reason—that the present charges are so high that many people cannot afford them.

The sixth reason is probably the strongest. If the company is actually making a huge profit, and you can demonstrate that it is, then picking up the garbage at lower rates would still allow the company to make a profit.

The statement in the seventh reason, that the dump is polluting the nearby streams, is a fairly serious matter. Most people agree that pollution is a bad thing. But it takes money to clean up pollution. This statement sounds like a reason for raising rates, not lowering them. You'd better cross it out.

Reason 8, that the company has no competition, is probably sound enough. If the city has given the company the only franchise, then the company becomes, in a sense, a public utility, and the city has an obligation to control its rates.

The fact that the owner of the company drives an expensive car and takes expensive vacations (see reason 9) may be a way of demonstrating reason 6, that the company is making a huge profit, but it's hardly a reason by itself.

As for reason 10, you may find the name of the company pretentious, but what it calls itself has nothing to do with how much it charges. Reason 10 is no reason at all.

Now what are you left with? If you discard reasons 2, 3, 7, and 10 and combine some of the others, you could come up with something like this:

1. The garbage company and its owner are making huge profits.
2. Unsightly and unsanitary conditions are the concern of the whole community.
3. The city, which has given the company the only franchise, has an obligation to control its rates.
4. Poor people who can't afford the high rates will dispose of their garbage somehow, by dumping it along the roadside or letting it pile up by their back doors.

All four of these sound like good enough reasons for wanting the rates reduced.

For the main idea sentence that private citizens must not be allowed to carry handguns, reasons may seem easier to find: Surveys show that most Americans are in favor of outlawing handguns. The murder rate in the United States is many times higher than it is in countries where such guns are against the law. You believe that many fatal accidents could be avoided if the guns were not so easily available. You also know that people who support handguns say that the Constitution says citizens have the right to bear arms. Your reasons might go something like this:

1. Surveys show that the majority of Americans believe that handguns should be outlawed.
2. The murder rate in the United States is much higher than in countries where handguns are illegal.
3. Many fatal accidents could be avoided if handguns were unavailable.
4. The Constitution refers to bearing arms against enemies of the country, not to owning guns for private use.

Some main idea sentences, however, can be supported by only one really strong reason. For instance, almost the only reason for thinking that men should help with the housework is that when both partners work, any other arrangement seems grossly unfair. Instead of looking for more, and weaker reasons, the writer's job is to find ways of showing the unfairness.

But the writer who wants men to share in the household chores and the care of the children must do more than say "It isn't fair." The paper must first demonstrate the unfairness and then show the improvements that will result from sharing. In the same way, before readers will consider that the garbage rates should be reduced or that handguns should be outlawed, the reasons must be supported. The four most common ways of **supporting reasons** are:

1. Giving examples
2. Citing statistics
3. Using authorities
4. Predicting consequences

Some of these methods of support work better with some reasons than with others. Use the ones that fit your reason best.

Beliefs must be supported by reasons, and reasons must also be supported.

Giving Examples

Most of the reasons that support your beliefs will be generalizations, and generalizations, as you discovered when you wrote definition papers, are always clearer when they are illustrated by examples. **Specific examples** not only make generalizations clearer, they are likely to make them more convincing, too.

More than fifteen years ago, public reaction to the Vietnam War showed how this principle works. We had all been told that war was horrible, that innocent people suffered, that the Vietnamese were not "the enemy" but human beings like ourselves. We knew all those things, but we didn't really believe them until the television news began to show the long lines of starving refugees walking hopelessly down a dusty road and Vietnamese children with their skin burned off. One picture did in sixty seconds what months of explanation couldn't do. More recently, the television pictures of emaciated children in Ethiopia, with protruding bellies and arms like matchsticks, have done more to make us realize the situation than all the headlines, "Thousands starve to death in Africa," have been able to do.

Most of us remember, when we're talking, that actually seeing something is better than an hour of abstract argument. We say, "Look, I'll show you," or "See for yourself." What is true for talking is true for writing as well. Usually we can't produce photographs to prove our point, but we can use words to create vivid pictures.

Suppose you're trying to prove that when people can't afford garbage collection, they will find other ways to dispose of their rubbish. Perhaps you begin with that statement and then try to explain it by more generalizations:

> When people can't afford garbage collection, they will find other ways to dispose of their rubbish. Lots of people in Granite City can't afford the present high rates. I know that a great many families are living below the poverty level. Retired people living on small pensions don't have enough money to pay the garbage company. People who have been unemployed for over a year can barely afford to buy groceries. These people have to get rid of the stuff somehow. Sometimes they just go out and dump it, and sometimes they just let it sit around.

This paragraph does make a beginning at showing who some of the poor people are, but most of it doesn't do much more than circle around the original statement. You need to let readers see one retired person, one family whose unemployment benefits have run out. Let them see what one backyard looks like, how one scenic roadside has been ruined.

You can show them old Mr. Dutton, who gets a Social Security check for $402 a month and spends half of it for rent. Let them see him spending $40 a week for groceries and $30 a month for the prescriptions he has to have. He doesn't have enough left to pay his phone bill, let alone have his garbage hauled away. And show your readers the Underwoods—both parents were laid off at the mill more than a year ago, and the only hot meal the three children get is the lunch the grade school provides.

Mr. Dutton has a heap of rags, rusted cans, and rotting newspapers beside his kitchen door. Rats can be seen running out of the pile, and stray dogs paw through it. Old Mr. Dutton may get a summons for creating a public nuisance and be charged a fine that he can't pay, but that won't get his garbage picked up.

The Underwoods, on the other hand, are trying to keep themselves decent and their yard clean, so Mr. Underwood loads the old car up once every couple of weeks and drives out into the country. He hopes nobody will see him as he tips the bags of garbage over the side. The potato peelings disintegrate finally, but the empty cans stay there, spoiling what was once a pleasant bed of ferns. He feels bad about it, but what else can he do? If Mr. Underwood's luck holds, he won't be arrested for littering.

It doesn't matter whether Mr. Dutton and the Underwoods are "real" people that you "really" know. Perhaps you have just made them up. But if there are lots of retired people living on about that amount of money and if there are several unemployed families facing the same kind of problem, these are perfectly fair examples.

As for the reason that expecting working wives to do all the housework is unfair, examples should be easy to find. Glenda Smith works from eight to five, her husband from nine to four, yet he sits in a lounge chair all evening with his feet propped up, watching hockey games on television. Anita Jones struggles over a stew, with a crying baby under one arm and a cookbook clutched in her other hand while Andy Jones, who boasts about his omelettes, won't go near the stove if Anita is at home. Pete Lang won't change the baby's diaper—that's "woman's work"—but he's all in favor of Pat changing the flat tire—that's "being self-sufficient." All these examples show one partner doing the work, the other partner taking life easy, a situation most readers would find not quite fair. But don't use the McNabs for an example, even though Grant never gets breakfast and seldom bathes the baby. He vacuums the house and does the laundry, and in spite of Grace's complaining, most readers would find that division of labor reasonably fair.

Specific examples help to convince readers by giving a clear picture of actual situations.

Citing Statistics

Carefully chosen examples can support your reasons by helping your readers to see the problem more vividly and understand it more clearly. But examples cannot include more than one or two cases. If your readers are to believe that the problem is really widespread, you must use some **statistics**—figures that show *how much, how many, how often.* For instance, the belief that the garbage company is making a huge profit seems to lend itself to statistical support. Since the company holds a city franchise, its financial statement is open to public inspection. If you find that the company showed a net profit of 23 percent last year, most readers will agree that the profit is "huge." If, on the other hand, the owner made only 4 percent above expenses, the reason might as well be discarded.

If you are maintaining that the possession of handguns should be illegal, you will need statistics to support two of your main reasons. Find a couple of those surveys showing that most Americans favor banning handguns and say what the exact percentages were. Find out what the murder rate in the United States was for the last five years and compare it to the rates in England and in Canada. If you can show that English and Canadian citizens are not naturally any more sweet-tempered and peaceful than the citizens of this country, those statistics will go a long way to support your belief.

Sometimes you can provide your own statistics by means of a simple investigation and a little arithmetic. If three of the six fatal accidents in Granite City last year were caused by children playing with handguns, you can argue that 50 percent of those fatal accidents could have been avoided. More often, however, you will need to depend on other people's figures. If you want to show the percentage of working wives, consult the most recent census figures. If you want to know how many of them work for their own satisfaction and how many because their families need the money, look at the Bureau of Labor Statistics or read some magazine articles. You can probably trust the statistics in national magazines, but unless you have done the counting and multiplying yourself, you must say where the figures come from. Give credit to the source of all your statistics by mentioning the public record, the book, the magazine, or the newspaper. If your source is a magazine or a newspaper, give the page and the date as well as the name.

Statistics help to convince readers by showing how many, how much, how often.

Using Authorities

Just as the library is useful in finding statistical support, so newspapers, magazines, and books can come in handy in finding **authorities** to support your reasons.

Sometimes, of course, you can find authorities without having to look them up. If you're still thinking about the possibility that garbage collection in Granite City should be free, you can call a friend in Shallikuk and ask how garbage is managed there. But your friend may not know exactly, and even if she does, she's not an impressive authority on city affairs. You would do better to find out who is mayor of Shallikuk, get in touch with him, and get his statement on how Shallikuk manages to pick up everybody's garbage at no charge without bankrupting the city. He may say that the City Council there believes that collecting rubbish is as much a city responsibility as paved streets and police protection, that all three of them should be supported by taxes. If he goes on to say that recycled rubbish pays for a big part of the collection costs, you have found another reason for believing that costs in Granite City should be lowered—the Granite City Sanitary Service is doing no recycling at all. The mayor of Shallikuk is a good authority—he knows what he's talking about.

Usually, however, it will be quicker to use the library. You can find statements both for and against the control of handguns by looking in the *Reader's Guide to Periodical Literature* under "gun control." You can find court decisions on peaceful protests by looking under "nuclear opponents" or "nonviolence," and if that doesn't turn up anything, the reference librarian may be able to help. Remember, however, that you can't quote just anybody. For a statement to be convincing, the person who makes it must be knowledgeable about the situation.

Authorities help to convince readers by backing up what you say.

Predicting Consequences

Predicting consequences means showing how much better (or worse) things will be if readers do (or don't) follow your advice. Predicting sounds like a simple thing to do. If men share the housework, then women won't be so tired, and rested wives are happier wives. If handguns are made illegal, fewer people will be murdered and fewer accidents will occur.

But what about the prediction that if garbage rates are lowered, more people will be able to afford the charges and those unsanitary piles and unsightly roadsides will disappear? Most of the unsanitary piles will disappear, but the unsightly roadsides won't go away by magic. And can you safely say that if people keep on hauling their rubbish out in the country, offenders can be arrested without fear of taking food from the mouths of hungry kids? Probably not, because no matter how much the rates are lowered, the Underwoods will still have to take some of their food money to pay the charges. If readers are to be convinced, they have to believe that what you say will happen will indeed happen.

In some kinds of predictions this is fairly easy. You won't have much trouble with the prediction that if the food and service in the cafeteria were improved, more students would eat there. Fresh, crisp salad; hot, appetizing sandwiches; and polite attendants at the counter could make all the difference. Asking a few students who now lunch on an apple from the corner grocery should give you some backing for that prediction. After all, the students who don't use the college cafeteria are the real authorities on what would happen if conditions improved, just as the students who do eat there now are the authorities on what will happen if the conditions don't get better.

But don't depend on a flat prediction, any more than you would depend on a flat statement of belief or an unsupported reason. Wary readers are likely to ask "How do you know?" You must show in some detail why your proposal will inevitably lead to the desirable consequences you predict—or why a failure to follow your proposal will inevitably lead to some consequences that most readers would find undesirable.

Predicting consequences helps to convince readers by showing them what will happen.

Dealing with the Other Side

No matter what logical reasons you have produced or how well you have supported them, there is still something to be said for the other side. Most problems are more complicated than they seem on the surface, and if some of your readers didn't disagree, you wouldn't have to persuade them. Here's where a bit of tact pays off. Instead of assuming that anybody who disagrees with you is an idiot, hardly worth bothering about, you can admit gracefully that your opponents do have reasons, even some that seem pretty good. You can, however, show why those reasons, looked at carefully, are not so good after all. **Dealing with the other side** openly can defuse its arguments and make your position more convincing.

If you ignore your opponents' reasons, if you leave it to chance, your readers may remember those arguments when you're not around to disprove them. A safer way is to get in first. Anticipate as much of the opponents' argument as you can. Then show what's wrong with it.

If you still want those garbage rates lowered, you can concede that wages have gone up, that the company did indeed purchase a new truck, and that the cost of maintaining the trucks has certainly not gone down. But you can also show that management has been poor, that the old truck could have been repaired rather than replaced, and that all the advertisements the company has been running, when there's no competition anyway, are a waste of money.

If you are writing in favor of making handguns illegal, you might say something like this:

> One of the major arguments against controlling the sale of handguns has always been that honest citizens won't have them, but criminals will. There used to be bumper stickers proclaiming "If guns are outlawed, only outlaws will have guns." It's true that honest citizens won't have guns, but it's also true that petty criminals won't have them either, if the penalties are severe enough. It's certainly true that a great many ordinary people who might have become criminals, just because a handgun was there when the argument got heated, won't commit crimes.

You already have material to combat another argument against control, that the Constitution guarantees the right to bear arms. You are ready to explain, not just that conditions were different in those frontier days, but that the constitutional provision was intended to cover muskets for use against an enemy, not small revolvers to be used against any suspicious-looking person who walks across somebody's lawn.

How might you deal with arguments claiming those peace activists should be arrested? As for the argument that a law is a law, and that anybody breaking it should be arrested without regard to how good their intentions are, you can point out that peaceful protests are protected by another constitutional guarantee, the right to free speech and peaceful assembly. You might also point out that some protesters welcome arrest as a way of getting more publicity, but that you believe the charge should be only a misdemeanor, with no penalties attached—an arrest no more serious than a parking ticket.

Considering what the opposition has to say can never weaken your position, and it can often strengthen it.

Dealing with the other side can help to convince readers by showing that you have considered the question carefully and are trying hard to be fair.

Planning the Paper

When you have worked out a clear main idea sentence stating your belief, found reasons to support it, and jotted down ways to support those reasons, your paper is fairly well planned. Before writing the first draft, however, you should reexamine your reasons to decide on the best **order**.

Look again at those four reasons for reducing the garbage rates in Granite City. Which is the strongest reason? Which is the one most likely to impress your readers? And which reasons are connected in such a way that they should come together? Perhaps the most effective reason is that the whole community is hurt when garbage is disposed of improperly, but that reason is closely tied to people not being able to afford the high rates. The other two reasons seem connected, too. If the profits are too great, the city should control them. Rearranged, your reasons will look like this:

First reason: The city, which has given the company the only franchise, has an obligation to control its rates.

Next reason: The garbage company and its owner are making huge profits.

Next reason: Poor people who can't afford the high rates will dispose of their garbage somehow, by dumping it along the roadside or letting it pile up by their back doors.

Final reason: Unsightly and unsanitary conditions are the concern of the whole community.

Notice that in this rearrangement the strongest reason has been saved for the last; what comes at the end of the paper is what readers are most likely to remember. But there's nothing absolute about this order. If you can think of another arrangement you like better, fine. And if as you write you see different connections, or if you think the support for one of your reasons is especially convincing, don't hesitate to abandon your plan and make a new one.

In general, the best order for a persuasion paper is to save the strongest reason for the last.

Writing the Paper

Many successful writers produce a draft of the main part of the paper before they write the introduction. On the other hand, some writers find that writing a really lively introduction puts them in the mood for the rest of the paper, in much the same way that a good introduction encourages readers to go on to the rest of the paper.

Whichever system you follow, however, remember that the **introduction** to a paper of persuasion must do double duty. It must *make a contract* based on the main idea sentence, letting your readers know what your belief is. This contract is the same kind of promise you began with in most of your earlier writing. In papers of persuasion, however, your readers not only have to be persuaded to agree with you, they often have to be persuaded to read your attempt. Even though you have chosen a topic that many people care about, chances are that most people are well satisfied with what they already believe. They don't much want you to change their minds. So your introduction must do more than make a contract—it must *get your readers so involved* that they can't stop with the first paragraph.

You might begin like this:

> Poor old Mr. Dutton went hungry for two months last summer. He had no meat, he had no fresh vegetables, and he had no milk. He ate his potatoes without butter, and even then there weren't enough to fill him up. What happened? Did his Social Security check fail to come? No, it arrived on time. The real problem was that Jack Dutton, who has been a good, hard-working citizen all his life, thought he had to pay that twelve-dollar garbage bill. When it got a bit colder, in October, he stopped paying the bill. He figured that when it wasn't so hot, the garbage wouldn't smell so much, so he started piling it up outside his door and spent the twelve dollars on much needed groceries. When good citizens like Jack Dutton are pushed to such extremes, it is clear that the garbage rates in Granite City must be reduced.

That introduction is both melodramatic and exaggerated, and you probably won't want to use it. Nevertheless, it's a great deal better than this beginning:

> Although I know that a lot of people maybe won't agree with me, I think the garbage rates in Granite City should be reduced, at least a little bit, because I think that a lot of people really can't afford to pay so much.

Good introductions find a middle ground between whooping and whining. Just as readers will be quick to see when you're overdoing it, so they'll be quick to stop reading if you underdo it too much, if you sound apologetic and uncertain. Show your readers a believable situation where change is needed. Then they will be more ready to consider your proposal for change:

> Last week I saw Jim Yates, who owns and operates the Granite City Sanitary Disposal Service, drive by in his new Mercedes, headed for two weeks in Las Vegas. The same day on the same road I saw Jack Underwood, who hasn't had a job for more than a year, throwing a sack of garbage from his old car onto a bed of ferns. I know that what Yates was doing is perfectly legal and Underwood was breaking the law, but I resented Yates and I sympathized with Underwood. If the company Mr. Yates owns would charge a little less, Mr. Underwood wouldn't be driven to such extremes. If we want to keep our roadsides clean and attractive, garbage rates in Granite City must go down.

Good introductions often begin by giving specific details and then working up to the main idea at the end of the paragraph. But if you can't think of a lively beginning, there's nothing wrong with a direct approach: "Men ought to help do the housework and take care of the children." This start is not very dramatic, but it's straightforward. It tells your readers without any shilly-shallying what your main idea is, and it's a good deal better than a beginning that tries so hard to be clever that your readers can't figure out what you do believe. The introduction below is unsatisfactory because it fails to make a clear contract:

> Glenda Smith is always tired, and no wonder. She gets up at six to make the coffee. Then she wakes her husband and kids, rushes back to the kitchen to keep the toast from burning, back to the bedroom to dress the baby, back to the kitchen to pack the lunches,

and somewhere between braiding sister's hair and putting the dishes to soak, she gets her own hair brushed. She's late to work because she has to take the baby to the day-care center. When she comes home worn out from a day at the office, she doesn't get to sit down with a drink or take a glance at the paper. There's dinner and dishes, diapers and dusting. Weekends are the same old story—mop the kitchen, change the beds, get the laundry done. It's the same thing over and over. Glenda never catches up.

This introduction gives plenty of specific details, but it never gets to the point and we never discover what the main idea is. What will improve poor Glenda's situation? Better planning? Quitting her job? Hiring some help? If the main idea is "Men should help with the housework," beginning with that plain statement and then going on to the details would be a great improvement.

The **conclusion**, as usual, must make the paper sound finished, but it always does it by *reemphasizing the main idea.* If you decide to get this emphasis by going back to the sentence you began with, it's a good plan to change the wording a little:

Introduction: Garbage rates in Granite City must go down.
Conclusion: Unless the rates go down, we'll continue to have people driven to dumping garbage in unsanitary and unsightly ways.

Introduction: Men ought to help with housework and child care.
Conclusion: When both partners work, it's unfair to leave all the household tasks to the woman.

Introduction: Private citizens must not be allowed to carry handguns.
Conclusion: Until handguns are made illegal, we'll continue to have unnecessary slaughter.

A single sentence, clearly and firmly stated, can be a convincing finish for a short paper. Beginning writers, however, are sometimes uneasy with short conclusions, and they are tempted to cloud their sentences with unnecessary words:

As I have tried to show in this paper, the garbage rates must go down, and if they don't *I'm pretty sure* Granite City will keep on having trouble.

In my opinion, then, men ought to help around the house, and when they don't, *it seems to me that* it's really not fair to the women who have to do it all by themselves, *usually.*

In conclusion, therefore, handguns should be made illegal *in spite of what some people think.*

You can see for yourself how these namby-pamby phrases weaken rather than strengthen the statements. No matter how brilliantly the reasons are supported, when writers end up apologizing, readers are likely to end up thinking, "Well, that writer isn't really sure."

If a single restated main idea sentence seems too abrupt, a summary conclusion may work better. A summary conclusion repeats the reasons, in the same order as in the paper, and then ends with the main idea:

The city, then, has an obligation to see that the company stops making huge profits for itself and begins charging reasonable rates—rates that even poor families can afford. When people are forced to use country roads and back yards as garbage disposal sites, it hurts the whole community. Those practices must be stopped. Garbage rates must be reduced.

Summary conclusions may not seem very exciting, but they are clear and definite. If the reasons have been convincing, the conclusion will be convincing too. Sometimes, however, you may want a livelier ending. If you can manage it without sounding corny, go ahead. This conclusion, for instance, will appeal to many readers:

That the same problem exists all over the place doesn't make it any better. If Glenda Smith's husband doesn't change his ways, she'll land in the loony bin or he'll land in the divorce court. And when I get married, if I ever do, there'll be a clear agreement on just what "woman's work" is—and I'll get it in writing.

Conclusions are important. Unless they are convincing, the effect of the whole paper can be destroyed.

Good introductions to persuasive papers do two things—arouse interest and make a contract.
Good conclusions reemphasize the main idea.

Subjects and Verbs

It won't be any surprise to you that in carefully edited writing, **subjects agree with their verbs**. Doubtless you've heard it for almost as long as you've been in school, and doubtless you see that yours do, most of the time. You know that when the subject is plural (when you're talking about more than one thing) the verb must be plural, too (it won't end in *s*). You know that if the subject is singular (only one thing) often the verb will end in *s:*

The subject interest*s* Craig.

The subject *does* not interest me.

Craig *has* read several books about it.

Prudence *is* reading about it too.

The grammatical rule of *agreement* between subjects and their verbs is not hard to grasp. But confusion sometimes arises when the subject gets separated from its verb, as in a sentence like this:

The subject, although it fascinates lots of people who like complicated problems, seem*s* dull to me.

Unless you are watching carefully, you may write *seem* instead of *seems,* because the closest word, *problems,* is clearly plural. Or you may write a sentence such as *He want to* because, in your spoken language, you don't always hear the *s.*

Problems like this are not as serious as muddy thinking or disorganized ideas, but some readers will take them very seriously indeed. Like misspelled words, more than one verb that doesn't agree with its subject may mark the writer as uneducated and, as a result, keep the readers from giving an argument the respect it deserves. If you have this kind of problem, get some help. The help can come from more practice in finding subjects and verbs and then checking them with considerable care. Or it can come from a friend who will help you read through your writing and point out where the problems are. Eventually, however, you will have to learn to do it on your own.

If your subjects and verbs don't agree, some readers will ignore what you're trying to say.

Two Sample Persuasion Papers

Hurrah for the Lottery

Introduction reminds readers of unpopular alternatives.

[1] Somebody once said that nothing is more certain than death and taxes. They could have said that nothing is more hated than taxes. People find sales taxes constantly annoying. They go to buy a shirt marked $8.99 and have to pay $9.62. They mutter and swear in the middle of April and try to find tax shelters or even decide to cheat on their income taxes. They hate property taxes so much that they pass referendums, like the famous Proposition 13 in California, to keep property taxes from getting any higher than they used to be. But the state does have to have money, especially for education, which everybody agrees is very important. The state lottery is the best way to raise money for education.

Introductory paragraph ends with main idea sentence.

Reason—lottery raises money painlessly.
  Supported by statistics showing how much.

[2] Last year alone the state collected more than $70 million in lottery ticket sales. Even after the prizes and expenses were paid, that left nearly $10 million the state was able to make without anybody complaining about taxes.

Reason—people enjoy the lottery.

[3] It wasn't just that nobody complained. The people who bought the tickets actually got some fun from

Supported by specific examples showing ordinary people winning.

spending that money. They liked thinking they had a chance to get rich, and they thought it could happen to them, just as it did to Connie Anderson, who spent ten dollars on a ticket that paid off a quarter of a million dollars. They can read in the paper that Connie Anderson has only a part-time job and was behind on her car payments. Now she can pay off the car and still have enough left to keep her comfortable for the rest of her life. A friend of mine knows a man in his own neighborhood who has twice won fifty dollars on a two-dollar ticket.

Reason—lottery is fair. Supported by authority from control board.

[4]   Johnson Lewis, who is on the state lottery control board, said last week in a radio interview that there has never been any sign of corruption in the state lottery. Unlike some other places people go to take a chance on winning something, the state lottery is perfectly fair and honest. Everybody who buys a ticket stands an equal chance of winning.

Arguments of opponents: Reason it's wrong—lottery gives ordinary people a dream.

[5]   Some opponents of the lottery say that the state has no business encouraging gambling, but people who want to gamble will do it anyway. Those who can afford it will fly off to fancy casinos, but most people don't have enough money to do that. If the state shut down the lottery, poor people would be shut out of one of life's harmless pleasures—dreaming of being a big winner.

Reason—without lottery taxes would go up. Supported by predicting consequences.

[6]   Even worse, if the lottery is discontinued, millions of dollars that are now paying teachers and buying school books would disappear. Classes would have to get bigger or else the sales tax would have to be raised again and nobody, including the people who don't like the lottery, would like that at all.

Conclusion repeats most important reason and main idea sentence.

[7]   Schools are important, and they do have to be paid for somehow. As long as people don't want their taxes to go up, a state lottery is the best way to raise money for education. It's painless and it's optional. Nobody is forced to buy a lottery ticket.

Here is another paper taking an opposite point of view:

What Does the State Lottery Teach?

Introduction begins with main idea sentence; goes on to give picture of who buys tickets.

[1] A lottery is a bad way for the state to raise money, even if hundreds of thousands of people are willing to buy the tickets. Last Friday the line at the Save & Buy Mart stretched outside and clear around the block. The people in line weren't there because hamburger was advertised twenty cents cheaper than any place else. They weren't there because surplus cheese was being distributed, though most of the people looked poor enough to be eligible for free cheese. They were there because it was the last chance to get in on the big sweepstakes and they were buying lottery tickets they couldn't afford.

Reason — chances of winning are very small.
Supported by statistics and authority.

[2] What are their chances for the big winning payoff? Not very good. Out of the more than $70 million that was wasted on lottery tickets last year, less than 50 percent was paid out in prizes. That cuts the chances in half right at the start. According to Elizabeth Summers, an accountant who has been studying the lottery results for more than two years, the chances of winning anything, even five dollars on a two-dollar ticket, are about one in ten thousand, and the chances of winning anything big are less than one in a million. The state is getting rich on false hopes.

Reason — not enough of the money goes to the state.
Supported by same authority and more statistics.

[3] Ms. Summers has also pointed out that a quarter of all that money never reached the state at all. Fifteen percent of it went to the out-of-state corporation that manages the games, and another ten percent went to the merchants that sell the tickets. The merchants are the ones making money on every ticket, not the people who buy the tickets.

Reason — lottery is paid for by poor people.
Supported by specific example.

[4] Worse than that, though, is that the people who buy the tickets are spending money they can't afford. None of the wealthy people are buying dreams of pie in the sky. They are shrewd enough to invest their money where they know they'll get some return. People who don't have much are the victims of this state shell game. A man who lives across the street from my parents buys ten dollars worth of tickets every time he gets a pay check. He said

to my father, "That's only 5 percent of my wages. If I win, I might get ten thousand dollars and that would be a 1,000 percent return on my money." His wife told my mother that there was more wrong with his reasoning than with his arithmetic. She said that ten dollars would make a big difference in the way she shops for food, but that if Frank just wants to blow the money, he could take her out to dinner some week. Frank may be enjoying his get-rich-quick dream, but his wife isn't.

Reason—state's position is illogical.
Supported by another authority.

[5]   In addition, the state is talking out of both sides of its mouth. In an article published in *The State Times* in February, Margaret Yorke, an ethics teacher at the college, said, "It is ironic that the government has declared it illegal for old men to enjoy a pinochle game for a penny a point in the back of a tavern, but finds it completely legal for the government itself to run a much bigger and more expensive gambling game."

Concedes that some of what other side says is so. Then shows that it is misinterpreted.

[6]   People who defend the lottery claim that it's a good thing because nobody is forced to buy tickets and some of the money goes to education. It's true that people who disapprove of gambling don't have to gamble, and it's also true that a certain percentage of the money—but only 75 percent—goes to the schools. But as Margaret Yorke says, education is supposed to teach logical thinking and decent values. Is teaching people to think they can get rich without working for it a decent value? Aren't we teaching them that gambling is wrong if the state doesn't get a share, but just fine if the state gets its cut?

Conclusion repeats the main idea and summarizes the reasons.

[7]   The lottery is an undesirable way to raise money because the chances of winning are too small, the state doesn't get enough of what is spent, the money comes from the people who can least afford it, and, most important of all, the lottery teaches illogical thinking and wrong values.

Key Words and Ideas _____

Here are some of the important terms and ideas discussed in this chapter. See whether you can answer these questions about them.

1. How is **rational persuasion** different from instinctive reactions and emotional appeals?
2. What questions should you ask yourself in deciding on a **topic** for a short **paper of persuasion**?
3. How can you recognize **main idea sentences for persuasion papers**?
4. What must you do to **support your belief**?
5. What are four common ways of **supporting reasons**?
6. How do **specific examples** help convince readers?
7. How do **statistics** help convince readers?
8. How do **authorities** help convince readers?
9. How does **predicting consequences** help convince readers?
10. How can **dealing with the other side** help convince readers?
11. What is usually the best **order** for a paper of persuasion?
12. What two things should the **introduction** of a paper of persuasion do?
13. What must the **conclusion** of a paper of persuasion do besides making the paper sound finished?
14. Why does it matter whether *subjects and verbs* **agree**?

Name _____

Exercises _____

Exercise 1. Main Idea Sentences.   Which of these statements are satisfactory main idea sentences for short papers of persuasion? If you think a statement is satisfactory, mark it *OK*. If you think it is unsatisfactory, rewrite it so that it might be usable. Don't worry about whether or not you agree with the opinion. You are not being asked to defend the statement, just to decide whether somebody else might use it. Be prepared to explain why the sentence you have written is better than the one it replaces.

> *Example:* My mother doesn't make my teen-age brother do enough work around the house.
>
> *Unsatisfactory because it's too narrow. Better:*
>
> Teenage boys should be required to help with the household chores.

1. The state should adopt a compulsory seat belt law.

   OK
   _____

   _____

2. Compulsory seat belt laws are an invasion of privacy.

   OK? Borderline.
   _____

   _____

3. I shouldn't be required to pay library fines if I have a good excuse for keeping a book overdue.

   NO
   _____

   _____

4. Should doctors be sued for malpractice?

   NO
   _____

   _____

5. American dairy farmers are paid for milk they don't produce.

_No._

6. It's a bad thing for people to be hungry.

Nothing to persuade

7. The Supreme Court said school officials should have a right to search students if the officials think the students are breaking the rules.

Not stating what they are trying to persuade

8. The college should make more low-interest loans available to students who can't afford textbooks.

_OK._

9. Some three-year-old children don't like to ride in car seats.

Nothing to persuade

10. The college newspaper publishes too much national news.

_OK_

11. I don't like rock music.

So what!

Name _____

Exercise 2. Finding Reasons for a Belief.   For each of these main idea sentences, find at least two reasons that might support the belief. Again, don't worry about whether or not you agree with the belief—for the moment, just pretend that you do.

> *Example:* Compulsory class attendance should be abolished.
> *Reasons:* (1) Students are mature enough to decide for themselves whether they need to go to class.
> (2) Compulsory attendance protects teachers who are dull and unprepared.

1. The college ought to provide more housing for married students.

1. More college age students are marrying.
2. Not providing housing is discriminatory.

2. Women drivers should take a course in simple car repairs.

1. Women would be able to avoid potentially dangerous situations - i.e. highway breakdowns - breakdowns after dark
2. Avoid repair shop rip-offs

3. Airlines should offer reduced fares to college students.

1. Would allow students to see their families more often
2. Would give students incentive to choose airline travel over other types of transportation

4. Smoking should not be allowed on the campus.

1. Health risks of second hand smoke

12. Helps Promote healthy lifestyles

5. Smoking should be allowed wherever the majority of students want it.

1. Students are adults capable of choosing whether or not to smoke

2. Non-Smoking areas already provided

6. The student council's cleanup drive is a useful contribution to the appearance of the campus.

1. Gives students incentives to keep campus clean

2. Contributes Helps to increase student awareness of situation

2. Helps the school to save money - allows clean-up money to be used elsewhere.

7. Grocery stores ought to have an adequate supply of advertised specials or give rain checks for the purchase of the same item at the advertised price.

1. Inconvenience to consumer when product is unavailable.

2. False advertising

Name _____

Exercise 3. Giving Examples. Here are some main ideas and reasons that support them. For each underlined reason, make up an example that will illustrate the reason.

> *Main idea and reason:* There's no reason that mothers with small children shouldn't work; <u>most babysitters look after kids just as carefully as their mothers do.</u>

Example illustrating the reason:

When Katie Kennedy was taking care of the two Smith children last week, she noticed that Willie kept using his left hand even though she knew he was right-handed. She found an infected sliver in his right thumb, got a neighbor to watch the baby, and took Willie straight to the doctor. By the time Mrs. Smith got home from work, the sliver was out, the thumb was bandaged, the baby was back, and Willie was cheerfully sucking the lollipop the doctor had given him.

1. The city should install a traffic light at Fifth and Maple; <u>that intersection is dangerous.</u>

   _____

   _____

   _____

2. Bay Center High School needs a new principal; <u>the present principal is much too strict.</u>

   _____

   _____

   _____

3. Bay Center High School needs a new principal; <u>the present principal makes no effort to keep order in the halls.</u>

   _____

   _____

   _____

4. Every college student should have some practice in operating a word processor. <u>Such a skill makes it much easier to get a job.</u>

_____

_____

_____

5. Don't shop at Sawyer's Cutrate Clothing Store; <u>their jeans fall apart.</u>

_____

_____

_____

6. Students should not be given true/false tests. <u>Such tests don't measure whether students understand the material.</u>

_____

_____

_____

7. Putting out misleading information in campaign literature should be against the law. <u>Voters tend to believe what they see in print.</u>

_____

_____

_____

8. Charging everybody a flat rate for telephone service is unfair. <u>Some elderly people make only four or five calls a week.</u>

_____

_____

_____

Name _____

Exercise 4. Citing Statistics.   Here are some main ideas and reasons that support them. For each underlined reason (1) say what kind of statistics would support it, and (2) suggest how or where the statistics could be found. Be specific in your answer. Saying "Look in the library" is much too vague.

> *Example:* The speed limit should be more strictly enforced; <u>speed kills.</u>
>
> *Kind of statistics* — the number of fatal accidents caused last year by driving over the speed limit.
>
> *Source of statistics* — a phone call to the State Patrol office; or a search in the library for the report of the National Safety Council.

1. The city should install a traffic light at Fifth and Maple; <u>that intersection is dangerous.</u>

Kind ____# of car/ped. accidents_____

____# of injuries due to these accidents_____

Source ___Urban Police Dept statistics - local newspaper___

Police accident reports stats

MS. CO

2. The college needs a bigger library: <u>chairs are often unavailable.</u>

Kind _____

_____

Source _____

_____

3. Putting a want ad in the college newspaper is a good way to get a job. <u>Many local people advertise there for part-time help.</u>

Kind ____# of ads that constitute "many"_____

#of people securing jobs in such a manner____

Source ___Survey of Ad section of local newspapers___

phone call to local newspaper ad dept.

4. The government is not doing enough to fight poverty. <u>The number of people applying for welfare in this city has gone up since last year.</u>

Kind ~~phone call or visit to Dept of Soc. Services~~

# of applications, % over normal

Source phone call or visit to Dept of Soc. Services

_____

5. Something must be done about acid rain. <u>Fish are dying in great numbers.</u>

Kind Type and # of fish dying

comparisons showing #'s before increase

Source DNR ,

_____

6. Bay Center High School needs a new principal; <u>the present principal is much too strict.</u>

Kind Comparisons of rules w/other area schools

specific rules that are too strict

Source interviews w/other local principals, school

board reports- ie. other complaints

7. Every college student should have some practice in operating a word processor. <u>Such a skill makes it much easier to get a job.</u>

Kind _____

_____

Source _____

_____

Name _____

Exercise 5. Using Authorities. Here are some main ideas and reasons that support them. For each underlined reason, say what kind of authority would be most convincing. You don't have to give actual names, but be more specific than "government expert," and explain what background the authority you suggest has in the area.

> *Example:* The speed limit should be more strictly enforced; speed kills.
>
> *Authority might be:* An experienced state patrolman (*He's been at the scene of many accidents.*)
> Admissions officer of a hospital (*She's admitted a lot of accident victims.*)

1. Students should not be given true/false tests. Such tests don't measure whether students understand the material.

Authority _____

_____

Background _____

_____

2. Bay Center High School needs a new principal. The present principal makes no effort to keep order in the halls.

Authority _____

_____

Background _____

_____

3. The college needs a new library. Chairs are often unavailable.

Authority _____

_____

Background _____

_____

4. Every college student should have some practice in operating a word processor. Such a skill makes it much easier to get a job.

Authority _____

_____

Background _____

_____

5. Something must be done about acid rain. Fish are dying in great numbers.

Authority _____

_____

Background _____

_____

6. The Department of Human Services should be given more funding. Many elderly people are being abused by their families.

Authority _____

_____

Background _____

_____

7. Television stations ought to limit the advertisements shown on children's programs. Some advertised cereals contain too much sugar.

Authority _____

_____

Background _____

_____

Name _____

Exercise 6. Predicting Consequences. Here are some main ideas and reasons that support them. Each reason is followed by part of another statement beginning with *if*. Complete the underlined statements by predicting the consequences that might follow.

Example: The speed limit should be more strictly enforced; speed can kill. If you drive forty miles an hour on glare ice, . . .

Prediction: your tires can't possibly hold the road. The car will skid out of control and go into a spin. You won't be able to avoid oncoming traffic, and with luck you will kill only yourself, not the people in other cars who have been creeping along at a safe ten miles an hour.

1. Bay Center High School needs a new principal. The present principal is far too strict. If she continues to suspend students for running in the halls, . . .

_____

_____

_____

_____

_____

_____

2. Postage rates for ads should be raised. Everybody gets too much junk mail. If the post office charged as much for advertising as it does for real letters, . . .

_____

_____

_____

_____

_____

3. Something must be done about acid rain. Fish are dying in great numbers. <u>If something is not done soon,</u> . . .

_____

_____

_____

_____

_____

4. Granite City needs more emergency shelters. Numbers of homeless people are sleeping in cars or under newspapers in the city park. <u>If nothing is done,</u> . . .

_____

_____

_____

_____

_____

_____

5. The recreation bonds must pass. The roof of the youth center is in deplorable condition. <u>If that roof collapses under heavy snow,</u> . . .

_____

_____

_____

_____

_____

Name _____

Exercise 7. Dealing with the Other Side.   Here are some questions, the answers to which will be a statement of your beliefs. First, answer the question. Then instead of finding reasons to support your beliefs, find reasons—one for each belief—that other people might use to disagree. Finally, show briefly what's wrong with the other side's reasons.

> *Example:* Does the college need a new library?
>> *Your belief:* The college must have a new library.
>> *Other side:* The gym is in worse condition than the library, and there's not enough money for both.
>> *Your answer:* Games may be important, but the real point of college is in learning, in books.

1. Should people who are hopelessly ill have a right to die?

Your belief _____

_____

Other side _____

_____

Your answer _____

_____

_____

2. Should the state refuse welfare money to pay for abortions?

Your belief _____

_____

Other side _____

_____

Your answer _____

_____

_____

3. Should citizens who shoot people they think are going to rob them be charged with murder?

Your belief _____

_____

Other side _____

_____

Your answer _____

_____

_____

4. Would a flat income tax be fairer than a graduated tax with a great many deductions?

Your belief _____

_____

Other side _____

_____

Your answer _____

_____

_____

Name _____

Exercise 8. Introductions.   Are the following paragraphs satisfactory as introductions to short persuasive papers? What will the main idea of the paper be? How has the writer aroused your interest? If you think the paragraph is unsatisfactory, explain why.

1. I probably won't have everyone's agreement, and I know that I'm not really an expert, but it seems to me that the college really does need a new library.

_____

_____

_____

2. "Fire! Fire!" is one of the most frightening cries in the world. The wail of a siren splitting the midnight air makes everybody who hears it shudder in their beds. Watching red flames shoot out from the windows of an old building can be fascinating, but it's horrifying, too. You can't help but wonder whether somebody is still in that building or whether there might be kittens forgotten in the basement.

_____

_____

_____

3. Almost any day you can see students trying to study in the snack bar. You can see them leaning against the walls in the hall, holding an open book. They sit on the steps taking notes. They have to study in these awkward places because all the chairs in the library are full. There's no question about it. We need a bigger library.

_____

_____

_____

4. The purpose of my paper is to show that funding for hot school lunches should be increased. That's about the only decent meal some of these children ever get.

_____

_____

_____

5. Once there was a little boy named Bobby. When Bobby was four years old he wanted a doll for Christmas so he could sing it to sleep and give it a bottle. But they gave him a toy pistol instead because he was a boy. Bobby's little sister Becky wanted a tool set. She liked to hammer nails and take screws out of things. But they gave Becky the doll because she was a girl. After a while Bobby grew up and got married, and his wife got angry with him because he wouldn't help with the baby. Becky grew up, too, and hollered for help every time she wanted to hang a picture. Both of them had unhappy marriages. Could the problems have started with that Christmas so long ago?

_____

_____

_____

6. There are at least a dozen reasons for voting for Martha Ebert for city treasurer, but I'm only going to talk about the three most important reasons.

_____

_____

_____

Name _____

Exercise 9. Conclusions. Read the following conclusions to short persuasive papers. If you think the conclusion is satisfactory, tell what the main idea has been and how the conclusion makes the paper sound finished. If you think the conclusion is unsatisfactory, explain why.

1. In this paper I have tried hard to show that the college really does need a new library.

_____

_____

_____

2. So the next time you hear the fire siren screaming in the night, just pull the blankets over your head and go back to sleep with the assurance that everything is being taken care of.

_____

_____

_____

3. If we want to keep the snack bar for snacking, the halls for a passageway, the steps for an entrance, we'll have to provide better places to study. A bigger library is the best way to do it.

_____

_____

_____

4. Unless we want millions of children to go hungry, to concentrate on their empty stomachs instead of their lessons, we must provide a free hot lunch program in the schools.

_____

_____

_____

5. Bobby didn't get his doll and Becky didn't get her tool set. They both learned that some things are right for boys and some things right for girls, and when they grew up they didn't forget that lesson.

_____

_____

_____

6. What children learn when they are very small, without anybody ever really putting it into words, stays with them all their lives. If parents want their children to grow up as fair-minded and well-adjusted individuals, they must stop teaching them stereotyped sex roles. And they can't start too early.

_____

_____

_____

7. To sum it all up, what I want to say is "Vote for Martha Ebert."

_____

_____

_____

8. Martha Ebert is qualified, she's experienced, and she's dependable. When you go to the polls on Tuesday, mark your ballot "Martha Ebert for treasurer."

_____

_____

_____

Name _____

Exercise 10. Subjects and Verbs.   Write a quiz on the agreement of subjects and verbs to be given to another student (or students) in your class. Write at least eight sentences, with only some of them containing mistakes that many readers would object to. Prepare an answer key for your quiz on a separate sheet of paper. After the other student or students have taken the quiz, see whether they agree with the key you have made. If you can't agree, get help from the teacher.

> *Example:*   The women in the class, with the exception of one woman, thinks men should learn to change diapers.
>
> *Your answer:* "Women" is the subject, not "woman," so the verb should be "think."

1. _____

_____

2. _____

_____

3. _____

_____

4. _____

_____

5. _____

_____

6. _____

_____

7. _____

_____

8. _____

_____

Name _____

Exercise 11. Finding a Topic for a Persuasion Paper.   Make a list of things that make you angry:

_____

_____

_____

_____

_____

_____

_____

_____

Make a list of changes you'd like to see made at the college:

_____

_____

_____

_____

_____

_____

_____

_____

Make a list of things that would improve your neighborhood or town:

_____

_____

_____

_____

_____

_____

_____

_____

Make a list of other things you strongly believe:

_____

_____

_____

_____

_____

_____

_____

_____

_____

Name _____

Exercise 12. Writing Main Idea Sentences.   Which of the possible topics you have listed in Exercise 11 are broad enough to interest readers? Which are narrow enough that you could cover them in a short paper? Pick two or three of those topics and ask questions beginning with "Should . . . ?" Then answer the question. The answer might be a good main idea sentence for a paper.

Possible topic _____

Question _____

_____

Answer _____

_____

_____

Possible topic _____

Question _____

_____

Answer _____

_____

_____

Possible topic _____

Question _____

_____

Answer _____

_____

Exercise 13. Finding Reasons and Supporting Them.   Pick one of the main idea sentences you wrote in Exercise 12 and list reasons to support your belief. For each reason, find one kind of support that would help to convince readers.

Main idea _____

_____

_____

Reason _____

_____

Support _____

_____

Reason _____

_____

Support _____

_____

Reason _____

_____

Support _____

_____

Why would anybody disagree with you? _____

_____

Why are they mistaken? _____

_____

Exercise 14. Writing a First Draft.   Write a draft of the paper you planned in Exercise 13. Put it away for a day or two and then reread it to see where you can make it more convincing. Show it to other students, if you like, and get their comments.

Exercise 15. Writing the Paper.   Write a finished version of the paper you've been working on. Then go back over it, making sure you can answer yes to all the questions on this check list:

Check List for Content

1. Does your introduction state your main idea clearly? _____

2. Have you done something to arouse the interest of your readers? _____

3. Have you given reasons for your belief? _____

4. Are the reasons arranged in the best order? _____

5. Have you given some support for each reason—examples, statistics, authority, or consequences? _____

6. Have you dealt with the other side? _____

7. Does your conclusion make your paper sound finished? _____

8. Does the conclusion restate your main idea or remind readers of what it was? _____

Exercise 16. The Final Step.   Read through your paper one more time, this time tending to the manners of your writing. Can you answer yes to all the questions on this check list?

Check List for Editing

1. Have you made sure all your sentences really are sentences? _____

2. Have you checked the important symbols of sentence punctuation—periods, commas, question marks? _____

3. Have you used quotation marks around all your direct quotations but not around indirect quotations? _____

4. Have you made sure your subjects and verbs agree? _____

5. Have you checked your spelling? _____

6. Have you said where your statistics come from? _____

7. Have you identified your authorities and made it clear why they know
   what they're talking about?   _____

8. Have you given a separate paragraph to each of your main reasons?   _____

Exercise 17. Introductions and Conclusions.   Write just the introduction and conclusion for another paper of persuasion. Exchange these with another student in the
class. Does the other student agree that the two hang together? Discuss how the introductions and conclusions might be improved.

Exercise 18. A Letter to the Editor.   Write a letter to the editor of either the college
newspaper or a local paper, suggesting some change you think should be made or
some policy you disagree with. Bring your letter to class and, if the other students
think you have made a convincing case, send the letter to the paper.

Chapter 10

Fair Persuasion

The world is full of persuasive writing. Some of it is open and aboveboard; some of it hides behind explanations and reports. When you think of persuasive writing, you probably think first of ad writers, for none of us can escape them. Ads are all around us. The radio shrieks at us about newer, bigger, better products. Television issues frank warnings about household germs and offensive body odors. Beautiful people in magazine ads beckon to us from beautiful cars parked on beautifully landscaped driveways in front of beautiful houses. Newspapers squeeze in a dribble or two of what happened around the world between the furniture closeouts and the grocery specials. Our mailboxes are jammed with circulars offering everything from life insurance to cemetery plots.

But ad writers are not the only people with a sales pitch. Politicians have something to sell, too. Millions a year are spent to persuade you that Senator John S. Goodsell is a plain, earnest farm boy who keeps a Bible on his desk and carries your particular interest engraved on the gold of his 100 percent patriotic heart. He persuades groups of laborers that he believes unions were made in heaven, and he persuades a group of business tycoons that he believes unions were definitely made somewhere else. In the Senate he tries to persuade his colleagues that the multimillion-dollar project for an earthworm sanctuary in his state will help to balance the budget, increase national prestige, and preserve a priceless environmental heritage.

Many other people try to persuade us, too. The public relations woman proclaims the merits of her organization, the president of the United Good Givers Association pleads for help in meeting the year's goal, the eight-year-old Girl Scout with the appealing smile coaxes you to buy her cookies. Indeed, so many people are trying to persuade us so much of the time that it's hard to think of anybody who isn't.

When you try to get other people to agree with you, and try to do it honestly, you give reasons for your opinion and support your reasons. It would seem, then, that when you want to act rationally rather than emotionally, you could expect supported reasons from people who are trying to make you agree with them. But how often do you get reasons? And when you do get them, how dependable are they?

Use Lovely Lady Facial Tissues.
It's the choice of television stars.

This advertisement, of course, is an attempt to persuade you to buy these facial tissues—the company knows you will have to buy them before you use them. The main idea sentence is, "Use Lovely Lady Tissues." The reason given to support the main idea is, "It's the choice of television stars." The name and claim suggest three things: that you are indeed a lovely lady and these tissues fit your personality; that if you use these tissues, you will be transformed into loveliness; and, moreover, that you will deserve to be a television star, whether or not you actually get to be one. The notion—an implied prediction—doesn't seem very sound when we state it plainly, but the advertisers don't expect you to state it plainly. They just want you to associate the glamour of television stars with the use of their tissues.

But look at what has been left out. The implication is that all television stars use it, but it only takes two to make a plural. The advertisers are hinting that a survey has been made, but if so, they have concealed the statistics. Nor do you know why the stars use these tissues. Maybe the Lovely Lady Tissue Company gave them a year's supply, and they hate to waste it. Certainly you are not told how the tissues are used. Maybe the stars use a handful of tissues to sop up their spilled coffee or wipe their dog's muddy paws. If you assume, as the advertisers hope you will, that the stars use the tissues on their faces, thus creating their dazzling complexions, you are being misled by a faulty cause-and-effect relationship.

And who is a television star anyway? The Cookie Monster and Lassie have both been television stars in their time, but surely the advertisers don't want you to think about them. Tansy Ragwort, who had a two-minute part in a soap opera two years ago, is called a star by her press agent. The language the advertisers are using is vague and indefinite.

But even if the stars were Joan Collins, Diahann Carroll, or Barbara Walters, would the reason be much stronger? You would ask a banker about a loan, a jockey for a racing tip, Julia Child about a recipe. They are experts on these matters. But what makes stars authorities on facial tissues? Do they blow their noses more than ordinary people? True, they wipe thick layers of make-up off their faces, but they do that with towels. In the matter of choosing a facial tissue, you are as much an expert as a television star. You have a nose, and a harsh tissue will not scratch it less, no matter how many television personalities might use the same brand of tissue.

You have a right to demand sound reasons from people who are trying to persuade you.

Slanted Words

The facial tissue advertisement relies entirely on people's willingness to respond emotionally to pleasant words. No advertiser would say, "With this paper you can wipe the grime off your face in a few hurried swipes. And when you're done fussing with yourself, you can just dump the paper in the garbage can." Instead, the advertiser says, "Lovely Lady Facial Tissue restores morning radiance. Its soft caress smooths away daytime cares. And when you are once again your fresh and lovely self, the tissue is disposable." *Radiance, soft, caress, smooth, fresh,* and *lovely* are all purr words that tend to put readers in a good mood, to soften them into buying the tissues.

People trying to sell a product are not the only ones who rely on emotional appeals; people trying to sell an idea often use the same technique. "These bleeding-heart sob-sisters want hardened criminals pampered and petted just because they're under eighteen." *Bleeding-heart, sob-sisters, hardened criminals, pampered,* and *petted* are all snarl words that tend to put readers in a bad mood, to harden them into agreeing that juvenile offenders should be tried as adults.

Persuasion that relies on emotion and **slanted words** is common, and it can be deceptive. When you wrote objective reports, you had some practice in avoiding slanted words. When you tried persuasive writing, you probably deliberately used a few slanted words in your introduction as a way of arousing interest. And it may seem to you that advertisers are just as entitled to use purr words and law-and-order supporters to use snarl words as you are to use colorful language in your examples. All of you are using vivid language for the same purpose: to create a picture in the minds of readers. But an honest argument does not stop with the picture; it goes on to give sound, supported reasons. Unfair persuasion often stops with the slanted words and colorful language. Using definite, specific language is a good thing, and there's nothing wrong with colorful words in the right place. You can be sure it is the right place by asking two questions:

> *Are the vivid words used to make the meaning clearer or just to get readers to purr or snarl?*
> *Is the appeal to your emotions or to your mind?*

Glittering Generalities

Glittering generalities are such sweet and general statements that we feel bound to agree—unless we realize they have no specific meaning. Glittering generalities slant by what they don't say. They are used by people who want to avoid definite statements.

For example, Senator Goodsell may leave more out of his campaign speeches than he puts in. The senator says he is for peace, prosperity, and patriotism. He says he believes in jobs and justice. Almost everybody will agree with these sentiments. Who is in favor of war, depressions, and treason? Who believes in unemployment and injustice? The senator is saying, in effect, that he is in favor of good things and against bad things, and since we too support good and oppose evil, we should vote for him. The senator hopes his listeners will react emotionally without stopping to ask whether the senator's more specific ideas of what is good agree with their own.

To avoid being taken in by such sweet generalities, you must insist on more specific information. In answer to the question, "Will you vote to extend unemployment benefits?" (a definite question) the senator says:

> That bill deserves the serious consideration of all thoughtful people. I believe in the old American values—honest work and a spirit of independence. And I have a deep sympathy for the plight of the unfortunate among us. I know what it is to be poor. My father worked hard for the bread we ate, and sometimes it was just bread. I cannot bear to think of a child going hungry. I know what it feels like. Unemployment is indeed a dreadful thing.

Do you know how the senator will vote? How can you tell? If you are in favor of extending the unemployment benefits, you may decide that the senator also favors the extension—after all, he's sorry for the unfortunate, and he doesn't like thinking about hungry children. But if you are against the extension, you could be excused for thinking the senator is against it too—after all, he thinks people should work hard, like his father, and be too independent to accept money they haven't earned. Unless you listen carefully, you may respond to these soothing evasions in the same way people respond to the ad writer's words, with emotion, not reason.

If you stubbornly insist, as you should, that the senator give a more definite answer, he may spoon out the sugar-coating of slanted words. Even though he plans to vote against the extension, he will not say, "Let those lazy good-for-nothing bums go out and get a job." He probably won't even say, "I think I'll vote against the bill." Instead, depending on how he sizes up his audience, he may say "The burden of taxation must be kept off the backs of American workers," or "All our citizens are entitled to the dignity that comes from self-reliance."

The ad writer gives you sugared words. Politicians often give you sugared words and sugared generalities. Both of them are appealing to you emotionally rather than rationally. Don't be persuaded until you get some supported reasons. What *examples* can the senator offer? What *statistical support* can he produce? Can he back up his stand by quoting *authorities* on unemployment and hungry children? What *predictions* is he making about the effect of the bill? If you don't want to be deceived, you must learn to tell the difference between honest and dishonest support. You can make a beginning toward telling the difference by asking:

> *Are the statements clear and definite or are they meaningless pleasantries designed to soothe people?*

Facts, Inferences, and Judgments

If you do force Senator Goodsell to give a more definite answer, you need to know what kind of statement he's making. Most statements made about the present or the past can be classified as *facts, inferences,* or *judgments.* (Statements made about the future are always predictions of one kind or another.) When you were writing objective reports, you learned to distinguish between *factual statements* (those that can be checked) and *opinion statements* (those that express the speaker's judgment). In between the extremes of fact and opinion are **inferences** — statements about what we think is or isn't so, did or didn't happen, based on some facts we do know. Sometimes inferences are so reliable that we can almost consider them factual statements. Sometimes they are so unreliable that they can lead us wildly astray.

We might begin with the old saying, "Where there's smoke, there's fire," to see how these three kinds of statements work. "Hey, the Christmas tree's on fire!" is, of course, a factual statement. You can check it for accuracy before you call the fire department. You can go into the living room and see. But if someone says, "There's smoke in the living room. The Christmas tree must be on fire!" the first half is a factual statement, the second half an inference. If there is a great deal of smoke and nothing else in the living room that will burn very easily, and if we agree that smoke is always a sign of fire, the inference is probably sound. At least, it's dependable enough so that you'd better call the fire department without looking to see whether it's the tree or the curtains.

"Abner smokes a pipe; he started the fire" is another inference, but this one is a good deal less reliable. It does relate to some facts. Abner is a pipe smoker. Abner was in the living room for an hour. And the Christmas tree did catch fire. Possibly Abner did leave a smoldering pipe too close to the dried-out fir branches, but it's also possible that the Christmas tree was too close to the fireplace, that little Gracie has been playing with matches, that the Christmas tree lights overheated. If the whole living room is destroyed, any decision as to how the fire started will remain an inference, although the fire marshall's inference, that faulty wiring was the culprit, will probably be the most reliable, especially if he discovers that the electric wiring behind the wall has fused. The statement that Abner has always been careless would, of course, be a judgment.

Because smoke and fire are physical things, we're on safer ground in dealing with them than we are when the old saying is applied to people's behavior. Sometimes you hear people say, "Where there's smoke, there's fire," when they're not talking about combustion at all. The neighbors have been gossiping about Rosita. She has an expensive new jogging outfit. She bought her mother the fanciest food processor on the market. She traded in her old VW for a sleek new sports car. Rosita is a cashier in the local bank. "She must be taking money out of the till," says Mrs. Grundy. "No other way she could be spending so much," says Mr. Busybody, whose brother manages the bank. "Where there's smoke, there's fire," says the brother and finds an excuse to fire Rosita because it's a fact that the bank's books were fifty dollars out of balance last Tuesday. The inference (that Rosita is taking the bank's money) was not investigated. The judgment (that Rosita is a thief) was based on the inference.

The kind of judgment (guilty or not guilty) that lawyers call circumstantial evidence is always based on inferences. Just after the drugstore has been robbed, Alfie Brown is seen running down the street as fast as he can go. Later Alfie is found to have a new transistor radio exactly like the one missing from the drugstore. Furthermore, the druggist, who was in the back room at the time, heard the thief coughing, and Alfie has a cold. The running, the radio, and the unidentified cough are the facts. That Alfie robbed the store is the inference based on those facts. Unless Alfie can show a receipt for the radio, the police may decide that the inference is reliable enough to justify an arrest.

There's nothing wrong with making inferences. We couldn't live or think without them. Inferences get us into trouble when we forget they are not facts, and when we forget to ask whether they are probable or merely possible. When people try to persuade us, it's important to know whether we're being given facts, inferences, or judgments, and to ask what's behind the judgments that are being made.

Facts *are statements that can be verified; they should be checked for accuracy.*

Inferences *are statements made about what isn't known based on what is known; they should be checked carefully against the known facts.*

Judgments *are statements about good or bad, desirable or undesirable, guilty or not guilty; they should be recognized as opinion and checked against the facts or inferences on which they are based.*

Honest Examples

Examples, because they have to be specific, are almost always factual statements. Like any other factual statements, they should be checked for accuracy. But even if they are accurate, they may not be **honest examples**. They can be misleading or unfair in other ways. Pushed into a corner, Senator Goodsell offers Josh Slacker as an unemployed person who doesn't deserve an extension of benefits. Josh has refused two jobs because he doesn't like working at night. His wife brings home a good paycheck from her secure position in the auditor's office. And their one child, far from being hungry, has a brand new bicycle. The senator says something about "the public trough." But this slanted and indirect reference to pigs gobbling up the public funds makes no mention of the five hundred people laid off when the paper mill shut down a year ago, people who have no chance at other jobs because there's no other large industry in the area. All the senator's facts about Josh Slacker are accurate, but Slacker is not representative of the five hundred other people in town who have not refused jobs, whose children don't have new shoes, much less new bicycles. The senator is misleading you when he uses such an unfair example.

On the other hand, Glenda Smith may be a fair example of a working wife left to do all the housework while her husband lounges in front of the TV. If you know several families in similar situations, and if you believe your readers will also know some, Glenda Smith is probably representative enough to be a fair example.

As you discovered when you wrote definitions of abstract terms, some words are so general and so subjective that they almost always require examples. The statement "John Smith is brave" needs an example to make clear what is meant by bravery. Does it mean that John Smith is completely without fear in all situations? Or does it mean that he is so eaten up by fear of spiders that removing a daddy-longlegs from the baby's crib showed considerable courage? When people talk about a *great revival of religion,* do they mean that more people are attending church every Sunday? That more people are giving money to charity and working toward peace? That more people are trying to force their religious views on everybody else? Only representative examples, carefully chosen, can make the meaning clear.

Sometimes the meaning of the word being used is clear enough, but the full force of what the word represents cannot be fully felt without a specific example. Even though most people understand what *explosion* means, the bare statement "Explosion damages Philadelphia neighborhood" will not disturb people nearly as much as the description of block after block in ruins, with dazed families staring at the ruins of what used to be comfortable houses. Statements such as "Four hundred killed in weekend traffic accidents" take on more reality with just one broken body, one glimpse of bloody pavement, and one set of grief-shocked relatives. Notice that these examples use definite, specific words *(ruins, dazed, broken, bloody)* that help us see a picture rather than words that stir our emotions vaguely *(American values, dignity, self-reliance).* If we respond to examples with sympathy or horror, it's because the language is vivid, not sugared. In dealing with examples, you need to ask:

Are the examples honestly representative of the generalizations they illustrate?

Do the examples make the meaning clearer or the picture more vivid?

Honest Statistics

Examples are honestly used when they lead to a clearer understanding or a more vivid realization, but they are dishonestly used when they tempt people to form a generalization based on only one example or one instance. It is unfair to argue that because one man in town doesn't want to take a night job, all the unemployed have refused chances to work. It is also unfair to say that because one commercial plane operated by Fairway Airways has crashed, everybody who buys a ticket from Fairway is in mortal danger.

Before you can make a reliable general statement, you must have enough facts to generalize about. One way of getting enough facts is to take a survey. Suppose you want to know how many students in your school have jobs. It is glaringly obvious that you can't say, "I work. Therefore, all other students probably work, too." It is equally obvious that you don't have time to ask all the students in school whether they are employed unless you drop all your classes and quit your own job. But you can take a survey.

Your aim is to come up with **reliable statistics**. But your statistics will not be very reliable if you question only the people in the coffee shop and then say, "Four of the forty people in the coffee shop at three o'clock Thursday afternoon said they have jobs. Therefore only 10 percent of the student body work." If your school has a student body of five thousand, a sample of forty students is not enough. Furthermore, the students in the coffee shop may not be representative of the whole student body.

Maybe at three o'clock most of the workers are at work. If you ask fifty people in the library at eight o'clock on Friday morning, 90 percent may say they have jobs.

A hundred out of five thousand might be a large enough sample, but if you ask only humanities students, you will not have a representative group. Maybe humanities students are less likely to be working than technical students. Your statistics will not be reliable unless you have used *enough examples* and unless those examples represent *a fair cross section* of all the students in school. If you ask a hundred students, if you make sure that they represent every department, and if you ask on more than one day and at different hours during the day, you may come up with a pretty honest estimate of the number of employed students.

Suppose your estimate shows that 33 percent of the student body work. When you present your statistics, be careful not to say "Many students work," or "A large number of students work," or "The average student works," or even just "Some students work." All these statements interpret the facts. One person's *many* is another person's *some*. Is thirty-three out of a hundred *many* or *some* or *a few*? And who is the *average student*? Remember that *average* and *typical*, like *good* or *bad*, *better* or *worse*, are opinion words. You are not justified in saying anything except "A survey of a hundred students shows that approximately 33 percent of the students on this campus work."

If your survey also deals with how much students work—whether they work full- or part-time—and if you discover that twenty-three of those thirty-three students work only an hour a day whereas the other ten hold full-time jobs and work eight hours a day, you may be tempted to report that students work for an average of about three hours a day. You have figured it out mathematically:

$$
\begin{array}{rcl}
\text{10 students at 8 hours} & = & 80 \text{ hours} \\
\text{23 students at 1 hour} & = & \underline{23 \text{ hours}} \\
 & & 103 \text{ hours}
\end{array}
$$

103 hours divided by 33 students = 3 hours and 4 minutes a day

It's plain, however, that no student actually works three hours a day, and the situation of the majority, who work only an hour a day, is quite different from the situation of those ten who try to combine a full-time job with full-time college attendance. People who know that "average" can be a deceptive word ought to ask how you arrived at that figure. Did you add all the hours together and divide by the number of people? That's called the *mean*. Did you line up all the responses in order, from most to fewest hours, and use the number that appeared in the middle of the list? That's another kind of average, called the *median*. Or did you give the number of hours that appeared most frequently? That's still another kind of average, the *mode*. Unless you're deliberately trying to deceive, you'll have to provide the actual figures: twenty-three students work an hour a day, ten students work eight hours a day.

Perhaps you added a third question to the survey and asked whether those hundred people thought working interfered with studying. Twenty-five said no, twenty-five said yes, and fifty were undecided. If the twenty-five who said no are not working, their answers are just guesswork. And even though you want to use your statistics to demonstrate that working does not interfere with studying, it's not fair to report that 75 percent of the people interviewed are not sure whether there is any connection between working and studying. People who realize that percentages can deceive are likely to ask "What do you mean by 'not sure'? Didn't anybody have a definite answer?"

When figures are used to prove a point, when someone has something to gain from the results of a survey, people should look at those statistics very closely. When Senator Goodsell hires pollsters to test his popularity, the pollsters' statistics may be open to some suspicion. His opponent has probably hired other pollsters to test her popularity, and their results may be quite different. In each case, the survey taker has a stake in the outcome, and sensible people will be cautious about believing the figures.

What's true for surveys is also true for statistical reports, whether they refer to experiments, investigations, or simple counting, but that's no reason to suspect all statistics. Science could not progress without using statistics. It was mathematical calculations that sent men into space. But good scientists are careful not to let their figures mislead either themselves or other scientists. They are careful to make sure that the statistics are honestly and accurately reported. Questions that can help you decide whether or not statistics are dependable are:

> *Is the sample big enough?*
> *Is the sample representative of the whole group?*
> *Are the results reported in specific, objective language with nothing left out?*
> *Does the person providing the statistics have anything to gain from the results?*

Honest Use of Authorities

Mentioning authorities who agree with you is another acceptable way of supporting reasons. But authorities can be misused, too. Using the name of a famous person who is expert in one field to give evidence for something in another field may be a misuse of authority. If you are looking for an expert on British policy during and just after World War II, you could hardly do better than Winston Churchill. But if you are looking for an expert on American foreign policy in the seventies, the role of women in society, or what to do with a colicky baby, it would not be fair to use Churchill, even though nearly everybody recognizes and respects his name.

If you need an expert on American foreign policy in the seventies, you can quote Henry Kissinger. If you're talking about women in politics, you can quote Geraldine Ferraro. If you're dealing with child care, you can quote Benjamin Spock. All these people are experts in these fields, and repeating what they say about foreign policy, women's political roles, and child raising is a perfectly **honest use of authority**, even though there may be other authorities who might disagree with what Kissinger, Ferraro, and Spock have to say.

It is, of course, possible for a person to be an expert in more than one field.

Ferraro knows a great deal about women in politics, but she also knows a lot about the damage publicity can do to private lives. Dr. Spock's books have given comfort to worried parents for more than a generation, but he has also had considerable experience in the antiwar movement. He's something of an expert there, too.

But expertise in more than one field is the exception rather than the rule. Usually, when authorities are quoted on subjects out of their main fields, the writer or speaker is trying to grab some of the glory associated with their names and graft it onto whatever is being discussed. We are urged to deposit our money in the Benjamin Franklin High-Interest Savings Bank, buy our used cars from the Abraham Lincoln Pre-Owned Car Emporium, or purchase our candy from the Martha Washington chain. We are told that one soft drink is better than another because the world-famous tennis champion says so. In each case, we can be fairly sure that authority is being misused. Franklin, Lincoln, and Martha Washington were dead for decades before these businesses were ever established. The business owners are simply taking advantage of Franklin's reputation for thrift, Lincoln's reputation for honesty, and Martha Washington's prestige as the first First Lady. The tennis champion knows about rackets, but no more about what quenches thirst than you do.

Neither is the imaginary *everybody* acceptable as authority. The case becomes no stronger if we say "Everybody knows that!" A moment's thought or a quick survey will show that *everybody* is an exaggeration. But even if a survey shows that 99.4 percent of the population believe they know it, the survey has not proved that it's necessarily so. Large numbers of people have supported actions we now think wrong: the Salem witch trials, the Nazi concentration camps, or the McCarthy Communist hunts of the fifties, for instance. Group hysteria is group hysteria, not rational thinking.

"Everybody says so" is not good authority, and neither is "I heard it on television" or "I read it somewhere." Television programs range from *M*A*S*H* to *Sesame Street,* from people shows to paid propaganda, and their purpose is often to entertain rather than to inform. Reading is a valuable habit, but not everybody who writes and gets published is a trustworthy authority. If a television or newspaper report begins, "An unidentified source . . ." or "A source close to the governor . . . ," careful people will be suspicious. Both the janitor and the cleaning woman may be "close" to the governor, but their guesses as to whether the governor will sign the tax bill are not much better than yours.

What happened in the past is not always good authority, either. "It's always been that way; why change now?" or "The founders of this country didn't say that" are not good reasons for being against a proposal made in quite different times, under quite different circumstances. People who say, "We don't need a welfare program. A hundred years ago people raised enough vegetables to feed their families. Why can't unemployed people do that today?" are not using acceptable authority. Conditions have changed in a hundred years. More people live in cities, and window boxes are not big enough to raise much corn. People who use the past as authority are often demonstrating nostalgia for a simpler life rather than displaying rational thought.

> *To decide whether authority is being honestly used, you can ask*
> *Are the authorities expert on the subject?*
> *Have they anything to gain by what they say?*

Honest Predictions

Predicting consequences is another frequent and acceptable method of supporting reasons, but **predictions**, even more than examples, statistics, and authorities, can be used unfairly. Attempts to foresee the future are always risky, but some can be a good deal more reliable than others. Suppose you say, "If I put a kettle of water on the stove and turn the burner on high, the water will boil." Almost everybody will accept this prediction. Suppose you say, "If I come to class every day and smile sweetly at the teacher, I will pass the course." Most people will want to ask a few questions. Suppose you say, "If we reelect Senator Goodsell, everybody in the country will get a good job, but if we elect Alice James, half the country will be unemployed." At this prediction, everybody should protest loudly.

Predictions that deal with the physical world are usually fairly safe:

Water will boil at 212 degrees Fahrenheit at sea level.

On January 28, 1990, sunrise in Kansas City will be at 7:25 A.M. central standard time.

Low tide in Chesapeake Bay tomorrow will be at 8:33 P.M.

Predictions that deal with the behavior of people are much less safe:

The senator's temper will boil if you mention extending unemployment benefits.

My uncle will rise from bed tomorrow at 7:25 A.M. central standard time.

My automotive teacher will sneeze at 8:33 P.M. tomorrow.

The senator may change his mind about the bill. Your uncle may oversleep. Your teacher may have recovered from the allergy that caused the sneezing.

Even so, if you are well acquainted with the habits of both your uncle and your automotive teacher, those guesses may be fairly dependable. If you are predicting something simple about somebody you know well, what you say may be accurate. But when you move to new situations and try to predict the results of something you have never experienced before, then your predictions become less reliable. When you try guessing about complex problems, in situations where a variety of causes might affect the results, your guesses may become wildly unreliable.

Predictions based on completely accurate statistics can also be misleading. Mark Twain once "proved" that by the year 2600 the lower Mississippi would be less than two miles long. He did it by beginning with some reliable figures showing how much shorter the river had become in the last 175 years and then extending those figures into the future. Mark Twain, who was deliberately making a joke, pretended that exactly the same process would continue to happen every year in the future. But people who are not trying to be funny can make the same kind of inaccurate predictions. Because there was such a great increase in the number of babies born just after World War II, many school districts thought the number of schoolchildren would continue to grow larger forever, and so they built a lot of new schools. Now some of those schools are standing empty or being torn down. Using the same kind of statistics and predictions, it would be possible to show that if the number of kindergarten children has decreased by 10 percent in the past ten years, a hundred years from now there will be no five-year-olds at all. Barring a nuclear holocaust, this prediction is obvious nonsense, but it can be pretty convincing if we extend it for only thirty years. Using what happened in the past to show what might happen in the future can sometimes be helpful, but only if we remember that conditions in the future are never likely to be quite the same as they were in the past.

Before you say "If we do *this, that* will happen" or "Because it's like this now, it will always be like this," remember:

Predictions dealing with the physical world are usually safe.

Predictions dealing with people you know well may be fairly safe.

Predictions dealing with new situations and new experiences are often not safe at all.

Post Hoc Thinking

Just as fair persuasion avoids simple-minded predictions about future events, so it avoids oversimplified explanations of what happened in the past. When you practiced writing causal analysis, you had some experience in how to tell whether one thing caused another. You discovered that most important human events have more than one simple cause. The old nursery jingle that begins, "Because of a nail, a shoe was lost, because of a shoe, . . ." makes good children's literature but not very good reasoning. No reliable historian would say that the assassination of Archduke Ferdinand was the *only* cause of World War I. No reliable psychiatrist would say that watching a lot of violence on television was the *only* reason fourteen-year-old Sammy Evans conked his grandfather with a beer bottle. Many events, in fact, have causes so deeply buried in the past that we can never be entirely sure what they were.

It's always tempting to think that because two events are related in time—first this thing happened, then that—the first thing caused the second. This temptation is behind most of the superstitions from which we never quite free ourselves, even though we know better. Once, probably, somebody walking under a ladder got hit with a bucket of paint, and it was easy to think the ladder had something to do with bad luck. Once, probably, somebody found a penny just after picking up a pin; it was equally easy to believe that the pin had caused good luck.

The faulty cause-and-effect relationships that give rise to superstitions are silly but harmless. Probably nobody was ever hurt by knocking on wood or refusing a room on the thirteenth floor of a hotel. But we can be harmed, or at least misled, if we fall for more serious examples of such bad reasoning. If somebody tells you that in September the teachers got a raise and in November the reading scores went down, so paying teachers more causes them to work less hard, you're justified in saying, "Wait a minute. That's a *post hoc* **fallacy**. There's no connection between the salaries and the scores." *Post hoc, ergo propter hoc* is a Latin phrase that means, "After this, therefore because of this." *Fallacy* simply means a mistake in reasoning. Remember:

> *Just because one thing happened before another doesn't mean that the first thing caused the second.*

False Analogies

Sometimes when you're puzzled by complex situations, you may try to simplify them by comparing the unknown to the known. Such comparisons can be dangerous if the differences are more important than the likenesses. A comparison can be fairly made only when the things being compared are alike in significant ways and when the differences have nothing to do with the comparison. It's probably fair to compare conditions at one college with conditions at another college if the two schools have the same kinds of students and teach the same kinds of courses in about the same way. It's probably fair to compare the results of fluoridation in two cities of about the same size in about the same location.

But if the people who are against fluoridation go on to compare the effects of swallowing fluoride with the effects of swallowing arsenic, they are using a **false analogy**. An analogy is unfair when it begins with things that are similar and then goes on to pretend that they are identical. It's true that both fluoride and arsenic (and table salt and aspirin and a good many other things we regularly put into ourselves) are deadly poisons when taken in large quantities. But medical authorities generally agree that fluoride in small quantities in drinking water is good for teeth, while even very small quantities of arsenic do no one any good. The differences are more important than the likenesses.

Let's examine another analogy. A year or so ago one politician, in commenting on the tobacco subsidy, said that if the secretary "continues to insist that tobacco kneel down and die at the altar of program consistency, then he is destined to become the Jim Jones cult figure of American agriculture." Is "program consistency" much like a religious altar? Can anybody force an industry to "worship" a proposal? And is an opponent of tobacco subsidies much like the cult figure who convinced nine hundred of his followers to commit mass suicide a few years ago?

Another politician, who favored extending more credit to agriculture, said that people who were against loans to farmers were "practicing a Marie Antoinette economics that is totally nonproductive." It's true that when Marie Antoinette was told that the citizens of Paris had no bread, she is supposed to have said, "Let them eat cake." That remark, of course, did not produce food. It's also true that farmers who can't afford seed will not be able to raise wheat. The French queen, however, spoke out of ignorance, just before the bloody revolution in which she lost her head. Those who oppose more farm credit speak from a concern over the federal deficit, and it seems unlikely that American farmers will rise up and guillotine members of Congress who vote against the subsidies. The two situations are different in important ways.

Analogies, like examples, are fairly used when they make a situation more vivid without distorting it or when they make meaning clearer. A professor who is trying to explain sound waves to a general physics class might compare sound waves to ocean waves. This analogy between something unfamiliar and something familiar is perfectly fair. It helps students form a picture in their minds of something they cannot see. It's also fair because the professor is pointing out that the two wave actions are similar but not identical. No sane person would carry the analogy so far as to suppose that a very loud noise might get people salty and wet.

In deciding whether analogies are fairly used, you need to ask two questions:

Are the things being compared alike in significant ways?
Do the differences have anything significant to do with the comparison?

Honest Reasoning

All the thinking we do can be roughly divided into two kinds: induction and deduction. **Inductive reasoning** means starting with specific things and making a generalization based on them. **Deductive reasoning** means starting with a general statement or belief and applying it to a specific thing or situation.

Usually these two processes of thought are so closely related and occur so fast that we aren't aware of how our thinking works. Tommy is late coming home from school, and Tommy's worried mother thinks to herself, "Something terrible must have happened!" Her thoughts, which she doesn't stop to analyze, go something like this:

> Tommy came home on time on Monday, Tuesday, Wednesday, and Thursday *(specific events)*.
> Therefore, Tommy always comes home on time unless he's had an accident *(inductive reasoning that produces a generalization)*.

Then Tommy's mother goes on:

> Tommy always comes home on time unless he's had an accident *(the generalization)*.
> Tommy is late today *(the specific situation)*.
> Therefore, Tommy has had an accident *(a deductive conclusion)*.

When Tommy does get home an hour late because he's been watching a truck being pulled out of a ditch, his mother goes through another deductive process:

> Children who worry their mothers should be punished.
> Tommy worried me.
> Therefore, I won't let Tommy watch television tonight.

Tommy follows the same process. He thinks to himself, "Mothers who love their children don't punish them for little things like being a little bit late, but my mother is punishing me." So he yells at his mother as he sulks off to bed, "You don't love me any more!" Neither Tommy nor his mother is aware of the thinking processes they have gone through, and neither of them has stopped to question whether their generalizations are reliable.

Both inductive and deductive reasoning are valuable and necessary. We can't do without them in ordinary life, and science uses them both. Almost all the discoveries of modern science have come from inductive reasoning. Let's take an imaginary situation. Suppose a man with a bad skin rash decides to dig the dandelions out of his garden. He works all afternoon, and when the last dandelion is gone, so is the skin rash. He rushes into the house to tell his wife that the dandelions have cured his rash. His wife, however, is a scientist. She is willing to guess that something in the dandelions might have caused the skin rash to go away—scientists call this kind of guess a *hypothesis*—but she also knows that the guess must be tested over and over again under very careful conditions. If hundreds of cases of the same kind of rash get much better when the same kind of dandelion is rubbed on them, the guess has been proved accurate, and medical science has a useful new generalization to work from: essence of the dandelion verticoma helps certain kinds of rash.

Applied science, on the other hand, usually works deductively. A doctor says to herself, "Certain cases of rash have been helped by rubbing them with essence of the dandelion verticoma. Eva Baldash has a hand rash. Essence of dandelion verticoma will probably help her." So the doctor writes a prescription for the essence, and if the generalization is accurate—if it has been tested often enough and carefully enough—Eva's rash will probably get better.

Inductive reasoning begins with specific things and arrives at a generalization.

Deductive reasoning begins with a generalization and applies it to specific things.

Inductive Reasoning

To test whether inductive reasoning is being used fairly, we do the same thing the scientist did in deciding whether dandelions can cure rashes. We ask whether a lot of similar but separate things have always produced the same result. Just as a statistical survey is reliable only if the sample is large enough, so a generalization arrived at inductively is acceptable only when there are enough occurrences to support it. Because cars always stop when they run out of gasoline, we can safely accept the generalization that cars won't run without gas. But if Senator Goodsell tells you that everybody is against requiring adults to wear seat belts—he's had three angry letters from motorists—you can point out that you know six people, at least, who think that requiring seat belts will save lives. The senator's attempt at inductive reasoning has led him to a bad generalization.

You are always justified in asking what's behind the generalizations that other people make, and you can expect that careful readers will question the generalizations that appear in your writing. Don't use words such as *everybody, nobody, always,* and *never* unless you can demonstrate that your generalization is really accurate. And don't make statements that can be interpreted as including everybody, even though you don't use the word. "A nurse knows what to do in an emergency" means *all* nurses in *all* emergencies. The generalization would be more acceptable if it said "most nurses" and "nearly always." If you say, "Men expect their wives to wait on them hand and foot," any reader who knows just one husband who makes the morning coffee and washes his own socks is likely to mistrust your whole argument, no matter how sensible the rest of it may be.

Before you accept a conclusion based on inductive reasoning, ask this question:

Does the generalization claim more than the specific events can support?

Deductive Reasoning

Checking whether deductive reasoning is being used fairly also requires two steps. First, you have to decide whether the generalization is dependable, and then you have to make sure that nothing has gone wrong in getting from the generalization to the conclusion. No acceptable conclusion can ever come from a generalization that is too broad. Anybody who starts with such a sweeping generalization as "Today's high school graduates can't spell" or "Dentists are out for all they can get" might as well stop right there. Any conclusion based on such all-inclusive statements is open to suspicion.

Even if the generalization is more carefully worded, and even if most people will accept it, the conclusion may still be faulty. Reasoning that begins with "Some dentists are out for all they can get" must not end with "Mother didn't need false teeth at all. Dr. Steinmetz just wanted the money." Mother may or may not have needed false teeth. The dentist may or may not have given bad advice for the sake of the money. Deductions that start with *some* or *most* have to end with *maybe, perhaps,* or *probably.* The conclusion can never be more definite than the generalization.

You must also make sure that whatever you're talking about really fits the generalization. It's accurate to say that all Americans over sixty-five are eligible for Medicare, but if all you're sure about is that Polly Riley looks stooped and wrinkled, it isn't fair to say that she can have part of her hospital bill paid by the government. Unless you can show that she's over sixty-five, it's unfair to shift from *looks like* to *is.* Honest reasoning requires that the conclusion say *perhaps.*

Another kind of shift occurs when we try to prove that something isn't so because it doesn't fit the generalization. When Senator Goodsell says "Americans believe in democracy, but Olaf Beubje isn't an American, so he doesn't believe in democracy," he hopes you won't see the shift. The senator is pretending that "All Americans believe in democracy"—not a very sound generalization anyway—is the same as "Only Americans believe in democracy."

Other kinds of shifts can lead to faulty reasoning, too. Sometimes the meaning of a word changes halfway through an argument. "If this is a free country, and they tell us it is, I shouldn't have to pay to get a driver's license" may sound reasonable until you remember that *free* in *free country* means the right to say what you believe and live where you please. It doesn't have anything to do with paying or not paying money.

Deductive reasoning goes on all around us all the time. We use it, and so does everybody else. Before we accept the conclusions, however, either our own or those of the people who are trying to persuade us, we need to ask two questions:

> *Is the generalization reliable?*
>
> *Has there been a shift between the generalizaton and the conclusion?*

Guilt by Association

Guilt by association is another very common way that faulty deduction can trick us into unreliable conclusions. The reasoning goes like this:

> All pigs have tails.
> All cows have tails.
> Therefore, cows are pigs.

The conclusion here is so obviously silly it's hardly worth discussing, but when this same kind of reasoning is applied to individuals or groups of people, what happens is not so obvious, and the results can be damaging and even dangerous.

A neighbor comments casually, "Known criminals eat lunch at the Double X Cafe. The new man across the street ate lunch there today. Looks like he's a criminal." Actually Ralph Upright has only been in town a week. When he was hungry, he went into the first place that sold hamburgers. But Mr. Upright will have trouble making friends if that neighbor spreads the word that there's something suspicious about his behavior.

In the United States in the fifties, when a Congressional committee was looking for Communists in every closet, many honest citizens lost their jobs and their reputations because of this kind of faulty reasoning. The argument went like this:

> Communists attended the meeting in Anderson Hall.
> John Doe was seen at the meeting.
>
> Communists are in favor of public housing.
> Jenny Doe thinks that public housing is a good idea.
>
> Communists write articles for *Better World* magazine.
> Jasper Doe wrote an article for *Better World* magazine.
>
> The Does are Communists.

Guilt by association, which can involve more than one kind of faulty reasoning, is still with us. Perhaps you hear somebody say, "Don't vote for Amy Kissell. Her husband did some business for Ashenden, Inc., and that firm was convicted for income tax fraud last year." Both of those facts are accurate. Jim Kissell did paint a building Ashenden owns, and Ashenden was fined for failing to report part of its income. The reasoning is faulty, but Amy Kissell may lose some votes. Such methods are smear techniques, not honest ways of supporting opinions or reasons.

Looked at one way, guilt by association is like analogy that has been carried too far. It fastens on a few similarities but completely overlooks the differences, and it destroys rather than increases our chance of understanding. Comparing sound waves to ocean waves does help us understand, and we know that the notion that sound waves can get people wet is absurd. Making judgments about people because they have something in common with other people we disapprove of does not lead to understanding, but it's often harder to see the absurdity. The rule to remember is this:

> *Just because two people or things are alike in one way does not make them alike in other ways too.*

Either/or Thinking and Other Bad Logic

It's easy to fall into the trap of supposing that if a thing is not so, its opposite must be; that if a thing is so, its opposite can't be. In many very simple situations, this **either/or thinking** is indeed logical. Either the basement light is on or it isn't. Either you missed the 8:30 bus or you caught it. Either you can pay the rent this month or you can't. And if you are expecting a baby, it will certainly be either a girl or a boy. But just as the causes of a complicated event are not simple, so more involved situations cannot usually be explained by saying "It has to be either this or that."

Senator Goodsell says, "Whose side are you on anyway? Either you're for me or against me." Nonsense. Perhaps you agree with the senator that some parts of the income tax law are unfair, but you surely don't agree that all income taxes should be abolished. "If you don't succeed in life, you're a failure." But lots of people go happily along, neither making a fortune nor landing on skid road. "The world is divided into good guys and bad guys." But unlike television serials, in real life most people are good sometimes, bad sometimes, and mostly somewhere in between. "Drugs are either helpful or harmful." But two aspirin tablets will cure a headache, and the whole bottle will land you in the emergency ward or the morgue. In times when war has seemed inevitable, some people have argued, "Unless we drop a bomb on them first, they'll drop one on us." So far, however, more reasonable people, aware of other possibilities, have prevented world disaster.

The old saying that there are two sides to every question would be more accurate if it said, "at least two sides." We need to be suspicious of people who say there are only two choices. Those people may be confused themselves or they may be deliberately trying to trick us.

Another kind of trick, sometimes deliberate and sometimes accidental, is to argue in a circle. **Circular arguments** begin with a belief or reason, but instead of supporting the first statement, they circle around until the original belief is used as proof of itself.

> "Senator Goodsell says the illegal immigration from Mexico can easily be stopped, and he's an authority on it."
>
> "What makes him an authority?"
>
> "He made two speeches about it."
>
> "Why did he make the speeches?"
>
> "Because he's an authority. He wouldn't be making the speeches if he didn't know a lot about it."

Sensible people will ask for more support than that.

Personal attacks are another way of arguing unfairly. Let's suppose that Senator Goodsell's opponent actually does know a good deal about the Mexicans who come across the border to work in the harvests. She spent a year with Cesar Chavez and she speaks Spanish fluently. When she asks the senator a specific question about the housing conditions of migrant workers, he responds by announcing that she was once almost expelled from college for leading a protest march against the draft. Instead of discussing the conditions under which immigrant laborers live, he has made a personal attack on his opponent, hoping voters will forget about the real issue and worry instead about his opponent's background. In the same way that arguing in circles can make people forget that nothing was proved, **name-calling** can make people forget what the actual discussion is about. Both methods of avoiding honest argument are illogical and unfair.

Remember that honest persuasion depends on supported reasons. Don't forget to ask yourself these questions:

> *Are there really only two choices?*
>
> *Is a statement being used as proof of itself?*
>
> *Is name-calling being used as a substitute for sticking to the point?*

Suspicion, Stampeding, and Sense

This chapter has covered several common errors in reasoning, and although the discussion certainly isn't complete, it does provide some important ways of distinguishing honest from dishonest support. It should help you to be critical of what you read as well as of what you write. But don't suppose that because there are so many ways to cheat, everybody who tries to persuade you is cheating. Lots of examples are lively and useful. Lots of surveys are carefully made and fairly reported. Many authorities are trustworthy. Many predictions, even the gloomiest ones, come true.

Nobody but a fool believes everything, and the person who doubts everything is only a little less foolish. You don't want to be railroaded into believing everything, but neither do you want bitter suspicion to keep you from believing anything. Asking for reasons and examining those reasons may not always make you comfortable, but it's a good deal better than being either a sucker or a skeptic. Although reason can be misused, it's important to remember that the human ability to reason soundly is what brought us out of the trees and into rocket ships. Sound reasoning is the only thing that can keep us from blowing both ourselves and the trees back to the amoeba stage.

Ask for reasons and what's behind them.

Offer reasons and say what they're based on.

Key Words and Ideas

Here are some of the important terms and ideas discussed in this chapter. See whether you can answer these questions about them.

1. What are **slanted words**? How can you tell whether vivid words are being used fairly or unfairly?
2. What are **glittering generalities**? How can you avoid being taken in by them?
3. What are **inferences**? How can you tell whether or not they are reliable?
4. What questions can you ask to tell whether **examples** are **honest**?
5. What questions can you ask to decide whether **statistics** are **reliable**?
6. What questions can you ask to tell whether **authority** is used **honestly**? How can you tell when authority is misused?
7. What kind of **prediction** is likely to be reliable? What kind is unsafe?
8. What does *post hoc* thinking mean? What is a **fallacy**? How can *post hoc* fallacies be avoided?
9. What is meant by **false analogy**? What two questions can you ask in deciding whether things are being fairly compared?
10. What is the difference between **inductive** and **deductive** reasoning?
11. How can you tell whether the results of **inductive reasoning** are dependable?
12. How can you tell whether a conclusion reached by **deductive reasoning** is acceptable?
13. What is **guilt by association**? How can it be recognized and avoided?
14. What is **either/or** thinking? When, if ever, should it be used?
15. How can you recognize a **circular argument**?
16. What is **name-calling**? Why should it be avoided?
17. How can you escape being either a sucker or a skeptic?

Exercises

Exercise 1. Slanted Words. What slanted words do you find in these advertisements? If you eliminate all emotional language, all personal appeals, and all glamour by association, what solid information is left? Rewrite each advertisement, including only factual statements.

1. ALPINE SPRING—a subtle blend of old-world sophistication overlaid with the freshness and fragrance of a new-world spring, hinting of dogwood, trilliums, and dog-tooth violets. Wear it with assurance. It's more than allure, it's the beauty of beginnings, the promise of passion. At all leading stores. $20 an ounce.

2. HOW TO FEEL RICH WITHOUT SPENDING MUCH

Nothing can do it quicker than the new Winner 999.

It's handsome, it's cozy, it's comfortable, and it looks big.

You don't have to count pennies to save money. You just know that a car like that will go—and keep on going.

Sit in it, touch it, stroke it. Listen to it. It purrs like a contented cat. What could you ask from a car that the Winner 999 can't give you? Windshield guards slide smoothly to keep down the smear. Defoggers cooperate gently, both front and back. Softly cushioned seats recline when you're tired, come forward easily when you want to sit straight in the car all your friends will envy.

Multimotors has been building classic cars for more than thirty years. You can depend on them to know what YOU want. They care about looks, they care about quality, and they care about YOUR money.

Don't wait—see a Winner 999 today.

Exercise 2. More Slanted Words. Find three advertisements that depend on glittering generalities and slanted words. Underline the factual information. Then bring the ads to class and be ready to explain how they work.

Exercise 3. Glittering Generalities. How many glittering generalities can you find in these letters to the editor? How many slanted words? If you eliminate all the emotional language, how much information is left?

1. CONGRATULATE THE YOUNG

Dear Editor:

It's time somebody took the trouble to congratulate some of our wonderful young people on the splendid job they are doing.

Newspapers only seem to care about running the kids down and printing all the bad news about them. But I have lots of examples to prove that most kids are well-behaved, polite, and thoughtful. They are a credit to the parents that have brought them up in the good old-fashioned way.

Let's stop hearing about the hole in the doughnut and start hearing something about the good wholesome food that surrounds it. Let's hear it for all the good kids out there!

Reader Who Likes Kids

2. TEEN-AGERS A DISGRACE

Dear Editor:

Today's teen-agers are a disgrace to the country. They're dishonest and disreputable. They disregard the comfort and convenience of everybody but themselves. The high schools are rampant with drugs—and worse. If some of our cowardly parents would get the courage to forbid rock music, which encourages every vice, from homosexuality to cocaine to free sex, we might get back to the fundamental values that made this country great.

A Grieving Grandfather

3. AGAINST FOUL LANGUAGE

To the Editor:

I'm sick and tired of hearing people, especially women, use all those four-letter words they shouldn't even know. I know some words to call those blankety-blanks, but I'm too well-trained to use them.

John Jones

Name _____

Exercise 4. Facts, Inferences, and Judgments. Which of these statements are fact, which are inference, and which are judgment? If you think a statement is either an inference or a judgment, decide how reliable it is and give reasons for your decision.

> *Example:* There's a button missing from my raincoat; the cleaners must have lost it.
> *Statement* — inference
> *Reliability* — doubtful, unless the speaker is sure all the buttons were on when the coat went to the cleaners.

1. The back door to the office was left unlocked Saturday night.

Statement _____

Reliability _____

_____

2. The janitor was the last person to leave the building.

Statement _____

Reliability _____

_____

3. The janitor forgot to lock the door.

Statement _____

Reliability _____

_____

4. The janitor is careless.

Statement _____

Reliability _____

_____

5. On Monday, a calculator was missing from the secretary's office.

Statement _____

Reliability _____

_____

6. Somebody got in through the unlocked back door.

Statement _____

Reliability _____

_____

7. The calculator was stolen.

Statement _____

Reliability _____

_____

8. The secretary was working on her income tax this weekend.

Statement _____

Reliability _____

_____

9. Probably the secretary borrowed the calculator.

Statement _____

Reliability _____

_____

Name _____

Exercise 5. Honest Examples.   In these sentences, each of the underlined terms is followed by an example. If you think the example is fair, mark it *OK*. If the example doesn't seem to fit the underlined term, replace it with one of your own that does fit. Then compare your responses to those of other students in the class.

> *Example:* The Rockford family is going through a period of hard times. They could only afford one trip to Europe last year.
>
> *Better:* The Rockfords' car was repossessed, they're two months behind on the mortgage payments, and the youngest girl just broke her leg.

1. I had a long wait in the dentist's office. I got there at 10:30, but the dentist didn't take me until 10:40.   _____

_____

_____

_____

2. Mrs. Quincy likes highly spiced foods. She puts Tabasco sauce in her coffee and cayenne on her oatmeal.   _____

_____

_____

_____

3. Jane's husband is a cheapskate. He insists that they can't go out to dinner until the monthly bills are all paid.   _____

_____

_____

_____

4. Mr. Paratus is very patriotic. He never disagrees with the president.   _____

_____

_____

5. The woman across the hall is a <u>liar</u>. She told her four-year-old daughter that Santa Claus is real.   _____

   _____

   _____

   _____

6. Mr. Clutz has <u>no manners</u>. When I went to dinner at their house, he
   didn't admire <u>my new dress</u>.   _____

   _____

   _____

   _____

7. Harry's wife is <u>disloyal</u>. When he wrecked the car she said it was his
   own fault.   _____

   _____

   _____

   _____

8. Old Mr. Arbuthnot is very <u>generous</u>. He offered his guests a second
   cup of coffee after dinner.   _____

   _____

   _____

   _____

9. The third grade teacher is <u>too strict</u>. He won't let the children interrupt him when he's talking.   _____

   _____

   _____

Name _____

Exercise 6. More Honest Examples.   For each of the following generalizations, provide examples that make the generalization more vivid. The point of this exercise is to give enough details in concrete enough language so that readers see, feel, smell, taste—in short, react—as you do. Give the bland statement some life.

Example: The children were neglected.

When I arrived at ten in the evening, the children were alone in the apartment. There was neither heat nor milk. The baby was crying listlessly, uncovered, and smelling as though he hadn't been changed since morning. The four-year-old was in the kitchen eating cold oatmeal, his nose running and his pajamas wet. Over the whole room there was an odor of stale beer.

1. Many family farms are being foreclosed.

_____

_____

_____

2. Nuclear war would be a total disaster.

_____

_____

_____

3. The living room was always spotless.

_____

_____

_____

4. The park is beautiful in the spring.

_____

_____

_____

5. The motel room was very uncomfortable.

_____

_____

_____

6. Mrs. Schollfist is a disagreeable woman.

_____

_____

_____

7. That was an exciting movie.

_____

_____

_____

8. Six-year-old Jane is very self-reliant.

_____

_____

_____

9. The meeting got out of control.

_____

_____

_____

Name _____

Exercise 7. Honest Statistics.   Look at the following statements and the statistics that support them. If you find that the statistics are reliable and that they support the statement, mark them *OK*. If they are unreliable or unconvincing, explain why you think so. Then compare your answers with those of other students in the class.

> *Example:* Lilac Groves is a prosperous area. The average family income is $30,000.
> *Response*—Can be misleading. Are there a few very rich families and many well below $30,000?

1. Use Albin's AntiAcid Pills. Four out of five doctors interviewed recommend them.   _____

_____

_____

2. Be sure that your dog gets distemper shots. The County Animal Control Board reports that there were fifty-four cases of distemper last year and 60 percent were fatal.   _____

_____

_____

3. Dobermans are better watchdogs than shepherds. I asked twenty people who own Dobermans which breed best kept marauders away and seventeen of them said Dobermans.   _____

_____

_____

4. It's apparent that most Americans dislike spinach. The United Cooperative of Lettuce Producers made a survey.   _____

_____

_____

5. The Senate overwhelmingly approved the measure. The vote was eighty in favor, two opposed.   _____

_____

_____

6. Most of the people in this area are in favor of a woman's right to choose. Out of more than three hundred people interviewed, 60 percent said they believe in the right to choose abortion.   ———

———

———

7. Community college students are twice as old as students on other campuses. In *American College Students: Norms for 1985,* it is reported that "all institutions" have 0.7 percent students thirty years of age and older, while community colleges have 1.4 percent.   ———

———

———

8. If the cost of living increased 4.5 percent last year, why should a loaf of bread that cost $1.00 two years ago now cost $1.29? The government index must be wrong.   ———

———

———

9. According to figures recently released by a consortium of insurance companies, Americans born in 1980 have twice the chance of living to be eighty that their grandparents had.   ———

———

———

Name _____

Exercise 8. Honest Use of Authorities.   Decide whether the following are acceptable as authorities on these subjects. Give reasons for saying yes or no. Then compare your answers with those of other students in the class.

Example: Julia Child endorsing a food chopper.
Response — Acceptable; she's a recognized expert on food preparation.

1. Your math teacher on a shortcut method of finding square roots.

_____

_____

2. Everybody knows that jogging is good exercise.

_____

_____

3. General Electric Company on why electric heat is better than gas.

_____

_____

4. Barbara Woodhouse on training puppies.

_____

_____

5. Truck drivers should be given stricter driving tests. I heard on TV that several of them regularly get speeding tickets.

_____

_____

6. The coach of the Olwaca basketball team says the team is unlikely to win the championship this year.

_____   _____

_____

7. James Monroe warned that the United States should stay out of European affairs. If we'd listened to him, the embassy in Lebanon wouldn't have been bombed.

_____

_____

8. Eating alfalfa sprouts can cure rheumatism. I read it in a book.

_____

_____

9. Senator Goodsell says that Pronto Pizzeria serves the best pizza in town.

_____

_____

10. Mrs. Alvin Wright, who has three teen-age children, says that *Don't Wait for Tomorrow* is an obscene book.

_____

_____

11. Education is not necessary for success. Thomas Edison never graduated from high school.

_____

_____

Name _____

Exercise 9. Honest Predictions.   Decide whether or not the following predictions are reliable. Mark each one yes or no and give reasons for your answer. Then compare your decisions with those of other students in the class.

> *Example:* When I get out of college I'm sure to get a good job.
> *Response*—No; predictions dealing with new situations aren't safe.

1. My cousin, who had dinner with me last night, has come down with measles today, so I will have them in about two weeks.

_____

_____

2. There will be a full moon Saturday night.

_____

_____

3. I smashed a fender on the new car. My father will probably never let me drive it again.

_____

_____

4. Those climbing roses will bloom all summer.

_____

_____

5. Unless the emissions from midwestern smelters are controlled, acid rain in the Northeast will get worse.

_____

_____

6. If the Equal Rights Amendment should ever pass, men and women will have to use the same bathrooms.

_____

_____

7. If you pick the baby up when she cries, you will spoil her.

_____

_____

8. You'd better take a raincoat if you go to Seattle in March. It almost always rains there in the spring.

_____

_____

9. Prayer in the schools will help to reduce vandalism.

_____

_____

10. If we build more and bigger missiles, no enemy will dare to attack us.

_____

_____

11. I'm going to put out snail bait to help get rid of the slugs.

_____

_____

Name _____

Exercise 10. *Post Hoc* Thinking. Which of these cause-and-effect statements are convincing? If you think the statement is acceptable, mark it *OK*. If you think a fallacy is involved, explain what's wrong with the statement. Then compare your answers with those of other students in the class.

> *Example:* I drank a cup of coffee for dinner and I didn't sleep a wink all night.
> *Response* — OK if drinking one cup of coffee always keeps you awake.

1. I gave Roger some steak last night, and this morning he bit the garbage collector. That's what happens when you feed dogs rich meat. _____

_____

_____

2. The power failure was caused by lightning, which struck a power pole. _____

_____

_____

3. The refrigerator didn't work last night. There was a power failure. _____

_____

_____

4. Power wasn't restored until this morning because the repair people didn't like to go out in a bad storm. _____

_____

_____

5. We had a bad winter because the squirrels stored more nuts than usual. _____

_____

_____

6. Representative Oglethorpe didn't run for reelection because his doctor advised against it.   ———

_____

_____

7. Just because Senator Goodsell is a friend of the vice-president, he
was reelected easily.   ———

_____

_____

8. The only reason the Wearever Shoe Factory went bankrupt is that
this country is importing too many shoes from Brazil and Italy.   ———

_____

_____

9. Whenever church attendance goes down, robberies go up.   ———

_____

_____

10. Mary Able was made office manager only because she's female.   ———

_____

_____

11. Watching violence on TV caused Henry to trip Henrietta on the
stairs.   ———

_____

_____

Name _____

Exercise 11. False Analogies.   Examine the following analogies. If you find the comparison fair, mark it *OK*. If you find it unfair, say why.

> *Example:* Failure to reelect the mayor during this crisis is as dangerous as changing horses in midstream.
>
> *Response:* Unfair. A city crisis is not like a fast river, and the problems of a city are not like a single horseback rider.

1. If you think of the sun as an orange and the earth as a marble moving in an ellipse around it, you can get a fairly good notion of the earth's movements during the year.

   _____

   _____

2. Professor Scholl is a bear in psychology, so I suppose Professor Vincent is, too. They look a lot alike.

   _____

   _____

3. There is no real difference between teachers and the people who patrol school crossings. Both of them have to keep students in order. The patrol people work for minimum wage. Why can't the teachers?

   _____

   _____

4. Careful parents punish their impertinent children. Why shouldn't the government jail the people who criticize it?

   _____

   _____

5. You can't cure poverty by giving people here and there a job any more than you can stop cancer by putting a Band-Aid on it.

_____

_____

6. Even a good bureaucracy tends to abuse its powers. It's like a dead mackerel in the moonlight. It both shines and stinks.

_____

_____

7. Watching TV at home is exactly like going to the theater, except you don't have to pay.

_____

_____

8. Cleaning spark plugs is much like cleaning the oven. Neither is very hard, but they're both dirty jobs to be put off as long as possible.

_____

_____

9. Buying a Viva Salon dress is as good as inheriting money; it makes you feel special.

_____

_____

10. Training a child is no different from training a puppy. Once you start, you have to keep at it.

_____

_____

Name _____

Exercise 12. Induction and Deduction.   Which of these statements are based on inductive reasoning, which on deductive? Mark each statement *I* for inductive or *D* for deductive and explain your decision.

> *Example:* I'll probably get a promotion. My supervisor gave me a good evaluation.
> *Response:* D. Based on the generalization that everybody who gets a good evaluation gets promoted.

1. I know Betty Bancroft is an American citizen because she voted in the last election and only citizens can vote.

_____

_____

2. Fourteen people in Prairie View had mumps last month. Prairie View is having an epidemic.

_____

_____

3. I got A's in all four subjects I'm taking. I'll be on the honor roll this semester.

_____

_____

4. I've pressed the doorbell four times and nothing happens. The doorbell must be out of order.

_____

_____

5. I've pressed the doorbell four times and nothing happens. The Browns must not be home.

_____

_____

6. The surgeon general has determined that cigarette smoking is dangerous to your health.

_____

_____

7. People who smoke three packs of cigarettes a day are more likely to have heart attacks than people who don't smoke.

_____

_____

8. All *Lobelia verticia* have six petals, usually pink.

_____

_____

9. This lobelia has six pink petals. It must be a *Lobelia verticia.*

_____

_____

10. I heard the phone ring three times and then stop, so I knew it was my sister calling.

_____

_____

Name _____

Exercise 13. Honest Reasoning.   Which of these conclusions are acceptable? Examine the wording of each statement carefully and then mark it either *OK* or *No.* If you think a statement is unfair or unacceptable, explain what's wrong with it.

> *Example:*   Ethel Barnes is sure to be against the new tax. I know most social workers are against it, and she's been a social worker for two years.
> *Response:*   No. The reasoning shifts from "most" to a definite conclusion about Barnes.

1. You won't be able to start that fire. Wet wood never burns, and this wood is probably wet.

_____

_____

2. We all agree that everybody should have the right to work. This proposal is called a "right-to-work" law. Obviously, we should vote for it.

_____

_____

3. I'm afraid that big dog will bite. I've always known that barking dogs don't bite, and that dog is not barking.

_____

_____

4. My grandfather drank a quart of beer every day of his life, and he always went right to sleep after dinner. Beer is good for insomnia.

_____

_____

5. Cars that use chains seldom get into accidents. Johnny has chains on his car, so I know he's safe.

_____

_____

6. Taking aspirin usually cures headaches, so it will probably cure mine.

_____

_____

7. Water freezes at 32 degrees. The temperature was below 15 degrees last night, so how do you expect to get water from that outside faucet?

_____

_____

8. I know at least six people who cheated on their income tax. Nobody is honest any more.

_____

_____

9. My girl friend will sure be mad at me for not keeping our date last Saturday.

_____

_____

10. Jane Simpson must have a lot of money. She drives a Mercedes.

_____

_____

Name   _____

Exercise 14. Guilt by Association.   Is the support used in the following statements fair or unfair? If you find the reasoning acceptable, mark it *OK*. If you find it faulty, explain why.

>   *Example:*   Susie must be unreliable. Her brother was arrested for shoplifting.
>   *Response:*   Faulty reasoning. Susie need not be like her brother just because they are members of the same family.

1. Of course we used concentration camps in World War II. Those people had Japanese ancestors, didn't they?

   _____

   _____

2. Dr. Gillis charges too much for an office visit. Don't go to Dr. Adams, either; they both graduated from Emerson Med School.

   _____

   _____

3. The Benjamin Franklin Insurance Company must be pretty good—their rates are lower than the Surety Insurance Company for the same coverage.

   _____

   _____

4. The Benjamin Franklin Insurance Company must be pretty good—their billboards have the cutest babies on them and the family in the photograph looks so cheerful and happy.

   _____

   _____

5. I don't care if the American Civil Liberties Union does support the Bill of Rights. They defended Communists and Fascists, didn't they, when the police tried to shut down a meeting?

_____

_____

6. In the names of Jefferson and Roosevelt, I urge you to vote in favor of this progressive proposal to widen Main Street.

_____

_____

7. We must do away with violence in this country, even if the police have to use tanks and machine guns to do it.

_____

_____

8. I'd trust him anywhere; he goes to the same church I do.

_____

_____

9. I wouldn't trust her with my money. She admits she's an atheist.

_____

_____

10. Watch out for the kids that went to Grant High. I knew a boy from there who beat up my kid brother.

_____

_____

Name _____

Exercise 15. Either/or Thinking and Other Bad Logic.   If you think the argument used is acceptable, mark it *OK*. If you find it unacceptable, say what's wrong with it.

> *Example:* If Henry doesn't show up by ten o'clock, we can be sure he's had a wreck.
> *Response:* Probably unacceptable; perhaps the traffic was badly congested, or he had a flat tire.

1. Don't tell me the car almost started. Either it did or it didn't.

_____

_____

2. We must penalize every student who comes late to class. If we don't, nobody will ever get here on time.

_____

_____

3. A woman is either honest or she isn't. I know that Jackie Smith told her husband she had to work late one night when actually she was out buying him a birthday present.

_____

_____

4. All we have to do to prevent unemployment is make sure everybody who is able to work gets a job.

_____

_____

5. Artie Arbuckle: "The fifty-five-mile speed limit ought to be more strictly enforced."
    Annie Arbuckle: "What about that speeding ticket you got last year?"

_____

_____

6. If things don't get better, they're sure to get worse.

_____

_____

7. Investing in the stock market is a good way to lose money. The stock market is always a gamble. A few gamblers win, but most of them lose. So if gambling is a bad risk, you're likely to lose money.

_____

_____

8. I don't care how much that guy knows about programming computers. I know he was divorced last year and I wouldn't hire him on a bet.

_____

_____

9. If the government forces us to install an antipollution device, we'll shut the factory down.

_____

_____

10. Unless the garbage collectors get a two-dollar raise, garbage will rot in the streets.

_____

_____

Exercise 16. Taking a Survey.   Working in a small group with other students in the class, plan a survey of the attitudes of your fellow students on some problem of current interest. Be sure that the plan shows the questions you will ask and how your sample will be chosen. Then take the survey. Use the results of the survey as support for a paper on one side or the other of the problem. Decide with other members of the class whether the results of the survey or the article based on it should be sent to the student paper.

Exercise 17. Advertisements and Arguments.   Write an ad for some product, real or imaginary. Then write an argument supporting the same product or explaining why your advertisement is misleading. Share both the ad and the article with other members of the class.

Exercise 18. Campaign Literature.   Write a campaign blurb for some political candidate, real or imaginary. The candidate can be running for a campus office or a local, state, or federal position. Then write a letter to the editor of the paper supporting the same candidate, using fair persuasion only. Ask members of the class to analyze the differences between the two.

Appendix One/
Summarizing

Jason has a long discussion with his father about borrowing the family car. Later in the day he summarizes the argument for his sister Jennifer: "He said no." Jason has captured the main point in three words, but when Jennifer asks why, he is able to provide some supporting details: "Oh, he talked about the speeding ticket I got last year, and the time you backed into a railing and bent the fender, and then he said he might want to use the car anyway—something might come up."

You have been making this kind of summary all your life. You have been listening to other people talk, and if you got the point of what they were saying, you could without much difficulty tell somebody else what had been said. In the telling, you shortened the original a lot or a little, repeating what seemed to you to be the highlights of the discussion. Such summarizing is simple, natural, and easy. And for ordinary situations, especially those in which you are genuinely involved, this system works very well.

The ability to summarize effectively, in fact, is one of the skills that makes a good listener. Perhaps you've heard somebody say, in the middle of a committee meeting, "If I understand it, this is what you're saying . . ." and then put neatly into three or four sentences what the other person's position has been. Such summarizing makes the work of the committee move more smoothly—and those abilities may get the summarizer appointed as chair of the committee next time around.

Summarizing Lecture Notes

Knowing how to listen carefully and summarize accurately can help you in college, too, both in the group work you may be doing in some of your classes and in the lecture notes you should be taking in some of the others. When you take notes on a lecture, your job is just the reverse of what the teacher probably did in preparing the lecture. The teacher knew what the main point of that half hour's presentation would be and what supporting material would be used to back up that point. All good lecturers work from a plan, sometimes short enough to fit on a three-by-five-inch notecard, and, as they speak, they add more explanation, give more details, and provide examples. The notes you actually jot down in class may include far too much of the additional explanation, but when you transcribe those notes after class—as you should, to straighten them out and fix them in your memory—the result should be fairly close to the plan with which the teacher started. You can review your summaries whenever a test is announced, and they are bound to help, even if the test is multiple choice or short answer. They will help even more in essay tests because you will have a ready-made plan tucked away in your head.

If you are not sure how these note-taking summaries work, ask your English teacher to give the class a thirty-minute lecture. Take notes as the teacher talks, turn those notes into an orderly outline of the lecture, and compare what you have done with the work of other students in the class and with the plan the teacher was working from. The notes won't all be alike, but everybody in the class should agree on the main point and the most important divisions.

Summarizing What You Read

Just as summarizing class lectures will help in understanding and remembering the material, so will summarizing what you read for each class, whether it's in a textbook or an outside reading assignment. The same principle applies, except that in reading you can go quickly through the material the first time, getting an overall idea of what is being covered. Then you can go back and take notes. Suppose in your Women's Studies class the assignment is to find something on sexism in language and make a very brief report to the rest of the class. You find this article in a collection of essays:

Sexism in the Language of Marriage

[1]   One of the few songs I remember from the halcyon era of the fifties starts out with the bold claim "Love and marriage go together like a horse and carriage"! I was a teenager then and I thought it was a wonderful song. But today in my more cynical adulthood, I might be tempted instead to think of a threesome consisting of love, marriage, and sexism. . . .

[2]   For example, when I at last received a regular faculty appointment at Arizona State University, where my husband had been teaching for two years, my father came to a celebration dinner with a package under his arm and a twinkle in his eyes. He had brought a present. It was a pair of pants for Don. They were handed over with the good humored explanation that since we were now equal, he just wanted to remind everyone who was "to wear the pants in the family."

[3]   This old cliché about *the pants in the family* is just one of the hundreds of ways that the language reminds us of the different expectations we have for the man and for the woman in a marriage. Some of these attitudes are revealed through our everyday language, in the ways we divide various aspects of marriage into male and female domains. . . .

[4]   "Ladies first" goes the old saying, but except in the phrase *ladies and gentlemen* we seldom follow this advice. Instead we have such pairings as:

Mr. and Mrs.	men and women
he/she	sons and daughters
his and hers	husbands and wives
Sonny and Cher	kings and queens
Jack and Jill	brothers and sisters
Fibber McGee and Molly	guys and dolls
boys and girls	actors and actresses
George and Martha Washington	host and hostess

[5]   This kind of male-female pairing is so set in our minds that it becomes automatic. I recently read that someone chided the National Organization for Women because their charter started out with "We, men and women . . ." instead of "We, women and men . . . ," which would have more accurately reflected their membership as well as their philosophy.

[6]   It is the general pattern in English for male words to come first. We make an exception only when something is so closely related to what we think of as the feminine domain that, without even realizing it, we switch over and break the pattern, putting the female first as in the following pairs, which all have to do with family relations and marriage.

bride and groom	mother and child
mother and father	aunt and uncle . . .

[7]   We went to a large wedding reception in a hotel the other night and the directory of events posted in the lobby read, "Cynthia Jenson Reception: Fiesta Room." I'm sure it was partly for the sake of efficiency that the sign maker didn't use the more complete "Cynthia Jenson and Robert Marshall Reception: Fiesta Room." During the couple's married life there will be hundreds of times when efficiency in listing their names is called for, but this announcement of the reception will probably be the last time Cynthia's name will be chosen over Robert's.

[8]   . . . The male's prenuptial party is called a *bachelor party* as compared to the female's *bridal shower.* And a woman considers herself a bride for a whole year after the wedding, while a man considers himself a groom only on the day of the wedding. . . .

[9]   At prenuptial celebrations, men look backward while women look forward. It is as if each sex wants to emphasize and honor the state it considers ideal, hence men stress the single state and women stress the married. At a bridal

shower, the entertainment consists of looking to the future through gifts which will enhance the comfort and the glamour of the new home. Games are played which revolve around daydreams predicting a romanticized future for the couple. At the bachelor party, the entertainment consists of looking to the past. It is one last fling with *the boys,* a nostalgic celebration in honor of *single blessedness* and freedom from the sex-related constraints usually thought to go along with marriage. The comments and the jokes made at both the bridal party and the bachelor party reflect our underlying attitude that marriage signifies success for a woman but defeat for a man. Perhaps this is one of the reasons society seems to ignore the marital status of men. Our consciousness of whether or not a woman is married is shown by our use of two titles, *Miss* and *Mrs.,* as contrasted to the all-purpose *Mr.*

[10]   In English a man's wife is jokingly referred to as his *ball and chain.* A similar metaphor exists in Spanish. The word for wife is *esposa;* the plural *esposas* means handcuffs.

[11]   It appears that society has certain expectations and that as long as behavior is fairly consistent with the expected, it goes unnoticed. For example, it is expected that every woman loves and serves her family, but such behavior is unusual in a man. We mark the unusual behavior with a word *family man* but there's no such thing as a *family woman.* The same type of reasoning probably explains why we have the term *career woman* but not *career man.*

[12]   It is ironic that although we consider marriage to be a desirable thing for a woman, we also look on it as making her the property of her husband. This is probably a leftover from the days when women could not get jobs, and so getting married was a cause for celebration, just as we celebrate when children who cannot take care of themselves are adopted by responsible adults. Because proprietary attitudes toward women go back into the dim reaches of history, it is not surprising that the language reflects this idea of ownership.

[13]   The most obvious example is the traditional wedding ceremony, in which the clergyman asks, "Who gives the bride away?" The father of the bride answers, "I do." If the father is not available, a male substitute is found, usually an older relative or friend of the family. After the father both literally and figuratively hands the bride over to the groom, the clergyman says, "I now pronounce you man and wife."*

After you have read the article through quickly, the first question to ask yourself is what the writer is trying to do. Although it seems clear that she is not sympathetic toward sexist language, she is not trying to persuade us not to use it: the purpose is to explain. The next task is to find the main idea. Does it occur in the first two paragraphs? No, the stories she tells here seem to be introduction, a way of arousing our interest. The main idea is in the two sentences of the third paragraph.

*Alleen Pace Nilsen, "Sexism in the Language of Marriage," in *Sexism and Language,* ed. Alleen Pace Nilsen, Haig Bosmajian, H. Lee Gershuny, and Julia P. Stanley (Urbana, Ill.: National Council of Teachers of English, 1977) 131–6. Copyright © 1977 by the National Council of Teachers of English. Reprinted by permission of the publisher.

What are the important points she makes in the rest of the article? The examples she gives in paragraphs 4 and 5 seem to be support for the point she makes in paragraph 6: Except when we are referring to family relations and marriage, male words come first. Paragraph 7 is another example of that same point. Paragraphs 8 and 9 introduce another point: the words we use for the parties that take place before a marriage show what we think marriage means for women and for men. Paragraph 11 tells us that some words reveal our recognition of unexpected behavior. And paragraphs 12 and 13 show how the words in a traditional marriage ceremony reflect the notion of women as property. You realize, however, that the general statements the writer makes will not be clear without a few examples, so you select those you think are clearest.

Your notes will look something like this:

Purpose: Explaining

Main Idea: Ordinary language shows how we think about marriage as one thing for men, another for women.

Supporting points:
1. Words about men come first except in talking about marriage and family
   (Usual—Mr. and Mrs.; Jack and Jill; guys and dolls)
   (Family—bride and groom; mother and child)
2. Words for premarriage parties show attitudes
   ("Bachelor party" looks back to "single blessedness")
   ("Bridal shower" looks toward happy future)
3. Words in traditional marriage ceremony show women as property
   ("Who *gives* this woman"—"pronounce you *man* and wife")

Those notes should be enough for you to give a fair summary of the article if you are asked for an oral report. They leave out only one important piece of information—where the material came from. You add this information to your notes:

Author—Alleen Pace Nilsen

Title of article—"Sexism in the Language of Marriage"

Where found—In book called *Sexism and Language* published by National Council of Teachers of English in 1977, pp. 131–136.

Your notes now include everything you need to prepare a summary.

Good notes for a summary include
  the purpose of the original writing;
  the main idea;
  the main subdivisions; and
  the source of the material.

Putting the Notes into a Paragraph

If the teacher asks you to write the report instead of giving it orally, these same notes can serve as the plan for your paragraph. It ought to read something like this:

> In an article called "Sexism in the Language of Marriage," Alleen Pace Nilsen says that ordinary language shows we think about marriage as meaning one thing for men and a different thing for women. Except when we are talking about marriage and family, words that refer to men always come first. For instance, we say "Mr. and Mrs."; "Jack and Jill"; "guys and dolls," and so on. But when we talk about family or marriage, we say "bride and groom" and "mother and child." The words we use in talking about the parties that precede a marriage also show our attitudes toward it. We talk about a "bachelor party" for men and the guests kid the groom about leaving his state of "single blessedness," but we give a "bridal shower" for the woman and talk about her happy future. Finally, the words in a traditional marriage ceremony show that women are regarded as property. The minister asks who *gives* the woman to the man and ends by pronouncing them "*man* and wife," not "husband and wife" or "man and woman."

This paragraph is a fair summary of the article you have read. It is less interesting than the original because it has to leave out a great many of the examples, but it does follow the general rules:

> *To write a summary paragraph*
>   *keep the same order as the original;*
>   *keep the same proportions as the original;*
>   *use your own words.*

Using Your Own Words

Using your own words is important. It may seem difficult to repeat what somebody else has said or written in words that belong to you instead of to the original, but it can almost always be done. You may be reluctant to abandon the original words because it seems to you that the original expresses it better or more clearly than you can do—and often it does. Nevertheless, using your own words accomplishes two things: it shows that you understand what you are summarizing, and it keeps you from being accused of cheating.

There are always at least two ways of saying almost anything. One third-grade child demonstrated this possibility when she retold a familiar nursery rhyme:

> There used to be a tiny female child who got a small round piece of hair right in the center of the top part of her face. And when she was nice, she was wonderfully nice. And when she was naughty, she was terrible.*

*By permission of Leah Berman, Springfield, Illinois.

In summarizing material that is mostly explanation or persuasion, stopping to think for a minute or so will usually enable you to find another way of expressing the same idea. One method is to read the original, cover it up, and ask yourself how you would naturally say it. If you can't avoid using several words that are exactly the same as the original, you must put them in quotation marks. When you look again at the summary of the Nilsen article, you can see that Nilsen's examples are quoted to show that those examples belong to her, not to you.

In some other kinds of writing, however, the idea being expressed seems less important than the words used to express it. Look at this paragraph describing an industrial town in the last century:

> It was a town of red brick, or of brick that would have been red if the smoke and ashes had allowed it; but as matters stood, it was a town of unnatural red and black like the painted face of a savage. It was a town of machinery and tall chimneys, out of which interminable serpents of smoke trailed themselves forever and ever, and never got uncoiled. It had a black canal in it, and a river that ran purple with ill-smelling dye, and vast piles of buildings full of windows where there was a rattling and a trembling all day long, and where the piston of the steam-engine worked monotonously up and down like the head of an elephant in a state of melancholy madness. It contained several large streets all very like one another, and many small streets still more like one another, inhabited by people equally like one another, who all went in and out at the same hours, with the same sound upon the same pavements, to do the same work, and to whom every day was the same as yesterday and tomorrow, and every year the counterpart of the last and the next.*

The purpose of this paragraph is to set a tone and create a mood, as well as to provide a picture of what the town looked like. See how much is lost in this bare summary:

> Dickens said the town was red, covered with black smoke. It gave an impression of machinery, chimneys, smoke, and bad smells. The machinery never stopped, and the streets, the people, the days, and the years were all monotonous.

The summary is accurate enough, as far as it goes, but it misses the sense of evil conveyed by the original. This revision, which does contain some of the words Dickens used, is much better:

> Dickens said the town was made of old red brick, darkened by black smoke, "like the painted face of a savage." It gave an impression of machinery, with chimneys producing "interminable serpents of smoke," and a river "purple with ill-smelling dye." The buildings shook, and the machinery went up and down "like the head of an elephant in a state of melancholy madness." The streets were alike, the people were alike, and so were their days and years.

*Charles Dickens, *Hard Times* (London: Chapman & Hall, n.d.), p. 31.

What has been added are three of the images — the vivid comparisons — that Dickens used, and including them helps to give the flavor of the original paragraph. Notice, however, that one of the main rules of summarizing has been carefully followed:

> *Always use quotation marks if you repeat more than three consecutive words of the original.*

Using the Help That's Provided

In summarizing longer material — a whole chapter or even an entire book — you can often get a good deal of help from the subheadings, which provide a ready-made plan for your own notes. Look at any of the chapters in this book, for instance. The chapters are divided into sections, each with its own title in darker print. If you were summarizing one of those chapters, the titles would give you some clues as to what the summary should include. You will also see that this book gives brief, ready-made summaries at the end of each section, and you could put together a perfectly accurate summary of a chapter merely by using those italicized statements — in your own words, of course.

Many books of explanation, including most textbooks, include similar guides, as do many magazine articles. Using these guides will not substitute for reading the entire text, but it will show you what the original writer thought was important enough to deserve special emphasis. Examine some of the textbooks for other courses you are taking. What system does each book use for dividing the material into sections? If there are subheadings, can you, as you review the material for a test, tell yourself what the main point that follows each subheading is? That kind of mental summarizing is an excellent way to make sure that you understand and remember what you have read.

> *When taking notes for a written summary of longer material,*
> *take advantage of the clues given in the original;*
> *treat each section separately;*
> *take notes as you read; and*
> *keep the proportions right.*

Summarizing Graphs

Sometimes the material you read will include illustrations — charts, graphs, or diagrams. Such drawings are often a shortcut for long columns of numbers, and they certainly make it easier for readers to see relationships at a glance. But in written summaries you won't be able to copy the charts; you will need to understand what's being shown clearly enough to put the point being illustrated into your own words.

Look, for example, at this chart* showing the nuclear explosions that have taken place in the world between 1945 and 1982:

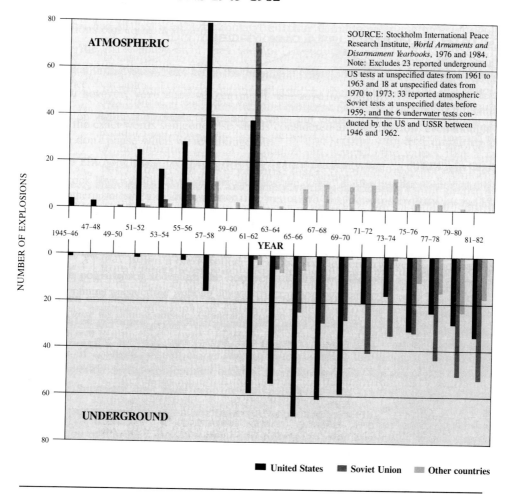

NUCLEAR EXPLOSIONS 1945–1982

SOURCE: Stockholm International Peace Research Institute, *World Armaments and Disarmament Yearbooks*, 1976 and 1984. Note: Excludes 23 reported underground US tests at unspecified dates from 1961 to 1963 and 18 at unspecified dates from 1970 to 1973; 33 reported atmospheric Soviet tests at unspecified dates before 1959; and the 6 underwater tests conducted by the US and USSR between 1946 and 1962.

■ United States   ■ Soviet Union   ▨ Other countries

Your summary might go something like this:

According to a chart printed in the spring 1985 issue of *Nucleus*, p. 5, the United States and Russia did almost all the nuclear testing between 1945 and 1982, though other countries did conduct a very few tests. Until about 1971, the United States did more tests

*"Nuclear Explosions 1945–1982." *Nucleus*, Spring 1985: 5. Reprinted by permission of the Union of Concerned Scientists.

than the Soviet Union (nearly eighty in 1958, compared to Russia's not quite forty that year), but since 1972 Russia has done about ten more each year than the United States.

Before 1963, all but one or two of the tests occurred in the atmosphere. Since the Partial Test Ban Treaty of 1963, however, all testing by the United States and Russia has occurred underground, though other countries continued a few atmospheric tests until 1980. The 1963 treaty did not halt the testing. It just moved the nuclear explosions from above the earth to beneath it.

Notice that the information in this summary is not nearly as complete as that in the chart. Summaries can never give as many details as the original. Notice, nevertheless, that the summary emphasizes two things: first, what has been done by the two superpowers, since the bars showing their activity are by far the most prominent part of the chart; and second, the shift from atmospheric to underground testing, since the chart makes that change very apparent. Notice, too, that the summary includes one thing that the chart does not show: the reason for that 1963 shift. The summary might be confusing without that information, so the writer took that one fact from the article that accompanied the chart.

Being able to interpret graphs fairly and accurately is an important skill. Test your ability to do it by finding a different graph in another textbook or a magazine article and bringing it to class. Working with another group of students, try to summarize what the graph shows. Then compare your summaries. Have all of you included the same information?

The rules for summarizing a graph are not much different from the rules for any other summary:

> *When summarizing a graph, be sure to*
> *include the most important thing the graph shows—the main point;*
> *keep all your statements accurate, reporting honestly only what the graph*
> *shows; and*
> *tell where the information came from.*

Summarizing Fiction

In summarizing fiction, you will not have the same clues that helped to guide you through explanations and arguments. Certainly there won't be topic subdivisions in heavy type. Such useful separators as *further, second, next,* and *another reason* will be missing. There will be only the story itself.

Neither will fiction openly state the main point. When you wrote about your own experiences, sometimes you didn't put the main point into your paper, although you had to keep very clear in your own mind what it was. In the same way, when you read an account of what happened to other people, either real or imaginary, you will have to figure out what the main point is. You will not state it openly if you are writing a straight summary, but keeping the main point in mind as you write will help you decide what to put in the summary and what to leave out, just as knowing your own main point helped you decide what to include when you were writing a personal experience paper.

For instance, if you were summarizing the story "Little Red Riding Hood," it might help you to remember that the point of the story is that little girls who don't mind their mothers will get into trouble. Another point, perhaps, might be that little girls ought not to talk to strangers, no matter how much sweet talking the strangers do. If you think minding mother is the main point of the story, you will not want to leave out the mother's warning as she ties the strings on the little red cape and sends her daughter out into the big woods. If you think the main point is not talking to strangers, you will want to emphasize the way the wolf flattered the innocent little girl. What is true for summarizing a nursery story is true for summarizing a longer tale, although the point may not be quite as easy to find.

If you have read George Orwell's *Animal Farm,* you know that the main point, or one of them, is that people who seize power often forget their promises and become even worse tyrants than the people they overthrew. If you are summarizing *Animal Farm,* you will want to keep that idea in mind. Remembering it will remind you to include what the pigs were like before they got rid of the farmers and what they were like afterward. But you will not include that idea in the actual summary any more than you will include the comment that the pigs remind you of the dictators in El Salvador and South America. If you are asked both to summarize *and* comment on what you have read, then certainly you will put in what you thought the point was and who the pigs reminded you of.

> *In summarizing fiction, use the main point to help you decide what to include, but don't state the point unless the original states it.*

Summaries and Reviews

Even though you use your own words when you write a summary, you don't use your own ideas. In summarizing, your job is to restate the ideas and opinions of the original writer. When you are asked to comment on or evaluate what you have read, you will be writing a *review.* It's important to keep the distinction straight.

In reviews, you give your opinions; in straight summaries you keep your opinions out. At first the difference may be hard to see because a good review always includes some summary for at least two reasons. One reason is that the summary sections help readers who have not read the article or book being reviewed or who may have forgotten some parts of it. Another and more important reason is that your opinions, whatever they are, must be backed up by reference to the original writing.

To see how this works, let's look again at the children's story "Little Red Riding Hood." Here is a review that contains, as it should, both evaluation and summary. So you can see the difference easily, the summary sections have been underlined.

A Very Silly Story

Little Red Riding Hood, that old nursery tale grownups keep telling children, seems to me so silly that bright kids would laugh themselves sick when they heard it. What sensible child would believe stuff like that? Little Red Riding Hood, in case you've forgotten, is the story of a little girl in a red cape who walks through the woods to take a basket of food to her bedridden old grandmother. In spite of her mother's warning to go straight there without talking to anybody on the way, the little girl gets into conversation with a wolf who hurries ahead, gobbles up the grandmother, and disguises himself enough to fool the little girl.

In the first place, what was the mother doing, letting the child out alone? If the woods were so dangerous, why didn't she go herself or drive the child in the car? Even the child's name shows she wasn't used to walking—Little Red *Riding* Hood. And the mother must have known the girl was a little retarded. Some children I know can't tell dogs from wolves, but they can sure tell wolves from human beings.

Some versions of the story say the wolf just shut the grandmother in the closet instead of eating her. But if that's what happened, what was the matter with the old woman? Why didn't she pound and scream to warn the child? In the original version, after the wolf had eaten the grandmother, he dressed up in her cap and got into bed. Here's where it really gets silly. At the answer to the very first question, "Why are your ears so big, Grandma?" "The better to hear you my dear," you'd think the child might remember that the old woman could hear all right last week, when her ears were a normal size. But no. The stupid child just stands there asking questions until the wolf, who is almost as stupid as she is, gets out of bed and eats her up, or, in the version designed not to frighten the kids that believe the story, until a woodcutter comes, saves the child, and kills the wolf. Why didn't the wolf just eat her out in the woods where it would have been easy and safe? What's all this foolishness about dressing up in a lace cap?

If the moral of this story is supposed to be "Never trust a wolf," my kids would certainly not be convinced by it.

Notice that what the reviewer thinks is the main point of the story, mentioned in the last paragraph, is not the same as the reviewer's main point—that the story is silly and would not convince any bright child.

Books and articles are not the only things reviewed, of course. Newspapers and magazines are filled with reviews of movies, plays, musical performances, and even restaurants. But whether you are reviewing a book, a film on public television, a speech at a college convocation, or a rock concert, the guidelines are much the same.

A good review
*   identifies what is being reviewed;*
*   gives the reviewer's evaluation;*
*   backs up the evaluation with bits of summary or factual information; and*
*   gives credit to ideas taken from other sources.*

A Sample Book Review

1984 in 1985

Identifies what's being reviewed: gives author, title, publisher, first publication date, edition used for this review.

Also brief information about the author.

[1]   The novel *1984* was first published in 1949, just four years after the end of the Second World War. It was written by George Orwell, the pen name of an Englishman, Eric Blair, who is also famous for a short satirical novel, *Animal Farm,* and an essay called "Politics and the English Language," which is reprinted in a book of essays we studied. The edition of *1984* that I read was a paperback published by the New American Library, Signet Classics, in 1983, with a preface by the television commentator, Walter Cronkite, and an afterword by Eric Fromm.

Writer's opinion—relates ideas in the novel to events near the time it was first published.

[2]   The novel seems to show Orwell's concern over recent historical events. The picture of what happens when a dictatorship controls people's behavior and beliefs makes readers think of what happened in Germany under Hitler and Russia under Stalin. The fact that the novel takes place after an atomic war is a reminder of the fear and horror many people felt after the atomic bomb was dropped on Japan. Orwell is trying to show what could happen in the world, to us and people like us, if an atomic war destroyed the structure of our world and gave a small group absolute control to treat people like cogs in a machine.

This paragraph is all summary.

[3]   In Oceania, the world of *1984,* the Party keeps complete control by dominating everyone's actions and thoughts. People are forced to attend Hate Week and two-minute Hate Seminars. They join Anti-Sex Leagues and are taught that all sex, except to beget children, is wrong. Whatever people do, Big Brother is watching them, and almost all of them like being watched. It makes them feel cared for. The Party destroys facts and changes history. The few people not willing to give up their identity are punished. Nevertheless, Winston Smith, the main character, and Julia, who becomes his lover, try to preserve their identity and avoid the Thought

Police. The book is the story of their attempts to keep their love and their freedom of thought. But they cannot do it. When they are being tortured, they betray each other. Winston says, "Don't do it to me, do it to her," and we find out that Julia, in the same situation, does the same thing. At the end of the book, after Winston has been brainwashed, he sits in a cafe every evening drinking free gin and finally gets rid of his "subversive" memories. He learns to love Big Brother.

Writer gives general summary of what others have said, crediting Cronkite.

[4]   Last year, when the real 1984 arrived, there was a great deal of discussion of Orwell's book. Many people thought things were all right because we had no Big Brother in this country telling us what to think and watching what we do. People thought Orwell had exaggerated because, even though the world is piling up nuclear weapons he couldn't dream of, there had not yet been a nuclear war. Other people, like Cronkite in the preface to this edition, saw signs of Orwell's world in other countries, such as Iran under the Ayatollah.

Writer's opinion, backed up by reference to "goodthink" in the novel.

[5]   But it isn't just other countries that show indications of an Orwellian world. Most Americans get their news and many of their ideas from television. Just this year there has been an attempt to buy and control one of the major networks because a group of people think its ideas are too liberal and that the information that goes out to people should be controlled so that viewers will think the "right" things. That attempt did not succeed, but an organized movement all over the country to remove books from school libraries if the books contain ideas the protesters disagree with has been successful in several places. These attempts remind readers of the "goodthink" practiced in Oceania.

Writer's opinion, backed up by reference to "doublethink" in the novel.

Credit is given to Fromm for a specific example.

[6]   What is called "doublethink" in Oceania exists in some ways in this country, too. We have a weapon of war and destruction named "Peacemaker." During the Vietnam War, we read about our troops having to "destroy" a village in order to "save" it. Fromm, in his afterword, says we talk about "the free world," when we mean countries that support U.S. policy, even though some of those countries

are dictatorships and not at all free politically. All these words remind readers of Oceania's "war is peace" and "slavery is freedom."

Writer's opinion, backed up by reference to Big Brother.

[7] Recent developments in technology also provide opportunities for more control over individuals. We have computers that pile up more and more information about our private lives. We have gadgets that can tap into any telephone conversation and record what we say. The FBI keeps files on thousands of citizens. We have satellites in the sky that can read license plates in a parking lot, as Cronkite mentions. So far all this technology is not being used much against ordinary people, but the machinery for some Big Brother to watch us does exist.

Again, Cronkite is given credit for a specific suggestion.

Writer's opinion, with reference to what occurs in the novel.

[8] Technology has also produced machines and computers that are doing the work, and the thinking, that people used to do. Nowadays clerks in supermarkets and department stores just push buttons and the computers do the rest. Work is dehumanized and thus people are being dehumanized, too. Work for ordinary people is becoming more and more meaningless, just as it was in Oceania.

Conclusion summarizes the main points of the writer's evaluation.

The four parallel sentences beginning "It should be read as a warning . . ." emphasize the writer's beliefs.

[9] We have not yet reached the kind of world that Orwell describes, but we are closer to it in 1985 than we were in 1949. The book *1984* should not be read as a prediction that did not come true. It should be read as a warning that "Thought Control," or "Goodthink," could happen here unless we remember that ideas we disagree with have a right to be heard. It should be read as a warning that some signs of "doublethink" are already here and that we need to be especially careful to consider what the language we hear really means. It should be read as a warning that the technology for watching us already exists and that we must fight to see that it is not used against ordinary people. It should be read as a warning that we are being dehumanized whenever we forget that loving and caring and thinking are more important than being comfortable and supplied with material things. If people do not pay attention to Orwell's warning, we can lose our freedom gradually, without much noticing it, and learn to love Big Brother just as Winston did.

Final sentence refers to what the writer considers the main theme of the novel, "Big Brother is watching you."

Appendix Two/
Writing Longer Papers

Even though you have written ten or twenty successful short papers and been rather proud of your efforts, there's something about the announcement "term paper" that may make you forget everything you know about writing. It's true that you will have to spend more time on a long paper than a short one, and it's true that a bigger proportion of your semester grade may depend on how successfully you write it. But there is no need to fall into a state of hysterical alarm just because some teacher says, "Term papers will be due the last week of the semester," and casually adds, "Make it about two thousand words long." There's no need to count up on your fingers (two thousand words is about eight typed pages) and decide you can't possibly do it.

Actually, the main difference between a term paper (or a reference or a research paper, whatever it's called) and any other college paper is just that—length. You will be all right if you remember that you are almost never expected to produce eight pages out of your own unassisted head. For long assignments, it is usually taken for granted that you will get some of your material from magazine articles and books. There are some exceptions, of course, but those exceptions often make the paper even easier to write. Suppose you are taking a course in child development; your term paper may consist of the observations you have made all semester in the day-care center, together with the conclusions you have drawn from what you have observed. In that case, you will have known about the assignment from the beginning of the semester, and the careful day-by-day notes you will have taken will form the bulk of your paper. Or suppose you are taking diesel mechanics; your term paper may be a careful report of the repair job your group did on one truck. These two papers are not much different from the kinds of reports you may have to write when you are actually out on a job.

Whatever form your term paper takes, be sure to find out exactly what you are expected to do. If the assignment isn't completely clear, ask the teacher to repeat it or stay after class and get a fuller explanation. If the assignment is a reference paper—that is, one in which you are expected to use books, magazines, or other sources to collect your information—be sure to ask how the final draft of your paper should be arranged (see pages 389–408).

The Reason for Research Papers

No teacher, in an English class or any other course, asks you to do a research paper just to make life hard for you. Good research papers are more than an exercise in following what may seem tiresome steps, one by one, and then submitting the results in conventional form. Good research papers, like any other kind of looking and finding, can be an exciting experience in discovery.

They also provide good practice in making discoveries. People in hundreds of different kinds of jobs are required to find information—from the law clerk who hunts for old legal decisions to the lab assistants who helped Jonas Salk isolate the polio vaccine. The people who hold such jobs not only have to find information, they have to evaluate it and decide how it relates to the question with which they began. They have to locate, examine, sometimes discard, and always summarize accurately.

Good research always begins with a question. Unlike some other papers you have written, you don't start with a main idea and look for things that will support it. Instead, you start with a topic, ask yourself some questions about it, and set out to find the answers.

You'll do a better job, and stand a better chance of enjoying the process, if you begin with a question you really care about. In some classes, a general topic will be assigned, in much the same way that the investigations you do on a job will be determined by the needs of the job. If you are given a topic, narrow your question to the part you find most interesting. If that's impossible, ask your teacher whether you can change to some other topic related to the course, something you *can* get involved in. Most teachers don't really want you to waste your time on a topic that bores you.

If a topic has not been assigned, the possibilities are wide open. Are you curious about whether windmills are a real alternative to nuclear energy? Do you want to know whether there are too many, or too few, hospital beds in your area? What's involved in running a small weekly newspaper or a hot dog stand? Are you curious about diet fads or divorce laws or draft regulations? You might begin your search for a topic with a bit of brainstorming. Make a list of the things you do for fun. What do you know about the background of those hobbies—science fiction? soccer? symphony orchestras? Make another list of terms used in newspapers or news broadcasts about which you have only vague information: Alzheimer's disease, Nazi war trials, Indian fishing rights, the destruction of dolphins—whatever arouses your curiosity. One man who read that *Huckleberry Finn* had been banned in the Mark Twain Junior High School asked himself how widespread such censorship is. One woman who caught the tag end of a television program on acid rain asked herself how much damage it actually does and what's being done about it.

In working out your question, don't worry about making a world-shaking discovery. College students are not expected to do the kind of research that results in a cure for cancer or an idea nobody has ever had before. One writer commented not long ago that most of our so-called intelligence is not in our heads but in the libraries of the world. A research paper is a chance for you to find some of that accumulated intelligence in your own library, evaluate it, and use it.

Finding Material

Suppose you are interested in American Indian treaties. Before you decide that your main idea will be that most of the treaties were unfair to the Indians, or that almost all of them have been broken, you will need to spend a good deal of time in the library, finding out all you can about the treaties. Almost any library can give you three main kinds of help: the catalog of books, the magazine index, and the reference librarian.

You may want to try the catalog first. In some libraries this catalog is a huge card file; in others it is a set of big books or a computer screen you can manipulate yourself by following the directions that are given. Whatever system your library uses, the catalog will list all the books the library owns by author, by title, and by subject. Try the subject listing first. Look both under "Indians" and under "treaties." Perhaps the main entry under "Indians" will say "See native Americans"; then you try that listing. As you continue your investigation, you will probably find that all the treaties with all the native American tribes over more than two hundred years is much too broad a topic, so you decide to concentrate on treaties that relate to fishing rights in the Pacific Northwest. There have been some recent controversies about that. You will probably find that most of the books you're interested in are shelved very close together, under the same general classification number. Jot down a number or two and, if your library has open shelves—that is, if you are allowed to go where the books are shelved and look through them—find the right section and begin browsing through the books. If the library has closed shelves—that is, if you must take a call slip to the desk and have someone bring the books—you can still browse through several to see which will be most useful, but the process will be slower.

If you have decided to investigate fishing rights, you will want to find out what has happened in the last year or so, events too recent to be covered in books. This information can be found in the magazine index, the *Readers' Guide to Periodical Literature,* which is a series of bound volumes listing articles published in most magazines of general circulation. It comes out by the month; then the monthly editions are combined into big volumes, each of which covers two years. The best way to find recent material is by beginning at the present and working back toward the past. The front of each volume carries a list of the abbreviations used. *Sat R,* for instance, means the *Saturday Review,* and the numbers following it show the page numbers of the article and the date of the magazine. You can easily find out whether your library stores back issues of particular magazines either bound or on microfilm. When you have copied down the notations for the articles that interest you, take the list to a librarian who will get the magazines for you.

Finally, of course, you can ask a reference librarian for help. Reference librarians are there to suggest sources you haven't thought about—other more specialized indexes than the *Readers' Guide,* pamphlets, perhaps a subject listing that will lead to fresh information.

Other possibilities exist, too. If there's someone in your area who is an expert on your subject, you might try for an interview, either in person or on the telephone. If you are concerned about hospital beds, perhaps you know a nursing supervisor who can tell you how many beds were occupied last year. If you are writing about fishing rights, perhaps there's a lawyer who defended some Indians arrested for spearing salmon or a charter boat operator angry because the fishing season was closed early last year. If censorship is your topic, you might want to call the local superintendent of schools to find out how the district handles complaints about textbooks.

Taking Notes

Don't try to read all of everything you have found. Instead, glance rapidly through each book or magazine, trying to find material that relates to your specific question. If you are examining a book, use the index and the bibliography given at the end of the book. The bibliography can lead you to other books that may be even more helpful.

As you read, take notes on the information you think you will want. Most people find three-by-five-inch notecards are the simplest way to record information—that's why they're called notecards. But whether you use notecards or a notebook, there are a few standard procedures you ought to follow:

1. Make a complete list of all the books and magazines that provide you with any information. Put down the author, the title, the publisher, and the place and date of publication for each book. For magazines, be sure to include the date as well as the page numbers on which the article appears. If you have interviewed somebody, put down the person's exact name, position, and the date of the conversation. You will need this list when you make the bibliography for your paper.
2. Keep your notes brief but accurate; if you write too much, it will be hard to sort out the information when you begin to plan your paper.
3. Put the information you find into your own words or, if you can't always do that, use quotation marks when you copy more than three consecutive words from somebody else.
4. Be sure to record the exact source of every note you take. Nothing is more exasperating than having to go back through every source you've used, looking for where you found an important piece of information.

Here are two notecards on acid rain:

```
┌─────────────────────────────────────────────────┐
│ Gay, p.7                          emissions       │
│                                                   │
│                                                   │
│        U.S. — 30 million tons SO₂ a yr.           │
│              15 million tons NO₂ a yr.            │
│                                                   │
│                                                   │
│   60% from utilities                              │
│                                                   │
└─────────────────────────────────────────────────┘
```

Since the list of sources already gives the complete information on Gay's book, the notecard doesn't need any more than her name and the page number. The notation, "emissions," in the righthand corner will help the writer sort the cards when it's time to plan the paper.

```
┌─────────────────────────────────────────────────┐
│ Time, p.18                      EPA decision      │
│                                                   │
│                                                   │
│   EPA rejects petition from PA, NY                │
│   & Maine (1984)                                  │
│   Angry Maine gov, Joseph Brennan,                │
│   says administration is "saying,                 │
│   in effect, it's OK to dump your                 │
│   garbage on your neighbor's lawn."               │
│                                                   │
└─────────────────────────────────────────────────┘
```

This second notecard, covering information taken from a magazine, uses quotation marks because the writer wants to repeat exactly what the Maine governor said.

Planning the Paper

Once you have made yourself something of an expert on your topic, or at least have found out a good deal about it, you can reword your question, this time making it more specific. If the original question was, "Were the Indian treaties unfair to the Indians?" your new question might be, "How have court decisions affected the fishing rights of Northwest Indian tribes?" or "Should the initiative on steelhead fishing passed in 1984 in the state of Washington be declared unconstitutional?"

The way you answer your new question will be the main idea sentence of your paper. You have already found the support for it, so your main idea can rest firmly on the material you have collected. Now the job is much like the job of writing any other paper. You will make a preliminary plan, showing the order in which you think you will use your material. Here's where the headings on those notecards will come in handy. If you are writing about fishing treaties and have several cards that say "steelhead" and several that say "Chinook salmon," you can group them together. In fact, you can rearrange your notecards as often as necessary, then use the order of the notecards themselves as the beginning of a plan.

As you write your first draft, don't forget to include the source of the information from each notecard as you use it. Something very brief will do—(Gay 7) for instance. Then when you write your final draft, you won't be frustrated by having to flip through all those notecards to find the source of a quotation or a set of figures.

When you begin to write, remember that the introduction should make the limits of your topic clear and give readers an indication of what your purpose is. If your paper—the report of what you have discovered—is to be successful, it should have only one general purpose, but you will probably need to use many of the other writing purposes, too. (The exceptions, in most papers, are giving directions and personal experience.) You will need to *define* the important terms you use; you may find *comparisons* and *classification* useful; you will want to *analyze* how something works or what caused it. Even though you take a position for or against something— the steelhead initiative violates the intent of the Indian treaties, or school boards should not be allowed to remove library books without a full public hearing—you will need to *tell what happened* and you will need to keep your writing as objective as possible. You will need to support what you say by examples, statistics, authorities, and probably predictions. You will want your conclusion, whatever it is, to be logical. And without some careful *summary* of what you have read, you can't write the paper at all.

Don't expect that your first draft will please either you or your teacher. In longer papers, even more than in short ones, it's important to cut what sounds like too much, add more details, and play around with the arrangement until you are satisfied that you have the order and the proportions just right. Remember, too, that the language in reference papers is expected to be fairly formal. Don't use contractions and avoid, as far as you can, sounding at all personal.

The woman interested in acid rain began with a very broad question: "What about acid rain?" As she read, she changed the question to "What damage does acid rain do?" and then she discovered that what she really cared about was why so little is being done about it. Her final question was, "If acid rain is so dangerous, why don't we do more about it?" Her main idea sentence then was, "Considering what we know about how dangerous acid rain is, it's important to understand why so little is being done about it."

She wrote a first draft based on the way she had arranged her notecards, but when she read it over, she discovered it sounded far too rambling and was far longer than she wanted it to be. She decided to condense two big sections, one giving details on the methods of reducing emissions and the other telling about the early discoveries in Sweden. Then she could include more on what was really the point of the paper—opposition to control in the United States. She made a new scratch outline:

What acid rain is
What causes it
How it's measured
Where it is
Damage it does—
  Lakes and fish
  Forests and crops
  Water
  Health
  Stone and metal
Who's against controls—utilities mainly
  Ads
  Costs
  Blackmail
  Union allies—lost jobs
Also government
  Under Carter
  Under Reagan
    EPA, other statements and actions

A Sentence Outline

That rough plan was enough for her purposes and she pretty much followed it in the next drafts she wrote. Her teacher wanted a formal sentence outline, however, so here is the one she prepared, based on the final draft of the paper that appears on pages 389–408. Notice that she used complete sentences all through and that she never subdivided unless she had at least two subtopics.

Poison from the Sky

I. It is important to understand why so little is being done about acid rain.
II. Scientists know a great deal about acid rain.
  A. The causes, amount, and extent are all known.
    1. Tall stacks have greatly increased the spread of pollution.
    2. Tons of sulphur dioxide and nitrogen oxides are emitted each year.
    3. Acid rain has been found in most parts of the United States.
  B. Damage is widespread in the United States and Canada.
    1. The environment is being hurt.
      a. Lakes and fish are dead.

         b. Trees are dying.
         c. Many crops are susceptible.
         d. Cattle are at risk.
         e. Both drinking water and groundwater may be contaminated.
         f. Many humans die needlessly.
         g. Cultural monuments are decaying.
         h. Cars and planes are corroded.
      2. Acid rain causes great financial losses.
III. Methods of control do exist.
    A. Several methods are well-known.
    B. Some industries have shown methods can be used profitably.
IV. Little is being done for several reasons.
    A. Utilities and refineries fight against controls.
      1. Advertisements and articles play down the situation.
      2. Cost is used as a weapon against controls.
         a. Utilities exaggerate the cost of controls.
         b. Refineries threaten to shut down.
    B. The possibility of lost jobs has made unions allies of industry.
    C. Government actions have not helped.
      1. Under the Carter administration two things occurred.
         a. President Carter proposed a change from oil to coal.
         b. The United States and Canada signed an "agreement to agree."
      2. Under the Reagan administration deregulation has been emphasized.
         a. Stockman accused the press of creating a false crisis.
         b. EPA appropriations were cut.
         c. Reagan said the OSTP report does not represent the official view.
         d. EPA rejected a petition filed under CAA rules.
         e. The Supreme Court ruled that EPA does not have to follow CAA restrictions.
         f. The 1980 agreement with Canada has gotten nowhere.
V. We cannot afford to wait.
    A. Doran called present conditions a recipe for stalemate.
    B. Harris poll showed 80 percent of Americans want emissions controlled.
    C. We may be ruining the world we live in.

Giving Credit

Because many of the things you will be saying in a long paper really belong to somebody else—that is, you are depending on facts other people have gathered or statements they have made—you will need to let your readers know where your material came from. There are two standard methods of giving credit to the original author. The first method is used for specific borrowing and is indicated in the body of the paper, just after the borrowing itself. These specific acknowledgments used to be called *footnotes* or *end notes,* and students were required to give fairly complete information each time they referred to a source, either at the bottom of the same page (footnotes) or in a group at the end of the paper (end notes). A more modern method, based on the new *MLA* (Modern Language Association) *Stylebook,* is much simpler to use. Under this method, you give the author's last name and the page number in parentheses—(Gay 7)—for instance, much as you have already recorded it on your notecards. Then your readers can refer to the more complete information that will be given at the very end of your paper. To see how this system works, look at the sample paper on pages 389–408.

You must acknowledge this kind of specific borrowing whenever you use:

1. Statistics collected by someone else
2. A piece of information or an example that is not common knowledge
3. More than three consecutive words taken from someone else
4. Even your own slightly changed version of someone else's words

The test for common knowledge is not whether *you* already knew it, but whether someone fairly familiar with your subject would have known it. That Abraham Lincoln was born in a log cabin, was president of the United States during the Civil War, and when he was young, may have walked several miles to return a penny is common knowledge. What Carl Sandburg, a Lincoln expert, says about Lincoln's personal sorrows during the war years is not common knowledge, and if you use Sandburg's information, you must give Sandburg credit.

If you have carefully recorded your source on each notecard and remembered to transfer that information to each draft of your paper, you will not have any trouble. But don't decide it doesn't really matter. There are three good reasons to give credit wherever it is needed. One, of course, is to avoid being accused of plagiarism— trying to pass off what somebody else has written as though it were your own original work. The penalties for plagiarism in some classes and some colleges are very harsh: failure on the paper, failure in the course, or even dismissal from school. The second reason is so that readers who are genuinely interested in what you are saying can go to your sources and read more about it if they want to. The third reason is again self-protection: if some of the information you find turns out to be inaccurate, it's the original writer's fault, not yours.

The second method of giving credit, which comes at the end of your paper, is a list of everything you read or used in gathering the material for your paper. You have already kept this list, so all you will have to do is put the list in alphabetical order under the name of the author or, if no author's name is given for a magazine article, under the title of the article. The traditional name for such a list is "bibliography"; more modern practice heads the list "Works Consulted" or "Works Cited." If you include everything you read, use "Works Consulted." If your list includes only the material acknowledged in the body of your paper, use "Works Cited." For more specific information about how this list should be arranged, look at the "Works Cited" pages at the end of the sample paper on pages 407–408.

Using a Style Manual

Be sure to find out from your teacher what method of giving credit you should follow. Several different methods exist, and these methods are carefully explained in pamphlets or books called style manuals. A *style manual* not only shows how to acknowledge the sources of your material, it also gives advice on whether to use single or double spacing, how wide the margins should be, when to abbreviate, and other such matters.

If you are expected to use the new MLA style, or if the choice is up to you, you can probably find enough information in this section, with a little additional advice from your teacher. Or your college may have a preferred style manual; if so, the bookstore probably has it in stock.

Whatever system is recommended, be sure to follow it exactly. It may seem to you a little silly to fuss about whether credit is given in the middle of the paper, at the bottom of the page, or at the end; whether the name of the book you are referring to is underlined or left plain, whether it is followed by a period or a comma. Many teachers, however, care a lot about these details, and getting it right is only a matter of taking pains.

It's also important to have the margins the right width, the page numbers in the right places, and the title arranged in the right form. If you are using MLA style, leave one inch margins at the top, the bottom, and the sides of your paper. Page numbers go inside these margins, in the upper right-hand corner. Don't use a separate title page; instead, put your name, your teacher's name, the course number, and the date on separate lines on the left-hand side at the top of the first page. Double-space twice; center the title, just as you have been doing on your shorter papers; double-space again and begin the paper. Double-space everything all the way through, including your name and course number, all the quotations you use, and the list of credits at the end. Again, you can use the sample paper at the end of this section to see how your material should be spaced.

Even if your teacher does not specifically require that your term paper be typed, it's a good idea to type it, or have it typed, if you possibly can. Typing will make it look better, and every little bit helps. If you do have someone else type it, however, be sure to read the finished copy just as carefully as you read the paper before you gave it to the typist. If you find mistakes, correct them neatly above the line, using a caret (∧) to show where an insertion belongs. If there are enough corrections on a single page to make it look messy, have that page retyped.

And don't hesitate, naturally, to have someone else read and comment on your paper at any stage in its preparation. You, and you alone, are responsible for the finished product, but we don't know anybody who presented a master's thesis without having a friend or two read it first.

A Sample Research Paper

1

Madeline Gorini

Mr. Babcock

English 102

May 17, 1985

Poison from the Sky

   Visible pollution has been with us for a long time.
Anybody who approaches an industrial area by plane on a
clear day can see the smog hovering like a dirty blanket over
the city. But invisible and more dangerous is the poison in
the clouds, carried everywhere by the winds--acid rain.
Scientists know that acid rain is destroying lakes and the
fish in them, killing trees in the high forests, damaging
crops and livestock, contaminating drinking water, causing
thousands of unnecessary deaths every year, and ruining
irreplaceable cultural monuments. What scientists do not
know for certain is whether this destruction is irre-
versible. They do not know whether acid rain is gradually
making the Northern Hemisphere uninhabitable. Considering

Everything double-spaced

Two double spaces here

Title centered

Two more double spaces

General introduction

**Sentence shows order
in which damage will
be discussed.**

2

Main idea sentence.

what they do know, however, it is important to understand why so little is being done about acid rain.

Ironically, one of the main reasons for the great increase in acid rain was an attempt to control the visible pollution.

CAA is public knowledge.

In 1970 Congress passed the Clean Air Act (CAA), which called for new methods of pollution control. The Environmental Protection Agency (EPA), charged with enforcement of the act, allowed utilities to build four hundred smokestacks taller than two hundred feet, thirty-six of them more than eight hundred feet.

Numbers that can be expressed in not more than two words are written out.

In the same year, INCO, the huge Canadian nickel smelter, built the tallest stack in the world, a quarter of a mile high.

One main cause of acid rain.

These tall stacks did relieve pollution in their immediate areas, but high pressure systems in the sky carried the dangerous sulphur dioxides and nitrogen oxides on the winds, mixed them with clouds to form acids, and dumped them hundreds of miles from the original source.

Quotation is made part of writer's own sentence.

Dr. Walt Lyons, a meteorologist from Chicago, says that satellite photographs showing "smog blobs" moving great distances demonstrate that acid rain is "not just a local problem. Due to shifting weather fronts, it can be a problem on a regional, national--or even a global scale" (qtd. in Gay 33).

Readers are referred to p. 33 of Gay's book; "qtd." means what Lyons said is quoted by Gay.

Thirty million tons of sulphur dioxide and more than

3

fifteen million tons of nitrogen oxides are released in the
United States every year, two-thirds of the sulphur dioxide
and 30 percent of the nitrogen oxides from coal-burning
utilities (Boyle and Boyle 18-9). When these gases combine
with moisture in the atmosphere, the acidity of the resulting water (or snow or sleet or hail or dew) is measured on a
pH scale running from zero to fourteen, with seven being
neutral (distilled water). The scale is logarithmic; that
is, pH 5 is ten times more acid than pH 6, and pH 4 is a hundred times more acid than pH 6, etc.

    In the Midwest and as far south as the Carolinas, the
average rain is now pH 4.5. In the northeastern states
it is pH 4.3. In Raleigh, North Carolina, the rain is
sometimes pH 3, more acid than white vinegar (Boyle and
Boyle 15), and in Wheeling, West Virginia, one storm in 1978
brought a rain of pH 1.5, about the same as the strength of
the acid in an automobile battery (Pawlick 12). Acid rain
has also been found in Colorado, Idaho, New Mexico, Montana,
California, Washington and Oregon. Rain in Seattle measures
between pH 4.2 and pH 5.2 seventy percent of the time (Boyle
and Boyle 64), and rain on the coast of Oregon has been
recorded as low as pH 4.3 (Core). Scientists trying to
measure acid rain over Los Angeles could not do so because

**Statistics come from
Boyle and Boyle, pp. 18
and 19. Names of both
authors are given.**

**Although the writer
wasn't familiar with the
pH scale, it's common
knowledge to anybody
who knows chemistry.**

**How much acid rain
falls and where.**

**These pH figures are not
common knowledge so
sources are given.**

**Page number not given
for Core because this
was an interview.**

4

their instruments became so corroded that they would not register (Boyle and Boyle 65).

Transition from areas affected to first kind of damage—lakes and fish.

The damage done by this widespread acid rain was first noticed in the Adirondacks and in Canadian lakes. Where fish were once plentiful they had disappeared. According to the Office of Technology Assessment, 3,000 lakes and 23,000 miles of streams in the eastern United States have been "acid altered," and 17,000 lakes of fifteen acres or more and 117,000 miles of streams are vulnerable (Gay 19). Canada has lost fish in an estimated 4,000 lakes and will lose 48,500 more in twenty years if acid rain continues at the present rate (Boyle and Boyle 24). Salmon runs have been destroyed in both Nova Scotia and Maine (Boyle and Boyle 52).

"Three thousand" is not spelled out because some numbers in this paragraph are more than two words.

More explanation of what the damage is.

These areas have no heavy industry. They are dependent on the tourists who come for the fishing. More frightening than the loss of livelihood in the resort areas, however, is the fact that an entire chain of life is altered as the waters become acid. The decomposition of leaves and other organic matter is slowed. Simple organisms and insects cannot breed. Then frogs, toads, and salamanders which eat the insects disappear. Small animals, such as raccoons, skunks, foxes, and birds, which feed on amphibians, become scarcer. Then the numbers of larger mammals diminish (Howard and

5

Perley 68-9). Some of the fish and mammals die from metallic poisoning, but those deaths, too, are caused by acid rain because sulphur dioxide releases deadly aluminum from the soil into the water.

In the same parts of the continent, valuable forests have been destroyed. In Vermont's Green Mountain area, acres of two- and three-hundred-year-old red spruce have been wiped out (Gay 23). In Ontario entire stands of sugar maples died between 1976 and 1980. A series of interconnected causes were responsible--weakened root systems, an increase in harmful bacteria, greater susceptibility to wind damage--but all these causes are directly traceable to acid rain (Pawlick 46-50). Long-term losses to the lumber and paper pulp industries are too great to be calculated.

Plants other than trees are also affected. Studies done between 1956 and 1969 indicate that twenty-two staple crops, including some kinds of wheat, turnips, sweet potatoes, squash, spinach, rye, rhubarb, and alfalfa, are sensitive to acid rain. Monetary losses from these crops can be huge. Pawlick says that a 1 percent loss of soybeans in the eastern United States represents a loss of $53 million (79). Some industry representatives maintain that the acidification can be offset by lime and fertilizers, and a

Second kind of damage—forests.

Third kind of damage—crops.

Just the page number is given here because the source (Pawlick) is mentioned in the sentence.

6

Opposition's argument is shown to be false.

scientist employed by TVA went so far as saying that some crops are "addicted to pollution." It is true that nitrogen and sulphur in small amounts are essential to growth, but EPA's Dr. Norman Glass has pointed out that "supplying sulphur indiscriminately by using polluted masses of air instead of controlled applications of fertilizer is just that--fertilizer" (qtd. in Pawlick 82).

Fourth kind of damage—cattle.

Even cattle are not safe. Livestock grazing in areas where acid rain has fallen eat contaminated plants and drink water contaminated by toxic metals leached from the soil. Human beings may not be in immediate danger from eating the meat, but the possibility of long-range damage exists (Pawlick 83).

Fifth kind of damage—drinking water.

If what people eat may not yet be dangerous, in many places the water they drink is. After water has been standing in pipes, acid rain reacts on plumbing to such an extent that dangerous levels of copper and lead are released. Health officials in Ontario have warned residents in some areas that they must let their water run for a long time before they can safely use it. The water in roof catchment/cistern systems has been found to exceed safe standards. As Pawlick remarks, it is ironic that in Pennsylvania these catchment systems were installed by householders trying to avoid wells that had been poisoned by coal mines (110-20).

7

Another danger is that groundwater, on which most water
supply systems depend directly or indirectly, may also be
being contaminated. Little is presently known about the
effects of acid rain on groundwater, but authorities think
it is possible that acidified lakes and streams may be leak-
ing far underground and releasing lead and cadmium into
these essential reserves (Pye et al. 73).

More water damage—groundwater.

The song that was popular a few years ago--"Don't drink
the water and don't breathe the air"--may not be so far
wrong. The Office of Technology Assessment says that 51,000
Americans and Canadians die early and needlessly every year
as a direct result of sulphur dioxide pollution. Another
study done by two universities says that 187,686 people in
the United States alone die from sulphates (Pawlick 101,
107). Most of those who die have asthma or are old or very
young. But a recent study in Germany has found a possible
link between sulphates and infant crib death, and soluble
aluminum, mobilized by acid deposits, may be a factor in
Alzheimer's disease (Pawlick 108, 118).

Sixth kind of damage—human health.

Statistics come from two different pages in source.

Cultural monuments that cannot be replaced are also at
risk. When acid rain hits marble already covered with dry
pollutants from the air, it turns part of the marble to gypsum, a softer substance which washes off easily. Or the
acid rain forms a black crust which falls off in chunks.

Seventh kind of damage—cultural monuments.

8

One writer has suggested that city dwellers, who tend to be suspicious of environmentalists, may regard acid rain more seriously when they realize that among the world's buildings being eaten away are the United States Capitol, the Acropolis in Greece, and St. Paul's Cathedral in London (Winckler 92).

Last kind of damage— metal, cars, planes.

Metals are also seriously affected. What has happened to the Statue of Liberty has been well publicized, but less well-known is the destruction to cars and planes. In 1978 in Pennsylvania several hundred automobiles showed raindrop-shaped scars after a storm with a rain of pH 3, an acidity between vinegar and lemon juice (Boyle and Boyle 85). The Air Force spends more than a billion dollars a year taking care of corrosion. Acid rain is one of the main causes of damage to B-52 bombers, in which corrosion is so bad "you can pop the rivets right out of the wings with your fingers" (Pawlick 91-2).

Costs of acid rain damage.

Magazine article with no author named, so the title of the article is used.

In addition to the environmental damage, acid rain is expensive--nobody knows exactly how expensive. The National Academy of Science says acid rain does more than $5 billion damage each year in the United States (Tall Stacks 18). In 1978 the U.S. President's Council on Environmental Quality estimated that property damage is costing $2 billion a year, with an additional $1.7 billion in health costs (Howard and

9

Perley 106-7). In 1981 the United Nations Organization for
Economic Cooperation and Development said that strict emission
controls could save $1.2 billion in corrosion costs (Acid
Rain/UNESCO Courier 23). Russell W. Peterson, president of
the National Audubon Society, says that the measurable benefits of air pollution controls would outweigh the costs of
such control by $5 billion a year (Boyle and Boyle 126).

> **Both title of article and name of magazine included here, because title "Acid Rain" not enough to distinguish it from other sources.**

Methods of control do exist. The most common of these
is the installation of stack gas scrubbers, which can clean
out from 75 to 90 percent of the sulphur dioxide. Their
disadvantage is that they produce 3,500 to 4,000 tons of
sludge a day. In one utility this sludge has, in five years,
filled sixty acres to a depth of thirty feet (Pawlick 124-5).

> **What can be done about it.**

But there are also other possibilities: coal washing; fluid-
ized bed combustion; chemical coal cleaning; coal liquefac-
tion and gasification, a technique available since 1921; and
ocean-thermal-energy conversion, which converts the gas in
smokestacks to heat and electricity. One simple remedy is
to change from the "economical dispatch system"--using
electricity from older, dirtier plants first and switching
to newer, cleaner plants only when demand is high--to a
"least emissions system," which reverses the process but
would cut down on profits (Pawlick 135-41).

10

Examples of successful control.

That utilities and refineries which control pollution can be profitably run has been demonstrated.   In Japan both old and new utility plants are equipped with scrubbers, and the sludge is converted to marketable gypsum (Howard and Perley 115-6).   In Canada the Dow Chemical plant uses a cogeneration system to produce more electricity than it needs, and the Kidd Creek Mines, Ltd. in Toronto is 99 percent efficient in catching sulphur dioxide and processing it to salable sulphuric acid (Pawlick 143).   In the United States the Daggett plant in California uses an integrated gasification combined-cycle plant in which sulphur dioxide is 95 percent removed with no loss of generating capacity (Crawford).

No page number given because original article is on a single page.

How utilities fight controls—ads and statements.

In spite of these examples, both utilities and refineries have done all they can to deny their responsibility for acid rain and prevent any action.   In 1974 the American Electric Power Company, a pioneer of tall stacks, circulated an advertisement claiming that these stacks "disperse gaseous emissions widely in the atmosphere . . . over a wide area and come down finally in harmless traces." The ad went on to accuse "irresponsible environmentalists" of "taking food from the mouths of the people to give them a better view of the mountain" (qtd. in Boyle and Boyle 19; Howard and Perley 13).   A representative of the Edison Electric Institute, an association of electric companies, has complained

Ellipsis (. . .) shows that unimportant words have been omitted from the quotation.

Two different books contain the same quote.

11

that it is unfair to call the rain acid because the word "acid" has an unpleasant connotation that tends to make utilities sound evil (Gay 38). Governor James Rhodes of Ohio, the biggest coal-burning state in the country, talks about "no-growth environmentalists" who "latched on to acid rain as a rallying cry for a new wave of environmental hysteria" (qtd. in Boyle and Boyle 102). As late as 1984 Fortune published an article in which the writer introduced the "Smokey the Bear theory," maintaining that the government itself is responsible for the dying lakes and forests. By preventing forest fires, he said, the government has deprived the soil of the alkaline ash which can neutralize the acid (Brown 170).

Another tactic has been to exaggerate the cost of con-   **How utilities fight—**
trols. In Canada in 1980 great publicity was given to a   **exaggeration.**
clean-up cost of $10 billion spread over twenty years, but
when industry spokesmen were challenged to give more specific details, they said they could not remember where that
$10 billion figure came from (Howard and Perley 123). In
1984, when the Waxman/Skorski bill to require some controls
seemed to have some chance of passing in Congress, utilities
claimed the cost would be $200 billion rather than the $20
billion that has been estimated (Pawlick 162).

All these claims of astronomical costs have emphasized

12

How utilities fight— higher electric rates.

that the expense would be passed on to the public in higher electric bills. Some utilities have said that emission controls would raise the cost of electricity by 50 percent in the Midwest, but independent studies have shown that the increase would not be more than 7 to 10 percent, and the Office of Technology Assessment has pointed out that the states which need to make the largest reductions would still have some of the lowest electric rates in the country (Gay 38, 62).

How industry fights— blackmail.

Utilities have to keep running, but refineries have not hesitated to use blackmail. When the Ontario government proposed to clamp down on INCO's Sudbury plant, the worst offender in the Western Hemisphere, and the company said it could control emissions by closing the plant, the Ontario government backed down (Pawlick 171). Norando Mines, Ltd., in Quebec, has said that if anyone could demonstrate that it was doing serious harm to the environment "then we would consider shutting our operations down" (Howard and Perley 121).

Unions fear loss of jobs.

The possibility of lost jobs has made unions in both countries allies of industry. In the United States the United Mine Workers, whose membership is concentrated in the high-sulphur coal region, have opposed controls in the fear that utilities might use low-sulphur, relatively clean,

13

western coal, thus cutting employment in the mines and
creating economic disaster in Kentucky, Illinois, and
Indiana.

Attitude of UMW is common knowledge.

Whatever hopes there were of controlling acid rain got a
first blow when President Carter, faced with the oil embargo,
proposed converting more than fifty oil-fired utilities in
sixteen states to coal, thus increasing acid rain emissions
by 2 million tons a year (Pawlick 178). In 1980, nineve-
less, the United States and Canada signed a "Memorandum of
Intent Concerning Transboundary Air Pollution," in which
they pledged to try for a treaty and set up technical and
scientific work groups to study the problem.

Government actions— Carter administration.

When the Reagan administration, committed to deregu-
lation, came to power in 1981, hopes for immediate action
faded. David Stockman, director of the Office of Management
and Budget, accused the press of

Government actions— Reagan administration.

> . . . orchestrating a pretty careful strategy
> . . . written by reporters who know not a damned
> thing about pollution. . . . And they're writing
> such preposterous and absurd things . . . that
> will probably cause EPA or the Congress to lurch
> forward into an acid rain program (qtd. in Boyle
> and Boyle 96).

Stockman's statement is indented without quota-tion marks because it is longer than four lines; four periods show that a sentence in the quotation ended here.

14

Stockman went on to say that even if a few fish are dying
from acidity, that's not much loss compared to the tremen-
dous cost of controls to prevent it (Gay 9).

EPA attitude.

Not surprisingly, in 1981 appropriations for EPA were
cut by 26 percent, and it became clear that EPA officials
were not interested in adopting or enforcing regulations.
When William Ruckelshaus was sworn in as administrator of
EPA, both he and President Reagan said that acid rain would
be "met head on," but when Ruckelshaus submitted a plan to
reduce acid rain, Reagan vetoed the plan and Ruckelshaus
told Congress that the subject "needed more study" (Sibossin 18-20).

OSTP report.

As part of the "more study" approach, in 1982 the
White House asked the Office of Science and Technology Policy (OSTP) to review the current state of knowledge about
acid rain. When OSTP reported in 1984 that it was dangerous
to wait, saying that action must be taken in spite of incomplete knowledge, President Reagan announced that the findings of the report did not represent the official view
(Pawlick 164).

**Report deliberately
delayed?**

It has been suggested, in fact, that the White House
deliberately delayed the release of that report from April
until August, until after a House subcommittee, by a ten to

15

nine vote, had killed a bill to control sulphur dioxide emissions. The White House said that the April report was preliminary and had been sent back for changes. The only
changes, however, were some weakening of the wording, minor
changes on which the committee members were not consulted
(Sun).

The EPA continued to interpret the CAA as narrowly as
possible. When Maine, New York, and Pennsylvania petitioned
EPA to order the Midwest to reduce the sulphur dioxide carried into their states by acid rain, EPA rejected the petition, saying that the CAA could be invoked only against
specific pollutants and that the connection between Midwest
emissions and Northeast acid rain had not been shown. The
angry Maine governor, Joseph Brennan, declared that the
administration is "saying, in effect, it's OK to dump your
garbage on your neighbor's lawn" (qtd. in Dumping Garbage).

EPA rejection of petition.

The Supreme Court made genuine controls even less likely
when it ruled that EPA does not have to follow the restric-
tive rules of CAA but may instead "properly rely upon <u>the
incumbent administration's view of wise policy</u>" [italics
added] (qtd. in Sandler 45).

Supreme Court decision.

**"Italics added" means
that this writer has
added emphasis original
didn't use.**

Meanwhile, the 1980 agreement with Canada had gotten
nowhere, and relations between the United States and Canada

Relations with Canada.

16

have become strained.   Canada, with an economy heavily
dependent on tourism and forest products, is in the direct
path of emissions from Ohio and gets three or four times
more pollution from the United States than it sends south.
When pressure for the control of acid rain became a major
issue there, Canada established a ten-year program to cut
its own sulphur dioxide emissions in half.   The Canadian National Film Board produced a film, "Acid Rain: Requiem or
Recovery?" which the United States Justice Department
labeled foreign propaganda, demanding that the Canadian
board supply a list of all the individuals and groups in
this country who asked to see the film.   The requirement was
dropped after a federal judge declared the regulations unconstitutional, but relations with Canada were not improved
by the attempt (Gay 51; Pawlick 182).

Again, information comes from two different sources.

The 1980 "agreement to agree" had accomplished nothing
except reports, some of them useful.   Even so, in 1981 the
United States withdrew its support for one of the key work
groups, and Canadians complained that U.S. representatives
were not arriving at scheduled meetings or were sending new
people who knew little about either acid rain or the work of
the committee.   A treaty offered by Canada in 1982 was
refused by the United States.   Then late that year the

Canada offended.

17

United States called for these acid rain reports to be
reviewed by the President's Council of Science and Technology, ignoring the Canadian representatives entirely
(Gay 42).

Just before President Reagan's visit to Canada in March
1985, Canadian Prime Minister Brian Mulroney said that acid
rain should be at the top of the agenda; Reagan's response
was to say it was a question of "doing what is reasonable
and responsible after getting all the facts," and to suggest
that both countries appoint "acid rain envoys." There appeared to be no chance of a bilateral agreement (Political
Consequences).

Reagan's visit accomplishes nothing.

Acid rain continues to fall, and nothing happens to stop
it. As Charles Doran of Johns Hopkins University said,
"U.S. political parties are divided on this issue, regions
are divided, bureaucracies are divided. It is a recipe for
stalemate" (qtd. in Political Consequences). The public,
however, seems less divided. A Harris poll taken in 1981
showed that 80 percent of the public does not want air pollution standards weakened or reduced. Louis Harris testified
that

Beginning of conclusion.

A recipe for stalemate.

Public favors controls.

> This message on the part of the American people
> . . . is one of the most overwhelming and clearest

18

we have ever recorded in our twenty-five years
of surveying public opinion (qtd. in Boyle and
Boyle 127).

Conclusion—summary of damage.

We cannot afford to wait. Lakes and fish, forests,
water supplies, and soil are being hurt, probably permanently, and acid rain is already seriously affecting crops,
cultural monuments, and health. Sulphuric dioxide emissions which cause acid rain are increasing rather than
diminishing. It is understandable that people worry about a
nuclear holocaust, but perhaps they should be worrying just
as much about acid rain. It does seem possible, as Boyle

Prediction of possible consequences.

Slash (/) shows division between lines of poetry.

and Boyle say (129) that T. S. Eliot may have been right when
he wrote, "This is the way the world ends / Not with a bang
but a whimper."

19

Works Cited

"Acid Rain." UNESCO Courier Jan. 1985: 21-4.

Boyle, Robert H., and R. Alexander Boyle. Acid Rain. New
    York: Nick Lyons-Schocken, 1983.

Brown, William H. "Maybe Acid Rain Isn't the Villain."
    Fortune 28 May 1984: 170+.

Core, John. Telephone interview. 20 May 1985.

Crawford, Mark. "Utilities Look to New Coal Technology."
    Science 228 (1985): 565.

"Dumping Garbage on Neighbors." Time 10 Sept. 1984: 18.

Gay, Kathlyn. Acid Rain. New York: Impact-Franklin Watts,
    1983.

Howard, Ross, and Michael Perley. Acid Rain: The North
    American Forecast. Toronto: Anansi, 1980.

**Magazine article—
author's name not given.**

**Two authors. Notice the
periods after the authors'
names and after the title.**

**Magazine article—cita-
tion gives author, title of
article, name of maga-
zine, date and pp. of article; (+) means the article
skipped some pages.**

**Magazine article with
pages numbered from the
beginning of the year;
volume no. is given.**

**Magazine, no author
given; page numbers
start over in each issue;
use standard abbrevia-
tions for months.**

20

Pawlick, Thomas.   A Killing Rain: The Global Threat of Acid

   Precipitation.   San Francisco: Sierra, 1984.

"The Political Consequences of Acid Rain."   Maclean's

   18 Mar. 1985: 18.

Pye, Veronica I., Ruth Patrick, and John Quarles.   Ground-

   water Contamination in the United States.   Philadel-

   phia: U of Penn P, 1983.

Sandler, Ross.   "Reversals for the Environment."   Environ-

   ment Nov. 1984: 44-5.

Sibossin, Jim.   "The Agency of Illusion."   Sierra May/June

   1985: 18-21.

Sun, Marjorie.   "Acid Rain Report Allegedly Suppressed."

   Science 225 (1984): 1374.

"Tall Stacks."   National Voter [League of Women Voters] 35

   (1985): 1374.

Winckler, Suzanne.   "The Ungentle Rain."   House and Garden

   Nov. 1984: 88+.

When titles start with "the" or "a," the article is alphabetized under the next word.

Here "U" means university and "P" means press: University of Pennsylvania Press.

Publisher of magazine shown for clearer identification.

Appendix Three/
Writing Application Letters

You may conduct most of your business by phone, but that does not mean you don't need business letters. If you've called to let a company know you're not pleased with their services and want things changed, your message will go further if you follow the call with a letter to the right people. And if you want to get a job, you may use the phone to make the first inquiry about it, but you will certainly need to write a letter of application as well, both as a way of getting clear in your own mind what your qualifications are and as a way of presenting those qualifications in the most attractive, orderly, and efficient form. Clearly, business letters have an advantage over phone calls: letters can be kept, referred to, verified, reread. Phone calls can't. Letters last, phone calls don't.

For all these reasons, letter writing is important. Business letters should be clear, make a point (have a main idea), and be well organized and easy to understand, just like all your writing. If business letters differ from the writing you have already done, the main difference is in a slightly greater formality and a slightly crisper tone than you may have been accustomed to using.

Being formal, however, does not mean using jargon, difficult words for their own sake, or long involved sentences. No good modern business writer uses such out-of-date phrases as "yours of the 4th inst. duly received" or "hoping to hear from you soon, I remain, your obedient servant." Good business writing comes to the point and sticks to it. It seldom includes personal chit-chat, but neither does it avoid using "I" and "you" if the writer means *I* and *you*. The tone is straightforward and natural.

Form for Business Letters

The form in which business letters should appear follows a fairly regular set of conventions. The writer's complete address and the date are given in the upper right-hand corner of the page, usually in "block style," with the beginning of each short line directly below the beginning of the previous line:

> 426 William Tell Lane, Apt. 7
> Grove Oak, Michigan 49431
> January 12, 1987

The only exception to this rule occurs when letterhead (stationery with a company or organization name and address printed at the center top of the page) is used. Then the date is either centered under the letterhead or given by itself in the right-hand corner.

Down a few lines at the left-hand margin come the name and address of the person being written to. If you know the person's official title, you should include it also, as well as the name of the company. This information is usually in block form, too:

> Mr. Rutherford Oldstedder, Sales Manager
> Modernday Products Company
> 22015 North 16th Street
> Kent, Washington 98031

Next comes a courtesy greeting, called the *salutation*. If you are writing to a specific person by name, the greeting part is easy. Business letters always use "Dear," without any implication of affection, and go on to give the person's last name, followed by a colon:

> Dear Mr. Oldstedder:

On the other hand, if you are writing just to a company, the salutation becomes a little more difficult. It used to be customary to use "Gentlemen" for the salutation, but many people object to the idea that all companies are run by men. Nowadays, if you don't have the name of any individual, it is acceptable to omit the salutation entirely and start right out with the letter.

If you are using block form in the letter itself, as most modern business writers do, begin each paragraph at the left-hand margin. Divisions between paragraphs are shown by skipping a line.

Skip another line between the last paragraph of the letter and the closing, which can appear either at the center of the page, in modified block form, or again at the left-hand margin. Another convention requires that the closing include a set phrase such as "Yours truly" or "Very truly yours," although in modern practice "Sincerely" is often used. Then skip four or five lines, to leave room for your signature, and type your name directly below the closing phrase:

> Sincerely yours,
>
>
>
> Jennifer Doolittle

With some letters you will need to send material other than just the letter itself —a copy of a cancelled check, perhaps, a receipt, or a list of information. When additional material is sent with the letter, it's customary to add the information "Enclosure" or "Enclosures" at the bottom of the letter.

The spacing between your address, the name and address of the person being written to, the salutation, and the closing depends on the length of a single-page letter. The whole page will look better if the letter itself is placed about the middle of the page. In very short letters, therefore, the spacing will be greater.

If it is at all possible, business letters should be typed, but your signature should always be written.

Application Letters

Perhaps the most important business letter you will ever need to write is a job application. Being straightforward, natural, and honest is essential in an application. Even though you've been remembering your readers' needs in other writing, here you should go one step further and actually put yourself in the reader's place. For you, your letter means "I want a job with this company." For the employer, your letter means "The writer of this letter is (or is not) able to do a good job for the company." Since the success of your letter depends on pleasing the person who reads it, you must try to imagine what would impress you if you were doing the hiring. Your letter must do more than just say, "I want the job."

One way of pleasing the reader is to keep the letter short, usually not more than four or five paragraphs. If you can, keep it to one page. The letter should include this information:

1. How you heard about the vacancy (from an advertisement, a friend, or a placement service)
2. Your most important reasons for thinking you're suited for the position
3. A word or two about why you think the job would suit you
4. A brief statement about your present circumstances (status in school, reason for wanting to change jobs, etc.)
5. Mention of the personal information sheet you're enclosing
6. The best way to get in touch with you and a request for an interview

If you are answering an advertisement, you might begin by saying "I saw your advertisement for an administrative assistant in the March 2 *Daily News,* and I am applying for the position." Or if you heard about the vacancy from a friend who is employed in the same company, you might start with "Thelma Riley, who works in your department, told me that you have an opening for an administrative assistant. I am writing to apply for the job."

In explaining why you are qualified, follow any clues you have about the requirements of the job. If it's construction work (or any other work that may be physically demanding), be sure to say you are in good health—if you are—and add anything else that will make you sound healthy: the jogging you do, the volleyball you play, your experience as a logger or a recreation director or a furniture mover. If the job is in sales, think of qualities that relate to selling: your pleasing personality (as demonstrated by the college offices you have been elected to, perhaps); your active imagination (as demonstrated by a campus field day you helped to organize or the successful advertisement you wrote for it); your leadership ability (as demonstrated by your volunteer work with the Girl Scouts or the excursions for senior citizens).

If you have had actual experience in the kind of job you're applying for, certainly that experience is your best recommendation. Be sure to mention it, saying exactly when, where, and how long you worked: "From June through September 1985 I worked as research assistant to Mr. Oscar Salmon, at Dynamic Services in Wichita."

But even if you have never had any direct experience in the special kind of job you're trying for, there's no reason to give up if the job sounds interesting and you believe you could do it well. Most people have something in their backgrounds that relates to nearly any job. Think about what you have done in the past and show how that experience might qualify you for the position you want, but don't invent experiences you have not had. Dishonest claims will not only result in losing that job, if you should get it, but will also give you a reputation for unreliability that may disqualify you for other jobs.

Reading the "help wanted" advertisements can give you some useful clues. Look at the kind of words that appear over and over in the ads for accountants, for instance—"budget analysis"; "performance evaluation"; "managerial experience"; "growth potential"; "billing expert"; "long-range planning." If you want to be an accountant, and have had the necessary training, use some of those words when you write your letter. Whatever job you are applying for—in administration, sales, education, health services, or anything else—you will sound like a more attractive candidate if you use some of the terms you see in the ads.

If you are applying for a job as administrative assistant, for example, talk about some of your old experiences in some of the new, fashionable words. If you have been a camp counselor, you can justifiably say that part of your job was as "assistant administrator" in charge of thirty-five girls; that you arbitrated grievances, made time-flow charts, helped develop goals and objectives, were involved in short- and long-range planning, and helped with the final evaluations. Don't say any of that if it wasn't so, of course, but even if you just made out the summer schedules, deciding who got the canoes and who got the tetherball, you did some short- and long-range planning. And even if you just wrote to the parents at the end of the camp session telling them how well their daughters adjusted, you've done some evaluation and handled some correspondence.

Does the job you're applying for require you to work with the general public? Selling tickets to the sophomore play or collecting for the United Fund is "working with the public." Does the job ask for planning and management ability? If you've had a successful delivery route, or handled the budget for the annual awards banquet, you've done some "productive planning" and shown some "efficient management."

Once you have explained why you think you are suited for the job, mention why the job would suit you. Unless you are contented in your work, you won't be a very good employee, and most employers realize this fact. Don't say you look forward to selling automotive parts as your life work unless you really have no other ambitions, but do emphasize the parts of the job you would like. Say, for example, "I like working with the public and I enjoy methodical attention to detail."

Be sure to say what you are doing now. If you are going to school, say when you expect to finish. If you are working part-time, say where. If you are unemployed, you can just say, "I will be available to begin work at any time that is convenient for you." And of course, if you are answering an advertisement, you will have to include any other information the ad asks for. A request to "state salary expected" sometimes appears in job advertisements. Expected salary is awkward to discuss in a letter. You may ruin your chance at the job if you ask for too much, but if you ask for too little, you risk getting hired for less than the company would have been willing to pay. You can't ignore the specific request, but you might sidestep it by saying, "I would expect to be paid at the usual rates for beginning administrative assistants," or "The salary is negotiable."

As for how the employer can get in touch with you, be sure to give both an address and a phone number. If you are at school from eight to five every day, say "I can be reached at 892-4808 any evening after 5:30." Your letter should also mention that you are enclosing a personal information sheet, giving specific details about your education, experience, and references.

In deciding what order to use in your letter, begin with your best qualification. Is education or experience more likely to get you the job? If you've had experience in the field, then your experience is probably more important than your education. Or if your work experience is not very closely related to the kind of job you're applying for, you'll probably want to list your education first, especially if you have a degree or some training that does relate to the job. An offer to come in for an interview whenever it's convenient for the employer makes a good closing line.

Personal Information Sheets

A *personal information sheet,* or *résumé* as it is sometimes called, has two advantages. For prospective employers, it provides a neatly organized picture of your background. For you, as a prospective employee, it provides a permanent record that can be used over and over again as you apply for different jobs, with just enough change to keep it up to date.

Your personal information sheet should give complete and accurate information about

1. your work experience
2. your education
3. at least three people willing to act as references for you

It may also include additional categories called "Other Experiences" or "Organizations," if these seem suitable.

All this information could be given in your letter, of course, and some of it undoubtedly has been, but including all these details would make your letter far too long. The purpose of your letter is to highlight, draw attention to, or explain the information listed on your résumé. The letter is an opportunity to make sure an employer sees and understands the experiences and education that qualify you to do the job. The résumé provides this information in outline form, where it is easy to see and understand.

Each section of your personal information sheet should begin with the most recent event and move backward. Under job experience, give the name of the person or company you worked for last; the address; the name of your immediate supervisor, if it is different from the name of your employer; a description of the kind of work you did; and the dates of your employment. Ordinarily, your educational record and your job record taken together should account for your time after you got out of high school. If there are any large gaps, they may lead a possible employer to wild speculation about what you were doing in that unexplained year or two. You'd better satisfy that curiosity. You can say, "September 1981–May 1982, unemployed" or "August 1978–August 1979, stayed home with small baby."

Unless your record of full-time employment is fairly long, it is a good idea to mention all the jobs you have ever had—paper routes, baby-sitting, lawn-mowing. Though these jobs may seem unimportant and quite different from the job you are applying for, the habits of responsibility and self-control demanded by any regular work may be just what will sway the employer in your favor. If the list is long, you may want to group part-time jobs or those that you held for a short time under a section called "Miscellaneous Jobs."

Your educational record should begin with the school you last attended and work backward through high school. Give the name of the school, the city and state where it is, the years you attended, and the date of your graduation. Be sure to list any specific courses or groups of courses that you think the employer would be interested in. Your school may have had a specific program or offered specific courses that make your educational training more valuable than another applicant's.

Don't overlook any opportunities to mention something special you have done. If you have participated in activities or belonged to service clubs, be sure to mention them. Maybe you designed the float for the Founder's Day Parade; maybe you were a volunteer at the hospital or visited at the jail or served as president of the Parent Teacher Association. Maybe you coached a Little League hockey team for a season or two. Think of how you spent your time outside of class or after work. You may be surprised to discover that much of that time was spent helping others or organizing events.

Your three references should include at least one person you have worked for, and all three may be previous employers if you have worked for that many people willing to recommend you. If you are short of previous employers, include a teacher who knows you well. It's all right to include character references, too, but they should never be relatives, and they ought not to be such close friends that they would obviously be prejudiced in your favor. Don't give anyone as a reference, except previous employers, until you have asked that person's permission. For one thing, asking permission is an ordinary act of politeness; for another, you shouldn't take the chance of naming someone who might be unwilling to write a letter recommending you.

It used to be customary for résumés to include very personal details, such as age, race, marital status, religious preference, and sex, but Title IX of the Fair Employment Practices Act has made it illegal for employers to ask for such information or to require that applications be accompanied by pictures. Naturally, unless your given name is Lynn or Marion or Clare, your signature will make your sex obvious, and the date of your high school graduation provides a pretty accurate hint as to your age. If you are called in for an interview, your sex, race, and approximate age will be obvious. Nevertheless, most employers are required to disregard these matters, and it is better to omit such details from either your letter or your résumé.

Proofreading

You should already be in the habit of proofreading everything you write before you consider it finished, but in application letters careful editing and proofreading are particularly important. The care with which you prepare your letter may be the employer's best indication of the care with which you will do the job. Some ads even ask you to reply in your own handwriting, rather than typing the letter, since handwriting is another possible index of care and character. Whether you write or type, however, a sloppy, misspelled letter may prejudice the employer against you, even though the job you are applying for may never require you to do any spelling at all.

Other simple things that may determine whether or not you get a response from the company are the neatness of your typing, the form of your letter, and your ability to balance between boastfulness on the one hand and an apologetic over-modesty on the other. Don't worry about beginning your sentences with "I." After all, you are telling about yourself, and saying so straight out is better than awkward attempts at avoiding what would be the normal way to say it.

Don't hesitate to get help on the wording, spelling, or typing. Once you have gathered the information, decided what you want to say, and written a draft of the letter, get somebody else to read what you have written and make suggestions about improving it. Ask somebody else to read it even though you are pretty confident you have done a good job. Full professors writing for foundation grants get help on their applications, and unless they have secretaries, they often ask friends to do the typing for them.

Remember, the point is not how much you can do without help but how attractive you can make your letter. If your letter and résumé are neat, well organized, complete, and courteous, employers who value competence and efficiency will give your application serious attention.

A Sample Application Letter

The advertisement—from the *Daily Inquirer,* April 15, 1986:

> **TEACHER**
> 2 part-time positions in day-care center. Ages
> 2+ and 6–10 years. Experience necessary.
> Send resume to Box 340, Clearlake, Ark.
> 72013. An Equal Opportunity Employer

Writer's address and date.

501 Denton Street
Clearlake, Arkansas 72015
April 16, 1986

Address given in the advertisement—no name is given so no salutation is used.

Box 340
Clearlake, Arkansas 72013

Tells how she heard about the job.

Please consider this letter as my application for the position of part-time teacher in your day-care center, as advertised in the Daily Inquirer of April 15.

Gives details of education—the strongest qualification.

I will graduate from La Monte Community College in June 1986 with an A.S. degree in Child Care.   In addition to the courses required in the program, I have taken courses in child psychology, design, music appreciation, children's literature, and methods of teaching.   I am sure that Loretta Kingman, director of the Child Care Program, will be glad to recommend me.

Gives details of job experience.

Although I have never been a paid employee in a child care center, I interned for a semester at the La Monte Day Care

Center operated by the community college. During that time
I worked four hours a day at the center, from 8 to 10 a.m. and
from 5 to 7 p.m. During the morning I had full charge of
about eight three-year-olds and was responsible for teaching
them songs, games, and simple crafts. During the evening, I
told stories and supervised the play of children whose ages
ranged from two to eight.

When I lived in St. Louis I served for more than two years as
a volunteer in the Head Start Program, working individually
with kindergarten children to teach them recognition of letters and numbers. I have done the same kind of teaching
with my own two children, both of whom are now in school. In
addition, while I was growing up I had almost full responsibility for five younger sisters and brothers, since my
mother died when I was fourteen.

Mentions other related experience.

I will be available to teach any time in the day or evening.
My sister, with whom I live, can take care of my own children
before or after school or at night, and if you need someone
to start before the first of June, I am sure I can rearrange
my hours at the college.

Says when she will be available to work.

The resume you requested gives more details about my activities and outside interests. I will be happy to come in for an
interview at your convenience. My phone number is 860-5757
and I can be reached there any afternoon after 2 p.m.

Mentions résumé, asks for interview, and gives phone number.

Sincerely,

Augustine Green

Augustine Green

Enclosure

A Sample Résumé

Augustine Green
501 Denton Street
Clearlake, Arkansas 72015
Phone: (501) 860-5757

Education

La Monte Community College, Clearlake, Arkansas, 1985-6. Will re-
    ceive A.S. degree in Child Care, June 1986, with special course
    work in child psychology, children's literature, and design.

St. Louis Community College, St. Louis, Missouri, 1984-5, with
    course work in music appreciation and methods of teaching.

Y.W.C.A. Extension Center, St. Louis, Missouri, 1981-2. Evening
    courses in Women's Studies.

Adult Learning Center, Dayton, Kansas, 1976-8. Various courses in
    literature, history, and philosophy; no transfer credit.

Experience

Intern, La Monte Day Care Center, La Monte, Community College,
    Clearlake, Arkansas, September to December, 1985. Janet Chee,
    supervisor.

Volunteer, Kenworthy Head Start Program, 7411 Aukland Street,
    St. Louis, Missouri 63115, February 1983 to July 1985. Two
    afternoons each week.

Other Jobs

Waitress, Chat 'n Chew, 47 Main Street, Clearlake, Arkansas 72015,
    January 1986 to present. Jack Holmes, manager.

Cashier, Peterson's Steak House, 4612 Alleghany St., St. Louis,
    Missouri 63110, 1983-5. Martha Quigley, manager.

Sales Clerk, Robinson's Variety Store, 2610 Central Avenue, Dayton,
    Kansas 66773, 1976-8. Verne Robinson, owner.

Honors and Activities

Dean's Honor Roll, La Monte Community College, fall 1985.

Kiwanis Club Scholarship, fall 1984.

President, South Elementary School PTA, St. Louis, Missouri, 1984.

First place, clarinet playing, Kansas State High School Music
        Festival, June 1976.

References

Loretta Kingman
Director, Child Care Program
La Monte Community College
Clearlake, Arkansas 72030

Janet Chee
Supervisor, La Monte Day Care Center
La Monte Community College
Clearlake, Arkansas 72030

Keith Washington
Director, Kenworthy Head Start Program
7411 Auckland Street
St. Louis, Missouri 63115

Dr. Ruth Olson
Clearwater Pediatric Clinic
600 East Broadway
Clearlake, Arkansas 72022

Appendix Four/
Editing

Whatever you're writing, the first and most important step is to get your ideas down on paper as clearly, forcefully, and gracefully as possible. Make sure your paper says what you want it to say. Make sure you're pleased with what you have written. Then, and only then, you can go on to the final step: editing what you've written.

Editing, often called *proofreading,* means going back over your paper, checking for such things as spelling, punctuation, omitted words, typing errors, and so on. These represent the etiquette of writing—a set of conventions that have developed during the five hundred years since the printing press was invented. Like any other kind of good manners, their main purpose is to make other people comfortable, to make reading smooth and easy.

These conventions are important because many readers will form judgments about you and the value of what you say based on how carefully you observe their notions of writing etiquette. It's not much use arguing that these are surface matters, quite separate from the worth of your report or your argument. It's not much use offering such clichés as "Clothes don't make the man (or woman)" or "You can't judge a package by its wrapping." We do make superficial judgments about strangers in terms of their appearance, although first impressions usually tell us nothing of real value. We do reach for the pretty package before the one in the battered box. Most of us do enjoy a dinner more when the tablecloth is clean and the goblets glitter, even though we know these niceties can't compensate for soggy potatoes and a limp salad. A careful cook will first time the potatoes and chill the salad, then turn to serving the dinner as attractively as possible. Careful writers will organize their ideas and put them into words, then go back over what they have written to "make it look good."

For some writers, however, that plan is easier to make than to follow. How do you know what to look for? How can you tell what to change? Where can you get help?

Beginning writers certainly can't look for everything at once. The brief sections at the end of the chapters in this book give some quick help on a few of the questions that often plague inexperienced writers, but what's said there may not be enough.

Whatever your problem is—and most writers have some problems, some things they always have to look up—probably the best solution is to break your editing into parts.

What is sometimes called "mechanics" can be divided into five parts: spelling, punctuation, paragraphing, capitalizing, and smoothing out the wording. Go through your paper once, concentrating just on spelling. Go through it again, this time looking at punctuation. Next time look at paragraphs and capital letters. Finally, read it again, this time looking for words you may have left out or minor things you may want to change.

This advice does not mean, of course, that if you find a misspelled word while you're checking your paragraphs, or a missing word while you're checking for spelling, you should ignore it. It does mean that more than one reading is bound to help, that it's hard to look for everything at once. As you grow more skilled in editing and more sure of yourself, you will be able to combine some of these operations. Some very experienced writers, however, make a habit of reading their papers more than once, catching changes on a second reading that they missed the first time through.

As for where you can get help, there are lots of sources: your teachers, your friends, the other students in the class. The best and most permanent source, however, is a good college dictionary. Modern dictionaries are more than just lists of words and their meanings. You can use them for more than finding out how a word is spelled. Most dictionaries have sections on usage and punctuation, sometimes listed under the heading "Manual of Style." Make sure your dictionary is up-to-date; the conventions of writing change, just as other conventions do. Then get thoroughly familiar with all the kinds of help it can give you. Don't try to edit without your dictionary handy, and don't try to edit without using it.

Spelling

There's nothing magic or sacred about spelling. It's just a method of using symbols—letters of the alphabet—to represent the sounds we make when we talk. In an ideal system, we'd have a separate letter to represent every meaningful sound, and each letter would always represent the same sound, and only that sound. When you saw the letter *s,* for instance, you would know that it stood for the sound you hear in *sit* and never for anything else. Unfortunately, the system isn't that reliable. The letter *s,* as everybody knows, can represent several different sounds: *s*it, *s*ugar, *s*hould, bee*s,* grea*s*y (the way some Americans say it), or no sound at all, as in i*s*land. What's true for *s* is true for most of the rest of the alphabet. Letters do double duty or pop up in places where they don't seem to do anything at all. We have at least one letter we could dispense with entirely: *C* could be replaced by *s* in such words as *century* and *civic,* or by *k* in such words as *cat* and *come.*

Naturally, this bad fit between sounds and letters is not deliberate. Five centuries ago, before Caxton brought the printing press to England, people spelled words however they thought they sounded, and nobody made any fuss about it. The early printers, however, decided their lives would be easier if everyone spelled words the same way, so gradually they "standardized" the system, using the spellings they saw most frequently. Sometimes they were printing very old manuscripts, written when the sounds of the language were quite different. Englishmen used to say *night* so you could hear the sound represented by *gh*; they said *knight* so you could hear the *k* sound at the beginning of the word. The printers tried to make letters represent sounds, and they did a fairly good job of it for that time and that place. But the sounds of a language keep changing, and what seemed a logical spelling in 1480, in London, can seem pretty illogical in 1980, in Omaha, Nebraska, or Melbourne, Australia. And though the sounds of speech are always slowly changing, the writing system doesn't change much for either time or geography. That it doesn't change makes reading easier and spelling harder.

As for making the system fit the language better, there isn't much hope there either. George Bernard Shaw, the famous British playwright, left a million pounds to "reform" the spelling system, but the English courts threw that provision out of his will. One objection to change is that all the books in all the libraries would immediately become out-of-date and very hard to read. Another objection is that English has so many dialects, with so many differences in the way English speakers pronounce words, that it would be difficult to decide whose pronunciation to use. And a final objection, perhaps the most important, is that people who have learned the system just don't want things any different.

Nevertheless, if you think of yourself as a poor speller, here are a few facts that may comfort you:

1. *The ability to spell well is not a measure of intelligence, nor is it a measure of the ability to write well.* Apparently, good spellers are people with good visual memories: their minds "photograph" the appearance of words on a page, and they can produce that photograph when they need to write a word. These are the people who, when you ask them how to spell something, say, "Wait a minute. Let me write it down." They judge spelling by the way it looks. Other people, whose memories depend more on sound than on sight, have more trouble with spelling and have to work harder at it.

2. *Nobody can spell everything; all of us have some words we always have to look up.* The trick, of course, is to learn what those words are. If you can't keep the *i/e, e/i* problem straight, in words like *believe* and *receive,* just accept the situation and plan to use your dictionary every time these words occur. It's only when your list of uncertainties gets too long, when it contains too many of the words you use regularly, that you have a real spelling problem. The best—probably the only—solution here is to take a few words at a time and just learn them. Some people have had good luck by developing their muscular memories. Using a child's crayon, they write the word very large, over and over, until it is imprinted in their minds. Other people use a rote system, saying "*w, h, i, c, h* spells *which*" until the spelling becomes automatic. If you have a genuine spelling problem, try to really look at the letters in each word every time you edit.

3. *Most spelling difficulty comes in the ordinary words of daily life; more than 80 percent of the words in the language are "regular"—that is, they follow a logical*

system. More people have trouble with a word like *writing,* for instance, than with a word like *insoluble.* If you can learn the common words, the "hard," unusual words will take care of themselves. Even if they don't, you can use the dictionary for obscure words without slowing yourself down much.

4. *The spelling of "sound-alike" words always depends on meaning. Peace* and *piece,* for example, are not the same word at all. We just happen to say them the same way. With homophones—words that sound alike but mean something different —learning the difference takes two steps. First you become aware that the pairs exist (or quadruples, as in *since, sense, scents,* and *cents*). Then you determine which is which. For some pairs, memory clues will work. Some people use "piece of pie" to remind themselves that a part of something is always spelled *piece.* They tell themselves that their high school principal (the "main" person in the school) was (or was not) "a pal," to distinguish *principal*—meaning main or important—from *principle*— meaning a rule or basic law. You don't have to be told these tricks; you can invent your own. But if you can't find or invent dependable memory clues, you're back to the usual solution; when in doubt, use your dictionary.

I/E, E/I WORDS

5. *Finally, in spite of the apparent confusion, there are some spelling guides that almost always work.* One of them deals with *i/e, e/i.* If you use the whole jingle, instead of just half of it, you can spell more than a dozen common English words. It's a good idea to reverse the order of the jingle:

> When said like *me,*
>
> It's *i* before *e,*
>
> Except after *c.*

Changing the order will help you remember that the guide doesn't work for words like *friend* and *neighbor,* because they don't have the same sound as *me.* Then you can use the jingle where it will work: *receive, relieve, chief, niece, belief, grief, conceive,* and so on. This guide will mislead you in two words, *seize* and *protein.* And depending on where you live and what your pronunciation is, it could steer you wrong in three other words: *leisure,* if you say the first syllable to rhyme with *me* rather than with *met*; and *either* and *neither,* unless you live on the East Coast. Learn these exceptions, remember the pronunciation part of the old saying, and you will save yourself a good deal of dictionary checking.

Most of the other useful guides have to do with suffixes—adding endings to words you can already spell.

DOUBLING CONSONANTS

If a short word has one vowel,

followed by one consonant,

double the consonant when you add

-ed, -er, -est, -ing

It works like this:

trim + ed	becomes	*trimmed*
win + er	becomes	*winner*
hot + est	becomes	*hottest*
stop + ing	becomes	*stopping*

If the word has more than one vowel,

or more than one consonant,

don't make any change when you add

-ed, -er, -est, -ing

nail + ed	becomes	*nailed*	*suck + ed*	becomes	*sucked*
deal + er	becomes	*dealer*	*kiss + ed*	becomes	*kissed*
sweet + est	becomes	*sweetest*	*long + est*	becomes	*longest*
fool + ing	becomes	*fooling*	*match + ing*	becomes	*matching*

This same guide works for longer words *where we emphasize the last syllable:*

corral + ed	becomes	*corralled*
begin + ing	becomes	*beginning*

Kidnap and *cancel* usually don't double the consonant, *because we emphasize the first syllable* rather than the last one: *kidnaped, canceling.*

DROPPING -E

> If a word ends in *e*,
>
> drop the *e* before adding
>
> *-ed, -er, -est, -ing*

hop¢ + ed   becomes   *hoped*   sav¢ + ed   becomes   *saved*

saf¢ + er   becomes   *safer*   balanc¢ + ed   becomes   *balanced*

nic¢ + est   becomes   *nicest*   balanc¢ + ing becomes   *balancing*

writ¢ + ing becomes   *writing*   believ¢ + ing becomes   *believing*

Notice, however, that *write* becomes *written*; the consonant is doubled here because the pronunciation of the vowel changes.

This guide will keep you from writing, "Jackie hopped for a bike for Christmas" (when you mean wanted it), or "Jackie hoped all the way home" (when you mean bounced up and down).

hop + ed   becomes   *hopped*   hop + ing   becomes   *hopping*

hope + ed becomes   *hoped*   hope + ing becomes   *hoping*

WORDS ENDING IN -Y

> If a word ends in *y*
>
> 1. change *y* to *i* before
>   all endings except *-ing*
>
> 2. add *-es* instead of just *-s*
>   after the *i*

It works like this:

copy   becomes   *copy̸ + i + es*   (*copies*)   but *copying*

marry   becomes   *marry̸ + i + ed*   (*married*)   but *marrying*

carry   becomes   *carry̸ + i + er*   (*carrier*)   but *carrying*

snappy	becomes	*snappy̶ + i + est*	(*snappiest*)
happy	becomes	*happy̶ + i + ness*	(*happiness*)
mercy	becomes	*mercy̶ + i + ful*	(*merciful*)
cozy	becomes	*cozy̶ + i + ly*	(*cozily*)
merry	becomes	*merry̶ + i + ment*	(*merriment*)

The only place this guide does not work is where the *y* comes after another vowel instead of after a consonant, as it does in words like *day, honey, boy,* or *buy.* For these words remember this rule: if a word has more than one vowel, don't make any change when you add the suffix.

ADDING -LY

> When you add *-ly,*
> don't change anything else
> ### EXCEPT
> 1. when the original word ends in *y*
> 2. when you'd get three *l*'s together
> 3. when you'd get *le* and *ly* together

cold + ly	becomes	*coldly*		but *angry + ly*	becomes	*angrily*
live + ly	becomes	*lively*		but *full + ly*	becomes	*fully*
hopeful + ly	becomes	*hopefully*		but *terrible + ly*	becomes	*terribly*

APOSTROPHES/CONTRACTIONS

Apostrophes are another part of English spelling that worry many people. Actually, we use apostrophes in only two main ways:

> Apostrophes are used
> 1. to spell contractions
> 2. to show possession after nouns and a few pronouns (*anybody's*)

A contraction occurs when we shorten a word (*o'er* for *over*) or push two words together to form a single word (*don't* for *do not*). The guide for contractions goes like this:

To spell a *contraction*

1. Write the combined words as a single word.

2. Use an apostrophe to replace the letter or letters left out.

3. Make no other spelling change.

---

can ṇọt becomes *can't*	*would nọt* becomes *wouldn't*
it ịs becomes *it's*	*they ạre* becomes *they're*
I wịll becomes *I'll*	*I wọụld* becomes *I'd*
Bertha ịs becomes *Bertha's*	*that ịs* becomes *that's*
we hạve becomes *we've*	*who ịs* becomes *who's*

The only contractions in which we do change the spelling—*will not* becomes *won't* and *shall not* becomes *shan't*—seldom give anybody much trouble.*

APOSTROPHES/POSSESSION

We get into trouble when we make oversimplified, incomplete statements about the other function of apostrophes: "Use an apostrophe to show possession." That's accurate enough, as far as it goes, but it doesn't go far enough. We need to add something:

Never use apostrophes to show

possession in seven common English

pronouns: *you, he, she, it, we, they,*

and *who.*

---

*We also change the spelling in *ain't*, the contraction for *am not*, but most writers have been taught to avoid that one, except in quoted conversation.

All these pronouns have special possessive forms—*your* or *yours; his; her* or *hers; its; our* or *ours; their* or *theirs; whose*—and these pronouns are never spelled with an apostrophe.

You never use an apostrophe for the possessive of *I*, either, but since *my* and *mine* never have an *s* sound, the temptation to do so is not there.

This guide is simple and reliable. The confusion comes because we run into homophones. Several of these pronouns sound like contractions. It's hard to hear much difference between these pairs:

You're (contraction of *you are*) leaving *your* hat (belongs to you).

The typewriter came with *its* (belongs to typewriter) own cover, but *it's* (contraction of *it has*) been lost for a long time.

They're (contraction of *they are*) planning to sell *their* car (belongs to them).

There's (contraction of *there is*) some question about whether *it's* (contraction of *it is*) really *theirs* (belongs to them).

Who's (contraction of *who is*) going to decide *whose* (belongs to somebody) car it is?

Probably the only sure way to decide between *its* and *it's, your* and *you're, they're* and *their, who's* and *whose*, is to apply the kind of test illustrated in the sentences just given. If reading it as a contraction makes sense—that is, if you can substitute *it is, you are, they are, who is*, for instance—use an apostrophe. If that substitution doesn't make sense, leave the apostrophe out.

Here is a simple guide for using apostrophes to show possession in everything except those seven pronouns:

> Use an apostrophe for any relationship that can be put into an *of* phrase.
>
> Put the apostrophe after the end of the word as it stands in the *of* phrase.
>
> If the word in the *of* phrase doesn't end in *s*, put *s* after the apostrophe.
>
> If the word in the *of* phrase does end in *s*, add an apostrophe and nothing else.

mother *of Helen*   becomes   *Helen's* mother

problems *of everybody*   becomes   *everybody's* problem

friend *of the children*   becomes   the *children's* friend den *of the lion*   becomes   the *lion's* den

den *of the lions*   becomes   the *lions'* den

novel *of Dickens*   becomes   *Dickens'* novel

job *of Charles*   becomes   *Charles'* job

On the last two, some people write *Dickens's* novel and *Charles's* job, as you would probably hear it in speech, but either way is all right, and if apostrophes seem mysterious, you'll be safer with the *of* guide.

Using these spelling guides may seem like a slow process at first. And it is. But since you should never bother with them when you're actually writing—that would interfere with your thinking—the slowness isn't serious. And it's true that there are many spelling difficulties these guides don't cover. Maybe you can find other guides to help with words that bother you: in all words where *-phon-* means "sound," for instance, the *f* sound is spelled *ph*. But if you can't find the guides, or if the guides don't work, use your dictionary.

Punctuation

Punctuation marks are a set of symbols that try to reproduce in writing the pauses, the inflections, and the intonations used naturally in speech. Granted, the few symbols we have are clumsy and inadequate; still, they're better than nothing. Remember, using commas and periods and question marks in the conventional ways is not a matter of being "correct" or "incorrect"; it's a matter of helping your readers "hear" what you've written. If you don't believe that, try reading the following unpunctuated paragraph:

> just by learning to talk even if you hadn't learned to read and write you have become a master of a subtle and complex system the proof of your mastery is that you can understand what other people who speak your language say to you at least most of the time and they can understand what you say to them it is exactly this mastery of language that distinguishes the dullest humans from the brightest and most accomplished animals an animal may grunt howl whine scratch or even point to express what it feels at the moment but only a human being has words for feelings and only humans can talk about what they felt yesterday and what they may feel tomorrow only humans can talk about what happened the day before yesterday the past can make guesses about what may happen next month the future and can discuss things that have never happened and perhaps never will happen by language by using words humans have learned to get outside the present

It's obvious that using commas, periods, and capital letters in the usual places makes reading easier. What is a good deal less obvious is where "the right places" are. A lifetime of listening to people talk provides very little direct help. People don't go around saying, "That's what I mean period don't you agree with me question mark" unless they're sending an old-fashioned telegram or dictating to a stenographer they don't trust much.

That nobody ever goes around saying "period . . . comma . . . question mark" is only one reason people have trouble with punctuation. The other reason is that the usual directions are hard to follow. The "rules" are almost always written in terms that involve a good deal of specialized knowledge. The rules for using commas, for instance, are given to saying such things as "Use a comma after a subordinate clause at the beginning of a sentence" or "Set off nonrestrictive clauses with commas." That's fine—if you know for sure what subordinate and nonrestrictive clauses are.

Another reason the conventional directions are not much help is that the sentences offered as examples tend to look quite different from the ones we write ourselves. If you have a sample pattern to follow, it's fairly easy to insert commas into sentences like these:

Hoping for rain tomorrow_____we did not water the lawn.

My mother-in-law_____who once lived in Boston_____makes baked beans.

These practice sentences lie quiet and unresisting while you stick commas in them. The sentences you write yourself, however, may be wriggling and full of life, and they seldom follow a neat textbook pattern. If your sentences don't look much like the patterns in the book, that doesn't necessarily mean your sentences are bad. On the contrary, it may be a sign you are an effective and vigorous writer. There's no reason to limit yourself to a few simple patterns, even though the livelier sentences may seem harder to punctuate. If you don't understand the terminology the handbooks use, don't just give up. Remember that the basic purpose of all punctuation marks is to help you express what you mean, to guide your readers so they can read what you have written with intelligence and understanding. Your job is to decide where commas and periods will help, where they will hinder.

If the problem is a comma, for instance, one good way is to ask yourself whether, if you were reading it instead of writing it, a comma would guide you in seeing what parts of the sentence belong together. The short pauses we make in talking sometimes mean we need commas, but sometimes they mean we've just stopped to think. The pauses we make at the ends of sentences are a more reliable guide. Periods are symbols of longer pauses. When people talk, they pause briefly between one sentence and the next. When they have finished a "complete declaratory sentence," to use the handbook's phrase, they lower the pitch of their voices. When they have asked a question, whether or not they expect an answer, they raise the pitch slightly at the end of it.

Just as you know a great deal of English grammar even though you cannot use all the terminology, so you know almost perfectly how this system of emphasizing, pausing, and pitching your voice works, even though you may not be able to define such terms as "pitch" and "stress." To remind yourself of what you already know, try reading these sentences twice each, first as though you were making an announcement, and then as though the news were more than you could believe and you were asking if it was *really* so:

> John was elected president of his class.
> *John* was elected president of his class?

> Mary is going to marry George.
> Mary is going to marry *George?*
> Mary is going to *marry* George?

You, like everybody else, can hear a big difference. You are hearing punctuation, or at least, you are hearing what punctuation stands for.

That's why it will help to read what you have written aloud to yourself, listening carefully to your own pauses and your own intonation. When you lower the pitch of your voice and come to a full stop, put in a period. When you raise the pitch of your voice and come to a full stop, put in a question mark. When you pause a little, but not much, and change the pitch just a little, you *may* need a comma. That's when you should examine how the parts of the sentence are put together.

If you can find a friend to listen to you read, that's even better. When someone else is listening, you are likely to read a little more carefully in an effort to help the other person understand your meaning. No matter how carefully you put in the periods and question marks, however, you won't be able to catch all the variations of your voice. Punctuation marks can only hint at the shocked disbelief your voice showed when you turned "Mary is going to marry *George*" into a question.

PERIODS

It's important that you figure out some reliable way of identifying sentences, since knowing where one sentence stops and another begins is your readers' most pressing need. You can't do it by length. Some sentences are short, some very long:

> The doctor came immediately.

> Although there was no apparent reason for her discomfort, whenever Marcia tried to stand up, and especially if she stood up suddenly, her face would twist with pain, tears would streak her face, and she would fall back to the chair, whispering, "It hurts, mommy, it hurts me."

Some things that are not sentences are also fairly long:

> When it is time for little boys to go to bed, even though they have eaten a big dinner and everybody knows that they can't possibly be hungry . . .

People do say such things in conversation, either in answer to a question ("When do kids ask for snacks?") or as an invitation for someone else to ask, "Well, what does happen at bedtime?" Even though we might *say* something like "When it is time . . . ," if we write just that much, followed by a period, we'll confuse or annoy our readers. Before you use a period to punctuate a group of words beginning with "when," make sure you have said what happens after that *when*. Before you use a period to punctuate a group of words beginning with *because* or *although,* make sure you have included what occurred as a result of that, or in spite of that, whatever that was. As you edit, look at the words you have punctuated with a period to make sure your readers won't be left saying "So what?" or "What about it?"

PERIODS

1. are used at the end of all sentences, unless the sentence asks questions or makes an exclamation

2. show a falling inflection and a full pause

Periods are also used for most abbreviations:

P.M.   etc.   c.o.d.   Ms.   Feb.   U.S.S.R.   B.C.

If you're not sure what the abbreviations are, your dictionary can tell you. But ordinarily, except for time designations such as P.M. or B.C., or titles such as *Ms. Chisholm* or *Dr. Boneset,* we don't use abbreviations in the middle of an ordinary paragraph.

QUESTION MARKS

The other end mark you will need is a question mark. We hear lowered pitch at the end of statements, raised pitch at the end of most questions. Again, the first step is to read and listen. Even though the question you have written does not require an answer, even though it cannot be answered, you should still use a question mark:

When will people learn to live together in peace?

If listening to yourself read doesn't help enough, paying a little attention to English word order may be useful. When we shift from making statements to asking questions, we shift the order of our words:

Cuthbert *was* eating *cauliflower.*
        becomes
Was Cuthbert eating cauliflower?
Why *was* Cuthbert eating cauliflower?
What *cauliflower was* Cuthbert eating?

Whenever a group of words begins with such words as *is, was, are, will,* or *do,* or such words as *when, where, why,* or *what,* immediately followed by *is, was, are, will, do,* and so forth, it should be punctuated with a question mark. That guide works for quotations, too. Notice the difference in word order between these two statements:

Hazel asked, "Why is the tax so high?"

Hazel asked why the tax was so high.

The first one needs a question mark, the second a period.

QUESTION MARKS

are used for

1. full pause and rising inflection

2. changed word order that signals a question

COMMAS

Commas are separators, too, but they represent smaller divisions within sentences. We use them when we offer lists:

A frightened, trembling, tear-stained child stumbled down the steps of the bus.

Mushrooms, oysters, snails, rattlesnakes, and chocolate-covered grasshoppers are all considered delicacies by some people somewhere.

We use them when the main part of what we're saying is interrupted by something else. Interruptions can occur at the beginning, before the main part of the sentence:

Nevertheless, I won't answer that advertisement.

Slipping and skidding on the icy pavement, my grandfather finally made it across the street.

Whenever I have a bad nightmare, I feel jittery all the next day.

Interruptions can occur in the middle, separating one main part of the sentence from the rest. Whatever the purpose of these interruptions, they need commas at both ends:

My uncle, a nice old man with a long white beard, is coming to town next week. (interruption to explain)*

My uncle, however, will not stay with us. (interruption to show contrast)

I wouldn't do that, Mr. Peters, if I were you. (interruption to be polite)

Interruptions can come at the end:

Radial tires certainly give better traction, an important consideration if you're driving on ice.

Quoting the exact words someone else said is considered an interruption, even though we often don't pause when we're talking:

Patrick Henry said, "Give me liberty or give me death," and his words encouraged the southern states to join the revolution.

We also use commas between groups of words that could be sentences if they didn't contain connectors:

It's raining outside, *but* we'll go anyway.

Because it's raining outside, Grandma decided to stay home.

However, if connectors such as *because* or *when* come at the last part of the sentence, we often don't use a comma because the interruption is not very great.

Grandma decided to stay home because it was raining.

We use commas when we give dates or addresses:

January 4, 1823

1403 Newberry Street, Joplin, Missouri

*Notice, however, that in some similar-looking sentences we don't use commas:

My uncle, a nice old man with a long white beard, is coming to town next week. (interruption)

My uncle from Arizona is coming to town next week. (not an interruption because it's needed to distinguish between the uncle from Arizona and the uncle from Maine)

The uncle who always brings presents is coming to town next week. (again, not an interruption because it's needed to show which uncle)

COMMAS

are used to separate

1. the parts of a list

2. interruptions to the main part of a sentence
      at the beginning
      in the middle
      at the end

3. groups of words that could be sentences if
   they didn't contain connectors

4. parts of a date or an address

DO NOT USE COMMAS

Finally, another useful guide to commas is, "When in doubt, leave it out." Unnecessary commas sprinkled through your writing may bother your readers more than a needed comma or two will help. If you don't hear any interruption, it's better not to use commas:

The old doctor who delivered me is taking care of my baby now.

Too many unnecessary commas will drive some readers frantic.

When commas are used between two sentences that should be separated by a period or a connecting word, the resulting punctuation is known as a "comma splice" or "comma error." Committing a comma splice is not a capital crime, but teachers who are particular about punctuation often think it means you don't know what a sentence is, and they are so upset by this failure to use conventional punctuation that they may fail the paper. This is where examining how the parts fit together will pay off. Look at the following collection of words; the two parts need to be separated by more than a comma:

A COMMA IS NOT ENOUGH HERE: Many people believe solar energy is better than nuclear energy, the sun can heat our houses without hurting the atmosphere.

There are several ways to show how the parts do (or don't) fit together:

USE A PERIOD: Many people believe solar energy is better than nuclear energy. The sun can heat our houses without hurting the atmosphere.

ADD A CONNECTING WORD: Many people believe solar energy is better than nuclear energy because the sun can heat our houses without hurting the atmosphere.

REARRANGE THE   The sun can heat our houses without hurting the atmosphere,
WORDS: so many people believe it is better than nuclear energy.

These are usually the best solutions, but one other possibility exists, using a semicolon:

Many people believe solar energy is better than nuclear energy; the sun can heat our houses without hurting the atmosphere.

COMMAS

are *not used*

between two sentences *unless* the two sentences

are joined by a connecting word

(and, but, or, so, etc.)

Periods, commas, and question marks are the most essential kinds of punctuation, and the only ones we can really hear. All the others are visual conventions: symbols that give sophisticated readers a little more information than they would otherwise have.

QUOTATION MARKS

The most important visual symbol is the quotation mark. We use quotation marks whenever we write down *exactly what someone else has said or written*. We use these marks whether what was said is one word, three words, a sentence, a paragraph, or a whole page of someone else's writing. We do *not* use quotation marks when we repeat just the sense of what was said but change the wording slightly. It works like this:

Grandpa Squeers was always using strange oaths.
Grandpa Squeers was always saying "dadniggled" and "jumping jeepers."

The camp counselor warned the girls not to throw gasoline into a lighted bonfire.
The camp counselor repeated, "Never throw gasoline into a lighted bonfire."

Nathan Hale commented that he was sorry he had only one life to give to his country.
Nathan Hale said, "My only regret is that I have but one life to give for my country."
Nathan Hale said his only regret was that he had "but one life" to give for his country.

We use quotation marks to show the beginning of someone else's exact words and again to show the end. If the quoted words run to more than a paragraph, we use quotation marks at the beginning of each new paragraph, to remind readers that we are still quoting. We do not use quotation marks at the end of paragraphs, however, unless we have stopped quoting.

If what we're quoting already contains a quotation, we use apostrophes to show the inside quotation, so readers won't be confused by thinking too soon that the main quotation has ended. It works like this:

> Grandma Squeers said, "I wish Pa would stop using those funny words. I sure get tired of hearing 'dadniggled' and 'jumping jeepers.' "

We use a comma before beginning a direct quotation whenever the quotation is a complete sentence:

> Dr. Holmes said, "Hold still!"

But we don't need a comma if we are quoting only part of what was actually said:

> Dr. Holmes said something about "aggravated eye infection."

Use whatever punctuation is appropriate at the end of the quotation—usually a period. Periods and commas always go inside the quotation marks. Sometimes a question is involved, though, and you must decide whether the question mark goes before or after the quotation mark. Then you have to decide which part is the question, the whole sentence or just the quoted part. The whole sentence is a question when we write:

> Did Dr. Holmes say "aggravated eye infection"?

Here the quotation mark comes before the question mark. But the main sentence is a statement, and only the quoted part a question, when we write:

> Dr. Holmes asked, "What on earth did you do to that eye?"

Here the question mark goes inside the quotation mark, and we skip the period that would ordinarily belong at the end of a statement. It's a safe guide never to use two pieces of end punctuation at the close of a single sentence.

QUOTATION MARKS

are used

1. at the beginning and the end of someone else's exact words

2. at the beginning of each paragraph in a long quotation, but not at the end until the quotation is finished

Other punctuation marks such as colons, semicolons, parentheses, and dashes have specialized uses. They are fairly easily learned, but for most ordinary writing, commas and periods will usually do just as well.

COLONS

Colons are always a signal that something else will follow. We use them at the beginning of business letters, showing that the rest of the letter will follow:

Dear Senator Underwood:

Dear Bob:

We use them at the end of a sentence to show that an example is coming, as we have been doing all through this section. We also use them to introduce long quotations, especially when the quotation will be separated from the words that introduce it by an indented margin (see the unpunctuated paragraph on page 430). And we use a colon, occasionally, in an ordinary sentence to show that the rest of the sentence is just an explanation of what we have already said:

The plumber's excuse was not very satisfactory: merely that he'd been "awfully busy."

In all these places, even at the beginning of a business letter, you could use a comma without confusing your readers.

COLONS

1. show that something will follow

2. are often used
   at the beginning of business letters
   at the beginning of examples, long lists, explanations, and long quotations

3. can usually be replaced by commas

SEMICOLONS

Semicolons are sometimes used in place of commas in long sentences:

Jason Slumber has had a legal office in a corner of the Mercantile Building, at Fourth and Commerce Streets, since November 1960; but the office isn't well-known, since Mr. Slumber only comes in once a week and seldom has a client oftener than once a month.

Using a comma between "1960" and "but" would certainly not be either "wrong" or very confusing. All the semicolon does is warn the reader that the separation here is a little more important than the separations shown by the other three commas in the sentence.

Semicolons are also sometimes used in place of periods when two sentences are very short and seem to belong together:

> Jason Slumber is a wealthy man; he inherited a million dollars.

If you read that sentence aloud, you will hear something close to a period; you might as well put it in, just as you could put a period instead of a semicolon in the sentence you are now reading.

Probably the place semicolons are most useful is in separating the parts in a long, complicated list:

> Besides the bride and groom, the wedding party consisted of Roger Simpson, the bride's father; Eleanor Chamberlain, the bride's mother; Angus McDoom, the groom's brother; and Agnes Smith.

Here semicolons help readers to understand that the wedding party was made up of four people, in addition to the two that got married, rather than seven, as commas might lead readers to suppose.

SEMICOLONS

1. separate the parts of a complicated list

2. can otherwise usually be replaced by
    periods for big pauses
    commas for smaller pauses

In other words, you can do a lot of successful writing without worrying too much about semicolons.

DASHES

Dashes and parentheses are used for interruptions that really break into the main idea of the sentence:

> Clay is an extremely plastic material—far more plastic than most so-called plastics—and is easily shaped into pots.

If you are doubtful about using dashes, you have two choices in sentences like this. You can substitute commas, or you can rewrite the sentence:

Clay is an extremely plastic material, far more plastic than most so-called plastics, and is easily shaped into pots.

Clay is much more plastic than many so-called plastics. Because it is so moldable, it is easily shaped into pots.

PARENTHESES

Parentheses are not quite as easy to eliminate as dashes, since they usually give additional information, but they too can be replaced by commas or rewriting:

Some kinds of clay (the common varieties are explained in the introduction) can be found within twenty-five miles of any city in this country.

A kind of clay, one of the common varieties explained in the introduction, can be found within twenty-five miles of any city in the country.

The eclipse is predicted for 10:34 A.M., eastern standard time (7:34 A.M. in San Francisco).

The eclipse is predicted for 10:34 A.M., eastern standard time, which is 7:34 A.M., Pacific standard time.

The main thing to remember about parentheses is: *always use two.* The first without the second will leave your readers wondering when you are going to get back to the main part of the sentence, or whether they're the ones that missed something somewhere. Parentheses are sometimes used around whole sentences, or even several sentences. In that case, it's especially important that both of them be there.

DASHES and PARENTHESES

1. are used for interruptions

2. can usually be replaced by commas,
    except when the parentheses enclose a
    complete sentence

As you edit your papers, remember that the guides given here are just that— guides. Probably no two copy editors (people hired to make corrections in professional writing before it is printed) would ever punctuate a book in exactly the same way. All the copy editors try for is consistency and clarity. They want to use the same kind of punctuation for the same kind of thing, rather than jump from parentheses to dashes and then to commas. They want to make reading clear and comfortable. That's all you need to try for, too.

Paragraphs

If you have organized your paper carefully and followed the advice on pages 74–75 to move from one paragraph to another as you move from one section of your paper to the next, you probably won't have much trouble with paragraphs.

You might want to remember, however, that paragraphing helps readers in two ways:

PARAGRAPHING

1. provides a convenient separation of the parts of a paper

2. rests the eyes and makes reading easier

Because that's one of the purposes—to make your writing "look good"—try to avoid a series of very short paragraphs or any extremely long ones. If you find you have written a lot of two- or three-sentence paragraphs, try combining them into one. If they won't combine smoothly, you may need better transitions. And if you have a very long paragraph, filling a whole page or more, find a place to break it up. If you look carefully, you can probably see a natural division.

When you write in longhand, or type double space, the usual way to show paragraph divisions is by starting the first word of each new paragraph at least an inch in from the margin. When you type single space, as you do in business letters and some reports, skip a space between paragraphs and begin the first sentence at the usual margin, like this:

> We regret that 42 cartons of size C batteries in our last shipment to you were improperly labeled.
>
> The defective batteries are being replaced at once, by air mail special delivery, and we will appreciate your keeping the 42 cartons now in your possession until one of our salesmen can call for them.

Capitalization

Deciding where to use *capital letters* in modern English is not as much of a problem as it would have been a century or so ago, when many writers capitalized the first letter of every important word, as we still do in writing titles. Nowadays capitals appear in only three places:

1. We use a capital to begin a sentence—that is, after you have used a period or a question mark, begin the next word with a capital letter.

2. We use a capital to name specific, individual people or things:

   Jennie Jones   Fourth Street   the Singer Building

   Chief Justice Warren   the United States

   Words that are not used as part of the name are usually not capitalized:

   A street near the river is being torn up.

   The building Singer built has forty stories.

   Earl Warren was chief justice of the United States from 1953 to 1969.

   The first thirteen states were united in 1787.

3. We use a capital to begin the first word inside quotation marks whenever we are quoting a whole sentence of what someone else said:

   At the end of the conference, the governor commented, "Seems like I'm damned if I do and damned if I don't."

   We don't use capitals when we quote indirectly—change the words a little and omit the quotation marks:

   At the end of the conference, the governor commented that he seemed to be damned if he did and damned if he didn't.

CAPITAL LETTERS

are used

1. to begin sentences

2. to name specific people or things

3. to begin direct quotations

Smoothing Out the Wording

As you read your paper aloud the final time before you copy it, watch for words you may have left out by accident. (Read the final copy for left-out words, too; it's even easier to omit things when you are copying.) Watch for places that *sound* clumsy; often the ear can hear awkwardnesses that the eye won't see. You want to make your writing smooth and natural.

FORMAL AND INFORMAL LANGUAGE

Making it natural, however, doesn't mean making it sound just the way you talk. Many American dialects leave out both words and word endings that edited American English usually includes. Even though you normally say "Josh step right in front of the bus last night," the conventions of editing will require "Josh stepped."

All writers have to make this kind of adjustment, and the more formal the kind of writing, the more the adjustments they must make. It's lucky for most of us, both writers and readers, that American writing has become much less formal in the last few years. People used to be told never to use "I" when they wrote a paper. Now almost everybody would agree that when we're talking about ourselves, "I" is the most natural and therefore the best choice. We used to be warned about contractions, too. We were told that "don't" is acceptable in speech, but that in writing, we should always use "do not." Now most people think that the difference in tone between the rather threatening "do not" and the more comfortable "don't" is sometimes more important than formality.

SEXIST LANGUAGE

One thing you will probably want to watch for, and avoid, is sexist language. The old handbooks used to be very insistent about our using "he" or "his" if we began with "everybody." We were urged to write such things as:

When the speech was finished, everybody clapped *his* hands.

A careful writer will avoid using words that will offend some of *his* readers.

The women's movement has reminded us, however, that most audiences contain both men and women, and that it's insulting to assume that all careful writers are men. If you want to stop assuming that women don't matter, you'll try to avoid using "he" and "his" unless you mean men only. One easy way is to talk about people, rather than "a person," when people is what you mean, anyway:

Careful writers will avoid using words that will offend some of their readers.

If "everybody" seems inevitable, forget the niceties and write "their," just as you would say it. Surely all those people didn't clap the same pair of hands, anyway. Or you can fall back on "his or her," if you're really nervous about it. But just as careful writers avoid using such derogatory words as *Polack, nigger,* or *honky,* unless they deliberately want to be offensive, so careful writers will avoid sexist language.

Editing isn't an impossible job, although all the advice we've given here may make it seem to be. All it takes is care and practice. If you are uneasy about possible differences between the dialect you speak and the dialect you want to write, get a friend, or friends, to go over your paper and pay special attention to the suggestions they make. There's nothing wrong with that kind of help—remember the copy editors who go over those professional manuscripts.

Editing In-class Writing

So far we have been talking about the writing you do at home, when you have plenty of time to edit carefully and prepare a clean copy after all the changes have been made. But even when you're writing under pressure, for an essay test or an in-class paper, you're still responsible for some quick editing.

It's a good idea to get an inexpensive paperback dictionary and carry it with you. Most teachers, unless they're giving a vocabulary quiz, will be glad to let you use your dictionary to edit any kind of writing. (But maybe, unless it's an English class, you'd better ask.)

Usually you won't have time to make a second copy of what you have written, but you can make changes neatly by crossing out and writing above the line. Before you begin to edit, try to separate yourself from what you have written, even only slightly. Stop a minute; look out the window, or think of something else. Then read what your paper says, pretending that it's not yours at all. The more you separate yourself, the more likely you are to catch left-out words or silly mistakes, such as writing "life" when you mean "like." At best, a quick rereading will catch all those unnecessary confusions; at worst, the changes you do make will convince whoever reads your paper that you've tried to be careful.

Glossary

This glossary gives short definitions of many of the important words used in the text. It also includes some traditional terms that do not appear in the text but which students may remember from earlier classes or which teachers may sometimes mention.

abstraction—a word that refers to an idea, attitude, or kind of behavior; something that can't be seen or heard or touched: *mischief, imagination, democracy.*

accuracy—getting facts right and presenting them honestly.

active voice—a sentence that follows normal English word order; the first noun (or noun substitute) does whatever is being done: "The child beat the dog." (The child is doing the beating.)

adjective—traditionally, a word that modifies a noun. Adjectives can fit two patterns: "It was a _____ thing" or "It looked _____." And they can show comparisons: "a *quicker* route"; a *more graceful* action."

adverb—traditionally, a word that modifies a verb, an adjective, or another adverb. Adverbs fit the pattern "He worked _____." Some of them tell *when* or *where* (today, always, here, there, and so on). Most of them tell *how* (quickly, happily, and so on). Adverbs that tell *how* are usually formed by adding *-ly* to adjectives. Adverbs can also show intensity: "He worked _____ quickly." (*very, somewhat,* and so on)

agreement, in sentences—(1) making the subject fit with the verb: "A fire burns. Fire*s* burn." (2) making pronouns fit the nouns they refer to: "One *girl* ate *her* dinner. Both *girls* ate *their* dinners."

analogy—a comparison of two things that have at least one similarity.

analysis—a method of explanation that examines the parts of a process or event.

antecedent—see *pronoun antecedent.*

apologies, in writing—overuse of such phrases as "in my opinion," "it seems to me," or other wording that makes the writer seem unsure of what's being said.

apostrophe—a mark used (1) in place of an omitted letter or letters in contractions: *can't; aren't* (2) to show possession in nouns and some pronouns: *man's* hat; *anybody's* guess.

audience—the person or people who will read what's been written.

authority—a method of supporting reasons; someone whose comments or judgment will influence readers. Authorities are used honestly only when they are experts on the subject being discussed.

auxiliary verb (sometimes called helper verbs)—verbs that combine with the main verb to show differences in time, intention, or possibility:

> He *is* eating the pie.
> He *had* eaten the pie.
> He *might* eat the pie.
> *Did* he eat it?

bibliography—an alphabetical list of the sources used in preparing a paper; appears at the end of the paper; now usually headed "Works Cited."

brainstorming—writing down everything you can think of related to a topic or idea, in random order, without regard to importance; a way of getting ideas flowing.

capital letters—used to begin sentences, to name things or people, to begin direct quotations:

> *T*he man hollered at us.
> We went to the *W*hite *H*ouse.
> He asked, "*W*hy do you do that to me?"

causal analysis—an explanation of why something happens or happened.

cause and effect—an examination of whether one thing (or things) actually caused another thing.

circular argument—the mistake of beginning with a belief and, instead of supporting it, circling around until the original belief is used as proof of itself.

circular definition—an unsatisfactory attempt to explain meaning, in which one word is defined by another version of the same word: "A plagiarist is a person who plagiarizes."

clarity, in writing—the relationship between words, sentences, and paragraphs shown so plainly that there is no room for confusion and no question about what the writer means.

class definition—a method of explaining a word by putting it in a big group and showing how it differs from other members of the big group: "A chair / is a piece of furniture / with four legs and a back, used for one person to sit in."

classification—a method of explanation that shows the relationship between a number of things. Classification can group similar things together and then subdivide the group, becoming more specific at each step (sorting down), or start with a specific thing and place it in a more general group or groups of things (sorting up).

classification chart—a diagram showing divisions and subdivisions in a classification system.

clause—a group of words that have both a subject and a predicate. (1) *Independent clauses* are complete by themselves: "The bridge over the Columbia has been recently painted." (2) *Dependent clauses* are not complete when standing alone; they must be attached to an independent clause by a subordinator: "[When the bridge was being painted,] my car got spattered." Or by a relative pronoun: "The man [who was painting the bridge] just laughed."

colloquial expression—a word or group of words more frequent in conversation than in formal writing; sometimes refers to regional usage: "He *carried* her home from the dance" (Southern—meaning *escorted*) or "I *slept in* Sunday" (Northwestern—meaning *slept late*).

comma error—same as *comma splice.*

comma splice—a punctuation problem that occurs when two sentences are separated by a comma instead of a period.

Example: Comma splices are not as serious as confused thinking, many readers get upset by them, however.

The solution is to use a period, a semicolon, or a connector, or to rearrange the sentence:

Comma splices are not as serious as confused thinking. Many readers get upset by them, however.

Comma splices are not as serious as confused thinking; many readers get upset by them, however.

Comma splices are not as serious as confused thinking, *but* many readers get upset by them.

Although comma splices are not as serious as confused thinking, many readers get upset by them.

comparison—a method of explanation that points out similarities and differences.

conclusion, in writing—the last sentence or last paragraph of a paper; makes the paper sound finished.

conclusion, in logic—the result of a reasoning process. If you know that Alfred was born in Kansas, and that people born in Kansas are U.S. citizens, your *conclusion* would be that Alfred is a U.S. citizen.

conjunctions—connecting words. (1) Coordinating conjunctions (*and, but, or, nor*) can connect words, phrases, or sentences. (2) Subordinating conjunctions (*when, although, because,* etc.) connect dependent clauses to the rest of the sentence.

connecting words—can be either conjunctions or prepositions. In this book, *connector* usually refers to conjunctions.

connotation—the emotional overtones that collect around some words: *home* has a pleasanter connotation than *house; mother* than *stepmother;* etc.

consonant—the sounds we make when we partly stop the air with our tongues, teeth, or lips. English has about twenty-four consonant sounds and twenty-one consonant letters: *b, c, d, f, g*—all the letters of the alphabet except *a, e, i, o,* and *u.*

contraction—word that results when two words are pushed together: "She *isn't* coming." "*Mary's* coming tomorrow." Contractions are used in speech and in informal writing.

dangling modifier—see *misplaced modifier.*

data sheet—see *personal information sheet.*

deduction—the kind of reasoning that begins with a generalization and applies it to a specific thing.

definition—explanation of what a word or phrase means.

denotation—the meaning of a word, separate from any emotional overtones; all words have denotation whether or not they have connotation.

dependent clause—see *clause.*

details—the specific information that helps readers "see" the person or event being written about.

developing a paper—providing specific details, examples, and support for the main idea.

dialect—a set of variations within a language, great enough to be noticed but not great enough to keep the speakers of one dialect from understanding the speakers of a different dialect. Dialect differences can occur in pronunciation, vocabulary, and usage, and dialects can be regional, social, or economic. Everybody speaks a dialect, sometimes more than one.

direct quotation—repeating the exact words somebody else has said or written:

Martin Luther King said, "I have a dream."

directions—telling other people how to make or do something.

draft—the first or second version of a piece of writing, before the last revision has been made.

echo transition—showing the relationship between one paragraph and the next by repeating a word, phrase, or idea from the end of one paragraph at the beginning of the next.

editing—going over the final version of a paper to check for spelling, punctuation, pronoun confusion, etc.

either/or thinking—the fallacy of believing there are only two sides to any question or only two solutions to any problem: "If it's not this, it's got to be that."

end notes—like footnotes except that they appear at the end of a paper instead of at the bottom of the page; now usually replaced by a different method of giving credit (see *footnotes*).

example—a specific illustration of a general statement.

exclamation mark (!)—used after single expressions ("Ouch!") or after complete sentences to show excitement or emphasis. Exclamations are seldom used in college writing— usually only in quoted conversation and there very sparingly.

explaining—writing that tells what something is or how it works by defining, comparing, classifying, or analyzing.

fact—a statement that can be checked and has been found to be accurate.

factual statement—a statement that can or could have been checked, whether or not it's accurate.

fallacy—a mistake in logic or reasoning.

false analogy—a comparison that has been carried so far that it's misleading; pretending that two things which have some similarity are identical or will have identical effects.

fiction—writing that is about imaginary people and imaginary events: novels, short stories, etc.

final draft—the last version of a paper after the revisions have been made and the paper has been carefully edited.

footnotes—an old method of giving credit to other people's work, still sometimes used. Better practice these days is to give credit by putting the name of the author and the page number in parentheses in the body of the paper: (Emerson 62–3).

fragment—a part of a sentence that depends on something else to be understandable; the punctuation problem that occurs when part of a sentence is punctuated as though it were a sentence:

> *fragment:* "When a parent thinks a library book uses bad language or contains too much sex."

The solution is to attach the fragment to another sentence it belongs with or to add words to the fragment:

> When a parent thinks a library book uses bad language or contains too much sex, the parent complains to the teacher or the principal or sometimes the school board. (attached to another sentence)

> A complaint arises when a parent thinks a library book uses bad language or contains too much sex. (words added)

general words—words that refer to a group of things: *furniture* or *animals*. The more things a word refers to, the more general it is. *Furniture* is more general than *chair*; *chair* is more general than *recliner*.

generalization—a statement made about a group of people, or things, or covering more than one situation. Generalizations can be acceptable or unacceptable, depending on what kind of support there is for the statement.

gerund—the *-ing* form of a verb used in a noun position: "I like *skating.*" "*Being criticized* discourages some people."

giving credit—acknowledging ideas or words you have gotten from other writers. Sometimes credit is given in a quick phrase ("As Mayor Huddleston has commented . . ."). Detailed information on how to give credit in longer papers can be found in style manuals. The method used in this book is to list all the sources at the end (see *works cited*) and give specific credit in the body of the paper. The last name of the original writer and the page number of the book or article are enclosed in parentheses (Thompson 14). This notation refers readers to an entry in the list of works cited:

> Thompson, Louisa. *Understanding Word Processors.* New York: Brinker Books, 1986.

glittering generality—statements so sweet and vague that they have little meaning: "I believe in giving all people the natural dignity they deserve."

grammar—(1) the way a language conveys meaning: in English, grammar enables us to understand the difference between "Man bites dog" and "Dog bites man," for instance; (2) the analysis of that system: learning to define verbs, prepositions, etc., and examining how they work; (3) certain choices, more accurately called usage or *dialect variations:* the difference between saying "he doesn't" and "he don't," for instance.

guilt by association—a fallacy which results from thinking that because two people or groups like the same thing, know the same people, or do the same thing, they are alike in other ways too:

> Football players wear helmets.
> Mary wears a helmet.
> Mary is a football player.

homophones—words that sound alike but are spelled differently: *who's* and *whose*; *to, too,* and *two.*

independent clause—see *clause.*

indirect quotation—repeating what somebody else has said without using the exact words:

> The teacher said to turn in all the exercises.

induction—the kind of reasoning that starts with specific things and arrives at a generalization.

inference—a statement about what isn't known, based on what is known.

infinitive—a phrase made up of *to* + a verb: *to understand, to want,* etc. Infinitives are most often used in noun positions, but they can serve as adjectives:

> *To cry* is childish. (noun position)
> He wanted *to see* me. (noun position)
> The man *to see* is my uncle. (adjective position)

interruptions—words, phrases, or clauses that could be left out of a sentence without destroying the basic meaning. In writing, interruptions need commas to separate them from the rest of the sentence:

> *Without giving any warning at all,* my aunt threw a lamp at the cat.
> My aunt, *an old battleaxe,* threw a lamp at the cat.
> The lamp, *by great good luck,* missed the cat.
> The cat, *when it saw my aunt,* howled and ran away.
> My aunt often throws things, *a very dangerous habit.*

introduction—usually the first paragraph of a short paper; makes clear what the paper will cover and serves as a contract between writer and reader; usually contains the main idea sentence.

italics—in print, shown by slanted letters; in handwriting or typing, shown by underlining.

judgment—a statement expressing opinion: a *bad* idea; a *brave* action.

language—the oral symbolic system by which human beings communicate; written language uses an additional set of symbols (the alphabet) to represent the sounds of speech.

link transitions—words such as *first, next, after, however,* etc., that show relationships of time, space, or contrast.

linking verbs (sometimes called auxiliary verbs)—verbs that connect the first noun (the subject) to the second or the subject to an adjective; they operate much like an equals sign. The most common linking verb in English is *be* (*is, are, was, were, been*):

> That man *is* a scientist. (Both nouns have the same referent—point to the same person.)

Other linking verbs are *seem, become, look,* and so on.

> The man *seems* lonely. (lonely man)

logic—the process of thinking straight; careful reasoning.

main idea sentence—a statement showing what the writer means to say in the paper; usually includes the narrowed topic and indicates both the purpose of the writing and the writer's attitude toward it.

metaphor—an implied comparison: "A temper tantrum can be a safety valve."

misplaced modifier—a phrase in the wrong position, so readers can't easily tell what it belongs with:

> Apartment wanted by single man with bay window.
> Coming in on Highway 99, the lake looks enormous.

Solution: Rearrange the sentence:

> Apartment with bay window wanted by single man.
> Coming in on Highway 99, we thought the lake looked enormous.

mixed metaphor—two different implied comparisons used in the same sentence: "My aunt was *blinded* by her *thirst* for revenge."

name-calling—making a personal attack against those on the other side in an argument, instead of sticking to the subject being argued about; a side-stepping technique, always unfair.

narrowing a topic—moving from a very general subject to some smaller part of it.

natural-sounding language, in writing—using words that avoid sounding stilted or overly formal, but that also avoid the fragments and repetitions that occur in speech.

nonfiction—writing based on facts or actual events: textbooks, biographies, histories, news reports, etc.

noun—traditionally, the name of something. Nouns are words that

1. can fit the patterns: "The _____ seems interesting" or "I like _____."
2. can follow such words as *a, the, some, any,* etc.: an *apple,* some *difficulties*
3. can be made plural by adding *-s* or by a pronunciation change: two *girls;* three *peaches;* four *women*
4. can form possessives: Matilda's *shoes,* a dollar's *worth.*

object—in grammar, the noun or noun substitute that comes after a non-linking verb:

> The child smashed *the vase.*
> She hated *it.*
> She hated *having to dust it.*

objective writing—writing that keeps the writer's attitudes and opinions out.

operational analysis—explaining how something works by examining it piece by piece.

opinion statement—a statement that expresses the writer's attitude or judgment; *good, bad, beautiful, large,* etc., are opinion words.

opposition—see *other side.*

order—in writing, the logical arrangement of ideas and paragraphs. The most common are (1) *chronological* (arranged by time); (2) *importance* (usually saving the most important point for the end); (3) *spatial* (moving from one area to the area next to it).

other side—an opinion or recommendation different from the writer's; in persuasion it's a good idea to discuss the argument of the other side and show what's wrong with it.

outline—a formal plan showing what a paper will cover or has covered, usually divided and subdivided by the use of numerals and letters.

paragraph—a sentence or group of sentences that seem to belong together because they refer to something slightly different from what is discussed in the paragraphs that come before and after them. Paragraphs break up the writing and give readers a short rest. Typical paragraphs in public writing usually contain from three to eight sentences, although they can sometimes be shorter or longer. The first word of each paragraph is started about an inch in from the left-hand margin.

participle—a form of a verb used in an adjective position:

> The *crying* child is hurt. (present participle)

> The dog, *beaten* and *battered,* put its tail between its legs. (past participle)

passive voice—a rearrangement of normal English sentence order so that the noun or noun substitute that usually follows the verb becomes the subject of the sentence:

> The child smashed the vase. (normal word order—active voice)
> The vase was smashed yesterday. (passive voice)
> That valuable oriental vase was smashed by the child. (passive voice)

Passive voice is not much used in good writing. Ordinarily it is used only when the normal subject is unknown or unimportant (the writer doesn't know or care who smashed the vase) or when the writer wants to emphasize what would normally be the object of the verb (the smashed vase is more important than the child).

pedantic language—stiff, overly formal writing.

periodical—a magazine.

personal experience—a piece of writing about yourself and your own experiences, written in such a way that readers can see the significance.

personal information sheet—a personal record included with an application letter, listing education, experience, references, etc.; also called résumé.

persuasion—writing that tries to get readers to change their attitudes, beliefs, or behavior; argument.

phrase—a group of words that belong together but do not have both a subject and predicate:

> I went *to the store.* (prepositional phrase)
> I want *to see that man.* (infinitive phrase)
> The man *traveling on the train* is my neighbor. (participial phrase)

I hate *washing dishes*. (gerund phrase)

I *will be leaving* tomorrow. (verb phrase)

plagiarism—copying what someone else has written without giving credit to the original writer.

plan for a paper—a list of the ideas that will be in the paper, arranged in the order in which they will appear.

point of view—the attitude the writer takes toward the topic or, in description, the position from which the writer looks at what is being described.

possessive—in grammar, the relationship between two nouns or noun substitutes:

>the *mayor's* car (car belongs to the mayor)
>the *mayor's* decision (the decision of the mayor)
>*her* decision

post hoc—from a Latin phrase (*post hoc, ergo propter hoc*) meaning "After this, therefore because of this." *Post hoc* fallacy is the mistake of assuming that because one thing happened after another, the first caused the second.

précis—same as *summary*.

precision—being exact; finding the right words to express a definite meaning.

predicate—the part of a sentence that contains the verb and what follows it: "The train *went through the tunnel*." "Riding horseback *can be very tiring*."

predicting consequences—making a statement about what will or could happen in the future, based on what has happened in the past.

preposition—a connector that shows the relationship between a noun, or words filling a noun position, and the rest of the sentence: *to* the store; *behind* the desk; *by* asking questions; *about* the question you asked.

private writing—writing not intended for many readers or for unknown readers: love letters, diaries, etc.

pronoun—a word that can substitute for a noun. Common pronouns are divided into five groups: personal, interrogative, demonstrative, indefinite, and relative.

Personal pronouns:
I, me (my, mine)
you (your, yours)
he, him (his)
it (its)
she, her (her, hers)
we, us (our, ours)
they, them (their, theirs)

The words in parentheses are possessive pronouns, which substitute for possessive nouns:
>That book is *Elizabeth's*.
>That book is *hers*.
Possessive personal pronouns are not written with apostrophes.

Interrogative pronouns:
who, whom (whose)
whoever, whomever
which
whichever
what

Interrogative pronouns indicate questions. The possessive form (whose) is not written with an apostrophe.

Demonstrative pronouns:
this, these
that, those
such

Demonstrative pronouns refer to things that have been mentioned earlier. They do not have possessive forms.

Indefinite pronouns:
words such as
all
any
anybody (anybody's)
everybody (everybody's)
few
nobody (nobody's)
none

Indefinite pronouns refer to a group of things or people, even though conventional usage treats them as though they were always just one:
Everybody *is* angry.
Nobody (none of a group) *is* coming.
When these words have possessive forms, they *are* written with apostrophes.

Relative pronouns:
that
which
who, whom (whose)

Relative pronouns connect clauses to the rest of the sentence:
The police told the man/*whose* truck was blocking the fire hydrant/to get the truck out of there in a hurry.

pronoun antecedent—the noun for which a pronoun is substituting. In the sentence "I voted for the candidate who seemed the most honest," *candidate* is the antecedent of *who.*

pronoun confusion—(1) changing from one personal pronoun to another in the same sentence or same paragraph: shifting from *one* to *you* to *anybody; Example:* "One doesn't always know what they want, do you?" *Solution:* "You don't always know what you want, do you?" or, "People don't always know what they want, do they?" (2) failing to make clear who or what a pronoun refers to: In the sentence "Jack told Jim that he won the prize," who is "he," Jack or Jim?

proofreading—see *editing.*

public writing—writing that is intended to be read by other people: college assignments, business letters, job reports, articles for publication in magazines, etc.

purpose—what the writer hopes the writing will accomplish: giving directions, explaining, telling what happened, persuading, summarizing, etc.

"purr" words—words that express the writer's approval and not much else; words meant to put readers in a good mood (term invented by S. I. Hayakawa).

question—a sentence in which the word order has been changed so that an answer seems to be expected.

Was that the doorbell? (expects *yes* or *no*)
Why did you come so late? (expects an explanation)

quotation—the exact words someone else has said or written.

quotation marks—punctuation that shows that someone else's words are being repeated exactly:

He said, "I'm not coming." (direct quotation)

Quotation marks are not used in indirect quotations:

He said he was not coming. (indirect quotation—words slightly changed)

rational argument—an attempt to persuade that depends on reasons rather than emotional appeals.

reasons—in persuasion, ways of supporting a belief.

referent—the thing, idea, person, object, that is symbolized by a word: "The round red fruit you can actually eat" is the referent of *apple*; "a collection of behaviors" is the referent of *fright*.

relative clause—a kind of dependent clause that is connected to the rest of the sentence by a relative pronoun:

> The hamburger *that I like best* is made at Yummy's Drive-in.

> That's the man *who was elected yesterday.*

report—writing that tells what happened, without the writer's interpretation or judgment about the events.

résumé—see *personal information sheet.*

review—writing that evaluates a book, movie, etc. Whereas a report merely summarizes, a review includes the writer's opinion.

revising—going back over what you have written, rewording sentences, rearranging the order, cutting some things and adding others; revising is best done a day or so after the first draft has been finished.

run-on sentence—a punctuation problem that occurs when two separate sentences have no punctuation between them:

> Blow-outs can be serious they cause an inexperienced driver to lose control of the car.

Solution: use a period or rewrite the sentence:

> Blow-outs can be serious. They cause an inexperienced driver to lose control of the car.

> Because blow-outs can make an inexperienced driver lose control of the car, they can be serious.

salutation—the formal beginning of a business letter, usually followed by a colon.

> Dear Senator Goodsell:

sentence—a group of words beginning with a capital letter and ending with a period or question mark. Sentences can be long or short, but they must have a subject and a predicate, and readers must not be left with the feeling that there's something they haven't been told.

long sentence: Whenever my parents went away, whether it was just for an evening out or a week's vacation in the mountains, my brother (*subject*) cried, making so much noise that the neighbors came over to see whether he had been injured (*predicate*).

short sentence: My brother (*subject*) cried a lot (*predicate*).

not a sentence: whenever my parents went away, whether it was just for an evening out or a week's vacation in the mountains (Readers will ask "Well, what happened then?")

not a sentence: my brother making so much noise that the neighbors came over to see whether he had been injured (Readers will be confused by *making*; to turn this into a sentence, the writer must say *was making.*)

question sentences: Did your brother always cry? (*subject:* your brother; *predicate:* did always cry)

Why did your brother cry? (*subject:* your brother; *predicate:* did cry; *question word:* why)

sentence outline—a formal plan for a paper, in which all the ideas to be covered in the paper are written in complete sentences.

sexist language—using only masculine pronouns when both men and women are meant:

A writer must polish *his* writing.

Solution: change to the plural: "Writers must polish *their* writing"; or use "his or her" (but that's a bit awkward); or write, "Everybody must polish *their* writing" defying the foolish rule that says *everybody* is singular).

slang—street language or faddish use of new meanings for old words: *bad* to mean *good,* etc. Slang usually gets quickly out of date and disappears; but sometimes it becomes accepted into the language as a "regular" word. *Mob,* for instance, was once slang. In writing, slang should be used only for special effect; it should always be avoided in formal writing.

slant—in writing that pretends to be factual, creating a favorable or unfavorable impression by the choice of words or emphasis or even omission of some of the facts.

slanted words—in objective writing, words that influence readers' attitudes. (*old hag* instead of *elderly woman*; *staggered* instead of *walked*; *pleasingly plump* instead of *fat*)

"snarl" words—words that express the writer's disapproval and not much else; words meant to create an unfavorable impression on readers (term invented by S. I. Hayakawa).

source—the book, article, etc., in which the writer found the information being used.

specific details—precise information that makes general statements easier to understand or visualize.

specific statement—a statement made about a particular thing that happened at a particular time.

specific words—the fewer things a word refers to, the more specific it is.

statistics—numbers that show how much, how many, how often. They should be checked for reliability.

stereotyping—putting a label on a person or group of people that disregards their own characteristics:

Everybody from Edinburgh is stingy.

Nobody on welfare wants to work.

New Yorkers think nothing important happens west of Philadelphia.

stipulative definition—explanation, often through the use of examples, of how a word is being used in a certain situation by a certain person.

style manual—a booklet giving directions for margins, spacing, footnotes, bibliography, etc., in a formal reference paper.

subject, in writing—the topic being written about.

subject, in grammar—the part of the sentence that comes before the predicate in normal word order; the thing the rest of the sentence is telling about. Subjects can usually be recognized by using the predicate to ask a question:

Dinner is ready. (What is ready? *dinner* is the subject.)

When *you* are confused, *subjects* can usually be recognized by using the predicate to ask a question. (Who is confused? *you* is the subject of the dependent clause; what can be recognized? *subjects* is the subject of the independent clause.)

subjective writing—writing that includes the writer's attitudes and opinions.

subordinate clause—same as *dependent clause.*

subordinators—connectors that are used with dependent clauses; words such as *because, when, although, which, that,* and so on.

summary—in writing, a shortened version of what someone else has said or written, using the second writer's own words.

syllogism—the formal pattern of deductive reasoning that includes a generalization (major premise), a statement relating a specific thing to the generalization (minor premise), and a conclusion. The relationship between the three terms determines whether the reasoning process is logically valid or invalid. The most famous example of a valid syllogism is:

> All men are mortal. (major premise)
>
> Socrates is a man. (minor premise)
>
> Therefore, Socrates is mortal. (conclusion)

synonym—a word that means the same, or almost the same, as another word: *obese* is a synonym for *fat.*

tense—a grammatical term applied to verbs; indicates when an action took place. Tenses in English are

> *present:* She works. She is working today.
>
> *past:* She worked. She was working yesterday.
>
> *future:* She will work tomorrow. She will be working all week.

Other different time relationships are shown by other tense changes:

> She has been working all day.
>
> She had been working nights before she got this job.
>
> By next month, she will have been working there a year.

thesis statement—see *main idea sentence.*

title—the name given to a piece of writing. The title is centered at the top of the first page and important words in it are begun with capital letters.

tone—a reflection of the writer's attitude toward the subject and toward the audience, the people who will read what has been written. The tone of a piece of writing can be light or serious, humorous or straightforward, etc.

topic—the general subject the writing is about; the topic can be expressed in a word or a phrase.

topic outline—a formal plan in which all the ideas covered in the paper are expressed in a series of single words or phrases.

topic sentence—similar to *main idea sentence,* except that topic sentences show what the main idea of a paragraph is.

transitions—wording that guides readers from one idea to the next and shows the relationship between the parts of a paper.

usage—the choices available wtihin the grammar of a language. The difference between saying to a dog "Lie down" or "Lay down" is a usage difference; but the first has more prestige than the second.

verb—traditionally, a word (or words) that show action or state of being. Verbs are words that can fit the pattern: "They _____ well," or "They _____ it." Verbs can have *-ing* added to the base form.

vowel—the sounds we make by letting our breath come out of our mouths in a clear stream. English has thirty or more vowel sounds but only five or six vowel letters: *a, e, i, o, u,* and sometimes *y.* Every syllable must have one vowel sound in it.

works cited or **works consulted**—the list of books and magazines, sometimes including interviews or television programs, from which a writer has gotten ideas in writing a paper. *Works cited* means that the list mentions only the sources referred to in the paper; *works consulted* means that the list contains everything the writer has found useful, whether or not the material has been mentioned in the paper.

Index

*Numbers appearing in **boldface** indicate exercise pages.*

Abstract words, 68
Accuracy, 199, **219**
Advertisements, 316, **335**, **361**
Agreement of subjects and verbs, 282, **307**
Analogy, false, 327, **351**
Analysis, 165 ff.
  causal, 168 ff.
  operational, 166 ff.
Apologies, avoiding, 39, **57**
Apostrophes, 110, **129**, **130**, 427
Application letters, 409 ff.
  personal information sheet, 413
  sample letter, 416
  sample résumé, 418
Argument, *see* Persuasion
Audience, 14, **25**, **27**, 29, **62**, 76, 103, **117**, **124**, 137, **161**, 167, 208, **215**, **233**, 238, 268
Authorities, 276, **297**
  honest use of, 323, **345**

Bibliography, *see* Works cited
Block style, 410

Book reviews, 373
  sample book review, 375
Brainstorming, 4, **17**
Business letters, 409 ff.
  form for, 409

Capitalization, 442
Causal analysis, 168 ff.
Cause and effect, 169, **185**, **187**, 326, **349**
Charts for classification, 138, **157**, **159**
Check lists, *see* Content; Editing
Choosing a topic, *see* Topics
Circular argument, 333, **359**
Class definitions, 67, **83**, **85**, **86**
Classification, 133 ff.
Colons, 439
Commas, 141, **159**, 210, **232**, 434
Comma splices, avoiding, 436
Comparison, 101 ff.
  purposes of, 102
Completeness, 201, **222**
Conclusions
  application letters, 413

461

Conclusions *(continued)*
  causal analysis, 172
  classification, 140
  comparison, 109
  definition, 74, **100**
  directions, 35, **53**
  operational analysis, 168
  personal experience, 243
  persuasion, 281, **305**
  reports, 209
  research paper, 384
Connectors, 245, **259**
Consequences, *see* Predicting consequences
Content, check lists for, **63**, **99**, **127**, **163**, **181**, **195**, **235**, **265**, **313**
Contractions, 14, 110, **129**, **130**, 427
Crediting sources, 367, 386

Dashes, 440
Deductive reasoning, 328, 330, **353**
Definition, 65 ff.
  abstract words, 68
  class definitions, 67, **83**, **85**, **86**
  synonym definitions, 66, **81**, **82**
Details, *see* Specific details
Developing the paper
  causal analysis, 171
  classification, 139
  comparison, 109
  definition, 75
  directions, 33
  operational analysis, 167
  personal experience, 242
  persuasion, 279
  report, 208
Directions, giving, 29 ff.
  for a drawing, **64**
  for a short journey, **64**
Discoveries, in personal experience, 239
Draft of a paper, 4, 37, **63**, **99**, **127**, **163**, **181**, **195**, **235**, **265**, **313**

Echo transitions, 40, **55**
Editing, 41, 76, 421 ff.
  check lists for, **64**, **99**, **131**, **163**, **181**, **195**, **235**, **265**, **313**
Either/or thinking, 332, **359**
Emotional appeals, 317
Exact words, 39, **57**
Examples, 71, **89**, **91**, **100**, 172, 273, **293**
  honest examples, 320, **339**, **341**
Explaining, 6, 65 ff.

Fact and opinion, 203, **225**, **227**
Facts, 318, **337**
Factual statements, 203, **225**, **227**
Fair persuasion, 315 ff.
False analogies, 327, **351**
Fiction
  book review, 375
  summarizing, 372
Finding a topic, 9, **17**
Footnotes, *see* Giving credit to sources
Fragments, in conversation, 244, **257**

General words, 70, **87**, **88**
Generalizations, 71, **89**, **91**
Getting started, 1 ff.
Giving credit to sources, 367, 386
Giving directions, 5, 29 ff.
Glittering generalities, 317, **335**
Glossary, 447 ff.
Graphs, summarizing, 370
Guilt by association, 331, **357**

Homophones, 172, **183**, **184**
Honest reasoning, 328, **355**

In-class writing, 445
Indirect quotations, 246, **261**, **262**
Inductive reasoning, 328, **353**

Inferences, 318, **337**
Introductions
    as contract, 34
    for application letters, 411
    for causal analysis, 171
    for classification, 140
    for comparison, 109
    for definition, 74, **100**
    for directions, 34, **51**
    for operational analysis, 167
    for personal experience, 242
    for persuasion, 279, **303**
    for reports, 208
    for research papers, 384

Judgments, 318, **337**

Key words and ideas
    analysis, 176
    classification, 146
    comparison, 116
    definition, 80
    directions, 46
    fair persuasion, 334
    getting started, 16
    personal experience, 250
    persuasion, 287
    reports, 214

Language
    conversational, 244, **255**, **257**
    formal and informal, 444
    meaning in, 65
    natural-sounding, 243, **255**
    sexist, 364, 444
Lecture notes, 363
Letters, *see* Application letters
Library catalog, 381
Link transitions, 40, **55**
Listing ideas, 104, **124**, 269, **310**
Logical thinking, 315 ff.
Longer papers, *see* Research papers

Main idea sentences, 12, **21**, **23**, **25**, **27**
    distinguished from topic, 13, **21**
    for causal analysis, 170, **177**, **189**, **191**
    for classification, 137, **153**, **155**
    for comparison, 105, **121**, **123**
    for definition, 73
    for directions, 32, **49**
    for objective reports, 206, **233**
    for operational analysis, 166, **177**
    for personal experience, 239, **251**
    for persuasion, 270, **289**, **311**
    recognizing, **21**, **23**
    writing, **25**, **27**
Meaning of words, 65
Mixed purposes, 5
MLA Stylebook, 387

Name calling, 333, 259
Narrowing the topic, 10, **23**
Natural sounding language, 243, **255**
Notecards, 383

Objective reports, 197 ff.
Objectivity, 203, **225**, **227**
Operational analysis, 166 ff.
Opinion statements, 203, **225**, **227**
Order, *see* Organization
Organization
    application letters, 411
    causal analysis, 171, **193**
    classification, 138, **157**, **159**, **164**
    comparison, 106, **125**
    definition, 74, **97**
    directions, 31, **47**
    operational analysis, 167, **179**
    personal experience, 242, **263**
    personal information sheet, 414
    persuasion, 278, **312**
    reports, 202, 208, **223**
    research paper, 384
    summary, 368

Other side, dealing with, 277, **301**
Outline, 108
    for a reference paper, 385
    see also Planning the paper

Papers, *see* Sample papers
Paragraphing, 74, **93**, **159**, 442
Parentheses, 441
Pedantic language, 243, **255**
Periods, 209, **232**, 432
Personal experience, 237 ff.
Personal information sheet, 413
    sample, 418
Persuasion, 8, 267 ff.
    fair persuasion, 315 ff.
Plagiarism, 387
Planning the paper
    application letters, 411
    causal analysis, 171, **193**
    classification, 138, **161**
    comparison, 104, 106, **125**
    definition, 72, **97**, **119**
    directions, 30, **62**
    objective reports, 208
    operational analysis, 167, **179**
    personal experience, 241, **263**
    persuasion, 278, **312**
    research paper, 383
    summary, 367
Point of view, classification, 134, **148**,
    164
Possessives, 110, **129**, **130**, 428
Post hoc thinking, 326, **349**
Precis, *see* Summarizing
Precision, 199, **215**
Predicting consequences, 277, **299**
    honest predictions, 325, **347**
Private writing, 1, 3, **17**, 238
Process of writing, 3
Process writing, *see* Operational analysis
Profanity, 246
Pronouns, 40, **57**, 76, **95**, 110, **129**,
    130, 428, 454

Proofreading
    in application letters, 415
    see also Editing
Public writing, 1, 3, **17**
Punctuation, 209, 430 ff.
Purposes, in writing, 4
    identifying, **19**, **20**

Question marks, 210, **232**, 433
Quotation marks, 246, **261**, **262**, 437,
    455

Readers, *see* Audience
Reader's Guide, 381
Reasoning, *see* Inductive reasoning;
    Deductive reasoning
Reasons for a belief, 271, **291**, **312**, 315
Reference papers, *see* Research papers
Reports, *see* Objective reports
Research papers, 379 ff.
    finding material, 381
    giving credit, 386
    outline for, 385
    planning the paper, 383
    reasons for, 380
    sample paper analyzed, 389 ff.
    taking notes, 382
    using a style manual, 388
    works cited, 387
Résumé, *see* Personal information sheet
Reviews, 373
Revising, 4, 37, 76, 109, 140, 242, 384
    sample revisions, 43, 78, 113, 143,
    248

Sample papers
    application letter, 416
    book review, 375
    causal analysis, 174
    classification, 143
    comparison, 111
    definition, 77

directions, 42
objective reports, 211
operational analysis, 173
personal experience, 247
persuasion, 283
research paper, 389
Semicolons, 439
Sentence length, 38
Sentence outline, 385
Sentence punctuation, 209, **232**
Sentences, recognizing, 432
Sexism in language, 364, 444
Significance of experiences, 239
Slang, 246, **258**
Slant, 205, **229**, **236**, 316, **335**
Sorting up and down in classification, 136, **151**
Specific details, 34, 76, 109, 140, 168, 171, 207, 241, **253**, **263**
Specific statements, 71, **89**
Specific words, 70, **87**, **88**
Spelling, 172, **183**, **184**, 422 ff.
Statistics, 275, **295**
    honest statistics, 321, **343**
Stereotyping, 135, **149**
Sticking to the subject, 200, **221**
Study aids, 140, 363, 370
Style, 38, **63**
Style manuals, 388
    MLA Stylebook, 387
Subjectivity, 203, **225**, **227**
Summarizing, 8, 363 ff.
    fiction, 372
    graphs, 370
    lecture notes, 363
    notes for, 367, 370
    using help in texts, 370
    using your own words, 368

Supporting reasons, 271 ff.
Surveys, 321, **361**
Synonym definitions, 66, **81**, **82**

Taking notes, 208, 364, 383
Talking and writing, differences, 244, **255**, **257**
Telling what happened, 7, 197 ff.
Term papers, *see* Research papers
Titles, 36–*37,* **54**
Topics, how to find, 9, **21**, 29, **61**, 72, **97**, 102, **117**, **147**, **179**, 238, **263**, 268, **309**
    for research papers, 380
Transitions, 39, **55**

Word order, natural, 243, **255**
Wording, smoothing out, 443
Words
    abstract, 68, **97**
    connecting, 245, **259**
    general, 70, **87**, **88**
    meaning in, 65
    opinion, 204, **225**, **227**
    precision, 199, **215**
    slanted, 205, **229**, **236**
    specific, 70, **87**, **88**
    stilted, 243, **255**
    using your own, 368
Works cited, 387
    sample, 407
Writing in class, 445
Writing process, 3
Writing purposes, *see* Purposes

About the Authors

Elisabeth McPherson has taught in public community colleges for more than twenty years, most recently at Forest Park Community College in St. Louis, where for five years she was chair of the Humanities Division, and earlier at Clark College in Vancouver, Washington, where she was chair of the English Department. She has a BA from Washington State University and an MA from Reed College in Portland, Oregon; she has been a legal stenographer, a bookkeeper, and a librarian. In 1972 she was the first community college chairperson of the Conference on College Composition and Communication. Since then she has served on various committees of CCCC and the National Council of Teachers of English, most recently on the NCTE editorial board. She has also been the featured speaker at numerous English conferences across the country. In addition to her articles for professional journals and the texts written with Gregory Cowan, she was the author of the section on composition in *The Teaching of English,* the 1977 yearbook of the National Society for the Study of Education. At present she lives in Ridgefield, Washington, where she is writing and consulting on the teaching of writing.

Gregory Cowan was a teacher of writing for nineteen years at Clark College in Vancouver, Washington, Forest Park Community College in St. Louis, Empire State College of the State University of New York, and Texas A&M University. A nationally known speaker and conductor of writing workshops, he authored numerous articles and monographs on composition as well as seven textbooks with Elisabeth McPherson for Random House, where he was a consultant for eight years. At the time of his death he was coordinator of the rhetoric and composition graduate program at Texas A&M University.